The USS *Swordfish*

The USS *Swordfish*
The World War II Patrols of the First American Submarine to Sink a Japanese Ship

GEORGE J. BILLY

McFarland & Company, Inc., Publishers
Jefferson, North Carolina

Frontispiece: **Launching of the USS *Swordfish*, 1 April 1939, at Mare Island, California.** *National Archives, College Park.*

LIBRARY OF CONGRESS CATALOGUING-IN-PUBLICATION DATA

Names: Billy, George J., 1940– author.
Title: The USS Swordfish : the World War II patrols of the first American submarine to sink a Japanese ship / George J. Billy.
Other titles: World War II patrols of the first American submarine to sink a Japanese ship
Description: Jefferson, North Carolina : McFarland & Company, Inc., Publishers, 2019 | Includes bibliographical references and index.
Identifiers: LCCN 2019040316 | ISBN 9781476677743 (paperback) ∞
   ISBN 9781476636788 (ebook)
Subjects: LCSH: Swordfish (Submarine : SS-193)—History. | World War, 1939–1945—Naval operations, American. | World War, 1939–1945—Naval operations—Submarine. | World War, 1939–1945—Campaigns—Pacific Ocean. | Smith, Chester C., 1905–1976. | Lewis, Jack Hayden. | Parker, Frank M. | Barrows, Frank L. | United States. Navy—Officers—Biography.
Classification: LCC D783.5.S96 B55 2019 | DDC 940.54/510973—dc23
LC record available at https://lccn.loc.gov/2019040316

BRITISH LIBRARY CATALOGUING DATA ARE AVAILABLE

ISBN (print) 978-1-4766-7774-3
ISBN (ebook) 978-1-4766-3678-8

© 2019 George J. Billy. All rights reserved

No part of this book may be reproduced or transmitted in any form or by any means, electronic or mechanical, including photocopying or recording, or by any information storage and retrieval system, without permission in writing from the publisher.

Front cover image: *inset* "USS Swordfish SS-193," pen & ink and acrylic painting by Thomas Denton (courtesy of the artist, a submarine veteran); USS *Swordfish*, stern view, trials in San Francisco Bay, 13 June 1943 (National Archives)

Printed in the United States of America

McFarland & Company, Inc., Publishers
  Box 611, Jefferson, North Carolina 28640
  www.mcfarlandpub.com

To all the men who served on *Swordfish*

Table of Contents

Acknowledgments	ix
Preface	1
1. Chester Smith: The Quiet Hunter	3
2. Special Missions	30
3. Chester Smith Creates a Legend	51
4. Competing with a Legend	84
5. Hensel's Finest Hour	112
6. New Commander—Old Submarine	137
7. The Thirteenth Patrol	153
Appendix A: USS Swordfish	169
Appendix B: USS Swordfish *(SS-193) Crew List of the Thirteenth Patrol*	171
Appendix C: USS Swordfish—*Ships Sunk or Damaged*	173
Appendix D: U.S. Submarines SS 188–193— Compartments and Tanks	178
Glossary	181
Note Abbreviations	185
Chapter Notes	187
Bibliography	209
Index	217

Acknowledgments

During the course of my research, individuals at several institutions greatly enhanced my ability to obtain information. In particular, I thank Rear Admiral P.E. Tobin and Edward J. Marolda of the Naval History and Heritage Command, formerly the Naval Historical Center, for providing a Vice Admiral Edwin B. Hooper Grant. The grant enlarged significantly my opportunity to travel to archival centers. In addition, at the Command, Kenneth Johnson, Timothy T. Pettit and Tracy Wilson offered many helpful suggestions and greatly facilitated the research process, as did Davis Elliott at the Navy Department Library of the Naval Heritage and History Command, and Captain Charles Creekman of the Naval Historical Foundation. At the National Archives and Records Center at College Park, Maryland, Barry Zirby and again Kenneth Johnson guided my navigation to essential sources. Similarly, at the National Archives and Records Center in San Bruno, California, Robert Glass rendered valuable assistance in locating very useful information. I am indebted to the staff at the Library of Congress Manuscripts Division for their steadfast assistance in dealing with the Charles A. Lockwood Papers, and I thank Wendy Gully at the Submarine Force Library Archives in Groton, Connecticut, for ferreting out material relevant to *Swordfish*. In addition, I thank Richard Werking and Lawrence E. Clemens at the Nimitz Library of the U.S. Naval Academy for providing access to their unique holdings. I especially thank the staff of the Schuyler Otis Bland Memorial Library of the U.S. Merchant Marine Academy for helping me in countless ways and for obtaining helpful sources.

Staff members at other remote sites were instrumental in obtaining additional information. I thank members of the Columbia University Libraries Center for Oral History for sending the reminiscences of Admiral James Fife. I also thank John Crouse at St. Marys Submarine Museum for sending materials from the Ben Bastura Collection, and both Rachel Howell at the Dallas Public Library and Erica Block at Texas Women's University for information about Dorothy Heath Clary. In addition, I extend thanks to Carol Bowers at the University of Wyoming's American Heritage Center for assistance with the Clay Blair Papers. I thank the staff of the National Personnel Records Center, Military Personnel

Records, for providing the service records of my uncle, Michael Billy. I am also in debt to Joyce Giles, Director of the Mare Island Park Museum, for taking time to guide me through the navy yard where *Swordfish* was built and launched. A very special thanks go to Tom Gierer and Martin Gray of New York City Fire Department Marine Company Number 9, for permitting me to hear one of the World War II vintage General Motors Winton engines aboard their fire boat, *Firefighter,* identical to the diesel engines aboard *Swordfish*. Submarine veteran Chief Michael Carmody should receive a special word of thanks for creating an oil painting of *Swordfish* which appeared on the cover of *Polaris*, the World War II submariner's magazine. In addition, I thank Marine artist Thomas Denton for creating a colored illustration commemorating *Swordfish,* and I thank submarine veteran Donald Kane for providing helpful information.

I had the opportunity to interview former *Swordfish* crewmen named in the bibliography, and I thank them for providing invaluable details about incidents aboard the boat and for documentary materials. I am especially indebted to *Swordfish* veteran Arthur Myers for permission to quote from his poem, "I'll Never Forget," dedicated to the lost crew of *Swordfish,* and thanks to his wife, Mary Myers, for her support and permission.

Similarly, family members related to four of *Swordfish*'s commanders provided valuable information. I thank David Fields and Katherine Wikstrom for information concerning Karl G. Hensel; J. Reilly Lewis and Beth Lewis concerning Jack H. Lewis; Thomas Keeley, Wyatt R. Nocera and Ruth Smith regarding Keats E. Montross; and Donald B. Smith for information concerning his father, Chester C. Smith.

Family members and friends related to *Swordfish* crewmen have related details helpful for filling in the *Swordfish* story, and I thank the following individuals for sharing their memories and providing information: Mary Gladding concerning James M. Mayfield; Reid Kimbrough concerning Clifford F. Slater; Janice Langley concerning Marshall E. Cox; Robert R. Parks regarding his father, Joe Parks; Erin Faye Devine regarding Lloyd Henry Faye; and Marie Billy, Margaret Cudwadie, Helen Frazee, Ann Kirkman, Margaret Rand-Eastman, Walter Scull, Michael Sturtz, and Peter Zeleznik concerning Michael Billy. Also, I sincerely thank John C. Clary, son of Dorothy Heath Clary, for providing information and photographs of his mother, and thanks also to David Clary & Cynthia E. Clary for their support. I extend a special word of thanks to the members of the Runner Chapter of the Submarine Veterans of World War II, to the members of the Long Island Chapter of American Submarine Veterans, Inc., and to the members of the Naval Submarine League, who invited me to participate in their meetings. It has been a privilege to know them, and I thank them for treating me "like family." They provided a clearer picture of life on the boats.

A very special thank you goes to Laura Cody for her invaluable suggestions, her expertise in working on key technical aspects of the manuscript, and her untiring enthusiasm. In addition, I thank Ann Boyer for reading portions of the work and offering editorial comments. The following individuals deserve my gratitude for reading the manuscript and for offering suggestions: submarine veterans Lieutenant Commander Joel Ira Holwitt, Kenneth Jacobs, Brian Leonard, and Lieutenant Commander Jules Verne Steinhauer, and I thank four additional readers: James C. Bradford, Patrick J. Kelly, Gene Allen Smith and Marilyn Stern for their suggestions. I also thank Rear Admiral Paul J. Early, Rear Admiral Maurice H. Rindskopf, Rear Admiral L.R. "Joe" Vasey and Captain Channing M. Zucker for tracking down information, and I thank them for taking a personal interest in this endeavor. Eliz Alahverdian, former Director of Exhibitions at Adelphi University, provided essential help with maps. In addition, I express sincere gratitude to Dean Shashi Kumar, formerly of the United States Merchant Marine Academy, for his consistent support and encouragement, as well as Robert P. Gardella, Gary Lombardo and Joshua Smith. Over the years that this book has been in process, a large number of additional individuals have offered suggestions and information, attesting to their genuine interest in the efforts of the submariners in World War II. I thank them for contacting me. In particular, I thank Jeanine and Lori Allen, Susie L. Hoeller, Thomas F. McCaffery, and Craig R. McDonald.

Finally, I thank members of my family, my wife Valerie and my daughters Margaret and Christine, for reading the manuscript, for their helpful suggestions, and for their strong support during the years that this book was in preparation. Any flaws and errors are entirely my own.

Preface

Peering through his periscope aboard the USS *Swordfish* on 16 December 1941, Chester C. Smith ordered three torpedoes fired at an armed merchant vessel. With this successful attack, *Swordfish* became the first American submarine to sink a Japanese ship in World War II. This early success was the beginning of a story of 13 war patrols, which continued until January 1945, when *Swordfish* mysteriously disappeared.

Seven skippers commanded the *Swordfish*, and each commander conducted his war patrols in a personal way. Many were successful, but some returned "empty-handed." As the chief officer aboard *Swordfish*, the commander decided the ultimate fate of his crew and boat. The skipper put his indelible personal stamp on his patrol, and each foray into enemy water was a story in itself. However, the critical role of the commander did not diminish the importance of the subordinate officers and crew aboard. Every man was keenly aware that the fate of the boat depended upon each shipmate performing the very exacting duties assigned. The sea could be very unforgiving, and close encounters with the enemy were fraught with uncertainty. The reactions of crewmen recorded in this book gave testimony to the stressful conditions which defined life at sea.

Swordfish's war patrols illustrated the strategy which the U.S. Submarine Service employed to sweep Japanese merchant shipping from the seas. Pearl Harbor had changed everything. The Japanese attack of 7 December 1941 altered the balance of naval power in the Pacific and put the United States Navy at a disadvantage. After the attack, the Pacific Fleet was largely in shambles, and the prewar plan of ordering submarines to coordinate their actions as forward scouts for the larger ships was no longer workable. American naval planners fell back to a strategy of cutting Japan's logistical routes to the outer reaches of her island empire. Submarines went on far-ranging patrols and engaged in a war of attrition or commerce war (*guerre de course*). *Swordfish* and other submarines aimed to close off the supply lines of raw materials going to the Japanese homeland and to stop manufactured war material from going out of the home islands to conquered territories in the Pacific. The ultimate goal was to weaken the Japanese Empire's ability to wage war and to bring it down in defeat.

The German Navy attempted a similar strategy with U-boats in the Battle of the Atlantic. It failed. The flow of materials from the United States to Britain and Russia, and then to liberated Europe, continued.[1] In the Pacific, however, American submarine commanders pressed on with their war against Japanese merchant shipping, which at the war's end was so severely depleted that the goal of crippling Japan's war effort had been largely achieved. Sinking 1,113 merchant ships, American submarines were responsible for Japan's loss of 4,779,902 gross tons of shipping, amounting to over 60 percent of the Japanese merchant marine tonnage lost to hostile action.[2]

Swordfish played a significant role in the submarine campaign. Yet up to now there has been no extensive history of the legendary *Swordfish*, and this book represents an effort to provide such an account. Previously, many references to the boat were short and usually referred to her as the first submarine to sink a Japanese ship, or they briefly discussed the sparse details of her mysterious loss in 1945. Broader treatments of America's submarine campaign, such as Clay Blair's monumental *Silent Victory* and John D. Alden's exhaustively researched works, were essential for placing *Swordfish* within the wider scope of the Pacific sea war.[3] However, a full-length history of *Swordfish* deserved to be written.

My early connection with *Swordfish* began in 1944, when a submarine sailor greeted a four-year-old youngster as he was playing in a sandbox. I was the four-year-old, and my uncle, Michael Billy, was saying goodbye before returning to his submarine, *Swordfish*. Michael and his shipmates never returned from the 13th patrol, but the dim memory of that last farewell has lingered on. As I learned more about the famous *Swordfish*, the idea of writing a book evolved. The book has been both a professional endeavor and, in view of my uncle's membership in the crew, also a personal journey back to those perilous days aboard the submarine. The war patrol logs and the personal experiences described by veterans of *Swordfish*, before that last fatal patrol, make it very clear that the submarine's history included frequent challenges to human endurance and ingenuity. As a result of my learning about what occurred, this book tells the story of those daring acts. They constitute a remarkable chapter in the U.S. Navy's submarine war in the Pacific.

A technical note should be mentioned. Calling a submarine a boat stems from the early days of submarine design at the beginning of the 20th century, when the Navy Department issued contracts for construction of "torpedo boats" that could submerge. The term "boat" stuck, and it was used in World War II. In accord with the tradition, I have referred to a submarine as a "boat" rather than a ship.

1

Chester Smith: The Quiet Hunter

The launching of USS *Swordfish* on 1 April 1939 was an event both festive and momentous. She was decked out in bunting and surrounded by dignitaries, navy personnel and workmen. An eyewitness to the event was crewman George Valentine Brown, Electrician's Mate First Class. He described the launching at Mare Island Naval Shipyard in California: "She hit the water amid the wailing of sirens, and a pandemonium of cheers from a crowd of about three thousand spectators, and eased out into the stream pulling on the great drag chains which finally brought her to rest about one hundred yards off shore, where yard craft took her over."[1] The yard craft nestled *Swordfish* into her berth for fitting out.[2]

Swordfish's keel had been laid down on 27 October 1937,[3] and as a member of the new Sargo class of sleek-lined fleet submarines, she was an unmistakable statement of American naval power and technical know-how. The specifications of the warship testified to its serious purpose. She was designed with four torpedo tubes forward and four aft, as well as a three-inch, .50 caliber deck gun and several machine guns. Measuring 310 feet, one inch in length and having a standard displacement of 1,450 tons, the boat featured a product of the foremost American engineering, very powerful diesel engines. Housed in her hull were four engines, manufactured by General Motors (Winton), each capable of 1,535 horsepower. At a speed of ten knots, the diesels could drive the submarine for a surface cruising range of 11,000 miles. However, while chasing targets, the required surface speed would often have to be greater than ten knots. For propulsion while submerged, *Swordfish* depended upon four electric motors, each with 685 horsepower. Reserve power was stored in two 126-cell batteries. Designed for an operating depth of 250 feet, the boat had another important component thoroughly appreciated by the crew, air conditioning.[4] Although the interior environment could still heat up, the air conditioning made operations near the equator much more bearable. These features suggested that *Swordfish* was intended for long-distance patrols, for underwater endurance, and for deadly attacks. All that was needed was a willing skipper and crew.

It remained to be seen if Chester Carl Smith, the boat's newly designated captain, would provide the right leadership, and his appearance was most deceiving. A month earlier, while inspecting *Swordfish*, which was still under construction,

Electrician's Mate George Brown had stumbled upon a stranger emerging from the third Main Ballast Tank. Wearing grimy, rimless glasses and grease smudges on his youthful-looking face, the dungaree-clad mystery man appeared to be a recent ROTC graduate, an ensign at best. Brown described him: "He looked more like a Halloween scarecrow than a naval officer." However, as the two toured the submarine, Brown slowly realized that he was with his new commanding officer, Lieutenant Chester C. Smith. Smith inquired, "Aren't you going to welcome me on board, 'Sparks?'" Smith's face had a silly, childlike grin that conveyed a disarming sense of confidence, which Brown and his fellow crewmen would later understand to be genuine.[5] Outwardly Smith was deceptively mild-mannered and quiet, so much so that another veteran of Smith's war patrols described his appearance as that of the ineffectual cartoon character, Casper Milquetoast.[6] The self-effacing Smith defied the popular image of a submarine commander. Rather than a display of the bravado and assertiveness of some commanders, crew members saw in Smith someone who could be easily overlooked due to his characteristic silence. They saw him as not very demonstrative, but very level-headed and very smart.[7]

George Brown's encounter with Smith during construction was not unusual. Another crewman, Electrician's Mate Robert E. Dyer, described Smith's hands-on reputation: "He [Smith] crawled through the boat literally as it was being built in Mare Island for over a year. The finished product was a reflection of his capabilities as a submarine officer."[8] Smith knew what was inside the hull. This knowledge was reflected in his management style, as related by Dyer:

Chester Carl Smith. *U.S. Naval History & Heritage Command.*

> The captain's thoroughness and attention to detail during *Swordfish's* construction kept the crew on their toes in maintenance of the machinery and systems. If you had a casualty of an item that had to be reported to the captain, you'd better have your ducks in a row because he was going to ask a lot of detailed questions and the Lord help you if you tried to give him a snow job. He had a long memory.[9]

Smith was mild-mannered, but he was no "push over." He was a stickler on vital matters and, in order to understand his environment, was willing to get his hands dirty.

Born in 1905, the young Smith was frequently engaged in hands-on activities while working on a farm in the Midwest, activities that carried over into his willingness to engage in the hands-on activity of crawling through the interstices of *Swordfish*. Also at an early age, Smith displayed other personal characteristics. He graduated from the U.S. Naval Academy in 1925, and his participation on the Annapolis rifle team for three years was an early indication of his interest in marksmanship, a useful trait for a submarine commander. The success or failure of a war patrol would ultimately depend upon accurately hitting targets, i.e., enemy ships. Smith also displayed the attribute of a successful card player, a poker face. That is, Smith excelled at keeping his thoughts private and not revealing through facial expressions what he was thinking.[10] Much to the disappointment of his Japanese housemaids employed by Smith and his wife, Mary Baxter Smith, while living in Pearl Harbor before the outbreak of hostilities, Smith's reticent nature frustrated any suspected attempts to eavesdrop for military information, as he did not discuss navy operations in the maids' presence. Smith summed up his thoughts, "Must be waiting for me to spill something." Smith never did "spill the beans."[11] Chester Smith's close-mouthed nature also carried over into family relations, as his son, Donald Baxter Smith, related. Chet Smith was also extremely competitive. He kept a notebook of dates and numbers corresponding to his winnings at poker while at Annapolis. His success at card playing continued while stationed at Hawaii, where he hosted frequent card games among the officers. With the Japanese attack on Pearl Harbor, Smith would be engaged in a far more lethal activity, where his desire to score high in the "game" of sinking Japanese ships would prevail.[12]

Despite his young appearance, Smith was no newcomer to submarines, as Brown and his fellow crewmen would in time realize. After a tour of duty on the battleship USS *New Mexico*, he entered the Submarine School at New London. Smith served in the Asiatic Fleet aboard his first submarine, the *S-40*, from 1929 to 1932. During this period on the China Station, Smith gained knowledge of Pacific water conditions which would became second nature to him, as he later conducted war patrols. For his duty aboard *S-40*, the Navy awarded Smith the Yangtze Service Medal. In 1929, Smith married Mary Frances Baxter, and they started raising a family with the birth of a son, Donald. After earning a Master of Science degree in Engineering at the University of California, Berkeley, Smith returned to the Submarine Service as a lieutenant, and in May 1934, Smith resumed sea duty aboard the *S-21*, based at Pearl Harbor. A year later, he assumed command of the *S-23*. Smith's submarine experience continued as Division Engineer from May 1936 to June 1937 for Submarine Division 7, and was attached to the *S-23*, when it was flagship of the division. After a stint as Assistant Inspector of Naval Material in Ohio, Smith moved to Mare Island Naval Shipyard as designated commander of the new fleet submarine, *Swordfish*, where he encountered his electrician, Valentine Brown. The "kid" had more experience than Brown could ever have imagined. Still, Chester Smith's leadership skills were yet to be tested in wartime.[13]

Judging by subsequent results, the period of time between the commissioning of *Swordfish* on 22 July 1939, and the advent of her first war patrol on 8 December 1941, was very productive for Chet Smith and his new crew. They learned the unique characteristics of the boat and of each other. For the rest of 1939, *Swordfish* made ports of call on the West Coast, then went on to Pago Pago, the Samoan Islands, and finally to Pearl Harbor.[14] Although Smith's shakedown cruises were routine and relatively smooth, there was one embarrassing incident that marred the record. During a submergence in the Puget Sound area in August 1941, *Swordfish* grounded, shearing off both sound heads of the hydrophone and its shafts. However, the keel touched bottom with no apparent harm to the hull itself. After the incident, the boat headed for repair at Mare Island, where there were materials and experienced personnel.[15]

After the Mare Island repairs were made, Smith and the crew detected a new problem. There were unusual vibrations in the bridge structure and the periscope supports during submergence and at high speeds on the surface. The number two periscope would shake violently, and routine procedures, such as scanning the horizon or taking accurate ranges, were severely hampered. After the boat returned to the Mare Island yard, workmen stiffened the periscope housing, the main deck

USS *Swordfish* with her original structure prior to alterations to reduce her silhouette, 29 September 1939. *National Archives, College Park.*

and the conning tower, which corrected the problem. By 2 September, the Navy's Bureau of Ships could report the problem as corrected. Afterward, American submariners could identify the boat by the braces installed to stabilize the periscope shears.[16]

After the post-shakedown repairs at the Mare Island Naval Shipyard were completed, *Swordfish* embarked on operations out of San Diego, California, and Pearl Harbor. In particular, Smith had the crew concentrate on target practice, involving the use of torpedoes and the deck gun. For a brief period, the deck gun crew held a record for the time required to score a set number of hits on a towed target.[17] The process of "welding" boat and crew into a fine-tuned weapon proceeded until 3 November 1941, when *Swordfish* headed out of Pearl Harbor for Manila and Smith's previous duty station with the Asiatic Fleet. Accompanied by a tender, *Holland*, and fleet submarines *Salmon*, *Sturgeon*, and *Skipjack*, *Swordfish* carried warheads with the mission of reinforcing the Navy's presence in the Far East. Emerging from the 1939–1941 period was a crew and boat fit for action.

On the eve of the Japanese attack on Pearl Harbor, thousands of miles west in Manila, Chet Smith temporarily put aside his concerns and dined with submarine commanders: William ("Bull") Wright of *Sturgeon*, Mort Mumma of *Sailfish*, Dick Voge of *Sealion*, and Freddie Warder of *Seawolf*. Enjoying a dinner of Chateaubriand steak, chablis and crepes suzette, the quintet resolved to eat at the restaurant more often. As part of the U.S. Asiatic Fleet, each officer understood his role as protector of the Philippines, which the United States had held as a Far Eastern outpost since the Spanish-American War. What they did not know was that their roles in the war that commenced the next day would be grossly magnified. The destruction of the U.S. surface fleet at Pearl Harbor threw upon the submarine service the full brunt of confronting Imperial Japan. Instead of serving as forward scouts for the main battle fleet as originally intended, submarines were, at least for the time being, *the* battle fleet. The time for long, leisurely meals had ended.

Upon receiving news of the attack on Pearl Harbor on 8 December (7 December Pearl Harbor time), the submarine command urgently summoned Smith and the other submarine skippers to a conference aboard *Holland*. In the early morning hours, a coxswain knocked on Smith's door at the officers club and informed him of the emergency. Concerned for the safety of his wife, Mary, and son, Donald, he had sent them to the American mainland a month earlier and had moved his quarters to the club.[18]

Acting on his own before receiving official orders, Admiral Thomas C. Hart, head of naval forces in the Philippines, issued the order for unrestricted submarine warfare. Later that afternoon, the official order came from Washington. Orders for unrestricted submarine warfare represented the culmination of a long evolution in military planning against the most likely adversary in the Pacific: Japan. Recognizing Japan's aggressive foreign policy in the Far East and her expanding naval strength, American naval planners developed War Plan Orange, which envisioned a possible future engagement and defeat of Japanese naval forces and a subsequent naval blockade of the Japanese home islands. U.S. naval strategists believed that because Japan had a paucity of raw materials and limited resources of food, cutting off imported commodities would lead, in time, to Japanese capitulation. In the initial draft of War Plan Orange , American submarines would perform the role of forward scouts for the U.S. fleet and as combatants against Japanese military vessels, rather than targeting Japanese merchant ships. In fact, the London Naval treaty and the London Submarine Protocol of 1936 severely bound submarine tactics when attacking enemy merchant ships. Sacrificing stealth, submarines were required to warn enemy merchant ships of their impending attack, and rules required the removal of the crews before sinking the merchantmen. Under such circumstances, the ready realization was that the submarines were at a distinct disadvantage and subject to counterattack.

As the prospects of U.S. involvement in war increased in the early 1940s, American naval planners drew up plans which delineated possible use of submarines in an unrestricted war against merchant shipping. Facing the distinct possibility of a two-ocean war, involving Germany and Japan, American naval planners set aid to Britain and defeat of Germany as the top priority, while maintaining delaying tactics in the Pacific. Admiral Harold R. Stark, Chief of Naval Operations, provided details for this strategy in November 1940 in his Plan D, which President Franklin Roosevelt tacitly endorsed. For submarine warfare, the conclusion to Plan D shifted in operations from defeating Japan totally to engaging a limited war via an economic blockade. Embedded in this shift was the realization that the United States lacked sufficient naval forces to control the Western Pacific. In these circumstances, the main unit capable of extending naval operations against imperial Japan was the Submarine Service, but, most importantly, the strategy would implicitly require abandoning previous international rules, which fettered submarine effectiveness, in favor of submarine warfare, unrestricted and unrestrained.

The navy took another step toward unrestricted submarine warfare when Admiral Stark and his chief planner, Rear Admiral Richard Kelly Turner, incorporated into the navy's "Rainbow 3" war plans authorization for "strategic areas," where protecting U.S. forces meant the exclusion (i.e., sinking) of all enemy forces, including merchant ships and aircraft. The expectation was unrestricted submarine warfare, since all forces in these strategic areas were presumed to be hostile, whether they be military or merchant marine. Stark sent Rainbow 3 plans to the fleet commanders, including Admiral Hart. In 1941, it was understood that such strategic war areas would be immediately established at the outbreak of war, and by the end of November 1941, the top naval commanders prepared for an imminent conflict with Japan, including orders for unrestricted submarine warfare. As naval historian Joel Holwitt has noted, Hart's order for beginning unrestricted warfare was not an isolated decision, but was, as Holwitt states, "the culmination of a year of strategic legal and moral consideration by naval leadership."[19] Subsequently, Japan's unprovoked, surprise attack on Pearl Harbor swept away any legal considerations set down in international law, and submarine operations commenced.

The order sending U.S. submarines out on patrol to sink Japanese merchant ships was no longer a matter of choice. With the destruction of a major part of the U.S. Pacific fleet on December 7, the U.S. Navy command had to put into operation one of the few options available, a war on commerce or *guerre de course*. Historically, the advisability of conducting such a commerce war by the weaker of two naval powers was a concept espoused by French naval strategists in the 19th century. They recognized that their fleet could not match the strength of the British navy, their chief adversary, if a direct engagement should occur. As an alternative, they advocated a war of attrition on British commerce. They reasoned that such a protracted campaign was the surest means of subjugating Britain, because the island nation would find her commercial losses too costly and would capitulate. Britain maintained naval superiority and, despite French hopes, the French strategy failed. However, the concept of a war on commerce remained an option in naval planning, and after Japan's devastating attack at Pearl Harbor, the stark reality of America's reduced naval strength induced the American naval command to resort to the option of an unrestricted submarine war on the Japanese merchant marine, a *guerre de course*. To be sure, Japanese military vessels were also targets, but the emphasis would be on Japanese merchant shipping.[20]

With the commencement of unrestricted submarine warfare in December 1941, the unfettered sinking of enemy ships became the highest priority for American submarine commanders. The success or failure of each submarine patrol depended upon whether or not the commander sank enemy ships. The U.S. submarine command expected such outcomes, and it duly rewarded successful commanders with decorations and promotions. On the other hand, on several occasions the results-minded naval command transferred out of the Submarine Service commanders who returned from patrol empty-handed or warned them to be more aggressive. There was no formal point system, but expectations of the submarine high command were clear. In endorsements to a submarine commander's patrol report, the high command officers would note whether the commander had been sufficiently aggressive, and they kept tallies of ships sunk and Japanese tonnage lost, which indicated the effectiveness of each commander and of submarine operations in general.

The personal bent of many submarine commanders augmented the risk and reward policy instituted by the U.S. Submarine Service's high command. The leadership position of a submarine commander was voluntary and prestigious, but also dangerous. A commander's reputation was equated with how many enemy ships were sunk under his command—the more the better. As the war progressed and as a commander's count of torpedoed ships accumulated, the commander and crewman would display as a matter of pride a banner with symbols of ships sunk sewn on a field of blue. Also, the analogy of commander competition and sports rivalry was recognizable. As in a sports competition, within the Submarine Service there was undoubtedly a friendly rivalry as to which commander could rack up the most ships sunk. Nevertheless, when out on patrol in the lonely position of command, each submarine skipper would realize that his real competition was against the Japanese military forces intent upon his destruction. No doubt there was also a matter of self-interest attached to successfully sinking enemy ships. As noted, submarine commanders could look forward to recognition in the form of decorations and promotions. Therefore, keeping track of the sinking of enemy ships was of value not only to the submarine high command, but also to aggressive submarine commanders.

After the achievement of victory in 1945, submarine sinking statistics took on a different meaning as a U.S. joint army-navy committee studied them. Although criticized for being too reluctant to give credit for unconfirmed sinkings, the committee's assessment report clearly showed the high degree of devastation achieved by the Submarine Service. The tallies of enemy ships and tonnage sunk amply demonstrated the effectiveness of American submarine operations. American submarines destroyed approximately 60 percent of Japanese merchant shipping. The continuation of the development of the United States submarine operations during the Cold War was based in part on the recognized effectiveness of submarine sea power. In this sense, the impact of the number of ships sunk during World War II lasted well beyond the war years. However, at the outset of war Chester Smith had precious little time for contemplation.

Captain Wilkes gave each submarine commander sealed orders. Smith was ordered to take *Swordfish* to sea immediately to patrol waters off the coast of Hainan, China. Navy planners believed that Hainan would be one of the embarkation points for Japanese ships involved in attempts to invade the Philippines. The crew was alerted. Motor Machinist Mate Second Class Lloyd Faye remembered the Shore Patrol advising him and his shipmates to return to *Swordfish*. Faye says that at first, no one knew what was happening. News of the Pearl Harbor attack came shortly thereafter.[21] Another member of the crew, Robert E. Dyer, remembered where he was when he learned of the Pearl Harbor attack. In the early morning hours, he and other shipmates were ashore "touring" the cabarets, having just returned from a cruise around Luzon. They had not heard anything concerning the whereabouts of the Japanese aircraft carriers. Upon hearing the news of the Pearl Harbor attack, they took a launch to *Swordfish*.[22]

For the patrol, *Swordfish* received a limited supply of food, torpedoes, and fuel. Chief Firecontrolman Vernon Fields characterized conditions: "They were short, and all submarines were clamoring to get these essential things for a long war patrol. We just seemed to get our share of what we could and got underway."[23] Time was of the essence. Underscoring the shift to a wartime footing, a final procedure before departing involved offloading classified documents carried on board in peacetime, but put ashore in wartime to avoid capture by the enemy. Smith and

1. Chester Smith: The Quiet Hunter

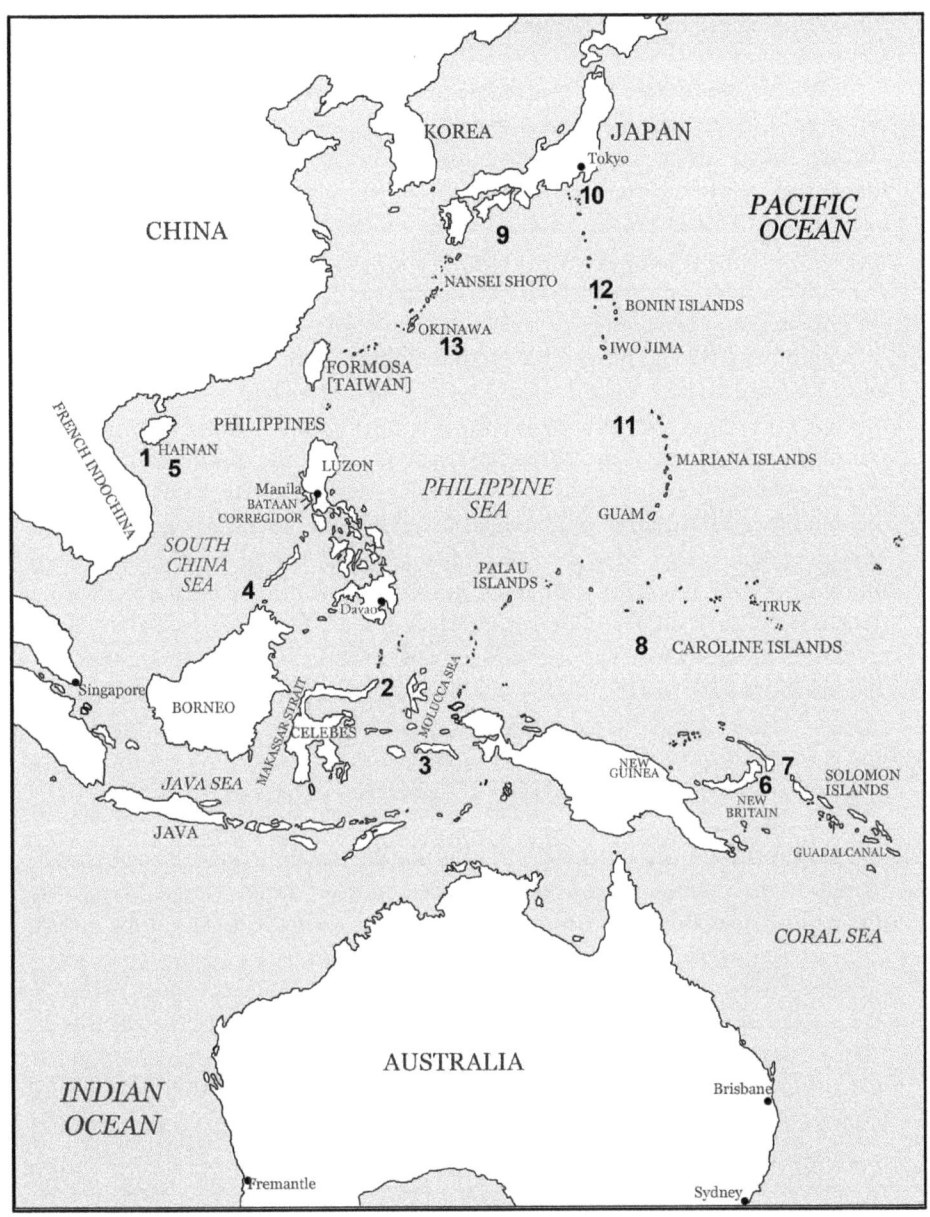

War patrols of the USS *Swordfish* (numbered). *Map by Eliz Alahverdian.*

a receiving officer meticulously accounted for each item in the transfer. Secrecy was paramount.[24]

When *Swordfish* set out from its anchorage at Mariveles in Manila Bay at 1425 hours on 8 December, the somber mood of the crew reflected the dark shadow that the Pearl Harbor attack had cast upon the Asiatic Fleet.[25] Although the commander and crew had trained for the rigors of combat, no one aboard could be certain of what lay ahead. The only certainty was that the world each seafarer had known beforehand had been torn in two and was truly a matter of the past. More than anyone else, the crew of *Swordfish* looked to their leader, Chester C. Smith, for guidance and assurance. He had been promoted to Lieutenant Commander in September 1939 and now was a wartime skipper. True, Smith was not the sole authority aboard. Each boat had a chain of command with a team of subordinate officers. Directly under the commander was the executive officer, the XO, who was responsible for the daily routines of the boat. Under the commander and XO, there were usually four other officers: the engineering officer, the diving officer, the communications and commissary officer, and the gunnery and torpedo officer. But as skipper, Smith knew that the fate of *Swordfish* and her crew ultimately rested on his shoulders. Out on patrol, his men would expect him to make the crucial decisions. At 1511, off the mined entrance of Manila Bay, *Swordfish* submerged, and Smith ordered a westerly course that would take the boat into Japanese waters and into submarine history.[26]

Michael Billy's Transformation

Meanwhile, 4,767 miles away in Hawaii, Michael Billy decided to volunteer for duty in the Submarine Service. While serving aboard the destroyer, USS *Flusser*, Fireman Michael Billy returned to Pearl Harbor from sea with American aircraft carriers and the escorting destroyers that were not present during the Japanese attack of 7 December. Billy had been in the peacetime Navy since August 1940 and had numerous friends at Pearl. In a very real sense, the Navy was like a family to Billy. He was one of seven children orphaned at an early age, and he found much comradeship in the Navy ranks. He also remained loyal to his siblings, sending home part of his paycheck to help them contend with the hard economic times still present. Another element was also present in Michael Billy, a deep sense of patriotism. In his home town of Rahway, New Jersey, Billy became familiar with local World War I veterans, who passed on to him and other young citizens their sense of dedication and service, which amounted to safeguarding democratic ideals and the American way of life.

By nature, Michael Billy was soft-spoken and mild-mannered, unless provoked, which brought out a deep determination to push back and to rise up to any challenge. In high school, he was a key player on the school's football team, where the need to defeat the opposing team provoked in him a deep resolve. The Japanese attack on Pearl Harbor was such an event. Seeing the carnage and destruction at Pearl Harbor raised Billy's ire and made an indelible impression on this 20-year-old. Many of his friends were casualties.[27] As with so many Americans, both military and civilian, the shock of the attack solidified in Billy's mind a resolve to avenge this brazen act. For Michael Billy and many other Americans, the Japanese sneak attack violated the American sense of fair play. The attack amounted to a foul attempt to humiliate and to "push Americans around" into submission. Americans of Michael Billy's generation bristled at the idea of accepting defeat at the hands of Japan, and they took up the challenge.[28]

Michael Billy made a fundamental decision. Desiring to avenge the attack, like so many other Americans, he sought an active role in the war effort. Not content to remain on *Flusser*, Billy volunteered for what he believed would be the cutting edge of the American response to Japan, the U.S. Navy's Submarine Service. In May 1942, he was assigned to the Submarine Service and entered the Submarine Service training school in New London, Connecticut. Ironically, Commander Karl Hensel, Officer in Charge at the school, would later become the skipper of *Swordfish* for her tenth patrol. After Billy completing training in September 1942, the Navy assigned him to USS *Gunnel*, which he expected to go to the Pacific. Instead, under the command of Lieutenant Commander John S. McCain, Jr., *Gunnel* went to the Atlantic, where, operating out of Scotland, she participated in preparations for the landings of the North Africa Campaign.[29]

Michael Billy. *Author's collection.*

As was usual for young sailors, while aboard *Gunnel* in Scotland, the 22-year-old Billy took an interest in the limited social activities while in port. There was a local dance hall which attracted many of the American servicemen on liberty, and illustrative of Mike Billy's determination to go there one evening, shipmate Robert MacDonald described how Billy was in such a rush to board the liberty boat that he fell into the water. The soaked Billy rushed back to quarters, and in a matter of minutes he appeared in MacDonald's borrowed "dress blues" and went off to the dance.

In order to utilize American submarines more effectively where surface targets would be more plentiful, the Navy transferred *Gunnel* to the Pacific theater of operation in 1943, but for the time being, Michael Billy remained in the Atlantic both for training at the Submarine School in New London, Connecticut, and for assignments on submarines *Barb* and *Blackfish*. During this period, Billy changed his classification from Fireman to Motor Machinist's Mate. Early in his youth, Billy had developed an interest in automobile and boat engines, and the Navy recognized his interest. Finally on 28 September 1943, Billy achieved his original desire to serve in the Pacific, where he applied his skills while assigned to USS *Drum*, and the Navy promoted Billy to Motor Machinist's Mate Second Class. When the Navy transferred Billy to *Swordfish* on 13 May 1944, he had already been in the Atlantic and Pacific theaters of operation, and he had served on several boats. By that date, *Swordfish* had endured the rigors of 11 war patrols and had gained a substantial reputation.

It should be noted that sailors had various reasons for volunteering for submarine duty. Many seafarers like Michael Billy believed they would be most effective in the war against Japan by serving on the boats. Some of them looked forward avidly to hunting down enemy shipping. Other submariners displayed an all-or-nothing attitude. They observed that submariners were seldom maimed or wounded. Either you survived intact or you died. There was no middle ground. Other sailors entered the Submarine Service because it offered a higher rate of pay. Another reason for joining the Submarine Service was the informal environment aboard the boats. While on patrol, the stiff formality usually observed on surface ships was, depending on the commander, often relaxed. Hot and humid conditions aboard often necessitated stripping down to minimal clothing with little distinction among the ranks.[30]

Although most of the men of the submarine force were volunteers, there were instances when the Navy found it expedient to fill in an empty position through an outright assignment. Here too, however, many of the men pressed into submarine duty remained on the boats. The close familial bonds among a submarine crew quickly took hold. Regardless of the initial motivation for entering the Submarine Service, the rigorous, mission-oriented training resulted in a very lethal fighting force. Initially, Japanese submariners believed that Americans would be too comfort-prone to endure the privations of submarine duty.[31] As the war progressed, the Japanese would learn that they were very much mistaken. American submariners, such as Michael Billy, were quite willing to forgo comforts in order to avenge the Pearl Harbor attack. In William Shakespeare's play, *Julius Caesar*, the revenge-seeking Marcus Antonius calls out, "Cry 'Havoc!' and let slip the dogs of war."[32] To paraphrase Shakespeare, through their hubris, the Japanese had unleashed the American dogs of war.

The Hunt Begins

While proceeding to the patrol area early in the morning of 9 December, Chet Smith sighted a steamer. *Swordfish* approached it on the surface. Smith thought he had come upon an aircraft tender traveling at 13 knots. However, comparison with silhouette charts of Japanese ships led him to conclude that he had in his sights a 3,900-ton merchant ship, and at 0057, the target was within a range of 1,000 yards. Smith went after his quarry with the methodical coolness of a master engineer, which he was. Aiming at the ship's foremast, Smith fired off two torpedoes with an interval of ten seconds. He had hoped to achieve a longitudinal spread pattern in the tracks of the two shots and thereby increase the chance of a hit. The torpedoes raced to the intended victim for a planned run of 700 yards and at a depth of 40 feet.[33]

By his surface attack, Smith had already defied standard submarine tactics, which early in the war called for deep, submerged attacks. Only after his assault did he order a dive in order to avoid a possible enemy counter-attack. Results of *Swordfish's* torpedoes came with the sound of one explosion heard in the maneuvering room. The noise of the submarine's dive prevented most of the rest of the crew from hearing the explosion, but the very audible noise of the Japanese ship's propellers had ceased to be heard by the listening gear.[34] At first, the close torpedo detonations startled the crew and were, as crewman Lloyd Faye reported, a "shocker." Faye remembered the shock waves putting out electric lights and breaking filaments,[35] and Donald Gaither recalled the tense atmosphere within the boat during this initial attack.[36] Vernon Fields added, "We were all very nervous during the attack, it being the first one and the first time any of us had heard a torpedo go off in fact."[37] Fred Kramer, an electrician's mate aboard *Swordfish*, along with other crewmen, cheered as word of the attack spread throughout the boat. They had been anxious to go on patrol and to torpedo enemy ships. The crew was proud of the fact that they were the first to do so. They understood the business they were in, and Japan's unprovoked bombing of Pearl Harbor had left no room for remorse.[38]

Just before temporarily losing depth control, Smith caught a fleeting glance of the damage. The stricken ship was sinking evenly, with evidence of a hit one-quarter from the stern. The vessel seemed to have broken in two, which produced a rise in the stern. With a characteristic economy of words, Smith reported the results of this first attack by an American submarine: "Propellers stopped. Stern seen to be bent up—ship settling. Considered sunk."[39] Approximately 20 minutes later, Smith was able to make a periscope observation and reported no ship in sight. At 0151, *Swordfish* surfaced to continue its journey to the assigned patrol area. As far as Smith was concerned, he had sunk an enemy ship, although he could not be certain. His months of training and activity aboard *Swordfish* in peacetime paid off in this first attack. The soft-spoken, quiet-mannered Smith demonstrated very early his willingness to seize opportunities when they came his way. If Smith had, indeed, downed an enemy ship, as he truly believed, he was the first American submarine skipper to do so, closely after the attack on Pearl Harbor.[40]

The next day, 10 December, brought another opportunity. At 0225, *Swordfish* sighted a steamer at a distance of six miles. Smith felt he could have overtaken the ship in a three-hour pursuit, but he calculated that *Swordfish* would have been too close to another submarine's lane, and he chose not to complicate matters or "gum up" another boat's operation. He elected to abandon the chase, but with regret.

Smith earnestly tried to get to his assigned patrol area by the morning of 12 December. With the engines revved up, *Swordfish* proceeded at 18 knots.[41] However, yet another opportunity lured *Swordfish* off its course. At 0525 on 11 December, a steamer was spotted five miles distant and traveling at 10 knots. The target appeared to be a Japanese merchant ship of approximately 3,500 tons. Smith commenced a surface attack similar to his first attack of 9 December. At a range of 1,270 yards, he ordered two torpedoes fired at a ten-second interval. His plan was to achieve a longitudinal spread to increase the opportunity for a hit. Aimed at the ship's foremast, the torpedoes were set to run 1,300 yards at a depth of 40 feet. As a precaution, *Swordfish* submerged, and the crew listened. No explosions were heard, and no change in the speed of the enemy ship's propellers pointed to one result—a miss. The commander concluded that a yaw in the submarine while on the surface caused enough change in position at the time of the firing of the torpedoes to cause the miss.[42]

Smith was confident in the firing data. As in the first attack, he had employed an ingenious piece of American technology that helped aim at the target. Known as a Torpedo Data Computer (TDC), torpedomen could use this device to key into the "fish" essential information concerning the intended target and to plot its course. The TDC measured the angle of approach, the ship's speed and distance, and other factors. After doing these calculations, the computer provided up-to-the-second information for directing the torpedoes on their course. The TDC was wired to the torpedoes right up to the time of firing and could pre-set turns in direction after the "fish" shot out of the torpedo tubes. The TDCs gave American submarine commanders a major advantage during World War II, and the disappointed Smith was certain it was not the TDC data that stymied his success.⁴³ With two precious torpedoes expended and nothing to show for his diversion from his passage to the patrol area, Smith resumed his journey.

Anxious to get to his designated patrol area by 12 December, Smith surfaced to achieve greater speed. However, at 1926, he had to slow *Swordfish* to 10.5 knots because he could not maintain adequate lookouts in the rough seas that the boat encountered. Smith barely made his goal as *Swordfish* entered the patrol area at 2200 on 12 December. Throughout the following day, Smith encountered several steamers and a destroyer. However, he chose to confine himself to sizing up traffic, as the boat stayed submerged in the middle of the patrol area, approximately 12 miles south of Hainan Island. Under the cover of darkness, that evening the boat surfaced. The crew made the boat ready for action.⁴⁴

The crew did not have to wait long to come upon a decent target. While searching near Hainan Island on Sunday morning, 14 December, *Swordfish* came upon a steamer estimated at 9,200 tons and traveling east at 12 knots. Smith followed the practices of his two previous night surface attacks. He quickly moved into position. Seven minutes after sighting the steamer, he aimed for the ship's foremast and fired two torpedoes. The estimated range was 2,000 yards, and the torpedoes were set at 40 feet. Taking a bit longer between firings, the interval was 10.5 seconds. As was his custom, he desired a longitudinal spread to maximize his chance for a hit.⁴⁵ Moonlight gave a brightness to the scene that was not to Smith's liking. He ordered a dive to avoid being spotted and fired upon. On the way down, no one heard an explosion due to the noise of the dive, but previous propeller sounds had ceased. Five minutes later, sounds of gurgling emanated from the direction of the Japanese ship. Seeing nothing in his periscope, the skipper concluded that one or both torpedoes found their mark. The ship was either damaged or sunk.

On the same day at 0907, *Swordfish* sighted a small coastal steamer of 30 tons, but Smith elected not to attack. He was seeking a more substantial target for his precious torpedoes. Fortune beckoned. At 1751, *Swordfish* came across another merchantman that fitted the silhouette for ships of 9,200 deadweight tons. It was going 14 knots and was 3.5 miles distant. Deeming the ship worthy of attack, in less than an hour Smith closed in to within 750 yards in a cautious, methodical, submerged approach. Concerned about being seen in daylight, Smith diverted from his recent pattern of surface attacks. Setting two torpedoes to run at 30 feet depth, this time the commander aimed at points on the hull 50 yards fore and aft amidships. He checked his TDC data. All was ready. The torpedoes were calibrated to run 700 yards to the target.

Smith sent off two torpedoes with an eight-second interval. An explosion 35 seconds later announced success. Apparently, only the second torpedo struck, but it was sufficient to cause the Japanese ship to stop, turn to the north, and list ten degrees to port. The explosion was audible to the crew, and Donald Gaither remembered that his crewmate, George Valentine Brown, was determined to hear a torpedo detonate. Brown prepared for the attack by stuffing cotton in his ears, but in his eagerness to hear a torpedo explosion, he removed the cotton and stood close to the pressure hull to listen. Gaither related that "he [Brown] jumped about two or three feet when the torpedo did go off because at that close range it sounded very much like a depth charge." In reaction, Brown shouted "Rig for depth charge, rig for depth charge!"

Smith could detect no further signs of settling or fire aboard the enemy ship. Intent on finishing off the victim, the commander approached her for a second submerged attack. Smith reported, "There were no further signs of ship settling, nor fire on board so at 1842 fired one torpedo, range 1,400 yards, zero degrees gyro, at MOT [middle of target]."[46] Again, set at 30 feet depth, the lone torpedo sped toward the wallowing vessel. The submarine's crew heard an explosion 55 seconds later, and Smith could observe the hapless ship sinking until darkness blotted out the scene. In his concise style, Smith reported, "Consider definitely sunk."[47] In order to avoid contact with the enemy rescue facilities ashore, *Swordfish* cleared the area.

On Monday morning, the submarine commander came across a new, sinister phenomenon at sea. While submerged near Yulinkan, *Swordfish* sighted a lone steamer eight miles in the distance. After a one-and-a-half-hour approach and closing to 6,000 yards, Smith spied a wholly different scene. Making four to five knots, the steamer plowed through the sea, displaying a huge Japanese merchant marine flag. This aged merchantman was listing ten degrees to starboard and presented a tempting target. Luckily for *Swordfish*, Smith also detected a Japanese destroyer weaving from side to side astern of what was obviously a decoy. Adding to the menacing scene, an enemy observation plane flew ahead of the decoy. Scrawled in the margin of Smith's war patrol report was the term "Q-Ship." The decoy vessel may have been an armed decoy ship known as a Q-Ship, which was specifically designed to lure submarines into proximity for their destruction.[48] Smith decided to hunt down the hunter and went after the destroyer rather than the decoy. He closed within 4,800 yards when three additional destroyers were sighted to the north, as well as numerous trawlers on patrol in the area. Moving to the side of discretion, the frustrated Smith declined to tangle with this little armada. Proceeding at four knots, he gave the order for *Swordfish* to clear the area.[49]

One for the Record Book

Adding to a patrol already full of surprises, on the morning of 16 December at 1143, Smith's periscope revealed a sight that he could have reasonably thought was the jackpot. While approaching at full speed a steamer that he believed was alone, Smith discovered a total of six merchant ships strung out in a loose column. Chasing the line of ships in a submerged attack, *Swordfish* achieved a minimum

1. Chester Smith: The Quiet Hunter 19

range of 2,800 yards for a torpedo run on the last ship in the column. The American commander gave orders for firing three torpedoes at the "forward goal post," the point amidships and the "after goal post," that is, the ship's upright cargo handling apparatus. Success was only partial, as he reported: "Premature explosion 35 seconds after first shot. Apparently one torpedo fired on arming. Second detonation 2–00 minutes after first shot."[50] Smith saw the ship halt and list ten degrees starboard. Confirming a hit, there was a fire amidships. Circling approximately four miles south of the damaged ship, Smith continued to watch her burn until he sighted a Japanese destroyer five miles distant and an observation aircraft in the vicinity.[51] The submarine commander decided it was time to leave and, descending to 120 feet, *Swordfish* headed southward. In his last sighting of the hapless victim, he noticed that the bow was, as he reported, "well down," and the list had increased to 20 degrees starboard. Also, heavy smoke rose from amidships, and Smith assumed the ship would soon sink. At 1927, *Swordfish* surfaced and reported by radio the passage of the column of transports.[52]

Submariners could not always confirm a sinking, especially when a hostile escort ship or plane made it advisable for the submarine to dive for cover. A sinking was officially confirmed largely after the war. However, when it was believed that a firing was successful in sinking a ship, it was, as *Swordfish* veterans described, a jubilant event similar to scoring a touchdown at a football game. There was cheering and a feeling of victory.[53]

The new day brought two familiar sights. At 0635, Chester Smith noted the blazing ship that *Swordfish* had torpedoed the prior day, which he had assumed was

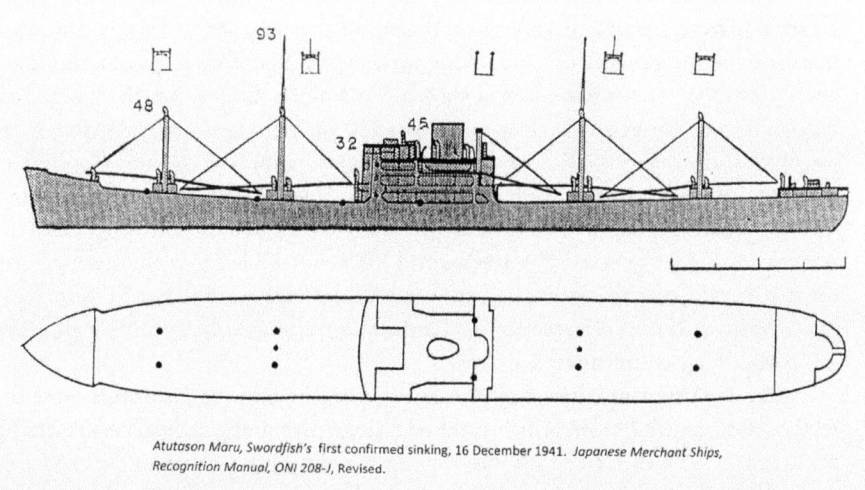

Atutason Maru, Swordfish's first confirmed sinking, 16 December 1941. *Japanese Merchant Ships, ONI 208-J*, Revised.

Atutason Maru, Swordfish's first confirmed sinking, 16 December 1941. *Japanese Merchant Ships, ONI 208-J*, Revised.

sunk. Apparently, the Japanese did not attempt to salvage the ship or its cargo, and it continued to burn and settle in the water, as it drifted toward the Indochinese coast. Seventeen minutes later, a much less welcome sight appeared in the periscope. The decoy ship and approximately 16 trawlers were proceeding in search of what they hoped would be an unsuspecting American submarine. Smith assumed the trawlers had sound detection gear. Overhead, one or two menacing aircraft supplemented the patrol of the trawlers, and a destroyer was sighted six miles in the distance, heading into Sama Bay.[54] Undeterred and unhindered, during the day Smith remained in the area, even though the danger of Japanese attack persisted in the form of patrolling destroyers and aircraft. The cool-headed Smith noted that he "had to dodge trawlers occasionally."[55] The skipper concluded that the neighboring sea was, as he put it, "too smooth and depth too shallow to proceed further" (without risking detection).[56]

At 1927, under the cover of darkness, *Swordfish* surfaced and exited from the vicinity. Smith resumed the patrol in the northwest corner of the patrol area and reported his last sighting that day, "When last sighted just before dark the hulk was still burning 30 degrees P[ort] and settling bow down."[57] The torpedoed ship of 16 December had not yet found its final berth, but eventually it did sink. Unknown to the crew of *Swordfish*, they had sunk (off Samar) the 8,663-ton armed merchant ship, *Atsutasan Maru*. Built by Mitsubishi Bussan Kaisha, Ltd, the ship was completed in 1937 and was used for air defense. The Japanese lost three crewmen and 25 gunners.[58] With this subsequently confirmed attack, *Swordfish* became the first American submarine officially to sink a Japanese ship in World War II. Smith's earlier efforts could not be confirmed.

Unfortunately, 19 December brought a repeat problem that would plague Smith and other American skippers throughout the early years of the conflict, premature exploding torpedoes. Patrolling submerged, *Swordfish* spotted a single Japanese destroyer accompanied by a trawler. Feeling confident, Smith attacked the destroyer. At a dangerously close range of 1,120 yards, he ordered the firing of two torpedoes, aiming at the destroyer's foremast and mainmast. *Swordfish's* problems erupted with a premature torpedo detonation 22 seconds after firing, very much like the premature explosion in the attack of 16 December. On the other hand, the American skipper guessed that the second "fish" missed because the alarmed crew on the destroyer maneuvered to avoid it.[59] Chief Firecontrolman Vernon Fields described the destroyer's reaction: "Naturally he retaliated by coming right down our torpedo wake, to the tube door."[60]

For the first time during this initial patrol, the crew of *Swordfish* came face to face with annihilation. Smith ordered a deep dive and a radical course change of 90 degrees. Within two minutes of firing the torpedoes, a rain of depth charges dropped on both sides of *Swordfish* for a total of eight shattering explosions.[61] To crewman Donald Gaither, the depth charging, as he noted, "made the deck jump under our feet." Stationed in the forward engine room, Gaither later remarked to a fellow machinist, "Anybody who says submarines aren't dangerous is crazy as hell."[62] Just as Gaither was expressing his sentiments, Chester Smith stepped into the engine room. Smith just smiled and continued his survey of possible damage. Starting out as an enlisted man, Ensign Gaither clearly remembered his initial depth charging. Gaither recalled his feelings at the time: "I was sure that once we were ever depth charged they would be sure to get us."[63] The Japanese attacker was dropping the depth charges from alternate racks, and it sounded oddly like the playing of a tune.[64]

Submarine veterans of World War II relate that a depth charge attack is unlike any other experience. Its harrowing nature is almost impossible to convey to others. The depth charging could go on for several hours, testing the endurance of the boat and the nerves of the crew. It has been compared to sitting in an oil drum whose sides are being banged with a baseball bat. During the ordeal, the crew usually remained motionless, except for required submarine functions. Absolute silence was demanded in order not to give away the boat's position by unnecessary noise. With the air conditioning turned off, the walls of the boat would sweat, and so would the crew. The decks would have a slick coat of moisture and would glisten. The knowledge that eternity could come with each detonation caused crewmen to turn inward. Some of the crew would pray in silence, others would think of family and loved ones, and, no doubt, some men would try not to focus at all.[65] For Lloyd Faye, the depth charging was a matter of both faith and fate. He stated that the submarine belonged to God; if the boat burst open, so be it.[66]

Locked in their solitary thoughts, silent and hardly stirring, the crewmen would wait. As a result of the general silence, the whir of those few mechanical systems still functioning was quite audible to the crew, and the sound signaled a very unusual time aboard the vessel. A growing faintness of depth charge explosions was like music to the submariners' ears, for it indicated the growing distance between the submarine and its pursuer, as well as the diminution of the deadly "ash cans."[67]

At times, a submarine would not have to wait, but could elude its pursuers. However, on 19 December, Smith could not steal away from his pursuers. At 1046, he reported, "Managed to sneak away for 15 minutes, but was heavy aft and did not want to pump. Settled on bottom at 174 feet and shut down all auxiliaries. DDs pinging."[68] Smith knew his pumps were noisy, and he elected not to risk attracting enemy vessels with anti-submarine listening gear. He later described the maneuver: "Our bottoming after the depth charge attack was not what we desired but we had settled there and felt that we couldn't do anything to get off." He added, "We didn't want to blow or use too much power on the propellers because of the mud that would be created, all in all, it was an uncomfortable feeling to be lying on the bottom with vessels on the hunt for us."[69] By 1300, the pinging of the sound detection equipment emanating from the destroyers had ceased, and two hours later Smith concluded that it was safe to resume the patrol.

Swordfish rose from the bottom. Cautiously raising the boat to periscope depth at 1607, Smith looked around. Nothing was in sight. *Swordfish* slipped away to the southeast corner of the patrol area. With the wrenching experience of the depth charge attack fresh in his mind, Smith sent off a message complaining about the torpedo exploding prematurely, giving away the submarine's location. A damage survey revealed nothing serious, and the boat continued the hunt.[70] The men of *Swordfish* had achieved the dubious distinction of withstanding one of the early depth charge attacks on an American submarine in World War II. Nevertheless, joviality returned among the crew as they realized that their skipper was not only adept in attacking the enemy, but also at evasion.[71] The crew's confidence in Smith continued to grow.

More Troublesome Torpedoes

Two days later, 21 December, the crew of *Swordfish* witnessed another problem with their torpedoes. The submarine sighted a steamer five miles away, proceeding westward and hugging the coast for protection. After tracking the target for a little more than an hour, *Swordfish* fired a single "fish" at a close range of 1,000 yards. Set at a depth of 16 feet, the torpedo missed. Analyzing the failure, Smith thought the depth had been set too deep or that the ship had spotted the incoming "fish" and maneuvered to avoid it. Smith observed, "The miss was probably caused by the torpedo running underneath the target because in looking through the periscope, I could see many people pointing over the side at the track of the torpedo as it approached them."[72] Unknown to American submarine crews in the early years of the war, the torpedoes had an inherent flaw in their depth-setting device, and the torpedoes would run deeper than the designated setting. Time and again, submarine skippers sent torpedoes that would pass under their targets at depth too deep to trigger a magnetic exploder, which was designed to react with the ship's steel hull.[73] Aboard *Swordfish*, Smith had assumed he fired at a ship that was lighter in the water than originally seen through his periscope, but the faulty depth setting could very well have been the "culprit." At a range of 1,000 yards, missing the target was possible, but less likely than at longer ranges.[74]

Lurking within the Mark 14 torpedoes used on the fleet boats was yet another flaw. Even when submarine commanders got the Mark 14s to strike the hull of a ship, many of them failed to explode. Unknown at the time, a faulty firing pin sheared on impact and resulted in a dud.[75] The Navy's Bureau of Ordnance had developed the Mark 14, with its Mark 6 magnetic exploder. In a defensive stance, the Bureau disdainfully refused to admit flaws in design, even though the torpedoes had never been tested in peacetime with "live" warheads. A stringent budget and bureaucratic smugness had militated against such testing. The Bureau blamed submarine commanders for improper utilization of the Bureau's creation.

Skipper after skipper complained about missed opportunities on their war patrols. Worse yet, after the torpedoes failed, the commanders and crew were subjected to the punishment of the counter-attack. The telltale bubbles from the faulty torpedoes often gave away the boat's location. Evidence of faulty torpedoes in wartime attacks with "live" warheads did not alter the arrogance of the Bureau.[76]

Admiral Charles A. Lockwood, commander of submarine operations in the southwest Pacific and, after February 1943, commander of all submarine operations in the Pacific, heard about the frustrations over the torpedoes from submarine skippers coming back from patrols. An exasperated Lockwood excoriated the Ordnance Bureau for its "head in the sand" attitude and complained, "If the Bureau of Ordnance can't provide us with torpedoes that will hit and explode ... then for God's sake get the Bureau of Ships to design a boat hook with which we can rip the plates off the target's sides."[77]

Reacting to Lockwood's relentless campaign to "debug" the torpedoes, the Head of the Bureau of Ordnance, Rear Admiral William H. P. Blandy, alternated between trying to placate the critical admiral and, at other times, accusing Lockwood of not recognizing his commanders' faulty procedures for employing torpedoes while on patrol. Although Blandy was sincere in his desire to locate defects in the MK14 torpedo and the MK6 exploder, it was left largely to Charles Lockwood and also to his subordinate, Captain James Fife, to ferret out the disabling defects. BuOrd was essentially reluctant to face the need to re-examine its "brain children," the MK14 torpedo and the MK6 exploder, regardless of the possible consequences for the submariners on patrol.

In 1943, Admiral Lockwood took the unusual step of conducting his own torpedo tests to get to the bottom of the problem. Risking his career and the wrath of the Bureau of Ordnance, Lockwood came up with sufficient evidence to compel the ordnance unit begrudgingly to admit serious mistakes in the Mark 14's design. Tests revealed that the Mark 14 had a poorly designed depth mechanism which caused the 14s to run ten feet deeper than their setting. Commanders were authorized to reset the depth. Similarly, magnetic exploders were disconnected in 1943 when it was realized that the sensor of the exploder often caused premature detonations. Finally, Lockwood's tests indicated that the standard firing pins of the contact exploders would jam, especially upon contact with an enemy hull at a direct 90-degree angle. A lighter firing pin was installed.[78]

It is not known how many boats were lost due to faulty torpedoes and subsequent enemy retaliation, but the submarine commanders knew at a very early date that the torpedoes were not working correctly. Concerning the premature explosions witnessed on his first war patrol, Smith spelled out the grave nature of the defect: "This condition is serious in that it discloses the position of the submarine for immediate depth charge attack and may thus readily cause the loss of the submarine."[79]

On 22 December, *Swordfish* came across new targets, but also her longest ordeal with danger thus far. Submerged and patrolling the same area as previously, at 0637 *Swordfish* picked up sounds of a propeller. When Smith raised the boat to periscope depth, the lens revealed a Japanese destroyer 2,000 yards away. Seven minutes later, the sounds and sight of a Japanese steamer within a range of 1,000 yards came into reach. The merchantman made several quick changes in course, but *Swordfish* continued tracking, intent on a kill.

Drawing on the experience of several previous attacks, Chester Smith displayed the sophistication of a master billiard player. At 0654, he ordered a salvo of two torpedoes fired for a run of 5,000 yards at low power in order to gain maximum effect. Smith revealed his intentions: "These had chance of hitting the steamer, the DD, or causing the steamer to veer into mine field to avoid."[80] If the Japanese ship was going to dodge the torpedo, Smith wanted consequences. As an added dividend, firing at such a long distance would allow the *Swordfish* to elude the depth charges of a counter-attack. After what must have seemed an interminable wait of nine minutes, three explosions were heard, and an increase of smoke from the Japanese ship was observed. Nevertheless, the American skipper doubted that he had damaged the vessel. Sighting a destroyer nearby and detecting the telltale pinging of two warships at 0730, he did not press the attack. A flat, calm sea increased the chance of seeing the boat's periscope.[81]

At 0905, Smith spotted a new steamer in ballast. He closed in for an attack but could not get within 5,000 yards of his intended victim. Increased anti-submarine activity forced Smith to halt his approach, and from that point onward, the Japanese created a day of hell for the men of *Swordfish*. At 0945, a Japanese aircraft commenced a depth charge attack. Rigging for depth charges, *Swordfish* dove to 135 feet and endured 12 explosions. In his understated way, Smith described the detonations as "quite close."[82] Only moments before, the skipper had scanned the horizon, and the aircraft attack came as a complete surprise. However, by 1115 a survey of the horizon via periscope indicated a seascape devoid of activity, except for the lonely white-caps on the surface.[83]

The boat lingered in the anonymity of a depth at 90 feet for 20 minutes before ascending to 70 feet for another scan of the horizon. The time of trial was renewed as an enemy plane again dropped a dozen depth charges in an effort to end the boat's life. Smith took the evasive action of diving hastily to 135 feet and also changing course 135 degrees. Even though *Swordfish* stayed at 135 feet for over an hour, the sea did not conceal her. At 1358, an aircraft unloaded eight more depth charges. After a tense passage of 90 minutes and hearing no propeller noises, Smith ordered the start of the drain pump to adjust trim. He had hoped to slip away. The enemy had other plans.

The sound gear aboard *Swordfish* picked up propeller noise, and at 1451, a destroyer dropped five more depth charges "fairly close," as Smith tensely related.[84] The Japanese pressed on with their hunt. One hour and 15 minutes after the most recent depth charge attack, either a destroyer or a fast torpedo boat on the surface crossed above the bow of *Swordfish*, traveled close to the starboard side, and passed astern. It dropped four more "ash cans" well astern at 600 yards distance. As daylight was nearing its end at 1655, the crew of *Swordfish* withstood yet another attack, this time probably from an airplane, as there were no propeller sounds from enemy ships. The aircraft delivered seven depth charges to close out an unforgettable day for the occupants of *Swordfish*.[85] The crew was delighted with the waning of daylight and of the attacks overhead.[86]

After keeping the boat at a depth of 135 feet for over seven hours, Smith surfaced under the cover of darkness and stole off to the southwest corner of the patrol area. He surveyed the damage. Upon examining the hull, the crew literally "sniffed out" an oily smell emanating from two broken bolts in a flange on the after-fuel filling connection.[87] Vernon Fields described the scene: "at night our men who knew the fuel oil system climbed in the superstructure and they rubbed their hands along the fuel oil lines, smelling their hands trying to detect the oil, which eventually led to the location of our leak."[88] There was evidence of oil in the area of the connection, and Smith concluded that the enemy aircraft had trailed a telltale oil slick back to *Swordfish*. Ensign Donald Gaither described the nighttime repair: "We were well flooded down, had to sit in water up to our waist to take this fitting off, put on new gasket, new threads, and make it tight. It was quite a job, and very scary, I know I was scared."[89]

Satisfied with the repair of the fitting, Smith put his men to work on another task. He had them prepare for the transfer of three torpedoes from the after torpedo room to the forward torpedo room. Chet Smith's decision to move torpedoes forward while surfaced was fraught with risk and complications. As Smith characterized the procedure, "This is considered [a] rather dangerous procedure but we needed them and thought that was the logical thing to do. Put them where we could use them." The shift required lifting the torpedo through a rear torpedo loading hatch and then, while on deck, wheeling the "fish" forward on a small cart and trucking it to the forward loading hatch, where a boom was used to lower the torpedo into the forward torpedo room, all while the submarine was subject to pitching and rolling in the open sea. In addition to contending with the sea, the shifting of three torpedoes took nearly two hours, and during that time the submarine was extremely vulnerable to attack, since the boat would not be ready to crash dive with one or more hatches open.

While on deck, circumstances were especially dangerous for the 12 to 15 crewmen detailed to perform the procedure. Torpedoes weighed over 3,000 pounds and a chance shift in a "fish" could result in a seaman's arm or leg being crushed into "jelly." Getting the men below in a sudden attack would also be a problem. Smith believed the crew would have to let the torpedo go and, as Smith put it, "hope for the best." While the boat dived, a loose torpedo on deck could rake the superstructure, causing any amount of damage. Smith could have left the torpedoes aft and resorted to possible stern shots, but the flexibility of having the torpedoes forward, in Smith's mind, outweighed the aft position, and Smith aimed to maximize every advantage. By 0330 the next morning, the torpedoes had been shifted forward and were made ready for more hunting, but in response to orders from the commander of submarines, Smith headed *Swordfish* to home port.[90]

Christmas Day, 1941, was spent at sea, and the crew of *Swordfish* had much to reflect upon. For the time being, they were at a peaceful juncture. They had mounted successful attacks and had survived repeated depth charge attacks, which had been a harrowing ordeal, especially for a crew that had no prior exposure to such danger. Their commander, Chester Smith, had shown his mettle and his unflappable composure. *Swordfish* had demonstrated its durability. The diesel engines had held up, and the hull had kept out the hostile sea. The crew could also reflect upon their collective experience as submariners welded together in the bonds of conflict. The intangible links forged among them were very much part of the success of the patrol.

Thinking of home, Chester Smith wrote a revealing letter to his father, Arthur L. Smith. Smith wrote that he was thinking of his relatives in Boise (Idaho) and said he was celebrating Christmas by writing a few letters. Smith went on to give his thoughts on the war. He wrote: "The outbreak of the war must have come as quite a shock to all of you. Now that it is in progress I hope that the people are taking it seriously and putting out every effort to prosecute it to a successful conclusion. War these days is not necessarily a function of the Army and Navy but of the whole nation. You may be well assured that we will do our part very seriously and energetically." Regardless of Smith's deceptively mild outer manner, his deadly earnest sense of mission was present. Moreover, he had realized that victory would require a national effort.[91]

As for the statistical record, *Swordfish's* maiden war patrol was surely a success. Smith and his crew were credited with sinking *Atsutasan Maru* on 16 December. In addition, *Swordfish* probably damaged the Japanese ship that she attacked twice on 14 December, *Kashii Maru*. Moreover, as noted, Smith believed he had been successful in sinking a ship on 9 December, although there was no evidence to corroborate a sinking. The disparity of claimed credit for a successful attack and subsequent confirmation was not unique to Smith's patrol. In order to avoid enemy retaliation after an attack, time after time, American submarine commanders were not able to linger long enough to observe their targets go under. Kenneth J. Keyser, a radioman on *Swordfish*, put the matter plainly, "But we can't ever stick around to see whether they go down."[92] In any event, *Swordfish's* record of being the first U.S. submarine to sink a Japanese ship in World War II stands with the confirmed sinking of *Atsutasan Maru*. *Swordfish* was the first.[93]

The 25th of December brought a message from the commander of submarines, which delayed temporarily the return of the boat. At 2330, *Swordfish* was directed to perform anti-submarine duty 30 miles from Corregidor prior to entering Manila Bay. Throughout the next day, *Swordfish* remained on patrol, noting at one point the blurred image of a destroyer, but unable to determine with any degree of assurance if it was friend or foe. Finally, at midnight *Swordfish's* bow turned toward the mined entrance of Manila Bay and passed the number two buoy. Twenty-two minutes later, the maiden war patrol of *Swordfish* ended as she anchored in 15 fathoms (90 feet) of water off Mariveles on the Bataan Peninsula. The following day, she moored at the island base of Corregidor.[94] When the boat was tied up alongside the dock at Corregidor, the crew took on stores and torpedoes, and the boat took on fuel while anchored in the bay. Donald Gaither recalled the press of the tasks at hand: "We were not able to go ashore and the only rest we got was rest that we got in the boat while lying submerged in Manila Bay, having to work all night getting fuel and stores aboard and getting ready to go out again."[95]

During their ever so brief stay, Smith and his crew learned details of the set of reverses that plagued the Allies after *Swordfish* departed for patrol on 8 December. Japanese naval units had sunk the British capital ships, *Repulse* and *Prince of Wales*, and Japanese troops had landed in Malaya. British forces retreated to Singapore, and the Japanese laid siege to Hong Kong. Moreover, a Japanese invasion force had overrun the stalwart but woefully outnumbered American forces on Wake Island.[96]

However, the most heart-rending action for the Asiatic Submarine Force took place in the Philippines. Within 48 hours after the attack on Pearl Harbor, Japanese air units destroyed most of the American air force while still on the ground. General Douglas MacArthur, head of the ground and air forces, failed to send the aircraft aloft to repulse the Japanese air assault. Thereafter, Japanese aircraft could bomb Manila and the nearby Navy installations at will. Submarines resorted to the practice of submerging in Manila Bay during the day to avoid being targets for enemy aircraft. Similarly, facing imminent danger and loss of the remaining surface units of the Asiatic Fleet, the head of the naval forces in the Philippines, Admiral Thomas C. Hart, on 9 December commenced ordering Navy surface ships to move out of Manila and head for the Malay Barrier. Japanese aircraft were making the Navy base at Cavite a shambles.[97]

Defense of the Philippines was placed in the hands of John Wilkes and the Asiatic Submarine Force. By 11 December, Wilkes had ordered 22 submarines to sea. His plan was for the boats to fan out east and west in a broad defense of Luzon, the main Philippine island. The aim was to catch enemy ships en route before they could land troops. As with *Swordfish*, some of the submarines were dispatched to Japanese-held bases where invasion forces were expected to originate. Other boats were stationed closer to Luzon as a defense perimeter.[98]

Fortune favored the Japanese. On 10 December, the first Japanese troops set foot on Philippine soil, and more troops followed at various points on Luzon. When a major Japanese force landed in the Lingayen Gulf, American submarines attempted to bypass Japanese Navy surface ships, in order to reach the landing craft. The navies clashed between 21 and 25 December without hindrance to the landings. The Japanese would not be stopped. Except for *Swordfish* and a handful of other boats, the American submarines were generally unsuccessful in either making enemy contacts or sinking ships. It was too little, too late. The one consolation was that crewmen on *Swordfish* and other submarines knew that they could still re-enter Manila Bay, proving to the Japanese that their surface blockade could not stop the submarines from coming and going. As one crewman expressed it, "That would be bad medicine for those kissers to swallow."[99]

The crewman's comment was an appropriate description of Manila Bay's virtues. The dimensions of the bay were impressive, constituting 30 miles in length and 22 miles in width. The depths were also significant. At the bay's entrance, the general depth was 182 feet, and at the bay's center, the depth measured 92 feet. Because of Manila Bay's expansive nature, the bay was not considered a safe haven during typhoons, but the waters were very suitable for the covert movements of American submarines.[100]

However, as the Japanese consolidated their positions and began to encircle Manila and Bataan, the prospect of maintaining American naval operations out of Manila Bay narrowed. Without adequate air protection, Manila was vulnerable to attack, and General MacArthur declared Manila an "open city." Enemy airplanes attacked American naval units, including two of the fleet submarines. The aircraft damaged USS *Seadragon* and bombed USS *Sealion* beyond repair. In addition, the submarine tender, *Canopus*, suffered a direct hit and was also lost.[101]

In the following days, American submarines became vehicles of escape rather than of attack. On 26 December, Admiral Hart boarded USS *Shark* with two staff officers to depart Manila for the Dutch base at Surabaya, Java. Similarly, concluding that the island bastions of Corregidor and Mariveles Bay were not viable as command posts for submarine operations, on 31 December, John Wilkes decided to move his staff out of the Philippines. The clinching act was General MacArthur's decision to destroy diesel oil stocks so that they would not fall into enemy hands. MacArthur's act of desperation denied American submarines the fuel required for their war patrols.[102]

In order to ensure that at least some of his staff would exit safely past Japanese forces, Wilkes divided his staff between two submarines, *Seawolf* and *Swordfish*. Wilkes elected to evacuate on *Swordfish* with nine staff members. Meanwhile, the other eight submarines in port loaded on submarine crewmen and technicians amounting to approximately 250 men. Many others could not be accommodated. All submarines that were not on patrol were ordered out of Manila. The 31st of December marked the last day of John Wilkes's command in the Philippines.[103] Slipping out of Manila Bay, *Swordfish* carried the Asiatic Submarine Command toward Surabaya to join American and Dutch forces. The trip was relatively uneventful. By 6 January 1942, *Swordfish* had reached Sacol Island. On the same day, *Swordfish* sighted another submarine. An exchange of signals revealed the USS *Shark*, and later, a destroyer was sighted eight miles in the distance. She was USS

Pillsbury, which rendezvoused to escort the *Swordfish* to port. Later, a harbor pilot clambered aboard to guide the submarine through the harbor channel to the navy yard at Oster Haven, Surabaya. Other units of the U.S. and Dutch fleets were present. On the following day, 7 January, John Wilkes and his staff departed *Swordfish*. Mission accomplished![104]

For the crew, Surabaya was the first genuine chance for liberty since the advent of war. However, even in Surabaya recreation was severely limited, because there was no relief crew to refit the boat. The regular crew was largely on their own in preparing the boat for further service. Even so, crewmen had the opportunity to spend a day at a mountain hotel and get a rest from their duties. Crewman Floyd Cooper remembered spending a day at the hotel: "We had dinner and a few drinks, and we greatly appreciated that." At the end of the day, they returned to the boat. The sailors' major complaint was not being able to speak the native language of the taxi cab drivers. The drivers took advantage of the situation by charging the "tourists" higher fees for needlessly going longer distances, a common experience of travelers. Nevertheless, the respite in the country was welcomed.[105]

2

Special Missions

Witnessing the hasty exit of his superior officer, John Wilkes, Chester Smith shoved off from Surabaya intent upon crippling the advance of the Japanese. The American crew departed with mixed sentiments. On the one hand, every crew member was forced to recognize the distasteful exodus from Manila. On the other hand, *Swordfish* had drawn blood on her first patrol, and the second patrol offered the prospect of further success.

Swordfish took the offensive on 16 January 1942, and the assigned patrol area seemed appropriate for good hunting. Operating south of the Philippines, the submarine prowled the waters of Piru Bay off Seram Island, Kema on Celebes Island, Davao in the Philippines, the Molucca Sea, the east coast of Mindanao, and the area off Manila Bay. The entire area was subject to Japanese invasion, and enemy vessels should be present. *Swordfish* would have to navigate around a tangle of islands surrounded by narrow waters with uncertain currents. The restricted waterways provided Smith with the opportunity to locate a target in the confines of narrow channels, but the waters also provided the Japanese with a more controlled area for anti-submarine operations. The chances for success and for failure were heightened.

In particular, the acute problem of torpedoes not hitting targets had to be resolved. Chester Smith ruminated on the dilemma and concluded that he was setting the torpedo depths too deeply, causing the "fish" to pass under the target. On the previous patrol, he had ordered the torpedoes to run at 40-foot and 12-foot depths. Smith decided to alter the settings so the torpedoes would run at shallower depths for actual impact, even though there was a significant risk of the enemy tracing the torpedo wakes back to *Swordfish*. Sometime thereafter, Smith made a further alteration concerning the warheads. Valentine Brown, an electrician aboard *Swordfish*, described changes which were contrary to procedures. Brown wrote: "Then, unofficially, Lieutenant Jim Clarke, Torpedo and Gunnery Officer, and the 'Old Man' [Smith] decided to immobilize the electrical firing device in the warhead."[1] They suspected that the premature explosions were caused, at least in part, by the warhead. Because there were no blueprints on board for the intricate wiring, through trial and error they managed to cut the energizing circuits from the warhead.² Unlike the navy's Bureau of Ordnance, which had developed the torpedoes in peacetime, Smith would be evaluating the validity of his modifications under the demanding conditions of combat.

Eight days into the patrol, *Swordfish* encountered a bit of bad luck. Smith believed that a log or large fish had struck outside the port side aft of the torpedo room, causing the rudder to move sluggishly and with noise while in hand operation. A two-degree left rudder setting became necessary to put the rudder amidships. The submarine's vulnerability had increased with this sacrifice of stealth.³ Nonetheless, Smith pressed on.

The next morning, 24 January, at 1015, while proceeding submerged in a calm sea along the north coast of Celebes Island, *Swordfish* sighted the first of two cargo ships anchored above Kema near Tanjung Merah (Cape Merah). Located at the southern entrance to the Lembeh Strait, the cape's waters are dangerously shallow, ranging in depth from 174 to 466 feet, with coastal areas that are shallower. In particular, a half-mile south of the cape there are shoals in depths of six to 18 feet of water. Any attempt by Smith to enter the waters in a submerged submarine 310 feet in length was risky.⁴

Japanese forces had already landed in the area, but ignoring the presence of ten seaplanes at anchor and several small boats, including a minesweeper and tender, Smith acted. He quietly moved into the lower part of the strait and entered the harbor channel, where workboats darted around the planes and ships. Not seeing a floating boom, Smith reasoned that there would not be mines in the channel. *Swordfish* hugged the Lembeh shoreline to achieve a favorable track and, more importantly, to avoid detection. Smith later remarked, "It's still something of a mystery to me that none of them sighted us."⁵

Inside *Swordfish*, tensions rose with each minute. Peering through the periscope, Smith could see the two ships at anchor, swinging with the current, first north, then east, then north again. Both appeared to be half-loaded. The submarine commander developed his plan of attack. He would fire with a zero degree gyro on a northbound course at a ship estimated to be 7,000 tons. Then, turning 90 degrees to the left, he planned to fire straight shots from the bow tubes at the second ship, estimated to be 10,000 tons. That accomplished, he would quickly swing further left to escape to the open sea. Smith could not determine the velocity of the current, so he decided to fire two torpedoes at each target.⁶ Decisions made, it was time to act. At 1238 hours, *Swordfish* fired two shots at the first ship at an interval of 11 seconds and a range of 2,100 yards. The "fish" were set to run at a depth of eight feet. The sound of two explosions reported results at 27 seconds and again at 42 seconds after firing. As Smith swung the boat round, he noted that the stricken ship was listing 20 degrees to starboard. The vessel had a vertical bow with long well decks, fore and aft, and two derrick masts. It was later learned that *Swordfish* had sunk a converted 4,124-ton gunboat, the *Myoken Maru*.⁷

Smith noted that the second, larger ship had four sets of twin derrick posts,

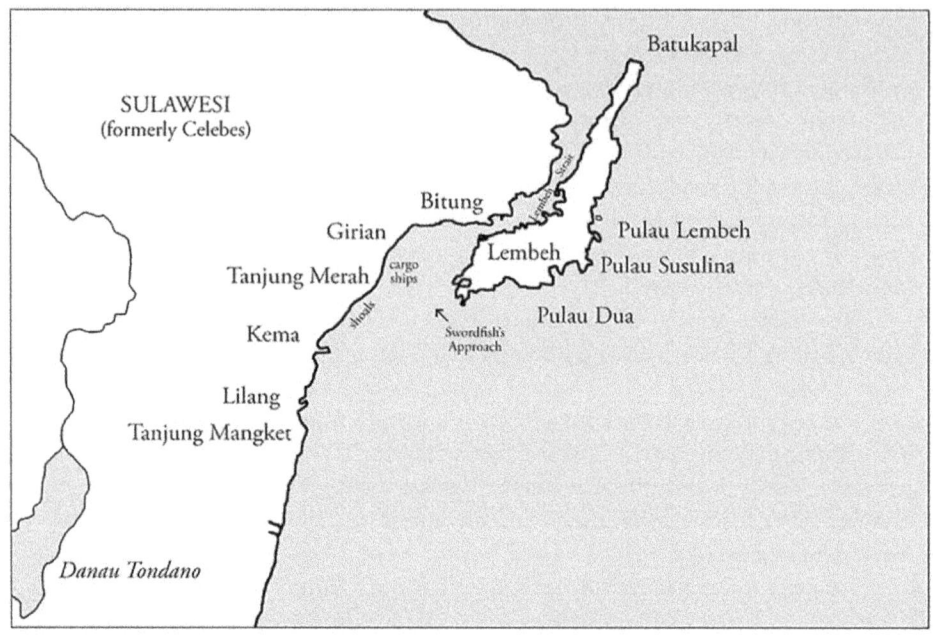

***Swordfish*'s attack in the Lembeh Strait (Selat Lembeh), 24 January 1943.** *Map by Eliz Alahverdian.*

a vertical bow, and a high forecastle. As planned, *Swordfish* dispatched two "fish" in straight shots at the second, larger merchant ship. The first torpedo was aimed midships and, allowing for a noticeable current, the second fish was aimed toward the bow of the cargo ship. Again, the torpedo depths were calibrated at eight feet. There was an interval of 27 seconds between the shots, and the range was set at 3,600 yards. Smith saw Japanese crewmen on the deck of the second ship pointing to the torpedoes as they sped to their target. Smith commented: "When last observed, about 90 seconds after firing first torpedo, the wakes of both were seen running true to target."[8] Sound gear picked up an initial explosion two minutes and 27 seconds after firing the first torpedo. A second bang was heard approximately 30 seconds after the first. *Swordfish* had attacked the 8,033-ton *Katsuragi Maru*, but it was unlikely that the attack achieved any significant damage. The Japanese ship participated in a subsequent force headed for Ambon on 30 January 1942, and met its demise when USS *Sturgeon* sent it to the bottom that October. The explosions heard aboard *Swordfish* may have resulted from the premature explosion of one or both of the torpedoes.[9]

Swordfish headed for the open sea and dived to 180 feet. She ran at full speed for four minutes before slowing to three knots. The crew silenced all auxiliaries and waited. The Japanese reacted in a brief frenzy. Immediately after the explosion of the first torpedo on the second vessel, sounds of 20 to 30 small explosions were heard overhead. Smith guessed that it was either a hail of gunfire or light bombs from aircraft. Some of the explosions were very near. The Japanese pressed on in a desperate attempt to counter-attack. When a heavy depth charge detonated, it shook the floor plates and flickered lights in the submarine's control room. Smith judged that the depth charge had been set deep and was most likely dropped from an aircraft, because there were no sounds of ship's propellers connected with the enemy action. However, during the next 40 minutes, the propellers of small boats were heard, although not nearby. Three more depth charges went off well astern, marking the conclusion of the Japanese counter-thrust. Smith wrote, "We were then not further annoyed, all boats probably being employed in rescue work."[10]

Smith subsequently reflected upon his achievement. He said,

> When we seemed to be leaving them well astern we were really very exuberant over our feat. It was not easy on any of us that an approach into a harbor for two and a half hours is a little bit nerve racking. During the latter part of this, in order to be sure that we were not heard, we shut down as much machinery as possible and run silently as possible. This meant that air conditioning equipment was shut down and we were all warm and a bit nervous.[11]

Chet Smith learned the consequence attached to his success as *Swordfish* headed toward Davao in the Philippines in search of more prey. After stalking a tanker for an hour and a half, the battle-weary Smith realized he was tracking a rock formation that looked like a tanker with its bow riding high. The ordeal of Kema Bay had had its after-effect. Indeed, one of the watch officers thought he had even seen smoke coming from the "target." Smith summed up post-attack conditions: "one must remember you do have a case of nerves."e a case of nerves."[12]

On the same day that *Swordfish* sank *Myoken Maru*, 24 January, the Japanese landed troops at Kendari, and they also landed forces at Subic Bay in the Philippines and at Kavieng, New Ireland.[13] The tide was still running in favor of the Japanese, but surrounding events did not stop Chester Smith in his hunt. *Swordfish* pushed on toward Davao.

Frustrated from his pursuit of a rock formation, Smith lost no time in chasing a real target two days later. At 0445, *Swordfish* sighted, three miles distant, the nemesis of all submarines, a destroyer. Revving up to a surface speed of 11 knots, *Swordfish* changed course to close the range in a daring surface attack. Within 14 minutes of first sighting the warship, Smith barked orders to fire two "fish" at an interval of eight seconds, with an estimated range of 1,700 yards. However, by the time the second torpedo was fired, it was already 22 minutes after the beginning of morning twilight and, as Smith related, "We were to eastward being silhouetted against a fairly clear horizon."[14] The torpedoes had run normally, but a long silence testified to two misses, and the sound gear noted no change in enemy propeller speed. These misses added to the sense of frustration. The one piece of luck was that the torpedoes probably passed astern of the destroyer. The enemy warship failed to notice the torpedoes or *Swordfish*. Chet Smith reasoned that the missed shots were most likely due to an inaccurate estimate of the firing bearing, "which," as he noted, "is difficult in a choppy sea when steering is not too steady."[15] A faulty gyro compounded problems of the attack; it was not successfully repaired until that evening.

When *Swordfish* surfaced briefly at 0518 to take star sights, the destroyer was nowhere to be found. All that Smith could do was notify two other submarines, *Snapper* and *Sailfish*, in the hope that they might catch the destroyer. Continuing north, *Swordfish* surfaced again that evening. As the submarine ploughed north through wind-driven seas with white-caps, the steadfast skipper declared, "Sea not too rough. Excellent submarine weather." Smith preferred an active sea, which helped to obscure the outline of the submarine.[16]

While traveling on the surface the following day, *Swordfish* sighted a steamer loaded with cargo ten miles distant. The submarine headed for the target at full speed. A torpedo was set to run 3,675 yards at a depth of 12 feet. However, as the commander gave the order to fire, the automatic gyro setting relay had opened, producing a greater than correct angle setting on the torpedo. Within minutes, the submarine sound gear picked up the torpedo running astern of the steamer for another miss. Frustrated again, Chester Smith noted his thoughts in the patrol log. He had closed the range to the target as much as possible before firing his long shot of more than 3,000 yards. The calculations of the TDC were, to use his words, "excellent." Bearings were checked closely for the last 15 minutes before firing. He was sure a hit would have been achieved had there not been a last-minute change in the gyro setting. After the torpedo passed astern of the ship, the steamer turned parallel to the track of the torpedo and began the evasive tactic of zigzagging its course. Smith wrote glumly, "No further attack was possible."[17] He sent his report of the contact to other submarines in the hope that they would have better hunting.

During the ensuing days, submarine headquarters transmitted two alerts to Smith, ordering him to select locations where convoys were expected to cross. Smith responded to orders, and, itching for action, he shifted three torpedoes from the after torpedo room to the forward torpedo room where, as he wrote in his log, "they would be more likely to be used in an aggressive style of attack."[18] But the convoys never appeared.

The fruitless searches must have tipped the scales in favor of greater risk-taking, because Smith's next move nearly doomed *Swordfish*. The following Monday, 2 February, Smith took the calculated risk of surfacing in the evening on a flat, calm sea, bathed by the light of a bright, full moon. While the submarine was clearing the north tip of Lembeh Island, at 1908 she stumbled upon several destroyers ahead on the port bow, approximately two miles distant. A couple of minutes later, the submarine crash-dived, but it was too late. The Japanese ships had seen the moon-lit silhouette of *Swordfish*. They headed for the submarine. Smith was diving to a protective depth of 250 feet, but when *Swordfish* was between 100 and 150 feet, depth charges rained down on the fleeing boat. Smith described the tense moments: "It appeared that there were 2 DDs and in the next 20 minutes 6 depth charges were dropped, several very close. All lights flickered and the ship was thoroughly shaken."[19] The Japanese pursuit continued as the harrowing sounds of a heavy ship propeller were heard overhead. About half an hour into the attack, one destroyer drew away to the southeast, while the other DD hovered close aboard, listening for a telltale sign of the submarine below. After a three-hour exercise of stealth, the submarine finally eluded the attacker as the destroyer departed northward. Smith surfaced and proceeded at first on battery power to avoid his smoke-producing diesel engines, but later risked detection by switching to his powerful diesels. Undeterred by the destroyer attack, he, too, headed north.

Early on Tuesday morning, *Swordfish* sighted yet another destroyer at a distance of 7,000 yards. In imminent danger, *Swordfish* plunged under the surface to avoid detection as the destroyer came within a distance of 3,000 yards, intermittently echo-ranging and listening. The destroyer did not pick up the location of the *Swordfish*, and the enemy ship departed in a northwesterly direction.

Chet Smith's next encounter with the Japanese displayed his true sense of daring and, in this instance, overconfidence. He ignored the presence of enemy warships and again surfaced after the departure of the last destroyer. He pushed ahead on the diesel engines in a northeasterly direction, and at 0140 the watches aboard *Swordfish* sighted a destroyer astern of the submarine. Even though a still sea enhanced visibility, Smith chose to remain on the surface and gamble on the destroyer not seeing his boat. He hoped that the destroyer would, as he expressed it, "go the other way."[20] It did not. The enemy ship headed directly for *Swordfish*, and Smith guessed that the destroyer was, as he described it, "following the wake that we left in the flat calm sea."[21]

Less than seven hours after the first destroyer attack, *Swordfish* was forced for a third time to seek refuge in the depths. Taking evasive action, the submarine changed course and listened for the destroyer. Sound gear revealed the ship coming within an estimated 3,000 yards, while apparently overrunning the wake of *Swordfish*. The destroyer swung around and dropped a single depth charge in the locale where *Swordfish* had submerged. Smith gave orders to change course 90 degrees and to head away. Surfacing at 0341, the submarine could still pick up the destroyer's faint echo-ranging. Proceeding on its engines, *Swordfish* left the destroyer behind, out of sight and sound.

Putting distance between the enemy ship and their boat, the crew of *Swordfish* reported damage sustained during their ordeal. The depth charge explosions had damaged the starboard bow plane, and the vertical rudder also appeared to be impaired. They had become very noisy during use underway, which curtailed their employment during escape tactics, lest the noise reveal the boat's location. They could be used only as a last resort. The starboard radio antenna was another casualty of the attack.

In mulling over what had occurred, Smith concluded that the Japanese believed that they had damaged his boat, and they were determined to finish her off or perhaps force *Swordfish* to the surface due to exhausted batteries. However, during the morning after the Japanese pursuit, *Swordfish* remained as long as possible on the surface in order, as Smith explained, "to crowd in a few more ampere hours in the battery."[22] Then submerged, the boat traveled at slow speed to conserve the battery.

Worse than the wear on the equipment, the bouts with the destroyers had an adverse impact on the submarine crew. Smith summed up the traumatic result: "The long period of being pursued showed its effect by the jumpy nerves of many of the officers and men of the crew during the next 3 or 4 days."[23] Although many of the crew's complement were combat veterans of the first patrol, the desperate hours so near to eternity had left their mark. The normally reticent Smith provided the historical record with a vivid example of a very tense crew. While on the surface at 2042, the weary lookouts sighted two destroyers at approximately 7,000 yards, and a dive was executed immediately. An hour passed without seeing or hearing the enemy. Smith came to realize that the imagined destroyers were actually distant islands, and he noted of the error, "This was apparently a slight hang-over of the jitters from the night before."[24] Sensing the "edginess" of his crew and knowing how much he had tempted fate, the skipper took a somewhat more cautious approach to hunting down the enemy in the 15-day period that followed.

Swordfish plodded slowly north toward Mindanao and then to Manila Bay. Now more cautious, Smith ordered "surface" only at night. However, during the night of 5 February, he increased speed to 16 knots in a determined effort to "catch" an enemy ship. But when the enemy vessel turned into the protective reaches of Cape San Agustin in the Philippines, Smith ceased the pursuit, explaining in the log, "It was bright moonlight with the submarine silhouetted, and undetected attack at reasonable range was out of the question. Decided to break off and headed eastward to clear the immediate area where anti-submarine activity could now be expected."[25] Smith had reason to be careful. That evening, *Swordfish* sighted three large cargo ships in column. When an approach was attempted, a Japanese destroyer headed toward the submarine. Smith "pulled the plug," but the boat's wake left an inviting trail, and a barrage of depth charges followed. Satisfied with driving *Swordfish* under, the destroyer returned to escorting the convoy.

Although now more cautious, Smith did not give up his quest for another target. Sailing on a northerly course off Davao, Mindanao, Smith laid out his plan of attack:

"This was the first day of patrol across what the C.O. [Commanding Officer] considers to be the most probable route between Japan and Davao. The latitude was chosen as that in which ships would be met in daylight if they were to arrive 40 miles from Cape San Agustin during darkness so that the Gulf of Davao would be entered with the least chance of attack by submarines."[26] In essence, Smith was trying to outwit the enemy, and in the classic tradition of the American West, he wanted to "head them off at the pass."

After six days of patrolling, while *Swordfish* was submerged off Davao on 14 February, a likely target was sighted nine miles away, bearing 265 degrees. Changing course and revving up to full speed to intercept, Smith hoped to get close enough for a shot. Observations of the target were taken intermittently as they neared. Finally within range at 2,800 yards, he estimated the enemy ship to be traveling at 13 knots. As was frequently his practice in previous attacks, Smith ordered a spread of two "fish" to be fired in order to increase the odds of a hit. Two minutes and eight seconds later, the first of the torpedoes ripped into the merchant ship near the stern, rather than its intended point near the bow. The second torpedo was aimed aft toward the stern but completely passed under it. Smith guessed that the target's speed was underestimated by a knot, resulting in the near-miss of the second torpedo. Through his periscope, the commander observed the stricken ship going down by the stern, and sounds of the propellers had ceased. He described the merchantman as having twin derrick masts, as well as a straight mast. Cautiously, *Swordfish* approached the target at slow speed to determine if the cargo vessel would sink. Between observations via periscope, he took *Swordfish* to a depth of 90 feet. The enemy crew had manned their guns, and Smith was also wary of being spotted by hostile aircraft.

Fifteen minutes later, a light explosion was heard in the vicinity of the enemy vessel, and Smith concluded that the ship was sinking. He judged another hit unnecessary, but he continued his vigil. However, the submarine's "sound" detected the noise of a heavy ship propeller close to port and getting nearer. Already at 90 feet, Smith took *Swordfish* deeper to avoid possible ramming of the periscope supports. After the heavy ship had gone, *Swordfish* ascended to periscope depth to return to observation of the recent victim. Much to the submarine commander's dismay, the torpedoed ship was fleeing the scene at approximately 12 knots speed. It was already 4,000 yards ahead when *Swordfish* gave pursuit. As the enemy ship pulled away, Smith declined to risk wasting another "fish."[27] He continued to watch the damaged ship as it headed for Pujada Bay with the most likely aim of beaching there. Smith could see that the bow was very high in the water, and just the deck line was clear of the water at the stern. The submarine commander guessed that the crew had pumped out the fuel tanks in order to keep the ship afloat, and he could not be certain it would sink. *Swordfish* had damaged a Japanese transport ship of 7,620 tons, *Amagisan Maru*, which had been pressed into navy service for the Japanese push southward.[28] When a destroyer was sighted in the direction of the damaged ship, Smith wisely abandoned the attack.[29]

Later that evening, Smith received orders to proceed north. Leaving the area, *Swordfish* headed toward the American stronghold on Corregidor Island at a speed of 14.7 knots. En route, *Swordfish* had a chance for a kill in the form of a small tanker five miles away. Smith commenced an approach. Eager for a hit,

Smith closed on the target, and the stern tubes opened to send two torpedoes at the Japanese ship. Torpedo runs were set at 875 and 1,000 yards. An explosion 35 seconds after firing the first torpedo signaled that something had gone awry. The detonation was at great variance with the estimated distance to the target. Smith was unsure as to why no hit was achieved, but he thought the explosion was an aircraft bomb rather than one of his torpedoes. He quickly took *Swordfish* into deep submergence and was denied a last look at the tanker. The submarine picked up what appeared to be an acceleration in the tanker's propeller, but it was soon identified as the sound of a different ship intent upon a counter-attack.

Within three minutes of Smith firing the "fish," the Japanese retaliated by dropping eight depth charges in groups of twos. Smith guessed that nearby land forms had obscured a 600-ton torpedo boat or a small destroyer that had come out to meet the tanker. Smith described the attack as "close but not close enough to cause any damage."[30] The submarine had taken refuge at 250 feet and stayed there while the Japanese used listening gear to ferret out the boat. Smith described the tense scene: "Further sound search by this vessel kept us down for over 3 hours as each time we started to periscope depth sound reported this ship getting closer."[31] Even after the Japanese ship gave up the search, *Swordfish* remained at 250 feet to avoid aircraft detection, which would have been enhanced by glassy sea conditions.

The submarine finally came to periscope depth in the afternoon, and heavy black smoke was noticed near the Bataan Peninsula and toward Subic Bay. Smith concluded that one of his torpedoes had, indeed, hit the tanker, and it was still ablaze. Observers on Corregidor had also noticed the smoke. Another sight also loomed up in the periscope, that of the searching enemy torpedo boat, but it was five miles distant and heading southward for Subic Bay. No doubt Smith would have continued his search for targets, but his superiors had other plans for *Swordfish*.

Very Special Passengers

Acting on a directive, at 1955 *Swordfish* surfaced off Manila Bay and quietly slipped into the bay to prepare for a secret mission. At the entrance to the Mariveles docks, *Swordfish* moored next to the Navy-commandeered tug, *Ranger*, where a fuel barge disgorged 44,900 gallons of diesel into the tanks of the submarine. In the early morning hours of February 20, a replenishment of 13 torpedoes was also loaded aboard. Before dawn, *Swordfish* settled onto the bottom of the bay and waited. That evening, *Swordfish* came to life. The submarine surfaced, and at the turning buoy she waited for a rendezvous with a motor torpedo boat that would come from the island of Corregidor at the entrance to Manila Bay. Measuring approximately four miles in length, the tadpole-shaped island stood like a sentinel, blocking Japanese conquest of the area. American and Filipino defense forces occupied a network of tunnels that honeycombed the island. As events unfolded, the "Rock," as Corregidor was called, became a refuge for military and civilian officials evacuating Manila.[32]

For weeks, Corregidor had been under severe attack by Japanese aircraft, and the outlook for holding out was grim. Wishing to avoid the humiliation of capture by the advancing Japanese, scheduled for boarding *Swordfish* was the president of the Philippines, Manuel L. Quezon, who was both aged and gravely ill with tuberculosis. Quezon personified Philippine freedom, and officials in the Philippine government as well as General Douglas MacArthur, the chief U.S. Army officer in the Philippines, believed that the Philippine cause was best served if Quezon evaded Japanese capture and lived. Colonel Carlos Romulo of the Philippine Army characterized his leader, President Quezon: "No matter what his bodily suffering might be, his spirit was indomitable."[33] General MacArthur had arranged with officials in Washington to have Quezon taken off Corregidor by a clandestine run through the Japanese blockade. Chester Smith was chosen for the task.

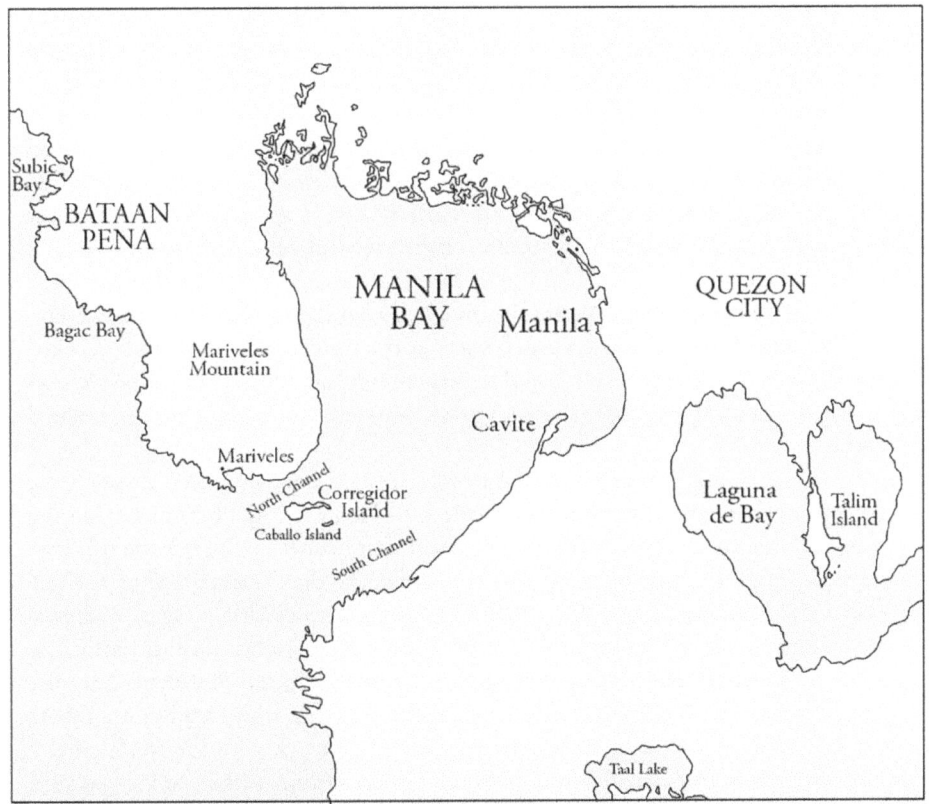

Manila Bay. *Map by Eliz Alahverdian.*

After an emotional farewell on Corregidor, General MacArthur and General Richard K. Sutherland held the frail Philippine leader upright until the motor boat arrived. The boat ferried the Quezons to deeper water, where *Swordfish* waited. Crewmen helped the president aboard and down the ladder into the submarine. Traveling with President Quezon were nine other passengers, including his wife, Dona Aurora Quezon; two daughters, Zenida and Maria; a son, Manuel Jr., and several members of the Philippine government and army. There was also special cargo of General Douglas MacArthur. MacArthur and his wife chose to stay on Corregidor with their son, but sent aboard *Swordfish* a footlocker containing personal items, such as the general's medals, investment securities, their wills, their son's birth certificate, his baby shoes, and photographs.[34]

For boarding, the hands not on watch formed a line from topside to bring the guests and their baggage below. During this process, an unexpected gift fell into the laps of the crew. As the gear was being passed along to temporary stowage in the boat, a packet wrapped in paper slipped out of the hands of one of the handlers and fell to the deck, breaking open. Out tumbled 100 pairs of men's "skivvies," size 48. The "accident" was most fortunate because there was a shortage of underwear aboard. When *Swordfish* hastily departed for her first patrol, she left behind a large amount of the crew's personal laundry, which had been sent ashore for washing. By the time the crew returned from the initial patrol, the Navy's shore-side facilities had been bombed out and the submarine tender, *Holland*, had already departed for Java and Australia. Recognizing the crew's shortage and this sudden "replenishment" of undershorts, the Chief of the Boat diverted the broken package aft for stowage in the after torpedo room. Later, a second packet of skivvies was discovered and was also sent aft for use by the crew. George Valentine Brown wrote, "With 200 pairs of skivvies to apportion out, all hands received 2 or 3 pairs each." Brown related that he had a 34-inch waist at the time, but "reefed" and "tucked" the shorts to achieve a fit. He noted that there were several additional packets on board which were not appropriated, so there was an ample supply for the original owner.[35]

At 2205, a PT boat escorted *Swordfish* as it cautiously exited through the bay's mine field, and the submarine headed for Panay, in the Philippines. During the 300-mile voyage, *Swordfish* did not encounter hostile forces, but the trip was, nevertheless, a trial for the Filipino passengers. The dust "kicked up" by the frequent Japanese bombings of Corregidor had aggravated President Quezon's tubercular lungs, so he moved around very little and wore pajamas the entire trip. The smell of diesel oil, permeating throughout the boat, affected President Quezon's breathing, and he was fitted with a Momsen Lung to help with respiration. Aurora Quezon and her two daughters were seasick and unhappy with the confined and hot conditions. In particular, one of the air conditioning units leaked its gas, and Smith was unable to obtain Freon for it. The unit was out of service very early in the patrol.[36] The sole, merry exception among the civilians was the 15-year-old

Quezon son, Manuel Jr. The skipper, Chet Smith, gave him a personal tour of the boat, and the youngster marveled at all the mechanical devices in this unfamiliar world. He also devoured the Navy food with great enthusiasm.[37]

With a sigh of relief, the passengers aboard *Swordfish* arrived at Panay at 0130 on 22 February, and the evacuation of President Quezon and his colleagues continued as they transferred to a motor tender, again under the cover of darkness. Manuel Quezon and his companions ultimately reached safety, completing the mission.[38] Notice of President Quezon's safe arrival in Panay was sent by a secret coded message which read: "Precious package arrived."[39]

The commander and crew of *Swordfish* did not rest. At 0242, the submarine swung north for Manila Bay to perform a second, secret evacuation. Two days later on February 24, *Swordfish* commander and crew again threaded their way through the outer mine field of Manila Bay and lay to off the turning buoy. The patrol boat, *Mary Ann*, a converted yacht, carried from Corregidor to the submarine Francis B. Sayre (High Commissioner to the Philippines), his wife, Elizabeth E. Sayre, and several other passengers, including the commissioner's young stepson, William Graves.[40] President Roosevelt had ordered the secret evacuation of Commissioner Sayre. Originally the commissioner was to be accompanied by three code breakers bound for Australia, but they were displaced by the commissioner's staff members. However, the Navy had one evacuee aboard. He was John C. Mueller, the representative of an engine manufacturer, who was familiar with submarine engines. The Navy wanted Mueller to assist personnel on submarine tenders in maintaining the engines.[41]

For Elizabeth E. Sayre, the High Commissioner's wife, entering the unfamiliar world of *Swordfish* was both a challenge and a salvation. After enduring two nerve-wracking months of Japanese attacks while in the defense tunnels on Corregidor, she would now endure life in the confines of a submarine, which was often submerged, a worrisome prospect for any newcomer. Nevertheless, *Swordfish* offered the last, best chance of escaping from the tightening hold of the Japanese advance on air, land, and sea. Many of the friends and associates that she was leaving on the "Rock" would never be seen again.[42] Before Sayre left Corregidor, Admiral Francis W. Rockwell grasped Mrs. Sayre's hand and assured her of Chester Smith's capability with these words: "Good luck. You are going out with our ace submarine skipper. He'll get you through."[43]

Descending down the narrow hatchways, the Commissioner, Mrs. Sayre, and the other passengers entered the compact world of the submarine with its maze of pipes, cables, valves, levers, lights, and switches. One of the evacuees, Ed Hester, likened the interior to living inside a time piece. Referring to the unusual noises emanating from the submarine, another civilian, Jan White, quickly added, "Make it an alarm clock."[44]

Accommodations were compact. Chester Smith shared his cabin with Commissioner Sayre, and several Navy personnel gave up their quarters. Mrs. Sayre and the other women "guests" were assigned to the petty officers' cabin with its four bunks, four meager storage drawers, and running water, a precious commodity after the paucity of fresh water on Corregidor. Because there were more men than bunks, the men were requested to "double up" with other men aboard in "hot bunk" ("hot rack") fashion, where there was a rotation of bunk use. On a shift basis, the ward room was used both for meals and for sleeping.[45]

However, Commissioner Sayre's 14-year-old stepson, William, had another preference for his sleeping area. The teenager chose a rack in the forward torpedo room. Joe Parks and the other torpedomen were amused by the youngster with whom they joked and cavorted. The boy eagerly absorbed the ways and means of the torpedomen's duties, much to their mutual delight. Graves also befriended a torpedoman in the aft torpedo room nicknamed "Jelly Belly," and this sailor made some coconut fudge for the young Graves. On several occasions during the trip, the sailor treated Graves to the fudge.[46]

One facility which proved a challenge to several of the newcomers was the ship's shower-bathroom near the galley. To operate it properly required multiple steps, and the procedure for operation on the surface was different from the protocols for operation while submerged. The passengers quickly dubbed this complex but necessary room the "execution chamber" or, as an alternative, the "torture chamber."[47]

By 0416, *Swordfish* was underway, once more navigating through the mine field in darkness and heading for the Dutch outpost of Surabaya, Java. Shortly after 0600 the next morning, Chester Smith greeted the commissioner's group, and Elizabeth Sayre recalled that "we were called in to breakfast with the Captain, a young, earnest, rather pale-looking man, whose quiet confidence soon gave us reassurance such as only master leadership can give. One look into those steady blue eyes made us realize that Admiral Rockwell was right—he was an 'ace.'"[48] Amea Willoughby, wife of Commissioner Sayre's financial advisor, described Chester Smith's honest, matter-of-fact manner: "He never gave us a 'there, there, now,' sort of answer, but came out with a straightforward explanation of what had happened or might be expected to happen."[49] Smith was genuine.

During the journey, the boat followed routine procedures by traveling submerged by day and on the surface at night, when detection was less likely. As *Swordfish* proceeded, Elizabeth Sayre and her fellow passengers became aware of a distinct feature of submarine life in tropical waters—the heat and humidity. The buildup of heat inside the submarine was unrelenting. Sayre recorded her thoughts: "The air got hotter and more foul as the long hours dragged by. It was almost impossible to sleep longer than fifteen minutes at a stretch. We would lie in our bunks, which soon became pools of perspiration, getting up now and then to take a sponge bath to relieve our burning skin."[50] Noting that the inside humidity would reach 90 percent at times, Amea Willoughby described how most of the passengers stripped to the bare minimum of clothing. Most male passengers followed the customary practice of the crew by going bare-waisted in shorts or cutoff pants. The women wore shirts and shorts, and as Willoughby declared, "Even to wear socks was a torture."[51] Prickly heat was common, and many of the "guests" kept damp towels handy to pat off the perspiration. The final hours just before surfacing in the evening were the most challenging, as Willoughby wrote, "So foul was the air that we found ourselves unconsciously taking quicker, shallower breaths."[52]

The heat and humidity did not spare the crew. Sayre noticed that some of the crewmen had heat rashes caused by the excessive perspiration. Yet the men proceeded with their duties as if unfazed by conditions inside the boat. Sayre set the scene: "In all the torrid days near the equator, when we suffered so that we could neither read, write, nor think, the men went about their jobs with concentrated effort."[53]

When *Swordfish* crossed the equator, all but one of the civilians aboard received certificates commemorating their historic passage. The crew decided to have some fun with the remaining civilian, young William Graves. One of the engineers dressed up as King Neptune and, in a mock trial, they initiated Graves into the select group of individuals who have crossed the equator. The crew presented a list of "crimes" that included the shameful offense of "bubble dancing," that is, erratic handling of the boat's bow planes, as indicated on a bubble gauge. Previously the crew had given Graves a chance to get a feel for the bow planes by letting him have some "hands on" experience. For his "offense," Graves described his fate: "I was sentenced to swab the control room deck with a damp handkerchief and to serve coffee to the duty watch." William Graves never forgot his initiation.[54]

The rise in temperature, combined with the meager privacy in such close quarters, made a daunting task out of the usual daily practices of washing. Even so, Mrs. Sayre and the other women aboard made an ardent attempt to maintain standards of cleanliness, including the washing of clothes. Sayre described the scene: "In our cabin, we managed to do a little laundry and it seemed that our ceiling pipes and handles were always strung with intimate apparel drying—or trying to—in the breeze of our hard-working little fan."[55] Because space was so limited, washing and dressing for the women were accomplished in shifts.

For the crew, conditions were just as challenging. Normally, the crew did not shower while on patrol. There was insufficient fresh water for such a "luxury." Food had been loaded in the crew's shower, and the crew used buckets and sponges to wash down. To alleviate heat rash, crewmen would take alcohol from the torpedoes and swab down. Usually, they wore cutoff dungarees or shorts and t-shirts or bare skins. At meals they wore the t-shirts. Electrician's Mate Fred Kramer related that after ten days on patrol, the smell of body odor was ever-present, but as he stated, "We all smelled alike."[56] Together with the prevalent odor of diesel oil, the smells aboard the boat were quite pungent. The smell of garbage was added to the mixture until it was deemed safe to discard it without revealing the whereabouts of the boat.⁵⁷ Kramer stated, "We did the best we could."⁵⁸ He noted that once in a while, on the way back from patrol, a crewman would shower.⁵⁹ However, this was an unlikely event with so many extra individuals present on this patrol. Machinist Mate Lloyd Faye resorted to an alternate method of coping. To keep clean, he washed down with clean fuel oil. For contending with the heat while sleeping, "Henry," as he was known by shipmates, preferred to lie on the deck plates rather than to sleep in a sweaty bunk.⁶⁰

Occasionally, when a hatch was opened at night, a waft of fresh air would be felt, but save for a small portable fan in her cabin, Elizabeth Sayre and her companions had little relief from the heat. Before the trip ended, the temperature inside the submarine would at times climb to 96 degrees Fahrenheit. Normally fleet submarines, such as *Swordfish*, offered some relief through air conditioning. However, as with the previous Quezon mission, the air conditioning malfunctioned.⁶¹

A bright spot in shipboard conditions was the food. After spending weeks of eating a limited menu on Corregidor, the submarine food seemed bountiful and delicious. The civilians feasted on frankfurters with sauerkraut, sandwiches, powdered eggs, canned fruits and vegetables, sliced ham, curried chicken, and canned milk. For dessert, they were served such delights as pumpkin pie, layer cake, and chocolate milk.⁶² Added to the convivial atmosphere, Smith made certain that one or two of the boat's officers shared meals with the visitors. A lone drawback was the drinking water. The water came from condensers and, although potable, it was described by one of the civilians as lukewarm and sometimes khaki-colored. Nevertheless, the "guests" drank all they could get, and on occasion a little ice was available to cool it off.⁶³

As she met the officers, Amea Willoughby collected impressions. She described Chester Smith's reaction when news of an award for him of a Navy Cross reached the boat. There was jubilation throughout the submarine, but Smith was characteristically quiet about the award. She wrote, "He looked quite pleased, but also a bit embarrassed."⁶⁴ Other officers had different personalities. Lieutenant David Sloan was a former football star with a vivid sense of humor. He confided to Mrs. Willoughby that he favored a life around horses. Quieter and more serious was Lieutenant John Hyde, who had the task of navigating past the hazards in Philippine waters and in the Dutch East Indies with its narrow straits. Other officers included Lieutenant Lyle Strickland, who, according to Willoughby, also gave the impression of being serious-minded, and Lieutenant J. E. Clarke, who had a wry sense of humor. Then there was W. H. McClosky, whose tall, lanky frame was a liability on the cramped boat. Nevertheless, McClosky and the other officers had certain common traits, which Willoughby described as "alertness, scrupulous attention to detail, and courage."⁶⁵

Chester Smith found it necessary to avoid encounters with ships and aircraft in order to deliver his passengers safely. For the passengers, the most alarming episode occurred in the evening of Monday, 2 March, when *Swordfish* sighted what appeared to be a Japanese destroyer three miles off the port bow. This nemesis of submarines was headed for *Swordfish*, and Smith took her down. As the boat was rigged for depth charges, Mrs. Sayre described the hurried procedures of the crew closing valves, securing hatches, screwing bolts, and barking quick commands. The chief engineer advised the passengers to stay in their bunks and gave them cotton for their ears. All ventilation ceased, including Sayre's portable fan, and the boat settled into a disquieting stillness. After what seemed like an endless period to the civilians, the all clear was given.[66] *Swordfish* proceeded on course.

On the same day, Smith received a change in orders: proceed via Sape Strait to Fremantle, a suburb of Perth, Australia. The proximity of enemy forces on Java prompted the switch in destination. By Wednesday, 4 March, Smith attempted to make better time by running on the surface during daylight on a clear, calm sea. However, the change in routine was brief, and progress was impeded the next day as a change in course was made to avoid an enemy submarine reported 150 miles north of Exmouth Gulf. In addition, by nightfall evasive dives had to be executed twice in order to elude unidentified aircraft. For a skipper with Smith's aggressive instincts, the need to avoid the enemy rather than attack must have been difficult.

A change in weather also proved a challenge, especially for the "landlubbers" aboard. On 5 March, the boat was plowing through choppy seas with a brine-laden spray coming over the bridge. For the next two days, Smith reported the same weather conditions: "Wind and sea continued from south causing spray on bridge and considerable reduction in speed."[67] Elizabeth Sayre reported on the rough seas: "We had to spend considerable time in our bunks, for we couldn't stand on our feet or even sit erect! The officers came down from the bridge dripping wet, but with a fine color in their cheeks."[68] Some of them had gotten a deep sunburn or weathering due to the spray and sun. By 8 March, the strong winds began to abate, but the sea remained choppy. Much to the relief of the passengers, *Swordfish* reached Fremantle the next day. She made a rendezvous with an escort vessel and the submarine, *Stingray*, but suffered one last tedious delay as fog prevented entry into the harbor.

After anchoring for several hours, the submarine finally sailed into Fremantle harbor, where Vice Admiral Glassford met High Commissioner Sayre and his party. They bid farewell to the officers and crew of *Swordfish*. Sayre wrote, "We were almost sorry to go. For two weeks we had been living with heroes. I wonder if we shall see them again."[69] As for the submarine's crew, they came on deck and displayed their joy at making port. Amea Willoughby described the scene: "The crew, like children just out of school, sparred with each other and swung the AA gun from side to side in some sort of game. They squinted too, in the unaccustomed sunlight."[70] At 1123, *Swordfish* eased alongside the mother tender, USS *Holland*, and moored. Mission accomplished!"[71]

Considering the special missions of evacuation, for Smith and his crew, the war patrol was certainly not routine and clearly not what could be expected or desired. Their top priority was to close with and destroy the enemy. The words "retreat" and "surrender" have never been popular in the American lexicon, and the missions of evacuation had raised the specter of such odious events. Nevertheless Chet Smith and his crew could be proud of their role in saving lives. The care and concern of commander and crew were long remembered by the evacuees. In recognition of the special missions, *Swordfish* was awarded a Navy unit citation for the Philippine Island Operation. The commander and crew were awarded battle stars. Smith held true to the main business at hand. On 17 March 1942, Smith telegrammed to his wife, Mary Baxter Smith, and concisely stated, "Still Hunting Japs." The special missions had been necessary, but the hunt was still foremost in his mind.[72]

But for now, the crew could rest. And rest they did. Traditionally gracious as hosts, the Australians at this time fully recognized that the American submarine crews were part of a last line of defense against the Japanese, who were edging closer. The tensions mounted by the frequent "close calls" and the privations of having too many people aboard *Swordfish* in too little space gave way to the release of anxiety normally associated with returning to port. As Floyd Cooper described, "there was plenty of good food ... there were plenty of women, dances, plenty [to] drink."[73]

Swordfish had tied up on the gently flowing Swan River at Perth, which contained numerous black swans. Valentine Brown, a member of the commissioning crew, along with the other "plank owners" still on board, decided to give *Swordfish* the nickname of "Black Swan," because of her sleek black hull. They likened their boat to one of the graceful water fowls. For a 25 cent glass of beer, Brown entertained his Aussie friends with a song the crewmen had composed in honor of their boat. The words were set to the melody of "The Caissons Go Rolling Along." The lyrics were as follows:

> "Take her down deep as hell
> We don't need your diving bell
> And the *Swordfish* goes rolling along."[74]

As late as May 1943, when Quartermaster Leymon ("Denny") Dennis came aboard, *Swordfish* was displaying a flag with a black swan on it. However, as the submarine continued her patrols, the image of a graceful swan gave way to a more bellicose picture. The boat's subsequent battle flag depicted a fierce swordfish clutching a torpedo.[75]

The strains of a patrol with episodes of depth charging and crash dives had affected not only the crew, but also *Swordfish* herself. In addition to the malfunctioning air conditioning, other significant functions showed signs of wear and tear. At the conclusion to his war patrol report, Chester Smith described equipment problems that required solution while in port. In particular, Smith was concerned with noises originating from malfunctioning equipment. The sounds betrayed the submarine's position when in deep submergence. The C.O. cited the bow planes as never being particularly quiet, but after the depth charge attack of February 2, movement of the starboard plane produced a loud knock. This was especially true when submerged at 250 feet, a depth commonly associated with taking evasive action while under attack. In his direct, laconic style, Smith declared: "This condition is serious when trying to evade searching destroyers."[76]

Smith went on to discuss the rudder problem that cropped up on 23 January after an unidentified object struck both the port side of the hull and the propellers or rudder. Here again, noise was the major concern. Smith described steps he had taken to avoid detection: "This rudder noise is so noticeable that when the ship is being hunted by DDs the Commanding Officer will permit movement of the rudder only when deemed particularly urgent and the DDs are at some distance away. This is unsatisfactory and dangerous." Smith believed dry docking would be required to accomplish a repair.[77] Another noise problem involved the trim and drain pumps. When *Swordfish* was in deep submergence, both pumps would pound badly with sounds that Smith suspected were not from mechanical misalignment, but probably from pressure waves that produced water hammer. He recommended the installation of air flasks in the discharge lines while in port.

Making matters worse were two additional noise problems which left the boat vulnerable to detection. Crewmen had been trying to reduce excessive noise that occurred while raising and lowering the number two periscope. Smith, the trained engineer, believed that either the motor and gear foundation were insufficiently stiff or the gears themselves were the noisy culprits. He emphasized that corrective action was, as he put it, "imperative to increase the military value of the vessel." Other problems were related to the periscope hoists, bow planes, and stern planes. During the past three months, numerous aligning studs had broken in connection with the brakes for these components. Smith believed the problems were suggestive of faulty alignments resulting from worn brake disks and linings. The brakes were excessively noisy, and Smith called for a thorough overhaul while at Fremantle.[78]

The list of defects and damage did not end there. Smith noted the faulty gyro compass which required repairs while under way. Other malfunctions involved a leaking high pressure air valve and considerable leakage of seawater into the control room, caused by a depth charge attack. The submarine's air conditioning, whose malfunction was so vexing to both the Quezon and Sayre groups, had to be addressed. The number one air conditioning unit was not working for most of the patrol due to a loss of gas, and a replenishment of Freon was not available during the patrol. Smith requested tracking down where the leaks were located, sealing them, and replacing the gas, if available.[79]

Finally, there were problems with the number one main engine, even though it had operated only 700 hours since the last overhaul. Smith reported that the engine was producing a "smoky" exhaust almost continuously when pushed up to and above 80 percent load. The engine was plagued with broken piston rings on one of the pistons, a seized bearing on another, and a cracked liner on yet another. In addition to impeding speed while on the surface, the smoke-laden exhaust was a telltale sign of the submarine's presence, especially when sailing on the glassy seas that Smith noted in his patrol report. The CO recommended a thorough overhaul of the engine, as well as of number three engine, which had been operating for 1,300 hours since its previous overhaul.[80] Although the engines were sturdy and could take much punishment, they were, along with the other parts of *Swordfish*, subjected to hard use. The rigors of the first and second patrols, along with the evacuation of John Wilkes and his staff, left their marks on the submarine. Like a veteran warrior, the submarine was battle-tested, but it displayed scars from the ordeal.

Smith, himself, had been tested in battle in two war patrols, and he proved to be a superb commander. Showing flexibility, he had a remarkable ability to proceed quietly with his attacks, to choose his targets well, and to deftly utilize his questionable torpedoes. He generally fired off two per ship in order to ensure a hit. His ability to shake off enemy ships looking for *Swordfish* was also evident to his crew. Even with noisy components, he knew how to use the submarine's quality of stealth both for the attack phase and the evasion phase of encounters with the enemy. Smith was quite willing to endure the enemy's counter-attacks as long as he was able to get in his attack on an enemy ship first.[81] Over time, the crew realized that their skipper would "bring them home," a vital concern for the submariner. Smith's ability to adjust to the various special missions that he was obliged to carry out was also to his credit. The same could be said for the crew of *Swordfish*. They had performed well under a variety of challenges. Undoubtedly the mutual respect between Smith and his crew was growing, and the bonds among the men of *Swordfish* were strengthening.

Corregidor

Going into harm's way, Smith and his men had evacuated high-ranking officials and military officers from the clutches of the Japanese. The tragic scene of Allied forces giving way to advancing Japanese forces was played over and over again. Now, desperate circumstances dictated an ever more challenging mission for Chester Smith and his hardy crew. For her third war patrol, *Swordfish* was ordered to deliver provisions to the island of Corregidor, which was under heavy Japanese siege. The American bastion still stood defiantly in the path of Japanese conquest, with American and Filipino forces holding out in underground tunnels, but they were low on food, ammunition, and medicine. Controlling the air and circling waters, Japanese aircraft and ships made it suicidal for U.S. Navy surface ships to attempt any form of relief.

Swordfish was one of several American submarines ordered to slip by Japanese forces and supply the battered Corregidor garrison. Setting out from Fremantle, Australia, on 1 April, *Swordfish* carried in her hull 40 tons of food, including beans, rice and flour, as well as ammunition for Corregidor.[82] A second part of her mission involved making a shuttle trip from Corregidor to Cebu in the central Philippines and then, laden with supplies, returning to the "Rock." Smith was dubious about the use of submarines for ferrying cargo because of their restricted free space. However, he understood the dire straits the Corregidor defense forces were in, and orders were orders.[83] Chet Smith was not alone in his doubts about employing submarines to deliver supplies to Corregidor. Admiral James Fife expressed a similar outlook: "Of course all of these things at that time diverted the submarines from what they were supposed to be doing, and it caused considerable irritation and friction.... If we'd had a good torpedo and our submarines would have been effective in knocking out Japs, why, then there would have been some better reason, some good reason for objecting to these trips into Corregidor."[84]

On 1 April, *Swordfish* headed north for the Philippines at flank speed.[85] But matters took a turn for the worse when the Bataan peninsula fell to the Japanese on 9 April. The next day, the submarine command sent the following message to Smith's boat: "Until further orders SWORDFISH operate offensively against enemy in the vicinity of AMBON."[86] The mission to Corregidor had been aborted, along with a similar mission given to the USS *Searaven* (SS-196). The degree of danger had become too great. After a relentless deluge of fire from massed Japanese artillery on the Bataan coast and steady bombardment from the air, the exhausted Corregidor garrison surrendered to invading Japanese forces on 6 May 1942. Once again, Smith and his crew were forced to witness an American defeat, and they were deeply sorry to learn of the misfortune.[87]

Meanwhile, *Swordfish* went on the offensive, but with a distinct disadvantage. In order to provide for the carriage of the foodstuffs intended for Corregidor, the boat left Fremantle with only eight torpedoes, one in each tube. Also, large-caliber ammunition was reduced to 25 rounds and small arms ammunition reduced to a minimum. As the submarine threaded its way through the Malay Barrier toward the island and bay of Ambon, a disturbing picture came into focus. *Swordfish* encountered several Japanese destroyers, patrol boats, and a minesweeper, indicating that the Japanese were continuing their advance southward. Endeavoring to cut the Japanese supply chain, *Swordfish* sought the preferred targets, merchant ships, but none came into range.[88]

Prospects of finding viable targets turned bleaker, and *Swordfish* headed south for a return to home port. All that Smith could show for his efforts were observations of Japanese naval activity and more problems with his boat. Noises arising from the bow planes, noted in his previous patrol report, still threatened to compromise stealth, as the hammer rapping noise at a depth of 250 feet had persisted. Again, he called for an investigation. Similarly, the two gyro rotors replaced after the second patrol had failed again, causing a variable error of 1.5 degrees.[89]

The aborted mission to deliver food to the starving garrison at Corregidor, the fruitless attempts to catch up with Japanese merchant ships, and the ominous presence of Japanese warships added up to an exercise in wretched frustration fraught with danger. The patrol had not gone well. On the morning of 1 May, *Swordfish* eased into Fremantle, ending this dismal third patrol. Almost immediately a relief crew set to work to prepare the boat for her next patrol. Smith had no time for his favorite leisurely pursuit, playing poker. There was too much to be done to ensure that *Swordfish* would be ready for another foray against the enemy.[90]

3

Chester Smith Creates a Legend

During the early months of 1942, the special missions required of *Swordfish* reflected the dark days faced by the United States and her allies. The Japanese string of victories continued after the attack on Pearl Harbor. In February, the British stronghold of Singapore fell, and in the same month, Japanese naval forces delivered a humiliating defeat to Allied naval forces in the Battle of the Java Sea. The fall of Bataan and Corregidor confirmed further the presence of Japanese military power. However, by mid–May 1942, there were some indications of American success. On 18 April, James Doolittle's bomber raid on Tokyo demonstrated that the Japanese home isles were vulnerable, although the attack itself was primarily a booster of American morale rather than the cause of much damage to the enemy. Then, in the Battle of the Coral Sea, 4 to 8 May, an American naval force stymied a Japanese attack on Port Moresby, thereby reducing the threat to Australia.[1]

With these events in the background, Chester Smith and his crew returned to *Swordfish* after barely two weeks in port. The reader might ask what impelled these seafarers to return to submarine duty after enduring the deprivations and dangers of a war patrol, especially the harrowing experience of a depth charge attack. When the author posed this question to veterans of *Swordfish*, they were quick to answer. A link much stronger than Navy orders or regulations drew these men back to their boats. There was a deep sense of loyalty to each other and a concern not to let their fellow crewmen down. While bouts of tedium or tension might lead to petty bickering or one crewman getting "ticked off" at another, major divisions were avoided. As veterans will note, a truly contentious shipmate did not last very long aboard the boats. While at sea, the men knew they depended upon one another for survival, which forged a deep bond among them. Back ashore, the crew members would go out in groups to the various places of enjoyment, such as the bars, and after engaging in bouts of drinking and reveling, petty differences were forgotten. The submariners knew they were a breed apart. The informality aboard the boat and the congenial association ashore was very much like a family or fraternity. *Swordfish* crew member William P. O'Briant described the camaraderie: "With the crew you had friends to go out and get drunk with. It was a family.

When aboard a submarine, it was a hell of a good family!"[2] At the scheduled time to return to the boat, they usually came.[3]

There was also the personal side of serving in the Submarine Service, which, with few exceptions, was an all-volunteer unit. Once a sailor joined this prestigious group, it was a commitment seldom willingly abandoned. At war, serving aboard the submarines was known to be dangerous, and any sailor who wore the Submarine Service dolphin insignia on his uniform sent out a silent message: he was part of a very select team of very daring individuals. The attrition of American submarines continued throughout the war, and close to 22 percent of the men serving on the boats were killed while on patrol. Out of a total of 16,000 men who made war patrols, 375 officers and 3,131 enlisted men perished.[4] Choosing to leave the Submarine Service could be interpreted, in the inner workings of the mind, as cowardice.[5] At bottom, this was a matter of self-respect or, as one *Swordfish* veteran described it, a matter of machismo.[6] In addition to the dolphin insignia, there was a more stark indication of a sailor in the Submarine Service. Upon his return from a patrol, a submarine sailor usually had sheet-white skin or, as sometimes described, a ghostlike pallor. While on patrol, a submarine came up to the surface primarily at night, which denied the submariner the benefit of sunlight, as well as vitamin D. There was no mistaking him when he had just returned from a war patrol.[7]

A phenomenon which drew submariners to serve on *Swordfish* was the prestige of Chester Smith and his crew. The skipper and crew had rising reputations for being successful in sinking Japanese ships. Indeed, many crewmen looked forward to doing so without regrets. For the adventurous submariner, *Swordfish* was the boat to sail on.[8]

Routinely, some crewmen rotated off a submarine after three to six patrols. It was the Navy's practice to "pepper" crews, slated for new construction or for submarine refit, with experienced seamen. New sailors would, in turn, "learn the ropes" from the seasoned submariners, whether they were in new construction, in refit or aboard currently operating boats, such as *Swordfish*. As a result, some of the original crew, the "plank owners," began to be transferred to other duties.[9]

Swordfish embarked from Fremantle with the purpose of impeding Japan's southward advance. On 15 May 1942, the crew let slip the lines for the fourth war patrol. At last, Smith and his crew were unfettered by the diversion of a special mission. The submarine command directed the boat to the South China Sea with simple orders: sink enemy ships.[10] Eight days into the patrol, 23 May, while passing through the Makassar Strait, crewmen sighted smoke, and with it came the opportunity to supplant the luckless third patrol. Smith gave orders to go ahead full-speed, and the chase was on. The target was a 6,500-ton cargo ship which was zigzagging in an evasive maneuver. Not wanting to let the ship sail out of range, Smith gambled on a long shot, as he related, "Fired two torpedoes at minimum obtainable torpedo run, 3,400 yards." The enemy ship must have seen the wakes of the torpedoes, because it apparently reversed engines, and the torpedoes passed ahead of its bow. Thus alerted, the cargo ship immediately turned away before *Swordfish* could fire again. The submarine gave chase, but the Japanese ship had sailed out of range.[11]

A second opening for a hit came the evening of 24 May, when an enemy ship sailed directly toward *Swordfish*. This time Smith was not taking chances. He waited until the target was very close and swung the submarine around for a stern shot at an estimated range of 1,000 yards. This time Mother Nature spoiled the set-up. The chagrined Smith explained: "This would have been highly satisfactory except that the target was lost in a rain squall and darkness during the turn and was not sighted again."[12] For several hours, the crew of the submarine searched in vain for the elusive target, but found nothing.

The USS *Seal*

In the vicinity of Balabac Island, there was another American submarine on the prowl, USS *Seal*. Her skipper was Lieutenant Commander Kenneth C. Hurd, and during the sequence of events that followed, the paths of *Seal* and *Swordfish* may have crossed. On 28 May, at a position of Latitude 07–33 North, Longitude 116–22 East, *Seal* spotted a ship which she initially thought was a destroyer, but was later discovered to be a prime target, a tanker. Submariners knew that petroleum was the lifeblood of modern mechanized warfare, and sinking tankers could affect the outcome of the war. Hurd described the ship as 450 to 500 feet long and approximately 1,700 to 1,900 tons. The ship had a straight bow, a bridge extremely far forward with a low stack, and a superstructure on the stern. There was a foremast rising from goal posts forward of the bridge and another set of goal posts and mast well aft. The target appeared to be one-half to three-quarters full.[13]

After they temporarily lost sight of the target, it came within range for *Seal* to fire two torpedoes at 2252. Both fish missed, and three minutes later, *Seal* sent off two more torpedoes. They resulted in a single hit and a very heavy blast just forward of the bridge on the starboard side of the maru. There was no flame, but spray from the blast shot up as high as the mast, and the ship was seen to settle at the bow. Although the engines had slowed down, the ship kept on sailing and eluded *Seal's* attempt to come within range for another shot. As the hours slipped from 28 May into the early morning hours of 29 May, *Seal* once again sighted the damaged tanker. Diving at 0228, *Seal* came within 6,000 yards of the ship. Hurd observed that the bow was already submerged, and the damaged ship was backing. A large oil patch covered the sea as *Seal* made her bid for the "end game."[14]

As *Seal* approached her target, *Swordfish* also moved into action. Early in a moonlit morning of 29 May, *Swordfish* was southwest of Balabac Strait at Latitude 7–33 North, Longitude 116–18 East, and was cutting through a slightly choppy sea. At 0150, a vessel loomed up in sight of *Swordfish*, eight miles distant. Chester Smith decided to investigate. As with Hurd, Smith initially thought he had sighted a destroyer, which, after diving, he viewed through his periscope as lying-to. Smith closed the range to the target and prepared for an attack. At 0240, *Swordfish* fired off two straight bow shots at an estimated range of 1,600 yards. As was Smith's practice, the first torpedo was aimed one-quarter inside the ship's bow, and the second torpedo, one-quarter of the length inside the stern. Sound gear reported an explosion one minute and 25 seconds after firing the first shot, and a narrow column of water shot up one-quarter length from the bow—a hit![15] At approximately the same time as *Swordfish's* attack, the submerged *Seal* had closed in to finish off her prey. Suddenly at 0251, a sharp explosion came from the direction of her target. The tanker's engines had started up and then stopped. A series of smaller explosions was picked up by *Seal's* sound gear.[16]

Meanwhile, as *Swordfish* moved closer to a range of 600 yards, Smith was surprised to discover that his victim was a tanker. The enemy ship's bow was slightly down, but it did not appear to be sinking, and there was no list.[17] The target was estimated to be a ship of 3,500 gross tons and 350 feet in length. The tanker had a bridge well forward and a single funnel aft, with two masts and two kingposts aft of the bridge. Smith described a cruiser bow and a continuous well deck. He gave additional details, "Ship appeared over-loaded with bow well down, so that main deck was horizontal."[18] It was a very worthwhile target, but it was refusing to sink. The men of *Swordfish* were not to be denied their success. Smith turned his boat around to bring the stern tubes to bear. At 0253, *Swordfish* sent a "fish" to deliver the *coup de grace*. Fifty-six seconds later, smoke and spray could be seen near the tanker's stern. Within two minutes, the ship was gone. The sinking of the tanker had broken the streak of unsuccessful attacks. The *Swordfish* was once more on the prowl.[19]

However, unknown to the men of *Swordfish*, at approximately the same time, *Seal* was coming up to periscope depth. At 0257, a very heavy explosion shook the *Seal*. It had come from *Seal's* intended target, which was approximately 1,500 yards away. A series of rapid, smaller explosions followed, but gradually died out. Peering through his periscope, Hurd caught a glimpse of the sinking ship just before it went under. In his patrol report, Hurd remarked, "The heavy explosion was too mushy for a depth charge, but I wondered if *Swordfish* could have been there and fired torpedo into his other side. Believe his boilers exploded."[20] Hurd thought the other sounds were detonating ammunition, but there were no signs of a fire. Sounds of the breaking bulkheads gave evidence to the death throes of the Japanese ship.[21]

In view of the similar circumstances connected with the attacks of *Seal* and *Swordfish*, there is a question of whether or not the two submarines had gone after

3. Chester Smith Creates a Legend 55

the same target. The patrol reports gave similar descriptions of the tankers, and the two submarines were in the same area. Also, they performed almost simultaneous final approaches to their targets. If this is so, Hurd and Smith deserved joint credit for sinking the same tanker, later identified as *Tatsufuku Maru*, a 1,946-ton tanker that had departed Labuan on 28 May and was bound for Sandakan.

There was no clear-cut agreement concerning the events of 28 and 29 May. In his endorsement of the patrol report of *Seal*, Charles Lockwood stated that an investigation of the positions of *Seal* and *Swordfish* indicated that between 0250 and 0257 on 29 May, the two boats were approximately five miles apart. He added, "practically simultaneously *Seal* sank a 7,000 ton tanker and *Swordfish* a 3,500 ton tanker."[22] Similarly, in Lockwood's endorsement to the fourth patrol report of *Swordfish*, Lockwood was lavish in his praise. Calling the patrol successful, the admiral cited how *Swordfish* "tenaciously hung on to ensure destruction of the enemy; on one instance to deliver the *coup de grace* and in the other to make a second successful attack after the first had failed." No word was mentioned of the *Seal* or of a simultaneous attack.[23]

In addition, the postwar JANAC assessment gave credit only to *Seal* for the sinking of *Tatsufuku Maru* on 28 May 1942, rather than 29 May. The report listed the maru's tonnage as 1,946 tons and the location of sinking as Latitude 7–27 North, Longitude 116–17 East. For 29 May, the JANAC report credited *Swordfish* with sinking an unknown maru, weighing an estimated 1,900 tons, at Latitude 7–33 North, Longitude 116–18 East.[24] On the other hand, Chester Smith initially maintained that the tanker he sank on May 29 had a weight of approximately 3,500 tons, but he was willing to accept the findings of the JANAC report. In any case, Smith steadfastly maintained that the ship *Swordfish* sank was not the same as *Seal's* victim, and he doubted that *Seal* and *Swordfish* were ever closer than 50 miles from each other. Smith also noted that there was a span of hours between *Seal's* attacks and those of *Swordfish*.[25]

Nevertheless, certain events confer credibility to the theory of a single target. According to *Seal's* war patrol report, she last fired torpedoes at her intended victim on 28 May. Thereafter, explosions emanating from her target's location on 29 May were most likely either secondary explosions resulting from *Seal's* attack of the previous day or the outcome of another attacker present, most likely *Swordfish*, since Kenneth Hurd suspected that *Swordfish* might be in the area. As early as 27 May, he spotted either another submarine's periscope or antenna, and he noted the possible presence of *Swordfish*. In two separate attacks on 29 May, *Swordfish* had fired torpedoes for hits on her target, which roughly matched the times when *Seal's* listening gear picked up sounds of explosions. Hurd himself believed it was *Swordfish's* torpedo which had finished off *Tatsufuku* on 29 May. In addition, the fact that Hurd and Smith gave somewhat similar descriptions of their intended targets helps to bolster the single victim notion. Although there is not enough evidence to assert unequivocally that *Seal* and *Swordfish* attacked the same ship, the coincidence of details makes the single target theory highly plausible, and the author believes that *Seal* and *Swordfish* deserve joint credit for sinking *Tatsufuku Maru*.[26] Moreover, according to Japanese sources, the maru sank on 29 May and not 28 May, as JANAC reports.[27] At bottom, one or both American submarines had diminished Japan's war-making capability by sinking *Tatsufuku Maru*. When the ship sank on 29 May, it carried with it 48 Japanese seafarers and the contents of its tanks.[28]

Another chance for *Swordfish* to mount an attack came in the night of 4 June, when in the bright moonlight, a destroyer six miles distant turned toward the submarine. Making heavy smoke, the destroyer closed at high speed. Smith's aggressive instincts came to the fore, and he went on the offensive. Submerged, at 0209 *Swordfish* fired four torpedoes from her stern tubes as the charging destroyer passed astern of the submarine. The estimated range and torpedo run was a dangerously close 400 yards. Smith tersely reported the sad results of his aggressiveness: "No explosions."[29] In his action report, Smith revealed his eagerness: "Snap attack. Too close on range. No time to get an accurate set up on TDC."[30] At such a close range, the torpedoes probably did not arm.

The destroyer retaliated. For two hours thereafter, the destroyer hunted the submarine, while Smith sought the anonymity of the depths at 200 feet. This tactic still left *Swordfish* in danger. As the submariners soon discovered, the pounding noises produced by the bow planes, when going deep during the second patrol, still persisted. Also, the submarine's trim pump made knocking noises when operating at 200 feet or more.[31] The Japanese pursuers finally moved away, and at 0449, *Swordfish* surfaced to continue her own hunt for targets. However, in sighting the destroyer again five miles in the distance and seeing it turn toward the submarine, Smith gave the order to take her down once more. Apparently the destroyer had not spotted *Swordfish*. Running silently, the submarine crew could hear the destroyer's propellers churning the waters as the destroyer passed overhead at intervals. Ten to 15 minutes later, it was gone.[32]

Pondering the attack on the destroyer, Smith admitted that he had made a hasty attack with the possibility of inaccurate data and control errors. Smith observed, "However, the target was so close it seemed impossible to miss."[33] He noted that the "fish" had older, lightweight warheads, thus alluding to a possible torpedo problem. Smith also speculated about his pursuer. He believed that the destroyer was not on a regular patrol and was not on convoy duty. Rather, it was possible that during the previous two moonlit evenings, an observer on one of the nearby islands might have spotted the silhouette of the submarine, and the destroyer was sent to hunt down *Swordfish*.[34]

On 6 June, off the east coast of Malaya, the Japanese presented Smith and his crew with a golden opportunity to add to their recent success of 29 May. Through the periscope, Smith could make out the faint image of smoke on the horizon 30 miles distant. He ordered "full speed." The command brought mixed results. The submarine surged forward with all motors operating at full tilt, but number three main motor showered the compartment with sparks. The crew quelled the sparks by reducing the faulty motor to low speed, and *Swordfish* continued the chase at a slower pace.[35]

As the submarine closed in on the smoke, the skipper made out a convoy of five cargo ships sailing in two columns and led by their escort, an *Amagiri*-class destroyer. It was 1,000 yards ahead of the merchantmen and between the two columns. The marus were periodically zigzagging in attempts to thwart any submarine from setting its sights and bearings. Relying on stealth to come within torpedo range, Smith chose a submerged attack by periscope in daylight. However, even under the surface, there was a risk of detection, as the periscope was briefly raised for observations and tracking. The sea was calm, and the wake of the periscope tube was quite visible. Amazingly, three more cargo ships came into view, belching smoke. The submarine commander could not tell if the new arrivals were pulling astern of the convoy to join it or passing by on their way south toward Singapore.[36] Smith did not wait to find out. The approach to the convoy had taken three and a half hours of tedious tracking, and the cluster of targets was too enticing. *Swordfish* had achieved close enough range for a long shot. Preparations were made for firing at the last ship in the near column, with a range of 3,200 yards. At 1626 *Swordfish* fired two torpedoes, set to run a full 3,300 yards. As was his usual tactic, Smith ordered the "fish" calibrated to hit the merchantman just inside the bow and just inside the stern.[37]

Without verifying results, attention switched to the next ship forward in the column. Ignoring the presence of the destroyer, Smith again sent two emissaries of destruction from the bow tubes for a range of 3,600 yards to the new target. Three minutes and 15 seconds after the firing of the first "fish," the submarine sound equipment and the control room picked up noise of an explosion. The location of the explosion was uncertain. There was no time for a periscope observation because *Swordfish* was coming round for stern shots, and preparations were in progress for firing from the stern tubes. Alas, no stern shots were fired due to the far range of the targets by the time of the full swing around. However, 26 minutes after firing, several explosions were noted in the distance. Smith wrote in the patrol log, "The reported explosions are characteristic of those emanating from a sinking ship."[38] Smith believed he either damaged or sank a 6,500-ton cargo ship, but he could not be sure.

By this time, *Swordfish* had taken refuge in the mud of the sea floor. Thrown off-guard by the attack, the destroyer escorting the Japanese convoy had taken four minutes to respond after the firing of the first torpedoes. The awakened enemy was at a range of 5,000 yards when it headed for the submarine. *Swordfish* went to deep submergence, which turned out to be unnervingly shallow. *Swordfish* hit the bottom at 140 feet, rather than the expected depth of 200 feet. Anxious moments followed.[39]

A Brush with Eternity

The searching destroyer dropped one depth charge 500 yards from *Swordfish* and then a second "ash can" 400 yards from the boat. Smith decided to remain on the seabed until after nightfall. He did not want to give away the location of his vessel by stirring up the mud while lifting off the bottom, and the noisy pumps would have "announced" the submarine's whereabouts. Moreover, *Swordfish*'s sound devices were stuck in the bottom mud and useless for detecting whether the destroyer was still searching nearby. Finally at 1910, Smith thought he'd surface, and *Swordfish* came off the sea floor.[40]

However, evasion from pursuers was short-lived. Within an hour and 20 minutes, the *Swordfish* again had to seek cover in the depths. A Japanese destroyer was sighted abaft the starboard beam at 3,000 yards. Echo ranging, the destroyer was searching for the intruder. *Swordfish* descended 170 feet, and the crew waited. Coming to the location where the submarine had slipped under the surface, the Japanese dropped three depth charges, which shook up the submarine and broke lights and gauge glasses aft.[41] To evade the hunting destroyer, Smith took *Swordfish* deeper and inadvertently bottomed again at 200 feet. Nothing more could be done. Compounding matters, both air conditioning units aboard the boat had been "bleeding" their refrigerant gas and, while submerged, interior temperatures had been rising to stifling levels. The men waited silently, hoping that the destroyer would weary of its quest and leave the area. Three hours later, it did.[42]

When the boat surfaced five minutes after midnight the next day, 7 June, hatches could be opened and fresh air could waft in. Smith ordered *Swordfish* south to clear the patrol area. The Japanese had hunted *Swordfish* for approximately seven and a half hours. After so much time in the deep, the boat's batteries required re-charging. The men also needed a "re-charging" away from contact with the enemy. Attention to the batteries offered a brief respite.[43]

Enduring the two depth charge attacks in shallow water had a marked effect on Smith's men. With these circumstances in mind, the normally reticent Smith stated clearly his concerns in his war patrol report:

> Operations in water less than the test depth of the ship have a noticeable effect on the officers and crew by increasing nervous tension. Our experience to date has caused us to believe that the depth charges have not been as near when the submarine is at a depth of 200 feet or more as when a less depth had been taken.[44]

For the next few days, *Swordfish* patrolled off the Malay coast and on to the Gulf of Siam. The submarine passed by locations with exotic names, such as Kota Bahru and Pulo Wai. But with the Japanese shipping present, the area was one of rank contention, and *Swordfish* was out to slow the Japanese juggernaut.

3. *Chester Smith Creates a Legend*   59

The Commander's Apprentice

As a hunting ground for enemy ships, the Gulf of Siam proved fruitful. While patrolling off Pulo Wai on 12 June, lookouts sighted a ship five miles in the distance. The crew of *Swordfish* sprang into action. Although the night was dark and visibility limited, the outlines of a maru could be discerned. The ship had masts fore and aft, with a bridge and high stack amidships.[45] *Swordfish* closed in on the target.

For training, Smith allowed one of his officers, Lieutenant D. K. Sloan, Jr., to direct the approach and attack from the bridge of *Swordfish*. Aiming at the maru's mast, at 0357 Sloan ordered two torpedoes fired at a 15-second interval. The estimated range was 1,400 yards. The dark night prevented tracking the torpedoes. No bangs, no spouts of white water marking a hit. Both "fish" had missed, and, apparently, the intended victim did not see the torpedo tracks. The cargo ship continued blithely along, unaware of its brush with annihilation. *Swordfish* still held the element of surprise, and Smith and Sloan were not about to let their target escape.[46] Increasing speed, they maneuvered *Swordfish* for another try. By 0434, the submarine was in position for a second surface attack. Again, the estimated range was 1,400 yards and, as before, two torpedoes were dispatched at a 15-second interval and a longitudinal spread. Depth was set at ten feet, as before. This time the officers abandoned the TDC for calculations. The bearings at the time of firing were eyeballed. The change paid off. Seventy seconds after the first shot, a torpedo slammed into the ship just forward of the bridge. Smith reported, "Believe second torpedo hit. Ship stopped and settled down by the bow and sank in twelve minutes." The persistence of Smith and Sloan paid off. *Swordfish* had sunk *Burma Maru*, a 4,584-ton cargo vessel.[47] Chester Smith complimented Lieutenant Sloan on the successful attack and noted the young officer's fine work in the war patrol report.[48] However, in all likelihood, after the torpedoes missed in the initial attack, Smith, the old master, took a more active role in "bagging" the prey. In particular, the swift, skillful move back into an attack position displayed the hallmarks of Smith's underlying, aggressive nature, when circumstances required it.

Smith ensured that the crewmen of *Swordfish* would not be disappointed. Indeed, although they had been pressed hard in this patrol, morale was very high.[49] Their efforts were paying off. Pearl Harbor and the fall of the Philippines were being avenged. Just as significant, with the sinking of the maru, one more link had been taken out of the Japanese logistical chain. The island empire's ability to wage war was slowly pared down with each sinking.

Preferring not to linger in shallow water for any length of time, Smith ordered a southerly course, but for the next five days navigation sights were hampered by poor visibility. Rain squalls and overcast skies were the culprits. The crew could not pinpoint the exact location of their boat. Unknown currents in these strange waters added to the challenge of pursuing a set course. On 16 June, Smith was able to write, "Finally obtained fix."⁵⁰ The crew discovered that their boat was 30 miles north of Sekatung Island in the South China Sea. The next day, Smith decided, as per schedule, to head home to Fremantle via the Balabac, Makassar, and Lombak Strait.

Added to the vexing problem of not knowing the exact whereabouts of *Swordfish* had been the problem of torrid interior temperatures while submerged. Leakage of the refrigerant had rendered the air conditioning units useless, and temperatures soared while submerged, a procedure necessary for cover during daylight travel. In the last three weeks of the patrol, over half the crew had suffered from heat rash. Smith reported, "Ten per cent were bothered by this enough to actually reduce their military efficiency slightly."⁵¹ The homeward trip for equipment repairs and rest for the crew had taken on increased meaning.

On 27 June, *Swordfish* reached the Celebes Sea and Smith got a chance for one more attack. Lookouts spotted a small interior land steamer on the port beam. The ship displayed a large Dutch flag painted on its hull. Smith elected not to investigate whether the flag was authentic or the steamer was a foe in disguise, estimating that an examination would consume one and a half hours during which *Swordfish* would be surfaced and vulnerable to aircraft attack. He observed that the cover of a partly cloudy sky would allow an enemy airplane to pounce upon the submarine with scant warning. Later, Smith chastised himself for not pursing the steamer: "The Commanding Officer now believes that this decision may have been a bit timid."⁵² Measured against the numerous aggressive approaches which he conducted in this and previous patrols, Chet Smith was certainly not a timid soul. In the present instance, he was overcautious perhaps, but not timid. He reasoned that safeguarding his boat and crew was more important than risking an air attack while investigating the possibility of engaging a minor combatant.

By July, *Swordfish* was considered in friendly waters and was proceeding toward Fremantle on the surface in daylight. Home port and relaxation were fast approaching. Possible death by "friendly fire" was also fast approaching. At 0914 on 2 July, an American PBY aircraft headed for the submarine in a most menacing fashion. Apparently the outline of the boat was not recognized as American. At three miles distance, the aircraft was sighted. Smith abruptly "pulled the plug" in a crash dive, and at the same time an emergency identification signal was fired. With Smith thinking the message had gotten through, at 1007 *Swordfish* surfaced, only to be driven down three minutes later. Again the plane headed for the submarine, and once more an emergency identification flare was fired. During the short time on the surface, Smith had intercepted the plane's message to its base. The eager pilot claimed that the submarine had sent off the wrong-colored flare. In his patrol report, Smith gave his rejoinder: "It is believed that the correct color was fired."⁵³ Upon surfacing at 1058, Smith sent a message to the PBY, informing him that his contacts were with *Swordfish*. There were no further attacks on the submarine. On

Independence Day, 4 July, *Swordfish* entered the Swan River and found its berth. Home port at last.[54]

The top submarine command recognized Chester C. Smith's extraordinary accomplishment. Admiral Charles A. Lockwood wrote his endorsement:

> This is another successful patrol aggressively conducted by *Swordfish*. It is worthy of note that on two occasions during this patrol *Swordfish* tenaciously hung on to ensure destruction of the enemy: on one instance to deliver the *coup de grace* and in the other to make a second successful attack after the first had failed.[55]

Officers in the Submarine Service often read the endorsements of the top brass along with the war patrol reports. The endorsements served a dual purpose. They called attention to the accomplishments of successful commanders. Secondly, other submarine commanders looked to the top command's comments for guidance as to how they should conduct their patrols. In particular, Admiral Lockwood's emphasis on conducting an aggressive, determined attack came through loud and clear. In charge of submarine operations in the southwest Pacific and later commander of all submarine operations in the Pacific, Admiral Lockwood loomed large in the minds of the submarine commanders under his authority. Known as "Uncle Charlie," Lockwood on several occasions replaced less aggressive submarine commanders with more assertive skippers.[56] Lockwood wanted his commanders to clear the Japanese merchant marine from the seas, and he declared, "Chet Smith is our ace." Lockwood added, "My ambition is a ship a day but we aren't up to it yet."[57] With Chester Smith, the admiral had no qualms. Smith and his submariners were quite willing to raise the score.

The patrol had been successful but long and exhausting. During the 51-day patrol, *Swordfish* traveled 9,752 miles, of which 1,510 were while submerged. The submariners spent 692 hours on the surface and 493 hours submerged. For their efforts, they sank two enemy merchant ships and possibly damaged or sank a third.[58]

The Price of Success

Nevertheless, there was a price to be paid for success. Chester Smith termed the morale of the crew throughout the war patrol as good. However, the rigors of the patrol had taken their toll. Smith noted, "Considering that the officers and crew had hardly a complete day's separation from the ship in eight months their morale is excellent. However, during this patrol there were several cases where outward indications of strain became evident."[59] Speaking to his superiors via the patrol report, Smith recommended rotating the crew sections to allow liberty. While in port, one section could take time off, and two other sections would stay aboard to maintain and secure the submarine. The conscientious Smith saw general benefits in this arrangement: "It is believed that the necessary work and security could be accomplished in this manner and that the morale and physical condition of the crew would be thereby improved."[60] Lockwood was cognizant of the "wear and tear" on the returning submarine crews. He wrote, "What impresses me most when these ships come in is that all hands look tired and thin. There has been no overhaul crew arrangement made as yet, nor rest camps. Men have not been available to form such crews but will start it soon and get the lads rested up."[61] During 1942, the submarine command began to implement a general system of relief that mirrored Smith's request, and eventually entire crews could be released for rest and relaxation during the refit periods. However, throughout the war there was a tug of war between keeping experienced men on the boats and sending them for shore-side submarine refit and upkeep duties.[62]

On the other hand, except for the outbreak of heat rash, the men's physical health had been generally good. As a general health measure, approximately half of the crew had been taking vitamins regularly, including all of the lookouts, who were constantly subject to the elements. Another 20 percent of the crew took the vitamins semi-regularly. Smith reported that about half of the crew displayed a noted improvement in physical condition.[63]

To shake off the rigors of the patrol, Chief Machinist's Mate Floyd Cooper remembered the officers urged the crew to go ashore and, as Cooper stated, "have plenty to drink and try and forget the ship for a few days."[64] With plenty of beverages available, Fremantle was a good port of call for following the officers' orders. However, three of the sailors decided to be a little more adventurous. Floyd Cooper, James Evans, and Donald Gaither went into the Australian bush to hunt kangaroos, which are viewed in Australia as a game animal fit for hunting, just as deer are in the United States. Gaither actually succeeded in "bagging" a kangaroo, but the hunt went awry when the three adventurers became lost. The submarine was notified, and crew members were being organized to search for the errant trio when they wandered back to their hotel in a condition Gaither described as "half-frozen and two-thirds starved, having been away from anything to eat for 24 hours."[65]

While the men recuperated, the condition of *Swordfish* was also a matter of concern. Under "Major Defects Experienced," Chester Smith described various malfunctions. The deep dives had revealed problems which were addressed after the previous patrol. The noisy bow planes and a noisy trim pump, replaced after the third patrol, jeopardized the requirement for stealth, especially when going deep to evade anti-submarine attacks. Both issues would have to be addressed again. The leaking air conditioning units were another problem that had to be solved. As mentioned, voyaging in climes so close to the equator made submarine interiors very inhospitable without air conditioning.[66]

However, the major "casualty" that resulted from the long and wearing patrol was Chester C. Smith. He had done well and could be very satisfied with his performance. However, while on patrol, he fell ill with a brutal cold. Smith was "laid low" and asked to "sit out" the upcoming war patrol. He believed the foul

3. Chester Smith Creates a Legend

Chester C. Smith receives a Gold Star Medal in lieu of a second Navy Cross from Admiral Charles A. Lockwood, aboard USS *Swordfish* at Fremantle, Australia, 1942. *National Archives, College Park.*

air, the smoky interior, and the diesel fumes aboard the boat would exacerbate his condition to the point where he would be ineffective as commander. In an informal, confidential agreement, Admiral Lockwood granted Smith's request to take a leave from sea duty with a promise to return him to command after the fifth patrol. Lockwood assigned Smith to command a shore-side relief crew, and he remained "on the beach" during the fifth patrol.[67] Speaking of Smith, George Brown remembered the crew's reaction: "It was a sad moment in our hearts aboard *Swordfish* when he was detached in Freemantle, West Australia, after we had completed our fourth successful run. We had other COs who earned a spot in our affections, but there was only *one* Chester C. Smith!"[68]

"Acey" Burrows

When Chester Smith was excused from sea duty in July 1942, Admiral Lockwood tapped Lieutenant Commander Albert Collins Burrows to command

Swordfish. Smith's misfortune provided Burrows with an opening to gain stature in the Navy. Albert Collins Burrows was born in Shawnee, Oklahoma, in 1905, and in 1923 he travelled east to enter Annapolis, where he was known to his classmates as "Acey" Burrows. When he graduated from Annapolis in 1928, the editors of *The Lucky Bag*, the class yearbook, provided insight as to how his classmates viewed him: "'Acey' is our foremost proponent of the power of words and has repeatedly proven his ability to handle them. Witticisms and superlative adjectives flow as freely from his exquisitely chiseled mouth as does the oil from a gusher of his native state." The editors recalled his penchant for antics in sea training, his mimicry, and his outgoing personality, which gained for him a wide circle of friends. *The Lucky Bag* added prophetically, "Slow to get started, 'Acey' is irresistible underway and behind a lot of surface nonsense hides a clear, cool mind and a capacity for quick sound judgment." The editors also noted that except for Burrows' weakness in mathematics, he had no academic concerns. He honed his ability to express his thoughts by being a Features Editor for *Log*, a student journal, and by working as part of *The Lucky Bag* staff. He was quoted as frequently saying, "Now here's the way I look at it...." He also found time to be a member of the water polo team, as well as participate in an assortment of student class committees. His classmates recognized his facile use of words, his wit, his popularity among his peers, and his intelligence.

He fit easily into the comradery of the Navy's corps of officers after graduation. Burrows made steady progress up the ranks in the peacetime service. Along the way, he gained both experience and association with senior staff officers, as well as earning a law degree. He had served on the staff of the Commander Submarine Squadron Five and later on the staff of Admiral Charles Lockwood when he was Commander of Submarines, Southwest Pacific. Burrows served in the 1930s on "S"-type submarines, and in 1942 he was attached to the USS *Seal* as Prospective Commanding Officer for one patrol.[69]

Now as Chester Smith's temporary replacement, "Acey" Burrows faced the loneliness that goes with command. Although subordinate officers could feed him information aboard *Swordfish*, he would be the final decider in all manner of things, including the tactics employed during attacks. But there was more than the Japanese to concern him. As a "rookie" commander on his first war patrol, Burrows had to deal with seasoned submariners who, in the course of four war patrols, had grown accustomed to Chester Smith's ways of command. Indeed, the crew had been very proud to serve with such a successful commander. Comparison between Smith and Burrows was inevitable. The crew would be watching.

There was also another observer: Admiral Lockwood. He would be gauging how effective Burrows was as commander. Lockwood needed to know if Burrows could sink enemy ships. *Swordfish* was yet another player in this drama. Burrows would have to deal with the peculiar characteristics of the boat. Going to sea in a strange boat would plumb the depths of his knowledge as a seafarer. Again, the crew and the high command would be watching to see if Burrows was "worth his salt." Finally, there was the sea itself, unpredictable, restless, and most unforgiving. Burrows' opportunity to make his mark was not a sure thing.

On 27 July, the mooring lines were slipped and *Swordfish* put to sea. Events of the first few days out of Fremantle did not augur well for the patrol. Burrows had re-organized crew assignments and changed diving procedures. After he gave orders to dive, an erratic descent resulted. Ensign Donald Gaither, who was in the chief's quarters, described how a locker came open and toilet gear spilled out on top of him. He went to the control room, where Burrows had taken charge. The commander ordered stop and then reverse. Gaither, who had gone on 11 patrols aboard *Swordfish*, remembered: "it was probably the highest angle [of descent]

Albert Collins ("Acey") Burrows. *National Archives, College Park.*

that I ever took on any submarine, we don't know how much it was but we know it was well over 30 degrees, everybody was pretty well scared."[70] The following day was no better. Burrows ordered a quick test dive. As the boat descended to 225 feet, a fuel transfer line burst, spewing fuel at the rate of 100 gallons per minute. Surfacing, the crew investigated the casualty, which was found to be badly corroded. A semi-permanent repair was made, and the patrol continued.[71]

As the patrol progressed, Acey Burrows displayed characteristics of command which stood in direct contrast to Chet Smith. Smith exhibited an informal, quiet, almost self-effacing style of command. Though he was tight-lipped and reticent, his crewmen willingly followed him because of his very evident ability to attack the enemy and to leave the scene of attack unscathed. His quiet confidence imbued in his crew the desire to meet his expectations. As Elizabeth Sayre noticed while aboard *Swordfish* for evacuation from Corregidor, Chester Smith had a deep sense of self-confidence. He epitomized quiet efficiency.

By contrast, the highly vocal, assertive Burrows established no such rapport with the crew of *Swordfish*. His quartermaster, Leymon Dennis, had previously served under Burrows when Burrows was berthed on USS *Holland*, and Dennis was charged with arranging for Burrows' transportation. Dennis described him as overbearing and never satisfied. According to Dennis, Burrows liked his privileged position as an officer, and he gave the impression of not respecting those who served under him. The easy comradery that Burrows had with his fellow naval officers did not transfer to his subordinates. Aboard *Swordfish*, contrary to the informal environment promoted by Smith, Burrows was more rigid, straight-laced, and an advocate of "spit and polish" appearances. Perhaps as a newcomer to *Swordfish*, he used this as a defense mechanism.

With his formality and authoritative demeanor, Burrows certainly obtained compliance with orders, but not the crew's enthusiastic support. In addition, Chester Smith, the engineer, had an impressive, intimate technical knowledge of *Swordfish*. As the designated commander, Smith had crawled through the sections of the boat while it was under construction. *Swordfish* was Smith's "darling." On the other hand, although Acey Burrows was well-trained and experienced in submarine operations, he seemed to be disinterested in technical matters, much as he had not been particularly interested in mathematics at Annapolis, preferring more the realm of words and expression. Electrician Robert Dyer, who served under both commanders, remarked that if you took Burrows back to the engine room, he was "lost" and showed no interest. Nevertheless, Smith and Burrows did have some similarities. In addition to both graduating from Annapolis, Smith and Burrows were both born in 1905, but whether or not the 37-year-old Burrows would be as aggressive as Smith would be answered in the ensuing days.[72]

Swordfish headed toward the Sulu Sea via the Makassar Strait, and on 8 August, Burrows had a chance to get his first "kill." Looking through the periscope just before dusk at 1825, the commander spotted masts over the horizon. Burrows ordered a change of course to close the distance and surface. By 2135, lookouts on the bridge discerned a faint, dark object one-half point on the starboard bow. Burrows approached the target but then hesitated. Instead of going in for an attack, he ordered a change in course to increase distance away from the Japanese ship. He wanted to move ahead of it in an end run without being detected. He planned to meet the enemy head-on and to maximize the availability of the target. By 2231, the Japanese ship was quite visible and within desirable torpedo range, which was approximately 1,200 yards.[73]

Again, Burrows hesitated, this time to lower his submarine's silhouette by venting her ballast tanks. The noise of the venting alerted the Japanese vessel, and it reacted. The ship increased speed and, with bow waves clearly visible, headed directly for the submarine. *Swordfish* quickly dived, and the would-be target passed overhead astern. At 2322, *Swordfish* was again on the surface and resumed the chase. Again the next morning at 0024, the enemy ship was quite close, and it once more headed toward *Swordfish*. The cat and mouse game continued as Burrows ordered "dive." By 0106, the chase would continue, but Burrows again hesitated. In reviewing his position west of Sibutu, he concluded that his submarine may have entered the patrol area of another American submarine.[74] Burrows decided to give up pursuit of the Japanese ship. He reasoned that in addition to possibly entering another patrol area, there was now poor visibility, and it was unlikely that the enemy ship would be caught off-guard since it knew of the submarine's presence. Later, in thinking over the encounter, the skipper regretfully concluded that he might have made a successful attack when the Japanese ship was suddenly picked up dead ahead at 0024. Burrows lamented, "The commanding officer considered that he errored in not firing at that time, while diving, and thus learns by hindsight."[75] After engaging in a seven-hour pursuit, Albert C. Burrows had very little to show for his and his crew's efforts, but the patrol was still relatively young.

On 15 August, *Swordfish* had another chance to score when the upper works of a ship were seen through the periscope. It was a maru of approximately 7,000 tons and was proceeding at a range of 14,000 yards. *Swordfish* gave chase, but to avoid detection, Burrows kept her submerged. The consequence was a slower pace of pursuit. One hour later, the Japanese ship passed ahead of the submarine at an approximate range of 7,500 yards. The vessel had been an enviable target—heavily loaded and unescorted. Burrows remarked, "To come so close and yet to be so far out was a bitter pill."[76] At 1913, the enemy ship had passed out of sight, but Burrows did not order surfacing to keep up the chase until after sunset. Upon surfacing, Burrows ordered a change in course in an effort to head the ship off at a later time, which never came. The enemy ship was gone.[77]

After two false starts, the next day Acey Burrows would not repeat the mistake of waiting too long to attack. Coming across a large, dark image directly ahead at a range of 3,000 yards, the submarine's crew scrambled to battle stations. Six minutes later, Burrows had misgivings about being on the surface with a bright, illuminating moon on his port quarter. Anxious about not giving up the element of stealth, Burrows ordered a dive to use a submerged approach. Although he could make out the target only temporarily and was unsure of the range to the target, he rushed his attack. Using only sound bearings and the TDC solution, he sent off, at 22 second intervals, four torpedoes in succession. The first detonation occurred four minutes and 55 seconds after firing the first torpedo. All torpedoes missed.[78]

Burrows acknowledged that the attack was in error because the calculated target course, speed, and range data were imprecise. The result was a waste of greatly needed torpedoes. To his superior officers who would read his patrol report, Burrows, the attorney, pleaded for understanding: "The lesson, however, has been learned and the only justification offered is an overly enthusiastic desire on the part of a new commanding officer to sink his first Jap."[79] Surfacing, Burrows again faced the vexing circumstance of not sighting his target, of not knowing where it went, and ultimately of realizing it had eluded him. The fates had been unkind.

In the hope of intercepting traffic from Hong Kong, Burrows continued his patrol in the vicinity of Macclesfield Bank east of the Paracel Islands in the South

China Sea. Opportunity knocked once more. While submerged during the afternoon of 17 August, *Swordfish* came across a fat prize, a 10,000-ton transport. The lens of the periscope revealed a picture which Burrows described: "Life rafts were everywhere visible about her passenger decks. One gun forward and one gun aft."[80] Clearly the transport was fitted out for carrying troops and was a highly desirable target. *Swordfish* increased speed. Burrows wanted to come within 2,000 yards. However, at 2,300 yards his eagerness got the better of him, and he ordered three torpedoes fired. The commander related the next events aboard the submarine. "Immediately after firing lost depth control and vessel started to broach. Ordered negative flooded and speed increased. Plummeted to 200 feet."[81] Reflective of his extreme concern about not being seen, Burrows emphasized that during the boat's rise, the periscope shears did not break the surface. While under, the sound men heard three delayed explosions, connoting that all "fish" had dashed along at deep depth and had missed.[82]

Thirteen minutes after the attack, Burrows exposed the deep mind-set which determined much of his conduct during the patrol. Rather than surface in daylight, he gave up the chase. Burrows provided an explanation for his actions based upon his obdurate aversion to daylight surface action. In his report, he wrote, "Discarded any hope of pursuit since target would have about two hours and twenty minutes run prior to my surfacing, and, in addition he would have proceeded south beyond limit of my area. This last would not alone, of course, have deterred my chasing him."[83] True to form, at 1930 that evening, *Swordfish* finally surfaced onto an empty sea.

During the days that followed, Acey Burrows set course to crisscross possible ship routes in the South China Sea, again around the Paracel Islands and Macclesfield Bank. Not finding enemy ships, he decided to reconnoiter Prattle Island within the Paracel group. On 27 August, *Swordfish* stood two miles off Prattle Island, and via periscope Burrows noticed an elaborately constructed radio station with two antennae and a staff bearing a Japanese flag aloft. He contemplated shelling or raiding the island, but hesitated without knowing the armament or number of personnel there. To gauge the size of any garrison and observe enemy harbor activity, he planned to station an observer for a day on a nearby island, but postponed the venture when stormy weather interfered with his plan, and the boat left. In the meantime, he had a detailed sketch made of the island.[84] Four days later, *Swordfish* returned to Prattle, and Burrows attempted to salvage the outcome of his patrol by mounting an attack on the island. On 31 August, the commander wrote in his patrol report, "Since original orders directed *Swordfish* to leave area today decided to request extension upon surfacing in order to await favorable weather for attack on Prattle."[85] In reply, Admiral Lockwood granted an extension until 5 September. To Burrows the task of reducing Prattle still required a full day of observation. In his usual cautious manner, Burrows wanted to gauge the strength of any garrison on the island rather than go in and lob a few shells at random. Almost as a plea he wrote, "It is devoutly hoped that *Swordfish* may be given an opportunity to do this job."[86]

Although Burrows was ardent in his desire to move against Prattle Island, it never occurred. Foul weather and reduced visibility ruined his step-by-step plan of observation and attack. Since he was unwilling to surface and engage in hit-and-run tactics, the passage of days prevented his more elaborate plan. Time simply ran out. Responding to orders, he started heading south for Australia, and the primary goal of sinking enemy ships once again became paramount. Near Ambulong Island in the Philippines during a pitch-black night, amidst a driving rain squall, lookouts on the bridge on 8 September noticed a white light. Burrows "pulled the plug" as much to avoid a collision as to escape detection. While the boat was under, the sound of heavy screws was heard as the vessel passed by. Knowing that he was in the last days of the patrol, Burrows ordered "surface" for yet another opportunity to score. He opened up speed to 14 knots in pursuit of the enemy ship. The driving rain had reduced visibility to 200 yards, but casting aside any concerns about a collision, he ploughed on into the early morning of 9 September.[87]

Evidently spotting *Swordfish*, the Japanese ship introduced what Burrows characterized as "a new trick to the binoculars of this vessel."[88] Intermittently, similar to creating a smoke screen, the enemy ship would emit a cloud of thick black smoke and then would pass through it. Burrows described the tactic as "a sort of masked zig."[89] Reaching a range of approximately 1,500 to 1,600 yards, Burrows ordered firing from bow tube number three, followed by a barrage from tubes four, one and two. Profiting from his previous hasty, inaccurate torpedo attacks, the submarine commander described the sequence. "All torpedoes were fired slowly and deliberately carefully allowing for the enemy's maneuver to avoid."[90] From the bridge of *Swordfish*, Burrows could observe the phosphorescent wakes of all four torpedoes.[91]

Even with such care in firing the "fish," the results were negative. Burrows believed one torpedo had gone under the ship's stern and another had hit the target. A loud explosion was heard, but the Japanese ship did not stop. Burrows thought perhaps he had attacked a Japanese destroyer, and the detonation may have been a depth charge. Whether the culprits in his attack were torpedoes with notoriously inaccurate depth settings or faulty warheads was unknown, but the close range and the care Burrows had taken left open these possibilities. In any event, after firing the last torpedo, *Swordfish* dived, and when she returned to the surface 30 minutes later, no ship was to be found. The hapless Burrows could only shake his head in frustration.[92]

The misfortune attendant with the fifth war patrol went beyond Burrows' decision-making. His officers and crew became quite sick. On 12 September, Burrows described the bouts with illness. "All officers and about 90 per cent of crew have been suffering from acute and persistent stomach disorders for past few days. Water suspected.... Malady characterized by constant dull pain in pit of stomach, frequent vomiting, inability to retain even liquids, general debility."[93] Burrows shifted to the electric distillery for water and radioed a request for medical treatment. Chief Torpedoman Paul Marvin recalled desperately attempting to administer a substitute for water. Marvin stated, "He [Burrows] mixed up some concoction of brandy and milk and gave it to the men, tried to help them out."[94] Contrary to the conclusion of Burrows, some crewmen aboard *Swordfish* believed that the crew's illness arose from the extension of the patrol and the need to "reach down" into the food lockers for the last items of food.[95] However, another crewman, Lloyd Henry Faye, asserted that it was not the food. Henry, as he was known by the crew, remembered seeing green flecks floating in the water.[96] Making matters worse, the air conditioning aboard *Swordfish* leaked Freon, as in the previous patrol. The entire stock of spare refrigerant was exhausted.[97] Without relief of air conditioning, inside *Swordfish* the pungent odors of vomit, sweat, bodily functions, and the ever-pervasive smell of diesel oil produced for days on end a thoroughly hellish environment, especially when temperatures rose near the equator. Worse yet, the pandemonium of men doubling over and retching, of groping for the toilet or a basin, and the chorus of groans and epithets challenged the normal orderliness of daily operations. No amount of prior training sufficed to guide Burrows though this ordeal.

After 55 days at sea, *Swordfish* finally returned to Fremantle on 21 September 1942, but with a very unhappy crew. When the submarine returned to home port, the medical officer's report identified copper poisoning as the cause of the abdominal troubles, confirming Henry Faye's observation of green flecks in the water. Certain copper fittings related to the distillation of water had to be replaced with brass elements. Most likely the diagnosis of the medical officer was correct. However, no one knew for certain, and the alternate explanation of tainted food offered by crewmen provides a view of their disapproval of the extended days on patrol. Many crew members and some officers compared their service under Chester Smith with that of Acey Burrows, and Burrows came up wanting. The lack of successful attacks during their extended patrol and the clumsy nature of operations in general led them to judge Burrows as an inferior commander. The widespread illness had further exacerbated conditions of morale.[98]

Albert Carl Burrows did not return to a hero's welcome. His superior officers gave a scathing critique of the patrol, not only as an evaluation of Burrows, but also as a way of giving guidance to other submarine commanders who would read the patrol report. The so-called "endorsements" were, then, an indirect way for Admiral Lockwood and his subordinates to give instruction of how to conduct a patrol. The commander of Submarine Squadron Two, James Fife, dissected the defects of Burrows's patrol. Fife wrote in his endorsement that 11 torpedoes had been expended with no positive results. Fife added, "A more serious consideration is that four valuable targets were allowed to escape."[99] In recapitulating the various attacks on enemy shipping, Fife analyzed mistakes made. Regarding the ship contact of 8 August, Fife asserted that Burrows should have gotten off a shot at 2135 rather than wait until the next morning at 0024. Moreover, Burrows had allowed the target to slip away due to his ill-timed decision to trim down the submarine just before the attack. The noisy venting procedure alerted the enemy vessel. Fife concluded, "it is evident that the commanding officer [Burrows] has now learned his lesson in this respect."[100] Again, according to Fife, Burrows was not sufficiently aggressive during the encounter of 15 August. In order to keep up with the Japanese vessel, *Swordfish* should have surfaced and used the power of her diesel engines. The attack the next day was flawed because Burrows chose a submerged sound attack with inaccurate firing data.

Fife continued to pick apart the patrol. He noted that, during the attack of 17 August, firing torpedoes at an excessive range along with probable control errors resulted in failure to sink the Japanese transport. Again, sensing Burrows' desperation in wanting to achieve a successful attack, Fife believed Burrows had used poor judgment in his final attack: "The failure on 8–9 September can be attributed to expending four torpedoes on the tracer bullet principle based more on hope than good attack technique."[101] The endorsement also noted that in two of the cases of enemy ships, Burrows gave as partial reasons for abandoning the pursuits the fact that his boat was entering into another submarine's patrol area. Fife did not accept this excuse and rebuked Burrows for giving this reason. Fife emphasized the point to Burrows and wrote, "it is improbable he will again make this error.[102]

As commander of submarines for the southwest Pacific, Admiral Charles Lockwood added to Fife's critique with his own criticism. However, he took into account Burrows's inexperience and wrote, "The Fifth War Patrol of the *Swordfish* was the first one made by a relief commanding officer and shows lack of experience and seasoned judgment."[103] Lockwood offered some more brief comments. He stated bluntly that Burrows had spent too much time submerged, and the admiral set down general guidelines for war patrols: "Daylight surface cruising enroute to and from station and in the assigned area when in the open sea must be employed with due regards for anti-submarine measures in order to increase the length of the time on station and to enlarge the area searched."[104] Clearly, Lockwood was doing more than correcting Burrows's actions. The endorsement was a statement of general policy, which other submarine commanders would read and, if they were wise, follow.

Lockwood also used the Burrows endorsement to point out the need for inter-submarine communication. He noted that regarding *Swordfish's* encounter with the enemy on 17 August, there was no record of Burrows attempting to contact any nearby submarines. From Lockwood's point of view, such communication warranted breaking radio silence. In closing, Lockwood observed that none of the chased enemy ships took offensive action against *Swordfish*, and the ship sighted on 9 September probably was unarmed. The expectation was that Burrows could have done damage to the enemy if he had been more aggressive.[105] Indeed, the underlying message of both Fife and Lockwood was that their submarine commanders were expected to conduct aggressive war patrols where closing with and sinking enemy ships was the prime goal. Anything short of this objective was unacceptable.

Evidently Albert Collins Burrows, ever the attorney, pleaded his defense with expertise, as Admiral Lockwood permitted him to remain in the Submarine Service. However, in a private conversation, Lockwood informed Burrows in no uncertain terms that he had one more chance to show his worth as a submarine commander. In a letter to James Fife, Lockwood related his earnest warning: "I had a long talk with Acey before he sailed. If no wishbones, curtains for Acey."[106]

Burrows confirmed Lockwood's faith in him in brilliant fashion, but not aboard *Swordfish*. Burrows went to sea again as commander of USS *Whale*, where he sank several enemy ships.[107] In a letter to Admiral Lockwood, James Fife summed up Burrows' rapid turn in fortune: "When Burrows came back from his trip with *Swordfish* I told him that no one would cheer louder than I would if he produced results on his next attempt. In view of recent results by *Whale* it was a great pleasure for me to write him with a big pat on the back and no doubt you have done the same."[108] For successful patrols aboard *Whale*, Burrows was awarded the Navy Cross, a Silver Star Medal, and two Gold Stars in lieu of second and third Silver Star Medals. Providing a window into his meritorious conduct, the citation for the Navy Cross reads in part: "For extraordinary heroism in the line of his profession as Commanding Officer of the USS *Whale* on patrol in enemy controlled waters. By his skill, courage and determination he succeeded in sinking four freighters for a total of 33,506 tons."[109] Burrows was making his mark. The citation for his second Gold Star reads: "For gallantry and intrepidity in action as Commanding Officer of a United States submarine on war patrol in enemy controlled waters. In the face of strong enemy opposition he conducted aggressive, skillful attacks, resulting in the destruction of 10,000 tons and damaging 17,000 tons of enemy shipping."[110]

Acey Burrows further raised his esteem among his fellow Naval officers by graciously agreeing to share the sinking of a Japanese ship with Captain Roy Gross of *Seawolf*, similar to the circumstances when *Seal* and *Swordfish* appeared likely to have sunk the same ship in the fourth patrol. As a result of the attack of 17 January 1944, Gross acknowledged that *Whale* had "assisted" in sinking an enemy ship, and Burrows in turn elected to share with Gross and *Seawolf* credit for the successful attack. As Edward L. Beach so artfully described the results, "There was glory enough for all."[111] After the war, JANAC gave Burrows official credit for sinking four ships in the single year in which he commanded *Whale*.

In biographical sketches of Burrows, such as newspaper accounts, Burrows' command of *Swordfish* is seldom mentioned. Most likely, Burrows would have liked to omit his whole experience aboard *Swordfish*. However, it was aboard *Swordfish* that he first experienced the lonely responsibility that goes with commanding a submarine. It is well to bear in mind that going to sea on a submarine war patrol was an act of courage in itself, and being in command demanded more qualities, including good judgment. Taking into account his command of *Whale*, it is evident that Acey Burrows had truly learned from his errors while aboard *Swordfish*.

Subsequent to his command of *Whale*, Burrows commanded two surface ships, USS *Shenandoah* and USS *Tappahannock*, and served in various shoreside administrative positions, including in 1950 in the Office of the Chief of Naval Operations, Navy Department, as the Head of Harbor Defense and Mine Warfare branch. Upon his retirement in 1963, the Navy promoted Albert Collins Burrows to the rank of Rear Admiral. As Burrows' classmates predicted in the 1928 edition of *Luck Bag*, "Acey" Burrows did indeed have a slow start, but as *The Lucky Bag* also foretold, he would be "irresistible underway" once he got going.[112]

Smith Returns

During the closing months of 1942, victory in the South Pacific hung in the balance. Fierce naval and air engagements in the Solomon Islands were part of an American counter-offensive against entrenched Japanese forces, and on her sixth patrol, *Swordfish* sailed into the contested waters. In September the crew of *Swordfish* had welcomed back their old commander, Chester Smith. After finishing a refit of the major work items, *Swordfish* set off for its new forward base in Brisbane, with a stop at Sydney to pick up torpedoes. The requirements of war did not permit much liberty in Brisbane. The submarine arrived there on 29 October, and Smith's new commander, Rear Admiral R. W. Christie, assigned *Swordfish* to patrol south and west of Bougainville Island in the Solomon Islands. *Swordfish's* task was straightforward, as stated in the war patrol report: "Intercept and destroy enemy shipping."[113] The submarine departed for the Solomons the very next day, and six days later she was in the patrol area, looking for targets.

Unfortunately, the crewmen of *Swordfish* were not entirely prepared to take the offensive. Smith observed sickness that would plague his officers and crew throughout the patrol, so much so that he could rate his men as only in fair condition. He noted, "Thirty percent of those on board were at some time during the cruise sick enough to vomit while almost one hundred percent were troubled with quaky stomachs at one time or another."[114] The most critical period of illness occurred from 6 to 10 November, when approximately 20 crewmen were vomiting and two men went to "sick bay" in their bunks and never resumed normal duties. This period of maximum illness occurred soon after a foul, iodine-tasting batch of water was put into use, and, recalling the water problems of the previous patrol, Smith identified contaminated drinking water as the cause of illness. He ordered water samples taken for analysis when they returned to port.[115]

In a rare instance of candor for Smith, he elaborated further on the two major "casualties." The skipper related how these bed-ridden crewmen had severe stomach pains and could not retain any food or liquids, though they were administered Amphogel, soda, Paragoric, and a mixture of soda and rhubarb. Finally, intravenous feeding revived one of the crewmen. On the other hand, the second sailor was less fortunate. Eventually he could eat solid food, but he began to display signs of a more serious malady, the sores of syphilis. The drinking water could not be labeled the culprit in his case. The workforce aboard the boat was further diminished when a third sailor had to be confined to his bed for a week due to a mild case of yellow jaundice. Although beset by the toll of sickness, the crew did receive a modicum of relief from the now-functioning air conditioning units. The repair time in port resulted in a better working system, which provided a much more bearable environment.[116]

A bright spot in the patrol was new technology in the form of SD radar, designed to search the air and provide warning of approaching aircraft. This new radar device operated via an antenna that could be extended above the surface while the boat was submerged. Intending to stymie surprise attacks by enemy aircraft, the Navy installed SD radar on the boats during the early years of the Pacific war. This defensive radar system provided an early warning of approaching enemy aircraft, thus allowing a submarine to dive before the adversary could pounce upon an unsuspecting boat. The SD radar operated through a ship antenna attached to the periscope, and it provided a multidirectional sweep of the approaches to the boat. However, by 1943 submarine commanders suspected that the multidirectional SD radar was enabling Japanese aircraft to follow the radar signal back to American submarines. Thereafter it was used sparingly.[117]

With a boat filled with sick men and new radar, Chester Smith "waded" through early November searching, searching, ever searching for a viable target close enough for *Swordfish* to do its own pouncing. Meanwhile, the Japanese were also searching by means of air patrols, sub-chasers, and general surface patrol boats. Traffic in the Solomon Sea practically guaranteed an eventual encounter between the submarine and the Japanese.

Responding to orders from submarine headquarters, *Swordfish* changed patrol areas off the coast of New Britain Island. When ship movements were ascertained through the decoding of enemy messages, the U.S. Navy would employ a secret communications system called ULTRA (short for Ultra Secret) to order American submarine commanders to locations where enemy ships would most likely be present and the approximate time when they would be there. It was up to the submarine commanders to utilize the information for successful attacks, if, indeed, the ships could be located. Much to the peril of the Japanese, as the war progressed, American intelligence personnel became more and more adept at decrypting the messages that the Japanese sent to their navy and merchant ships.

The change in patrol area proved fruitful. Late in the afternoon of 13 November, the commander spotted through the periscope two merchantmen in a loose column at a distance of 1,000 yards apart and led by a sub-chaser. All ships zigzagged to thwart a submarine locking in on their bearings. As a further anti-submarine measure, the escort was echo-ranging continuously. *Swordfish* began to track the ships at a general distance of 3,500 yards. During the initial stages of the approach, *Swordfish* was able to gauge accurately the speed of the targets, but after sunset at 1826, the darkness foiled attempts to use the rangefinder for accurate observations. By 1917, *Swordfish* was in attack position and firing. Smith's plan was to fire four torpedoes, two at each ship. He employed his usual method of firing a spread of torpedoes at eight-second intervals, with the point of aim being one-quarter of each ship's length inside the stern and one-quarter of each ship's length inside the bow. Unfortunately, Smith had hurried the third shot and the bearing was not matched with the TDC or the gyro angle, although, by his estimate, it was not far off. Sound equipment on *Swordfish* picked up one explosion a few minutes after firing the first shot, indicating a possible hit, but three additional explosions heard at a distance later suggested that the other three "fish" had missed, traveling to the end of their runs. Smith acknowledged that the angles on the bow (vis-à-vis) the targets were probably in error.[118]

Now it was the Japanese turn to go on the offensive. In the darkness, Smith was barely able to see the merchant ships, and the sub-chaser was totally obscured. Apparently the sub-chaser was unaware of the presence of *Swordfish* until, as Smith believed, one torpedo had exploded against the merchantman. It was only after the three other torpedoes had exploded, ending their long, uneventful runs, that the enemy escort vessel showed signs of knowing the position of the *Swordfish* and headed toward her. Hearing the sounds of the incoming propellers, Smith went deep and rigged for silent running in expectation of a counter-attack, never knowing for certain if he had sunk the merchant ship.[119] The Japanese obliged with a depth charge that detonated overhead, but too shallow to jar the boat or inflict any damage. Smith wrote, "It wasted no time in locating us and dropped one depth charge apparently overhead while we were at 250 feet running silently. Although the search seemed to be continued for about 40 minutes by alternately eco-ranging and listening we drew gradually away running silently in the wakes left by the convoy." Smith, the old master, had showed his expertise.[120]

During submergence, the sound operators aboard *Swordfish* detected propeller sounds from only a single merchant ship and from the escort, suggesting that one cargo ship had been sunk. Moreover, when *Swordfish* emerged from the deep, she was alone. Smith reported, "Nothing in sight although the ship should have been seen if it were still stopped and on surface."[121] Heavy rain squalls closed in all around to obscure visibility, and Smith concluded that further searching for the convoy was fruitless. He ordered a change in direction to avoid patrols and in order to search southerly traffic lanes, as well as to charge the batteries.[122]

As November wore on, fighting intensified in the vicinity of New Britain as well as off Savo Island near Guadalcanal, and *Swordfish* witnessed an air assault on the Japanese stronghold of Rabaul. The night sky was lit up with flares and anti-aircraft fire. The fireworks lasted approximately five minutes, bearing witness to the ferocity of the contest.[123]

At approximately 25 minutes past noon on 17 November, while patrolling up and down the constricted waters of St. George's Channel, Smith came across just the kind of traffic he was seeking. He spotted a Japanese convoy in the distance consisting of two freighters followed by a 4,400-ton tanker, traveling approximately 1,000 yards apart in a loose column. Leading the column was a sub-chaser, and a second escort was on the side toward *Swordfish* off the port beam of the middle freighter in the convoy. All the ships were zigzagging as an evasive measure.[124] When the convoy was sighted, Smith was uncertain that his boat would get close enough for a shot. Since *Swordfish* was submerged, for propulsion Smith was relying upon the limited energy in the batteries. Nevertheless, he ordered an acceleration in a bid to catch up to the Japanese. The skipper described his actions: "When picked up it appeared almost impossible to get in an attack. High speed running on normal approach course brought us finally within reasonable range of the last ship, a 4,400 ton tanker."[125] Making matters precarious, the sea had swells of about four feet, which forced Smith to raise the periscope higher above the surface in order to see the target, thus possibly alerting the escorts.[126]

The sub-chasers were echo-ranging continuously, and at one point when the second sub-chaser was about 2,000 yards distant, it appeared that it had picked up the presence of *Swordfish*. Smith described his evasive maneuver. "We turned toward to present a minimum sound target and it was apparently given up as a false contact."[127] This nearby escort crossed the bow of the submarine at about 1,500 yards ahead, and Smith decided it was time to attack. He wrote, "It was decided to fire four torpedoes from bow tubes at the tanker in order to ensure at least one hit."[128] In characteristic fashion, he opted for a spread of torpedoes fired at intervals of eight seconds. At 1325, *Swordfish* fired one torpedo aimed half the length astern of the ship, another inside the stern, another just inside the bow, and the fourth torpedo half a length ahead of the bow. The estimated range was 2,400 yards. The torpedo depths were set at zero feet with the expectation that they would run at ten feet. Whether or not Smith had in mind the faulty depth setting inherent in the torpedoes is uncertain, but he was taking no chances on the "fish" running too deep.[129]

One minute and 34 seconds after firing the first torpedo, there was one explosion. Smith observed the hit, which was just forward of the stern at the break of the poop deck. Smoke and steam billowed from the stricken ship. Observing the tanker for two and a half minutes, Smith saw that the stern was settling in the water and that it was heavily loaded. Smith was certain he had achieved a "kill." He declared, "From previous experience of a torpedo hit in a similar position on a tanker the Commanding Officer has no doubt about the sinking of this ship in

3. Chester Smith Creates a Legend 77

less than 10 minutes."[130] As for the other three torpedoes, they had missed the ship and detonated at the end of their runs. Unfortunately for Smith and his crew, the tanker could not be watched until it sank.

Following the wakes of the torpedoes, both sub-chasers immediately headed for the *Swordfish*. The attackers dropped two depth charges each, but the detonations were further than 500 yards away, and Smith had already taken evasive action. Diving to 250 feet, he ordered silent running and brought *Swordfish* under the wakes of the convoy, co-mingling any noise from the submarine with the sounds of the turbulent wakes above. Enemy echo-ranging continued astern, but the submarine silently slipped away from the scene. Suspecting that aircraft would come to assist the sub-chasers in the search for the disruptive submarine, Smith kept *Swordfish* deep for three hours. Upon returning to periscope depth, smoke from a sub-chaser was spotted. Smith suspected that the enemy boat had come out of Wide Bay on an anti-submarine mission, and a searching enemy aircraft was also spotted. *Swordfish* once more took refuge in the depths until sunset. At that point, there were no sound contacts and nothing to be seen.[131]

During November, the U.S. and Japanese navies waged a series of battles near Savo Island, but after the fierce engagement of Tassafaronga on 30 November, the naval contest for Guadalcanal largely diminished. Nevertheless, in the restricted waters of the Solomons, prospects for finding a target remained good. In this microcosm of conflict, *Swordfish* sighted several enemy destroyers, but traveling at 25 knots or more, the destroyers would, Smith regretted, never come within torpedo range.

Aircraft were another matter. Smith's boat had made several contacts with night-flying aircraft in the Huon Gulf area by sight, sound, and radar, but as Smith noted, "it is believed that most [contacts] were with own planes on patrol or going to and from bombing missions." *Swordfish* had been in the vicinity to cover the shoreline near General MacArthur's forces.[132] On 26 November, when an airplane flew over just astern of *Swordfish* and seemed to bank toward the boat, Smith ordered a crash dive. The plane looked like an American B-25 bomber and had crossed the bow of the submarine at an altitude of 500 feet. After surfacing later, one of Smith's officers, Lieutenant J. S. Clark, suggested that *Swordfish* use its aircraft detection radar. The suggestion was well taken. At 0230 the next morning, radar indicated an incoming aircraft and, diving to 120 feet, *Swordfish* registered the sound of a stick of four bombs exploding across the aft part of the boat. Fortunately, there was no damage and only slight vibration. Smith wrote in his patrol report, "Decided that our submarine headquarters would get a report of the bombing and straighten the matter out so that we would not be bombed by own planes in the future."[133]

In the days that followed, Smith had to resort to frequent dives after picking up contacts with aircraft. In several instances when the boat was diving after making radar contact, the aircraft closed the distance with the submarine as in an attack. On 2 December, American night bombing in the area of Buna was so intense that submarine headquarters ordered *Swordfish* to clear the area. Observers on the *Swordfish* could see flares in the direction of Buna, with bombing and anti-aircraft fire. Danger was lurking. On the same day as the advisory from headquarters, at 2143 an aircraft dropped a flare close astern to *Swordfish* and, as Smith noted, "obviously intended to illuminate us."[134] Again, flares in the vicinity of Buna from 3 to 6 December indicated activity in the area. In several instances, the submarine had to dive to avoid closing aircraft. Smith and his crew continued to search for targets, but they also remained very wary of approaching aircraft, both hostile and friendly. Clearly, the environment was very unhealthy for a combat vessel whose main defense was stealth. Although Smith was prepared to continue his quest for targets, when the designated date for departing the patrol area came on 12 December, Smith complied and turned *Swordfish* toward Brisbane. On the 51st day of the patrol, 19 December 1942, *Swordfish* entered the channel at Brisbane and moored at New Farm Wharf, ending the patrol.[135]

In comments on the sixth patrol, Smith's new task force commander, Rear Admiral Ralph W. Christie, congratulated *Swordfish* for, as Christie wrote, "making the most of her meager opportunities and for inflicting the following damage to the enemy:

SUNK......................1 freighter of 4,395 tons.
DAMAGED...............1 freighter of 6,332 tons.[136]

Christie gave credit for damaging the ship in the first attack on November 13 and credible evidence of a sinking of the ship in the second attack of 17 November. The endorsement also declared that the sunken ship was probably a freighter rather than a tanker. Christie complimented Smith and his men on the use on the newly installed radar system. A second endorsement by Admiral W. F. Halsey acknowledged that the ship in the attack of 13 November was probably sunk, but that, because the evidence was inconclusive, Christie's conservative assessment was preferable: that the Japanese ship was only damaged. As with Christie's report, Halsey complimented Smith on the use of the SD radar.[137] Subsequently, recognizing that Smith sank one ship and damaged another, the Navy awarded Smith a letter of commendation for the sixth patrol.[138]

While Smith was out on patrol, Charles Lockwood penned a letter to Commander W. J. Suits of the Bureau of Naval Personnel, which revealed why he had held on to successful submarine commanders, such as Smith, rather than rotate them to new construction. There were not enough prospective commanding officers available for promotion to skipper. Lockwood wrote, "Also there is a great reluctance on my part of sending back those who are especially good because we need them for the job of reducing Hirohito's tonnage." Lockwood included Chester Smith among the commanders he wanted to keep on patrol, but added,

> Naturally, I do not intend to hold on to them too long for fear that they may crack up. As you can appreciate they are under a continuous and severe strain, the major part of which

strain I believe is contributed by navigational problems for, as you know, they must pass through a lot of bad spots under the worst conditions and when they get back in they look pretty tired from loss of sleep and usually pretty gaunt.[139]

While rewarding Smith for his stellar performance as a submarine commander, his superiors found a way to keep Smith active. Perceiving that he could be utilized in a much broader role than that of submarine skipper, they promoted him to the position of Commander, Submarine Division Sixty-One. Smith's days as skipper of *Swordfish* had now ended. True to form, in his new position, Smith was an inspiring leader, and he expected results from the skippers in his command. They were expected to be aggressive, and if a submarine commander declined to be aggressive on two patrols, Smith relieved him. The skippers in Smith's division sank enemy vessels totaling over 250,000 tons, and they damaged many more tons of Japanese shipping. For his exceptional, meritorious leadership, Chester Smith was awarded the Legion of Merit.[140]

In his subsequent wartime service, Smith moved to duty in the headquarters of the Commander in Chief of the U.S. Fleet in Washington, D.C., and in the last months of the Pacific war, Smith served as Commander, Submarine Squadron Thirty and as Commander, Task Group Seventy-One Point Three, May 1945 to September 1945. For his excellent service, Smith earned another Letter of Commendation and the privilege to wear a bronze star on his commendation ribbon. In the following years, he filled various administrative positions, and during the Korean War he went to sea again as commander of the cruiser, USS *St. Paul* (CA 73). Continuing his Navy career, he was promoted to the rank of Rear Admiral. After 34 years of active duty, Chester C. Smith retired on 1 January 1959. Taking into account his combat record, upon his retirement the Navy advanced him to the rank of Vice Admiral.[141]

After his retirement from the Navy, Chester Smith continued to be active in an occupation related to submarines. He joined the Lockheed Missiles and Space Corporation in California in a division that involved program planning for the Polaris and Poseidon missile programs. In this capacity he worked until his retirement from Lockheed in 1970. Chester Smith passed away on 24 January 1976.

The foundation for Smith's Navy career was built upon his award-winning exploits as skipper of *Swordfish*. Right from the first war patrol, there was an unmistakable journey that circumstances obliged Chet Smith to take. On the first patrol, Smith became the first American submarine commander to sink a Japanese ship in World War II, and he kept on sinking enemy ships. On a special mission, braving the ever-tightening ring of Japanese forces encircling Manila Bay, Smith successfully evacuated his commander, John Wilkes, and his staff. Returning to Manila Bay, he evacuated the ailing president of the Philippines, Manuel Quezon, with his family, and, in yet another slip past Japanese warships, he rescued the American commissioner, Francis B. Sayre, and his group.

From the very beginning, the Navy recognized that Smith was no ordinary commander. For his skillful command of *Swordfish* during the initial war patrols, in which he was credited with sinking eight enemy ships, in March 1942 the Navy awarded Smith the Navy Cross and a Gold Star in lieu of a Second Navy Cross. The award citation noted his "heroism and outstanding courage."[142] In particular, the award cited Smith's second war patrol when, during January and February 1942, *Swordfish* inflicted heavy damage on enemy shipping.

Chester C. Smith (right) points out to R. D. Adams the 11 swordfish symbols, each designating a Japanese ship sunk by *Swordfish*, Perth, Australia. *National Archives, College Park.*

3. Chester Smith Creates a Legend

After Smith's successful fourth war patrol, the Navy awarded him a Silver Star for sinking three Japanese ships despite the presence of hostile destroyers in the vicinity. The citation read in part: "With great skill and aggressiveness, the Commanding Officer daringly penetrated a strong escort screen and, despite attacking destroyers, launched torpedo attacks which resulted in sinking of three enemy ships, totaling approximately 17,000 tons. He skillfully evaded strong enemy countermeasures and brought his ship back to port safely."[143] Smith's old prewar commander, Harley F. Cope, summed up Smith's qualities as a wartime skipper: "Coolness, courage, skill and daring are combined with perfect judgment in him. The Japanese can attest to his ability even under the most trying conditions."[144]

Recognizing the success of the five patrols under Smith's command, the Navy gave wartime credit to *Swordfish* and her crew for sinking 11 Japanese ships, totaling 68,000 tons, and another four ships damaged, equaling 27,000 tons. These totals made Smith the highest-scoring commander at the close of 1942. Because Smith's score could not be entirely confirmed by other sources, such as Japanese records (often incomplete), the postwar Joint Army-Navy Assessment Committee credited Smith with sinking only four ships: *Atsutasan Maru* on 16 December 1941, *Myoken Maru* on 24 January 1941, an unknown maru (probably *Tatsufuku Maru*) on 29 May 1942, and *Burma Maru* on 12 June 1942. Over the objections of Admiral Lockwood and other submarine commanders, the committee reduced the wartime scores of numerous submarine skippers, including Smith.[145] Nevertheless, by the end of 1942, Chester C. Smith had already become a legend and an inspiration for submariners out on patrol.[146]

Three of Smith's fellow commanders from the old Asiatic Fleet served with distinction. "Bull" Wright and Dick Voge either went on patrol or worked in administrative capacities within the Submarine Service. "Mush" Morton racked up a significant record of sinkings while in command of *Wahoo* before 11 October 1943, when a Japanese aircraft sank the submarine with all hands, including Morton. Another unfortunate commander was Mort Mumma. While on patrol, Mumma's boat was severely depth-charged, and the strain of command was too much for him. Mumma suffered a nervous breakdown and relinquished command to his executive officer. Mumma's career as submarine commander was over.[147]

Chester Smith was successful in another way: he achieved to a remarkable degree the loyalty and confidence of his crew. After Smith passed away, George Valentine Brown characterized the original crew's loyalty toward Smith when he wrote,

> And love him we all did—the entire "plankowner" crew in *Swordfish*. That "kid" lieutenant was destined to become somewhat of a Submariner's legend; the late Vice Admiral Chester C. Smith, USN (Ret.) did actually become the best loved skipper of all of us "plankies," and of others who were fortunate enough to later serve under his command. He was the type of skipper we'd all dreamed of serving with—one whom you could follow confidently and without hesitation through hell and high water.[148]

Brown added that on the war patrols with Smith, they often did just that.[149]

The same was true of *Swordfish*. She, too, had become a legend. She was the first American submarine to draw blood from the enemy by sinking *Atsutasan Maru*, and she went on to sink or damage other ships. The special missions into Manila Bay further added to the aura of a daring, successful boat. However, even the legendary *Swordfish* had its underside. At the end of the sixth patrol, Smith reported that the chronic binding noise of the bow planes noticed in the previous patrol had persisted in the current patrol. More work on them had to be done.[150] Similarly, the trim pump continued to be very noisy when operating below periscope depth. Smith declared, "Repeated overhaul and check of alignment during each tender refit have so far failed to improve the situation."[151] He called for further checking of the alignment of the pump and also expressed hope for the development of a pump with a better design. Smith's concern was not merely for mechanical efficiency. While he took evasive action to escape Japanese anti-submarine listening gear, the noisy bow planes and noisy trim pump sacrificed stealth. The commander also noted problems with oil pressure, and although there had been no piston seizures, the outlook was, as Smith stated, "not optimistic." On the other hand, the SD radar had worked extremely well. Smith credited it with saving *Swordfish* from several aircraft approaches. The radar would remain a valuable part of standard operations. *Swordfish* was ready for another refit, which commenced on 19 December. Smith remained in command during the refit and repair.[152] *Swordfish* would strike again.

As Christmas approached, the crew could look forward to a holiday ashore, and many of them went to a rest camp at a seaside resort near Southport, Australia. Donald Gaither reported the Christmas scene: "There were a lot of people up there for vacations and consequently there were a lot of girls around, everyone had a good time."[153] The merriment of a Christmas "down under" gave a welcome boost to morale.

The submarine officers back in Fremantle were not so fortunate. A minor crisis had developed. The Christmas and New Year's holidays were approaching, and there was a shortage of a favorite beverage, Scotch whiskey. In a letter to Captain M. Collins, Liaison Officer in Adelaide, Australia, dated 23 December 1942, Admiral Lockwood noted that for the previous four months a shortage of Scotch whisky had forced rationing of the spirits to approximately two drinks per month. Lockwood observed, "Although this situation is a bit grim for the submarine officers who are on patrol a good part of the time, we have been able to get along all right on the local whiskey and gin. Recently, however, we have found it impossible to obtain liquor of any kind due to the shortage of local stocks brought on by lack of transportation facilities."[154] In place of Scotch, Lockwood authorized a local firm to order three hogsheads of Australian whiskey and two hogsheads of gin, and he asked Collins to help with delivery of the alcohol to the submarine base.

He added, "I don't suppose there is anything that can be done about Scotch but if you know of any which might be procurable, we would certainly appreciate your aid in starting some out this way."[155] Clearly, Lockwood was striving to ensure that his officers on shore leave had the necessary ingredients to celebrate the holidays and to forget, at least temporarily, the traumas of the war patrols.

4

Competing with a Legend

In reviewing the results of the American submarine campaign against Japan in 1942, Admiral Lockwood congratulated the Submarine Force and noted the official results known at the time:

Total tonnage sunk—902,518 tons
Total tonnage damaged—409,008 tons
Enemy ships sunk—137
Enemy ships damaged—55

Nevertheless, Lockwood expressed his expectations. He wrote, "This record, while very good, is not as high as we hope to attain in the future."[1] Postwar historical research indicates that submarines sank a total of 884,928 tons of Japanese merchant shipping in 1942, which was only minimally greater than available prewar tonnage and replacements through new shipbuilding in Japanese yards.[2] It would be up to a new skipper on *Swordfish* to show what his boat could do to increase the tonnage sunk in 1943.

When Jack Hayden Lewis assumed command of *Swordfish* on 3 January 1943, he had a compelling reason to do well: his career in the Submarine Service was in jeopardy. Before coming aboard *Swordfish*, Jack Lewis was known chiefly as the skipper who smashed up the newly built USS *Trigger*. The mishap occurred 6 May 1942, during the Battle of Midway, when *Trigger* was on patrol. While standing watch on *Trigger* in the early morning hours, young Ensign Edward Beach stood aghast as he realized that *Trigger* was heading toward a reef, following a change in orders that put the submarine in immediate danger of grounding. He quickly reported land ahead and waited for the captain to appear. After a delay, when he finally did appear, wearing red goggles for preserving his night vision, Jack Lewis pored over the relevant chart, made no alteration in direction, and returned below. The commander failed to realize that the red-tinted goggles had blanked out red markings on the chart for the reefs.

As *Trigger* cut through the sea at 18 knots toward a rock formation, in desperation Beach later claimed that he repeatedly attempted to call for assistance or at the very least clarification of orders, until he was told to desist. Beach stated that

4. Competing with a Legend

just before the collision, Lewis appeared and ordered "reverse engines," but then in a fatal error, rather than hold to "reverse engines" or call for a drastic change in rudder, Lewis hurriedly ordered the sounding of a collision alarm. In the excitement, the chief of the watch in the control room sounded all the alarms, including the order to dive. *Trigger* surged forward with the dive order. Beach remembered vividly the loud, shrieking sound of the scraping metal hull as *Trigger* ploughed into the wall of the reef, and *Trigger's* trajectory: "Her bow shot skyward. Her sturdy hull screamed with pain as she crashed and pounded to a stop." Within *Trigger*, there was general consternation as lights went out and watertight doors temporarily closed.

As the morning light began to appear, the crew struggled to reduce the weight of the boat, to get her off the coral before the expected Japanese invasion commenced. They dumped fuel and emptied the trim tanks, with no success in getting *Trigger* free. To his embarrassment, Lewis had to call for assistance, and a small tug arrived from Midway lagoon. After two attempts to put a hawser on *Trigger's* stern, the tug fixed a line, and, with *Trigger* reversing engines and the tug straining to pull *Trigger* free, the submarine finally slid off the reef. The damage was readily apparent: a large, glaring hole in a pierced ballast tank, but no puncture of her pressurized hull. *Trigger* was judged seaworthy, and Lewis elected to proceed on patrol before going in for repairs. With all the excitement of the victory at Midway, *Trigger's* debacle was not an object of close attention, and Lewis kept his command.[3]

Surviving the Midway episode, Jack Hayden Lewis commanded *Trigger* on her patrol to the Aleutian Islands. The Japanese presence was evident by *Trigger's* observation of enemy destroyers and other ships. In one incident, two destroyers crossed the bow of *Trigger*. Whether it was out of caution after the ill-fated Midway collision or for some other reason, Lewis refrained from pursuing these opportunities. Ned Beach offered a condemnatory explanation for Lewis' dismal "track record." He recollected that Lewis was more interested in playing games of poker in the ward room than attending to his duties while the boat was underway. Lewis would involve others in playing poker, and the other players had to be reminded to stand watch. Beach found Lewis to be unpleasant during these bouts of cards, and he refused to play.

Another habit which Beach observed in Lewis was the commander's penchant for frequent dozing. This was a practice that the editors of *The Lucky Bag* for 1927 had also mentioned under the entry for Lewis, when he was at Annapolis. While *Trigger* was on the surface at night, Beach stated that Lewis would lie half-asleep on a makeshift bunk in the conning tower, while during the day when submerged, Beach claimed that Lewis frequently stayed in his cabin unobserved with the curtain drawn, leaving many of the operations to others. Beach provided his acidic assessment of Lewis as commander on the Alaskan patrol: "Our commanding officer, whatever his other faults, proved to be a good writer. From reading his report one would think we had covered the area well and behaved as an aggressively handled submarine should, but our superiors in the submarine force organization were not fooled."[4] The impression on Beach's mind was indelible, and clearly he had a very negative opinion of Lewis as a leader, no doubt influenced in part by Beach's personal involvement in *Trigger's* mishap at Midway.

Nevertheless, Lewis was next assigned to *Swordfish*. Because there was a shortage of skippers, Lewis was given another chance in which to gain the confidence of the submarine command. In his favor, Jack Lewis had substantial knowledge and experience. He also had a tenacity which suited him well as a member of the varsity football team at the Naval Academy, and for dealing with the uncertain turns of circumstance in submarine seafaring. Within three years of graduating from Annapolis in 1927, Lewis was a member of the Submarine Service, and his first boat was USS *S-15*, with duties of engineer and executive officer. At this time, he also married Dora C. Currie and started a family. After *S-15*, he filled various submarine-related assignments and training until the Navy appointed him commander of *S-31*. When *Trigger* was commissioned in January 1942, Lewis was tapped to be her first captain. Upon returning from Alaska, he was hospitalized with pneumonia, and when he was released *Trigger* was no longer available. Lewis was now chosen to apply his knowledge and experience for the seventh patrol of *Swordfish*.[5]

Under Lewis's command, *Swordfish* shoved off from Brisbane on 9 January 1943, and soon after, while proceeding in a moderate head sea, a crewman lost his balance and fell into the water. Within five minutes, he was rescued. For Lewis, the man overboard brought into memory a previous incident when Lewis saved a seaman's life. On 26 April 1934, while in the Canal Zone, then-Lt. (jg) Lewis witnessed a seaman, Francis Quigley, fall off the bow of USS *S-14* and strike his head on a working float. Lewis, who

Jack Hayden Lewis. *By permission of J. Reilly & Beth Lewis.*

was fully dressed, immediately dived from the seawall to rescue the unconscious Quigley. With the assistance of other crew members, Lewis brought Quigley to safety. The Navy awarded Lewis a letter of commendation which stated, "Undoubtedly Quigley would have drowned ... had not Lieutenant JG Lewis witnessed his fall, watched him and promptly dived to his rescue."[6] Later in 1946, the Navy awarded retrospectively to Lewis the Navy and Marine Corps Medal, the highest non-combat decoration for heroism. Regardless of any shortcomings in leadership that Lewis may have displayed on *Trigger*, his reputation for personal heroism was well-earned and untarnished. Nevertheless, the crew on *Swordfish* may have wondered if his unlucky mishap at Midway would repeat itself. Lewis lost no time in dispelling any brooding among the crew. Over the next few days, he ordered practice dives and deck gunnery practice. Lewis was preparing for any eventuality.[7]

Lewis faced challenges connected to the submarine itself. As early as 10 January, the number two periscope gears jammed when being raised and lowered. Chester Smith had mentioned this defect in his previous patrol report, but apparently the refit crew could not solve the problem. Lewis noted, "This periscope vibrates so much above four knots speed that it becomes useless." During the early part of the patrol, the packing around the periscope leaked enough to cause concern. Similarly, Lewis noticed loud noises emanating from the trim and drain pumps that the "old timers" in the crew had heard on earlier patrols. The pumps made loud sounds when submerged below 90 feet, thus sacrificing the element of silence. Lewis described the phenomenon: "On more than one occasion it has required 15 minutes to pump 500 pounds of water while making a noise like a blacksmith beating on an empty oil drum."[8] Nevertheless, Lewis recognized that even with her defects, *Swordfish* was the vehicle that could bring his reputation out of the shadow of his previous conduct aboard *Trigger*. He dared not turn back.

On the positive side, the abdominal distress that plagued the men on the previous two patrols was gone. During the last refit, a senior medical officer attributed the widespread sickness to inhalation of carbon tetrachloride fumes. Stowed below decks, the chemical was kept on board to clean electrical equipment. For patrol number seven, the substance was removed. The drinking water was untouched, and the crewmen remained in an excellent state of health. Two men came aboard with dengue fever, but within a few days they could perform their assigned tasks.[9]

In mid–January, Navy analysts noted the movements of Japanese convoys coming out of Truk and Rabaul and headed for the Solomons. The Navy alerted *Gato*, *Triton*, *Silversides*, and *Swordfish* concerning the activity.[10] By 16 January, *Swordfish* had reached her assigned patrol area in the vicinity of Cape St. George and St. George Channel. Japanese shipping activity beckoned. That evening, the sighting of a merchantman escorted by three small boats prompted action. The weather was clear, with a moon three-quarters full, and Lewis chose a night periscope attack to avoid being seen during the approach. However, at 0007 the following morning, Lewis wrote, "Either range was overestimated or speed was underestimated, or both."[11] *Swordfish* had lost sight of the maru. Although Lewis ordered "best speed" to try to catch the target, contact had evaporated in the darkness.

A day later, a second, more intriguing sight was beheld. At the entrance to St. George Channel, *Swordfish* came upon a 4,000-ton, lightly loaded cargo ship escorted by two destroyers. Reports of enemy aircraft rounded out the picture of surveillance. Puzzled by such a heavy escort, Lewis concluded that the merchant ship was a decoy. Too far from the submarine to make an approach, the ships passed out of range, resulting in another false start.[12]

Amidst rain squalls and lightning, on 19 January the Swordfish began to patrol a new area off Cape Hanpan, Buka Island. At 1540, pinging sounds followed by the sighting of three heavily loaded merchantmen, screened by two destroyers, finally ushered in another chance for an attack. The presence of a Japanese Kawanishi 97 aircraft added to the danger, as it flew toward the submarine. Lewis ordered "dive," and *Swordfish* plunged to 150 feet, but as the boat approached the targets, Lewis ordered periscope depth. He found one destroyer patrolling back and forth ahead of the merchant ships, while the second destroyer trailed behind the formation.[13] The submarine got into position for a stern shot. Visibility had improved, and at 1634 *Swordfish* commenced firing three torpedoes at the first and second merchant ships in the formation. Lewis observed one hit forward of the bridge of the first ship, and a second hit was heard eight seconds later. While the boat went into deep submergence, three bombs detonated, announcing the airplane's counter-attack.[14]

Mechanical problems and further Japanese retaliation ended the American attack. The crew of *Swordfish* discovered that they could not open the outer door to torpedo tube number six. Worse, the outer door to tube number eight would not close. Both torpedo tubes would be out of commission for the rest of the patrol. However, these mishaps were balanced by the gratifying sound of ten explosions in the direction of the targets. Lewis believed the sounds were the internal explosions connected with the death throes of a Japanese ship. New sounds were heard as the Japanese started their depth charging six minutes after the attack. For the next 13 minutes, the Japanese dropped a series of ten "ash cans," but *Swordfish* escaped unharmed. When the boat came to periscope depth an hour and ten minutes later, the searching Japanese plane dropped two more depth bombs, driving the submarine back again into the depths.[15]

While *Swordfish* was briefly on the surface before the second aircraft attack, Lewis sighted only one destroyer and one merchantman five miles distant. Coming back to the surface to recharge batteries later that evening, Lewis mulled over the attack. He could not explain the disappearance of the other Japanese destroyer and two merchant ships. Lewis speculated that perhaps he had, indeed, been very lucky. He wrote, "The remaining AK [merchant ship] was not one of the two fired at and appeared to be undamaged. It is certain that two torpedoes hit the leading AK and it is possible that the third torpedo hit the second AK since it was aimed at the bridge at a range of about 2,000 yards."[16] Jack Lewis and *Swordfish* received wartime credit for sinking one Japanese merchant ship on 19 January. Japanese records confirm *Swordfish's* sinking of *Myoho Maru*, a 4,122-ton merchant ship operated by the Japanese army. *Myoho* was in a convoy heading for Bougainville with the Japanese Army's 6th Division. A single torpedo had hit aft on the starboard side. The death toll included 61 of the 922 soldiers aboard, as well as 35 naval passengers, 3 crewmen and the loss of all equipment. The other submarines in the area, *Gato*, *Triton*, and *Silversides*, had also sunk enemy ships.[17]

On several occasions during the ensuing days, *Swordfish* made contact with enemy ships, but the distances proved too far for an approach. The distant sounds of bombs detonating on 23 January did not imperil *Swordfish*, but reminded the crew that they had to watch for aircraft. Foul weather on some days interfered with visibility. Another concern was fuel, which was beginning to deplete, and Lewis wrote in the log, "may be a problem to solve later."[18]

Then on 2 February, while patrolling in the vast expanse of the Pacific just north of the Ninigo Islands group and the Hermit Islands, *Swordfish* crew sighted smoke approximately 20 miles distant. The submarine submerged for an attack, but the men noticed that oddly, the targeted ship was not taking the usual evasive action of zigzagging. When *Swordfish* came closer, all became clear. It was a hospital ship. There were markings designating it as a non-belligerent, including a large red cross emblazoned on its hull. Lewis wrote in the patrol log, "Not identified until just prior to reaching a firing position."[19] According to Chief Fire Controlman Vernon Fields, Lewis was annoyed by this internationally protected target, and the submarine commander declared, "Somebody on our boat must not be living right." Fields observed Lewis as he attempted to provoke the ship into hostile action: "Captain almost porpoised right in front of him one time, trying to get him to either use a gun or change course, so we could have some excuse to torpedo him in case it was loaded with ammunition or troops, or something."[20] *Swordfish* permitted the ship to pass by at 1,500 yards while photographs were taken through the periscope.[21]

The next encounter was not so placid. On 7 February, an aircraft attack nearly put an end to *Swordfish*. At 0925, the submarine was proceeding on the surface when machine gun fire prompted the Officer of the Deck and the lookouts to face toward the sun. Out of the sun came a large, land-based bomber swooping down in a glide at a distance of 3,000 yards and an altitude of 500 feet. There had been no indication on the radar, and the lookouts were still on the bridge when the aircraft commenced firing. Lewis reported the tense moments: "About 15 seconds later, just after closing the conning tower hatch; the impact of bullets striking the bridge and conning tower were felt and heard. One large explosion was heard. Paint chippings were knocked off the conning tower."[22] The bullets had raked the boat from bow to stern.[23]

When the boat dived to 170 feet, the damage started to become apparent. The forward engine room hatch leaked, and battery ventilation ducts, forward and aft, were flooded. The safety tank was partially blown, and the depth decreased to 90 feet. However, another problem was noted. When the battery ventilation drains were opened, they were discovered to be under pressure, and the ducts could not be freed of sea water. Lewis suspected a rupture outside the submarine's hull.[24]

During the evening, *Swordfish* surfaced, and in the darkness the crew inspected the damage topside. They estimated that 20 hits of .50 caliber ammunition had riddled the bridge, fairwater, and superstructure. Damage included a hit in the forward engine room hatch skirt which did not penetrate but which cracked the metal, and a temporary weld was made. As suspected, there was also a hit in the battery ventilation duct forward of the conning tower, for which a temporary patch was fashioned. Two main ballast tanks sustained hits, and several dents in the conning tower plating indicated damage there. Sea conditions prevented a thorough inspection of the superstructure.[25]

Lewis informed the commander of Task Force 42 that *Swordfish* had sustained damage. Ironically, the submarine command replied by informing him that friendly reconnaissance aircraft were on patrol north of the equator from Guadalcanal, and the submarine should keep clear. In his log, the exasperated Lewis wrote, "Our previous instructions were to conduct surface patrol when practica-

Japanese hospital ship photographed through the periscope of the USS *Swordfish* during the seventh war patrol. *National Archives, College Park.*

4. Competing with a Legend

ble."[26] Lewis may have been referring to Charles Lockwood's endorsement to Acey Burrows' fifth patrol. As noted previously, in his endorsement, Admiral Lockwood had emphasized the need to patrol on the surface whenever possible and criticized Burrows for too much time submerged.[27] Aboard *Swordfish*, the Officer of the Deck and the two forward lookouts had positively identified the attacking plane as the same type as a U.S. Army Boeing B-17. A few days later, the submarine command stated that a "friendly" plane had strafed the submarine, which the aircraft had mistaken for an enemy boat. Indeed, the attacker was a B-17. The Army airmen had spotted a forward deck gun on *Swordfish* and falsely assumed that her silhouette was that of a Japanese submarine.[28]

The submarine command ordered *Swordfish* to proceed to Pearl Harbor, and she headed eastward. As Lewis had predicted, fuel consumption became an issue. Due to both the weather and challenging seas, headway became difficult. Also, he thought that the damage may have extended to one of the fuel tanks, because 600 gallons of fuel oil had been lost. Lewis described in the log measures he introduced to conserve fuel: "Heavy head seas and adverse currents have greatly increased our fuel consumption. Slowed to one generator engine at midnight to economize on fuel."[29] However, Lewis noted that the resistant sea was not allowing very much of a saving in fuel, even while using one generator engine, so he ordered a shift to two direct-drive engines. Limping along, *Swordfish* reached Pearl Harbor on 23 February. Tying up at Pier 4 at the submarine base, Jack Lewis and his crew could finally give a sigh of relief.[30]

In his patrol report, Jack Lewis did not hesitate to describe the trials he had with the submarine itself. He noted defects that were not related to the aircraft attack, such as the faulty periscope gears and the noisy trim and drain pumps. Other defects included leaks in the high pressure valve and other valves associated with the main ballast tanks. There were leaks in the air conditioning equipment, and Lewis called for a stronger unit. Malfunctions had also occurred concerning the bow planes, which would not rig out due to a blown fuse, a drain line, and a sanitary tank. Other problems involved the gyro compass, the SD radar, which experienced tube failures, and valve leaks associated with the main engines. As had Smith, Lewis warned that the insulation resistance measured low with respect to the main motors, and he noted that the armatures were due for renewal at the next overhaul.[31] The torpedo tubes were another problem. During *Swordfish's* attack of 17 January, the drain valve connected to torpedo tube number 4 produced a loud, chattering noise. The subsequent breakdown of torpedo tubes six and eight during the attack of January 19 undoubtedly altered the chance for further success in the encounter. Finally, there were the torpedoes. The torpedomen encountered a great deal of stiffness when setting gyro angles.[32] Collectively, all the above-mentioned problems added to the challenge of enemy encounters.

Then there was the matter of the American aircraft attack. Knowing his report would be read by his superiors, Lewis wrote, "A satisfactory identification insignia should be displayed to prevent attacks from own planes."[33] Lewis also recommended that submarine headquarters send more communications concerning changes in friendly aircraft activity. Admiral Lockwood addressed the performance of Jack Lewis. He noted that the patrol had been unfortunately cut short due to the attack by the friendly aircraft. Heeding Lewis's remarks, the admiral wrote that recommendations for preventing a repeat occurrence would be the subject of a separate report. In addition, Lockwood complimented the one attack on the convoy Lewis had made on 19 February, while contending with an escorting aircraft and destroyer. The admiral noted that the malfunctioning torpedo door added to the need for an overhaul. Lockwood credited *Swordfish* with sinking one freighter.[34]

The admiral's endorsement was welcome news for Lewis. Lockwood judged that Lewis had a successful patrol. Lewis had demonstrated his ability to sink an enemy ship, and under the very trying circumstances of the strafing by a friendly aircraft, he had brought the *Swordfish* back to port. The Navy awarded Jack Lewis a Letter of Commendation (and ribbon) for successfully sinking a Japanese ship. In general, the crew of *Swordfish* held a similar assessment: the patrol was a success.[35]

Unfortunately, fate was unkind to Jack Hayden Lewis. His next assignment was command of a new submarine, USS *Dragonet*, for her first war patrol. From the start, the boat had numerous mechanical problems, and it was nicknamed the "Reluctant Dragonet." While on patrol off Matsuwa To on 15 December, while *Dragonet* was submerged at a depth of 70 feet, the crew felt a jolt. For the second time in his career, Jack Lewis was skipper of a submarine that had gone aground, this time hitting an uncharted pinnacle of rock. As sea water rushed into the forward torpedo room, the men forward escaped and secured the watertight door. To Lewis's credit, he gave orders to force air into the flooded chamber, which pushed out much of the water, but the submarine was heavily damaged. Lewis was able to bring his boat to the surface, and he headed for port. Adding to Lewis's challenge for survival, *Dragonet* encountered a fierce storm which almost sank the boat. Lewis rose to the task and successfully rescued his own boat. In a strange way, Lewis's previous mishaps, going aground while in charge of *Trigger* and being strafed while in command of *Swordfish*, had provided instructive experiences, even though unwelcome, in handling emergency situations. The submarine crawled into the port at Midway on 20 December. In World War II, *Dragonet* had the dubious distinction of being the only submarine to survive while having a totally flooded forward torpedo room.[36] The French define *déjà vu* as having seen or experienced an event previously, and Jack Lewis could well understand the expression. As Lewis contended with the events of *Dragonet's* accident, undoubtedly the harsh memory of *Trigger's* Midway grounding came to mind. Certainly the specific details of *Dragonet's* mishap were different from those of *Trigger*, but Lewis once more had to suffer the embarrassment of going aground, even though his quick thinking and fine seamanship on *Dragonet* staved off further disaster.

For successfully bringing *Dragonet* safely back to port, Jack Lewis was awarded the Bronze Star Medal by the Navy.[37] Lewis also received many compliments for his handling of *Dragonet*'s emergency, and he remained commander of the submarine. Subsequent to repairs, in April 1945, *Dragonet* went on patrol. She performed lifeguard duty, rescuing from the sea four downed American aviators. During the operation, Lewis had to take evasive action to elude enemy forces. In recognition for his accomplishment, the Navy awarded Jack Lewis a letter of commendation, and he was subsequently promoted to the rank of captain. Thereafter Lewis came ashore, where he performed various administrative duties as an anti-submarine warfare officer. In 1955, Jack Lewis retired, ending a Navy career that included the disastrous groundings of *Trigger* and *Dragonet*, but also the successful war patrol aboard *Swordfish* and his resourceful, successful seamanship in saving *Dragnet* after her grounding. The rescue of the four aviators and his earlier rescue of a seaman, while Lewis was an ensign, were also positive actions to his credit. Unfortunately for Jack Lewis, when the Navy reviewed his overall service record, the Navy denied Lewis' application for the benefits of combat retirement, and the Navy declined to promote him to the rank of admiral upon retirement. The Navy's rebuff was a source of disappointment which Jack Lewis harbored for the rest of his life.[38]

Upon returning to Pearl Harbor on 23 February 1943, *Swordfish* was due for an overhaul. After undergoing three days of minor repairs at Pearl, the boat sailed to San Francisco for further work at the Bethlehem Shipbuilding Company.[39] Floyd Cooper described the homecoming: "When we came in to San Francisco we came under the Golden Gate Bridge with our battle flag flying, we had a blue and white flag with a swordfish running from one corner to the other, with Japanese flags for each ship that we had sunk during the patrols."[40] As the submarine pulled up to the dock, a large crowd of yard workmen and bystanders warmly welcomed the crew and asked questions about their exploits. In the hustle and bustle that ensued, there was mass confusion as sailors attempted to gather their gear and head for leave all at the same time. The exceptions were a handful of the crew who were, as Floyd Cooper remembered, "getting out and getting a few bottles of beer and not caring whether they ever got home."[41]

Frank M. Parker

Much to the disappointment of the crew, Jack Lewis bid farewell to *Swordfish* on 23 May. He turned over his command to Lt. Cmdr. Frank Mahlon Parker. Lewis had been very popular with the crew, and contrary to Ned Beach's critical assessment mentioned earlier, the crew of *Swordfish* had responded to Lewis's style of command.[42]

During the overhaul, workmen installed new equipment and repaired existing apparatus. In particular, the installation of SJ radar was a major addition. Developed by Western Electric Corporation, SJ radar vastly improved submarine offensive capabilities by providing American submariners with the ability to pinpoint enemy ships for night surface attacks. The new equipment emitted a focused radar beam, which allowed American submarine commanders to find targets. Because Japanese escort vessels often lacked radar equipment for detecting surface vessels at night, the American submariners could mount their surface attacks under cover of darkness with reduced risk, as well as with a greater chance of success. Few American submarines had the SJ radar on board in 1942, and only 30 percent of attacks were conducted at night. By 1944, with more installations of SJ radar, submarine commanders conducted 57 percent of their attacks on the surface at night. For *Swordfish*, the installation of the SJ radar showed great promise.

Other alterations included moving the number one periscope to the conning tower, lengthening the conning tower, moving the 3-inch gun forward, and installing two 20-mm guns. Below, a new battery was installed as well as new sound gear. In order to increase the efficiency of the air conditioning, the coils were brought inside the pressure hull. Floyd Cooper remembered the previous "sweltering" conditions aboard *Swordfish* because of unreliable air conditioning: "Very few times did we ever make a patrol during these first seven with the air conditioning operating satisfactory throughout the entire patrol."[43]

In addition, the men in the yard finally installed rebuilt armatures in the main motors. At the end of the sixth patrol in December 1942, Chester Smith had noted low resistance related to the armatures. Although he judged the situation as not critical at the time, he recommended the armatures of the main motors be baked and reinsulated.[44] Jack Lewis subsequently noted that the armatures were due for attention at the next overhaul. Workmen serviced the armatures.[45]

When Frank Parker assumed command of *Swordfish*, it was in effect a promotion for previous meritorious service. As executive officer aboard USS *Argonaut*, Parker helped ferry 121 U.S. Marine raiders to Japanese-held Makin Island for a lightning commando raid of 17–18 August 1942. Another submarine, *Argonaut*, carried 90 Marines to Makin. The purpose of the raid was to draw Japanese forces away from the American landings at Guadalcanal. Initially, the raid was deemed successful and was a morale booster, even though the Japanese did not divert forces from Guadalcanal as desired.[46] Nevertheless, for his participation, Parker received a Letter of Commendation, which read in part: "His planning and supervision of the difficult problems necessary for the successful accomplishment of the task assigned was inspiring despite seriously overcrowded conditions in the submarine due to the increase in personnel from the raider unit."[47]

During the Makin Raid, Parker had shown the degree of flexibility necessary to deal with the unforeseen rigors of command. He had witnessed the need to carefully develop military operations, including alternate plans. During the raid, alternate plans had to be improvised due to a breakdown of faulty gasoline motors for the rubber landing boats as well as a last-minute change in orders. Significantly, Parker also observed the war "up close," as seven wounded Marines were brought to *Argonaut*. The submarine, along with *Nautilus*, was transformed into a hospital with an operating room. Fortunately the wounded Marines aboard the submarines survived. Not so fortunate were nine Marines who were inadvertently left on Makin Island. After capturing them, the Japanese committed the atrocity of beheading them. In general, the Marine casualties were especially painful for the submarine crews because during this 56-day patrol, with 47 days submerged, the navy men and the Marines had formed a close bond. Some of the Marines actually stood watch during submarine operations. No doubt for the executive officer of *Argonaut*, the Makin raid left a lasting impression on Frank Parker.[48]

However, the toughening process which steeled Frank Parker to deal with the uncertainties and rigors of command had developed well before the Makin raid. As reported in *The Lucky Bag*, the yearbook for the Class of 1932, at the Naval Academy, Parker endured a great deal of chiding because of his short height. Known as "Shorty" and "Half-pint," Parker learned to live with his classmates' characterizations and was known as both "irrepressible" and "little but loud." Unfortunately, Parker's shortness kept him off the varsity basketball team, but it became an asset when he later came aboard the cramped S class submarines. At Annapolis, in class football, Frank Parker succeeded because opposing teams, as the editors of *The Lucky Bag* related, "didn't see him." The same would be true when Parker went on patrol with *Swordfish* in the grimmer contest in the Pacific.

During the 1930s, Frank Parker developed his navy career and started his family. Very early after graduating from Annapolis in 1932, Parker showed an interest in submarines, and in 1934 he attended submarine school in

Frank Mahlon Parker. *U.S. Naval History & Heritage Command.*

New London. Moving steadily along, he was designated a submariner in 1935, and in 1937 he qualified for submarine command. From January 1935 to June 1938, he served as Engineering Officer and Executive Officer aboard S-30, and in June 1940, he came aboard *Argonaut* as Engineering Officer and Executive Officer. During the same period, Frank Parker developed a family. Shortly after graduation in 1932, he married Katherine M. Zvanich, a former British subject born in Capetown, South Africa. They had two children, Cynthia and Frank Parker. Thus, by the time of the entry of the United States in World War II, Frank Parker was well-established in both his career and his family. He knew he wanted to serve in the Submarine Service, he was prepared to take on responsibility, and he was prepared to fight for home and country. After the Makin raid, the submarine high command judged Parker ripe for command of a submarine, and *Swordfish* was his reward.[49]

With Parker in command, major repairs on *Swordfish* ended in early June, and the boat underwent the finishing steps before returning to patrol—post-repair trials and the departure for Pearl Harbor. She arrived at Pearl on 25 June. However, tragic circumstances interfered with the start of Parker's departure for the eighth patrol. On 29 June, a fire broke out on the bridge and superstructure. Destruction included all electrical cables outside the pressure hull, numerous gaskets, and parts of the wood decking. The conflagration also damaged two key pieces of equipment, the SJ and SD radars.[50]

Parker was not to be denied his first wartime command. Crewmen from a tender, along with the submarine's force, worked diligently to set matters aright. Repairs made, Parker conducted training exercises and, after giving his men time for final preparations and goodbyes, he ordered departure of *Swordfish* for her eighth patrol on 29 July 1943. Arriving at the Navy anchorage at Johnston Island two days later, *Swordfish* topped off the tank with 12,643 gallons of fuel and departed the same afternoon. By 12 August, the submarine had reached its patrol area. *Swordfish* patrolled along the line between Palau and Rabaul, two heavily garrisoned Japanese bases. The objective was to interdict enemy supply ships.[51]

After finding no targets in the area, Parker moved to the area between Palau and Wewak, North Eastern New Guinea. Instead of finding an enemy ship, Parker thought *Swordfish* had an encounter of a different kind. While passing through a plethora of logs and trees floating in the area, the starboard propeller became noisy, and the skipper suspected that the boat brushed up against a log, clipping a propeller. The screw would pose a problem afterward. Still finding no enemy ships, Parker hoped for success by heading further westward toward Manokwari, in Netherlands, New Guinea. Located due south of Palau, Manokwari seemed a likely place to find ships on the north-south line from Palau.[52]

On 22 August, everything changed. At 0644, telltale puffs of smoke on the horizon summoned *Swordfish* to action. The submarine swung toward the potential target and surged forward. For tracking, the TDC trained on the puffs of smoke. The initial distance of 35,000 yards began to narrow, and by 0835, lookouts atop the periscope shears could discern three sets of masts.

During the approach, Parker displayed the same meticulous care in planning and flexibility in operation as he had shown during the Makin Raid. When the enemy ships altered course and moved to 12 knots, Parker revved up all four engines to achieve 16.8 knots. In textbook fashion, Parker intended to pull ahead of the convoy in order to meet it in the most favorable position and allow maximum time for an attack. The time-consuming process of an approach continued. To maintain the element of surprise, *Swordfish* stayed at a distance, keeping the mastheads just in sight. For a very brief period, the submarine even headed away from the convoy in order to check bearings. With the bearings fixed, Parker ordered "dive," and *Swordfish* slipped under the surface and headed once more toward the unsuspecting merchantmen. Parker had to rely heavily on his periscope rather than radar. He described the deplorable state of the radar: "The operation of the SJ radar was so poor that very little confidence could be put in its use even when it supposedly was in working condition."[53]

As the submarine drew nearer, the characteristics of the convoy came into focus. It consisted of three transports, escorted by a ship similar to a corvette and a smaller ship. As an anti-submarine measure, the convoy zigzagged every four or five minutes, and with each zig, the two larger merchant ships belched puffs of smoke. All ships appeared to be only partially loaded. Parker was intent on making this encounter the last trip for one or more of the ships. At a range of 1,500 yards, he singled out the second and third ships in the lineup for destruction. They were sailing along at approximately one-and-a-half lengths apart. At 1238, Parker judged the time was ripe, and he ordered the first of four torpedoes fired in succession. Two "fish" tore through the water for the first target, followed by two more aimed at the second transport.[54]

Parker and his crew dared not linger to view the fruits of their carefully planned attack. Performing a quick, routine sweep around with the periscope after firing, the commander saw imminent danger. Coming in rapidly on the port quarter, a third Japanese escort, previously unseen, lunged for *Swordfish*. The submarine went deep to 300 feet, rigged for depth charges, and waited for the counter-attack. A combination of deafening noises ensued, as a pattern of ten depth charges resounded close by, severely shaking up *Swordfish*. The escort had used the torpedo wakes as locators. However, there was one consolation. The crew heard the sounds of three torpedo explosions, marking the results of their attack.[55]

Subsequent sounds provided a picture of the surface action. Broad, high-level crackling and snapping noises suggested the breakup of one or more ships. The noises continued for several minutes and were heard in both torpedo rooms. The submarine sound gear picked up sounds of only one heavy screw from a single larger ship, but detected no other heavy screws. Propeller sounds of the three angry escorts were also evident. One of the escorts halted in the area of the intended targets and stationed itself there for a period of time, while pinging in an effort to locate the American intruder. The corvette joined the escort in the hunt. The other escort remained briefly where the attack had taken place, then left the scene with one or more of the merchant ships.[56] The American skipper could not be certain if he sank one or two ships, but the sounds indicated the high probability of at least one ship sunk. *Swordfish* had, indeed, sunk one ship, *Nishiyama Maru* (*Seizan Maru*), a 3,016-ton cargo ship operated by the Japanese Army. The vessel was part of a convoy traveling between Rabaul and Palau. One torpedo had passed under the hull, but a second torpedo hit by number three hold, killing seven aboard.[57]

Parker and his men put *Swordfish* through several evasive maneuvers, but they could not shake off the searching Japanese. A significant problem was defective steering apparatus, which substantially governed how much maneuvering *Swordfish* could perform. At 300 feet, the steering gear was binding, and the bow planes leaked excessively at the same depth. Making matters worse, the starboard propeller was excessively noisy above 100 revolutions per minute, making a quiet getaway difficult.[58] Machinist Mate Lloyd Faye concluded that the San Francisco refit team had, in his words, "messed up." The rehabilitation effort, regardless of good intentions, had only exacerbated conditions.[59]

The Japanese corvette and the remaining small escort closed in for the kill. One of the Japanese ships reacted to a false contact via echo ranging, and two depth charges rained down astern of the submarine. But then the smaller escort obtained a positive contact and stopped, while maintaining the echo ranging contact. This escort guided the corvette onto a firing course. The corvette dropped six more depth charges as it passed overhead. In all compartments of the boat, the men could hear the cadence of the passing screws—"whoosh, whoosh, whoosh, whoosh."[60] In the patrol report, Parker remarked on the expertise of the Japanese: "It was the unanimous opinion of all on board that this was the best executed depth charging that anyone on board had experienced to date."[61] The attacking escorts had demonstrated excellent teamwork and accuracy, but they did not follow through with the attack. They rationed the use of the depth charges and did not persist in their search. Had they done so, given the expertise of the Japanese, they well might have sunk *Swordfish*. After four hours of the boat's deep submergence, the pinging sounds of the escorts gradually faded away astern.[62]

For Quartermaster Leymon Dennis, the depth charge attacks were only partially remembered. He was so fatigued from the long ordeal of the tense tracking of the convoy, the final approach, and then the attack, that he could not keep his eyes open. During the Japanese counter-attack, he slept![63]

Parker wanted to be certain of no further depth charging, which had already damaged the starboard sound gear and had shattered glass throughout the boat. *Swordfish* remained submerged. Finally at 2013, all seemed safe, and the submarine surfaced to a moonless evening laden with heavy haze. In such poor visibility, Parker concluded that it would be useless, as he put it, "to locate the scene of the

4. Competing with a Legend 99

USS *Swordfish*, altered with a reduced silhouette, San Francisco, 13 June 1943. *National Archives, College Park.*

crime."[64] It had been a long ordeal. The final word of the attack, however, came over the radio from Tokyo Rose. Much to the amusement of *Swordfish*'s crew, she announced in English that Japanese ships had sunk the submarine. After this false announcement, the radio blared with a broadcast of the latest recordings of American popular music.[65]

A subsequent reconnaissance of Manokwari Roads revealed the area devoid of enemy activity, and after five days of fruitless searching, often with poor visibility due to heavy rain, *Swordfish* returned to the Palau-Wewak line. During this lull, the crew had the chance to address the propellers. On 1 September, *Swordfish* stopped completely for 15 minutes while the engineering officer examined the screws. Parker recorded the results: "No faults found but starboard screw is still very noisy over 100 R.P.M."[66] Problems continued, as two days later the commander reported that the SJ radar was out of commission.

The following day, 4 September, the lookouts spotted masts and a smokestack in the distance. It was time to act, regardless of mechanical problems. *Swordfish* dived and began an approach. a convoy of three merchant ships and an escort lay ahead. In *Swordfish*'s favor was the poor position of the escort, which was strung out 5,000 yards ahead of the merchantmen and too far forward for a quick response to any attack. Parker remarked that the escort was "definitely second-string."[67] Unable to get any closer than 8,000 yards submerged, Parker chose a different tack. He surfaced and switched to the diesel engines to achieve greater speed. Parker opened the range to 25,000 yards so as not to be seen. In the boat's log, Parker set down his plan: "Surfaced and commenced end around run hoping to get ahead in time for an attack before dark as a night attack was considered out the question with no SJ Radar and no moon with the probability of rain."[68] All Parker had to go on were the enemy ship's smoke puffs, from which he calculated the base course and speed. The odds of success were questionable.

By 1840, *Swordfish* had gained the desired position ahead of the Japanese, and the submarine dived to begin an approach for the second time. In a dilatory manner, the escort echo-ranged spasmodically at intervals of three minutes, interspersed with ten minutes of silence, just sufficient to catch the sounds of any submarine within 20 miles.[69] However, nature snatched away the chance for success, and Parker related what happened in his log:

"Fate was again unkind as a heavy rain set in which with the oncoming darkness defeated all chances for attack." Without the aid of the SJ radar and with poor surface visibility, the alternative of a shot by sound gear was all that was left. Parker judged that such action would likely result in the convoy taking a radical change in direction and *Swordfish* losing them completely. The better course of action would be, in Parker's estimate, to wait for a daylight attack the next day. The frustrated commander recorded the outcome: "The convoy passed overhead which was bitter medicine to take."[70]

Dawn brought another chance. With smoke sighted on the starboard bow, *Swordfish* surged to 17 knots, while tracking and gaining position ahead of the column. The boat dived to periscope depth, but because of the noisy starboard screw, Parker did not attempt to close the track to the target. At this point, the escort was plowing through the seas just ahead of one of the targets. The firing time was dictated by the convoy's last-minute zig away from the submarine, leaving the boat 3,000 yards from the targets. Not wanting to lose the convoy a third time, Parker quickly chose the largest of the three ships and sent off four torpedoes. The aim was to cover 100 percent of the target, although in actual fact the "fish" had a spread covering 60 percent of the ship's length. Range was set at 3,100 yards. In view of his careful tracking of the convoy, Parker was confident of the shots.

By exposing only a few inches of the periscope, *Swordfish* was well-concealed, but Parker decided to seek cover, since he could not see the escort. Just after observing all the torpedoes head, as he put it, "beautifully" toward the unsuspecting target, he ordered a dive to 300 feet and braced for the expected counter-attack.[71] The first sounds heard were not depth charges, but four torpedo hits audible throughout the boat, as well as by the sound gear. Judging by the escort's propeller sounds, the stunned escort was tardy in its reaction. Thirty seconds after the last hit, the escort altered course and followed in haste the tracks of the torpedoes. The escort's delay gave *Swordfish* enough time to move clear of the firing point, and the submarine was well out of danger when the escort sent overboard six depth charges. For half an hour, the escort echo ranged and stopped intermittently to listen for the submarine. The last action of the escort was to drop four more depth charges, "apparently," as Parker believed, "more for the record than on contact, and retired to his depleted convoy."[72] Parker was almost certain of sinking a ship. Brief high-level noises emanating from the torpedoed cargo ship had been heard until they were blotted out as the submarine pierced a strong density layer at approximately 240 feet.

After three hours, *Swordfish* returned to periscope depth, just in time to see two ships receding far over the horizon. In the patrol log, Parker added a terse note: "Passed through small amount of wreckage."[73] The torpedoes had done their jobs. *Swordfish* had sunk the 3,203-ton army transport, *Tenkai Maru*, which was on a Palau to Wewak run in convoy Wewak No. 8. In addition to 60 passengers, the ship was transporting ammunition, gasoline, and automobiles. One of the torpedoes hit the ship portside under the funnel, causing a fire, an explosion, and the loss of six lives.[74]

Swordfish continued in her patrol area until, as per orders, she set course for port at Midway Island. Frank Parker and his crew could look upon the patrol with much satisfaction. *Swordfish* had sunk two ships and had damaged, or perhaps sunk, others. However, on 13 September, fortune once more cast the dice in favor of *Swordfish*. Men on lookout sighted smoke, and forsaking a tranquil voyage home, Parker ordered a full power run toward the smoke. He resorted to his favorite tactic of pulling ahead of the enemy and getting into position of maximum advantage. Once in position, the submarine dived for a final approach at periscope depth. As *Swordfish* closed with the smoking target, Parker's eyes must have popped. Here was not only a large transport belching smoke, but with it were an escorting destroyer and another larger naval ship.[75]

Initially, Parker had focused on the transport for destruction, but he shifted to the largest ship, which he thought was a heavy cruiser. The crew set four torpedoes in the stern tubes to run at a depth of 15 feet. Range was estimated at 3,000 yards, and torpedoes were aimed for a divergent spread in the hope that one or more would hit the target. At 1632, *Swordfish* unleashed the four torpedoes. Parker attempted to watch the results of the shots, but with only six inches of periscope exposed, visibility was limited. Making matters worse, the speed applied at the time of firing caused the periscope to vibrate so radically that nothing could be seen. All torpedoes missed. Parker could not be certain if the torpedoes failed to hit because the target had avoided them or because he mistook the target to be a cruiser when in fact it was possibly a large destroyer with a shallower draft. If the target had a shallower draft, the torpedoes would have passed under the hull for a complete miss. In the Japanese counter-attack, submarine sound gear indicated

USS *Swordfish*, plan view amidships and aft, berthed in San Francisco for repairs, 13 June 1943. *National Archives, College Park.*

that two destroyers were dropping depth charges. One destroyer had been initially seen during the approach, and the second may have been the intended target or possibly a third escorting tin can. Parker and his crew could not be sure.[76]

After the submarine's attack, the two escorting destroyers dropped 13 depth charges in the area where they estimated *Swordfish* to be at the time of firing. Firing from the stern tubes had made it more difficult to predict the location of *Swordfish*. The escorts made no attempt to gain contact either by listening or echo ranging. Parker characterized the counter-attack as very perfunctory and intended only to keep the submarine submerged until the ships had passed. One of the enemy ships proceeded directly over the undetected submarine. After the sound of that ship's screws faded, *Swordfish* surfaced and searched the area for results—no indication of a sinking. Because the convoy was traveling at a high speed, Parker estimated that it was now beyond reach. Disappointed, he proceeded with the course set for Midway.[77]

The crew could begin to think of home port and the celebrating connected with their return. For Electrician's Mate First Class Fred Kramer and a select group of other shipmates aboard, preparations for the partying in port were more than a vague dream. Kramer and a few other crewmen operated a makeshift distillery for manufacturing whiskey. As a basic ingredient, they removed grain alcohol used in the torpedoes. To deter crewmen from drinking the alcohol, the torpedo manufacturers had added a pink solution so that whoever drank the liquid would become very sick. In the parlance of the submariners, the additive was called the "Pink Lady," and should not be confused with the cocktail bearing the same name. At times on other submarines, crewmen would use bread to filter out the "Pink Lady," but this was not always effective, and the men of *Swordfish* designed a still to remove the harmful additive.[78]

Kramer related that the distillery was built in the Navy Yard in San Francisco, when *Swordfish* was in for an overhaul prior to the eighth patrol. At Pearl Harbor, regular alcoholic drinks were expensive, and the torpedo alcohol was a substitute. After distillation to remove the "Pink Lady" additive, the alcohol was put into bottles or containers. Not everyone in the crew knew of the distillery. The electricians knew of it, and so did the men in the engine room. During the eighth patrol, the still was kept in the maneuvering room. Kramer and the other "distillers" operated the still only when the diesel engines were running, because of the fumes. When the after engines were running, they took in the fumes and burned them off. The crewmen shut off the alcohol burners when the engines were not running, such as when submerged.[79]

Fred Kramer said, "It was like making moonshine."[80] The distillers boiled the alcohol and passed it through a coiled copper tube. The coils screwed on top and were cooled with water to condense the alcohol. The condensed alcohol dripped and was collected in containers. The still was small and could produce about a fifth of whiskey. Fred Kramer and Yeoman Second Class William P. O'Briant, both veterans of the eighth patrol, maintained that the alcohol was for consumption in port. Once the submarine reached home port at Midway, the alcohol would be served. Regular alcoholic drinks were practically non-existent for the enlisted men, and the distillers prized their inventory.[81]

One last event intruded upon a peaceful return to home port. Six days after the encounter with the Japanese destroyers, on 19 September *Swordfish* made radar contact with an unidentified aircraft, which Parker assumed was friendly. The submarine was only 450 miles from Midway.[82] When the plane closed within five miles, *Swordfish* fired two identification flares and dived. As she passed to 130 feet for deep submergence, two depth bombs exploded close enough to shake the boat and trip the auxiliary breakers. Ship's cook, Robert Harrington, was in his bunk. He heard ricocheting noise off the hull, and he immediately went to his battle station.[83] For a short time, all auxiliary power was knocked out. Although the specific facts differed, as with patrols six and seven, once again while *Swordfish* was returning to port, aircraft attacked her. The next day, the eighth war patrol came to a close as *Swordfish* reached Midway.[84]

Frank Parker's superior officers heaped lavish praise upon the new commanding officer. They noted the great care and planning that Parker had shown in his attacks on enemy ships. In particular, Parker's boss, the commander of Submarine Division Twenty-two, Joseph A. Connolly, singled out Parker's eventual success, after repeated attempts, in sinking *Tenkai Maru*. The submarine high command gave *Swordfish* official credit for sinking one ship and damaging two others, but later evidence indicated that the submarine sank two ships, one each in the attacks of 22 August and 5 September. John B. Griggs, Acting Commander Submarine Force, Pacific Fleet, declared the patrol "successful" for the Combat Insignia Award.[85] The single remark of criticism came from Connolly, who chastised Parker for assuming that the airplane contact on 19 September was friendly and for not rigging for depth charging. It was an enemy plane. As general advice, he recommended that submarine skippers rig for depth charging when diving on any aircraft approach. Nevertheless, the Navy awarded Parker a Silver Star Medal for his leadership and intrepidity on the eighth patrol.[86]

Frank Mahlon Parker never commanded *Swordfish* again and never went on another submarine war patrol. In view of his success on the eighth patrol of *Swordfish*, it was most likely his choice. Yeoman William O'Briant recalled that Frank Parker had an arthritic condition. At times, O'Briant stood watch on the bridge, and he recalled that Parker's arthritis had slowed his movements to the point where the heavy-set skipper had trouble clearing the bridge. O'Briant believes it was the arthritis which caused Parker to relinquish his command. Parker was talkative by nature, and he had good rapport with the crew, although he caused them much anxiety at times because of his audacious tactics.[87]

Addressing defects which Parker pointed out, Joseph Connolly wanted repairs done during the routine refit period. In particular, Connolly noted that attempts to ascertain the reason for the excessive starboard noise at 130 rpms had not been successful. His patrol endorsement spelled out a solution: "Propeller will be replaced and all efforts made to prevent necessity for return to dry dock."[88] He added that the port steering gear and SJ radar would be thoroughly overhauled during the refit period.[89] Clearly, Connolly wanted to return *Swordfish* to sea as soon as possible. The repairs foiled Connolly's timetable. In the refit period, most of the problems with *Swordfish* were addressed. However, contrary to Connolly's plans, the repair crew at Midway could not quell the noisy starboard propeller or repair the rudder. Crewmen believed these were the noisy "culprits" that gave away the boat's location when she received severe depth charging during Parker's patrol.[90] These casualties required a dry dock. *Swordfish* journeyed to Pearl Harbor and entered a dock on 15 October. As Connolly had ordered, the starboard screw was replaced and the rudder repaired. Final work included the painting of the submarine's bottom.[91]

Frank Parker remained with *Swordfish* during repairs and brought the boat through the post-repair trials on 17 and 18 October. These trials included firing ten torpedoes at a net. He also conducted training from 19 to 21 October. Departing Pearl Harbor on 24 October, *Swordfish* arrived at Midway four days later.[92]

Meanwhile, the saga of the clandestine distillery had come to an end. While *Swordfish* was being repaired at Midway, the regular crew had neglected to hide the distillery, and relief crewmen appropriated the still for their own use on the island. For the regular crewmen, this "acquisition" by the relief crew was in a way fortunate. Before saying farewell to the regular crew, Frank Parker held a meeting with them. He asked his relieving skipper, Lieutenant-Commander Frank L. Barrows, to leave the room. He then informed the crew that he knew about the distillery, thus putting the crew on notice that disciplinary action was possible. Parker's veiled warning was sufficient, and use of a still on *Swordfish* ceased. After the submarine underwent a final set of exercises on 29 October, Parker bid *Swordfish* farewell. Frank Barrows relieved Parker as commander that evening. Parker's career as a wartime submarine commander was over.[93]

Parker's next assignment was as executive officer aboard the submarine tender, USS *Holland*. On *Holland*, he excelled in supervising repairs and the preparation of submarines for operations, and he earned an official Letter of Commendation for his outstanding work. His experience with malfunctioning equipment while commanding *Swordfish* had impressed upon his conscientious disposition the imperative, while aboard *Holland*, to prepare boats in as good shape as possible for their next war patrol.

Determined to stay in the Navy after the end of war in 1945, Parker continued in positions of leadership involving command of surface ships *Maryland*, *Hamner*, *Kankakee*, and *Cavalier*. He also spent close to three years as an instructor at his *alma mater*, the Naval Academy. His various decorations included recognition for military service during both World War II and the Korean conflict. Upon his retirement in November 1959, on the basis of his combat awards, the Navy advanced Parker to the rank of Rear Admiral. In particular, to use a phrase the sports-minded Parker would have liked, while serving in the Submarine Service, Frank Parker was definitely a member of the "first string," on *Argonaut*, on *Swordfish*, and on *Holland*. As recognized by his superiors, his efforts made a difference.[94]

While *Swordfish* was being refitted, the crew relaxed as best they could. Called "Gooneyville" because of the large flock of albatrosses present, Midway was far less popular than the more cosmopolitan Honolulu. Midway offered limited activities, such as swimming and various types of ball games. Card games, such as poker, were frequent. Yeoman William O'Briant remembered winning over $5,000 in one of the games in a big pot. On the other hand, Electrician Fred Kramer remembered losing all his money in a poker game. The Pacific oasis was lacking in one significant aspect of sailors' time in port—women. The dearth of opportunities to socialize and to forget the perils of the patrol was a shortcoming. However, all was not lost. Until it "disappeared," the crewmen of *Swordfish* made use of the product of their distillery to augment the limited supply of alcoholic drinks available. All in all, the brief respite "on the beach" was welcome.[95]

Frank L. Barrows

Frank Lloyd Barrows had reason to believe that *Swordfish* was ready for a war patrol. Workmen at Midway and Pearl had dealt with the known defects, and the post-repair trials and exercises normally would have revealed any glaring omissions that required attention. In addition, from 30 October to 1 November in the Midway area, Barrows received training as a new commanding officer. One noticeable defect, a malfunctioning hull ventilation blower, necessitated a further delay for repairs. Finally, Barrows and *Swordfish* were ready. He put *Swordfish* to sea for her ninth patrol on 8 November 1943.[96]

As with Frank Parker, command of *Swordfish* was Barrows' first assignment as a submarine skipper and a confirmation of the Navy's belief in his ability. Barrows had graduated from the United States Naval Academy in 1935, where his classmates called him "Butch." He had an interest in music and choral singing. He also was an avid weightlifter, and he enjoyed motorcycling. But his main interest was in seafaring, and he was progressing well. Prior to his assuming command of *Swordfish*, the Navy recognized Barrows' exceptional wartime conduct. For his outstanding service as executive officer aboard USS *Gudgeon*, Barrows was awarded a Silver Star Medal. The award citation stated in part, "his skill and courage materially contributed to the success of the missions during which an important amount of enemy shipping was sunk and damaged."[97] While serving on another boat, USS *Gar*, he was noted for his "coolness" and high devotion to duty while the submarine was taking evasive action to avoid enemy anti-submarine measures.[98] Frank Barrows was a logical choice as next commander of *Swordfish*. In contrast to their view of the loquacious Frank Parker, crewmen on *Swordfish* remembered the tall and lanky Barrows as being on the quiet side and reserved in personality. He was prone to keep his thoughts and emotions to himself.[99] How he would adjust to the loneliness of command remained to be seen.

Barrows' next assignment provided an excellent chance for an aggressive commander. *Swordfish* was ordered to skirt the southern coast of Japan's main island, Honshu. With ships going in and out of Japanese harbors, most likely there would be frequent targets. The risks were also abundant. There would be land-based air patrols, coastal naval units, and convoy escorts. Once departing Midway, with the passage of every mile, Frank Barrows would have to take into account both the opportunities and the dangers inherent in the patrol orders. By 17 November, *Swordfish* had reached the island of Aoga Shima, due south of Tokyo.[100]

The submarine had already encountered hostile aircraft, which required

4. Competing with a Legend 107

dives, and Barrows began to realize that all was not well with his boat. The repair work at Pearl had not eliminated entirely the troublesome propeller noise. Barrows reported: "Both propellers (or shafts) develop a swishing noise at about 100 RPM."[101] There were other noises that compromised stealth. The steering pump was very noisy, and Barrows termed the trim pump "excessively noisy at all depths."[102] Other problems with the steering system appeared. When taking a substantial down angle in a dive, the steering system leaked in many places, and air entered into it, requiring a daily venting of the system. Nevertheless, Barrows was not by nature a complainer. The quiet and reserved commander kept to himself, and *Swordfish* continued her northward course.[103]

The next day introduced the first of a series of events which sharply challenged the new commander. In heavy seas which caused the submarine to broach twice, the armature of the hydraulic pump motor burned out. As electrician's mate Fred Kramer related, "It took the heart out of operating."[104] Until the motor was repaired, the crew had to resort to manual controls for many of the operations. A fatigued coil had broken. For several days, the crew worked on the problem and finally jury-rigged another motor to keep the system functioning. While the crew contended with the breakdown and the weather, numerous small targets appeared: patrol boats, sail craft, and fishing vessels. Some were suspected of being lookout boats. Moreover, frequent contacts with hostile aircraft kept the crewmen alert and at times forced the submarine to dive.[105]

The 23rd of November ushered in two more breakdowns of machinery. The hull vent supply blower, which had broken down in early November, went down again. Compounding woes, the SJ radar caught fire. Barrows paused to set down the consequences: "SJ radar fire. Do not wish to encounter patrols without radar—will play southeast corner of area tomorrow."[106] In the midst of airplane contacts the next day, the list of the boat's casualties expanded. The stern planes jammed so badly that they could not be moved either by power or manually. Fortunately, the boat's planes were in a near-zero degree position. While the crew was still grappling with stuck stern planes, submarine headquarters ordered *Swordfish* to pursue a specific patrol course. Barrows complied.[107]

All the next day, the crew tried to free up the stern planes. Finally on the third day, the jammed planes freed themselves. Mystified, Barrows wrote, "What could it be?"[108] The crewmen isolated the binding as coming from the aft part of the boat. When they opened a gear box for the stern planes, they found nothing wrong except for some steel grindings, possibly from a cracked ball bearing. Barrows dutifully continued on the course prescribed by ComSubPac, but he was wary of placing very much reliance on the stern planes. Barrows professed his concern: "Stern planes appear to be operating normally but we feel that they cannot be trusted."[109] While the boat was taking evasive action, jammed stern planes could be deadly.

While *Swordfish* was submerged on the route set down by ComSubPac, a chance to score big came into focus on 23 November. Initially, the far-off sounds of three aircraft bombs in a period of ten minutes caught Barrows's attention. Later that morning, an aircraft carrier and three destroyers were sighted, clipping along at 20 knots at a range of 19,000 yards. *Swordfish* turned to catch the ships, but the Japanese interrupted the pursuit. The enemy dropped either a bomb or a depth charge, followed by eight depth charges, none close by.[110] Although no pinging was heard, sound conditions were good, and Barrows did not know if the enemy had detected *Swordfish* or a fish or were simply "plastering" the area out of suspicion. Two of the escorting destroyers detached themselves from the group to reconnoiter the area for 40 minutes, but they made no contact with the submarine. The destroyers lingered until midmorning before leaving. An hour later, *Swordfish* surfaced for its own reconnoitering and sighted two unidentified aircraft. Barrows concluded, "We think we will stay out of sight for a while."[111]

On 28 November, Frank Barrows made a momentous decision. Already beset by a cascade of material casualties and the unrelenting presence of Japanese patrols, he decided that the jammed stern planes were the tipping point. Regardless of patrol orders, Barrows had had enough. He wrote in his patrol log, "Decided stern plane trouble is too much potential hazard to warrant continuing patrol. Headed for Midway."[112] With his aspirations for a successful patrol dashed and contrary to orders, he headed for home port. After yet two more sightings of enemy aircraft and a suspicious patrol boat en route, on 5 December 1943, the luckless Barrows and the ailing *Swordfish* finally reached Midway.[113] According to Quartermaster Leymon Dennis, who was beside Barrows when *Swordfish* approached the lagoon at Midway, the submarine received a flashing light warning the boat not to enter the harbor. From Barrows' perspective, danger was imminent, and out of concern for his crew and the deteriorating capability of *Swordfish*, in desperation the skipper ordered Leymon Dennis not to "roger" the harbor warning. Instead, Barrows ordered to proceed into the lagoon. The squadron commodore and an armed guard of U.S. Marines greeted Barrows at the dock and escorted him to submarine headquarters. Apparently Barrows convinced his superiors of the gravity of conditions aboard *Swordfish*, and the ninth patrol was terminated. It should be noted that transiting Midway's entrance past the surrounding reef was inherently risky, and Barrows took a substantial risk in entering. While attempting to reach the inner harbor at Midway a few weeks later in January, USS *Flier* ran aground and was wrecked on the circular atoll.[114]

Although the nightmare of the ninth patrol was over, the consequences of the patrol were just beginning. Characteristically, Barrows accepted full responsibility for the unsuccessful patrol, even though circumstances were, to a marked degree, beyond his control. Broken in spirit, Frank Lloyd Barrows asked to be relieved of his command of *Swordfish*. His self-confidence had been badly shaken. However, his superior officers were not so quick to let him go. They recognized his innate ability and re-assigned him to new ship construction. Barrows presided over the building of USS *Moray* (SS-300), which was commissioned in January

4. Competing with a Legend

Admiral Nimitz presents Silver Star to Frank Lloyd Barrows. *National Archives, College Park.*

1945, with Barrows as commander. In June 1945, *Moray* performed distinguished service on her first patrol as part of a coordinated submarine attack group that involved five other submarines. Later, she participated with USS *Kingfish* (SS-234) in an attack on a convoy in which she was credited with sinking a whaler. Under Barrows' command, *Moray* received one battle star for her World War II service.[115]

As predicted in *The Lucky Bag* for 1935, Frank Lloyd Barrows elected to stay in the Navy after World War II, until retirement in 1955, when he was advanced to the rank of Captain. He worked in various positions, ironically including Operations and Security Superintendent at Mare Island Naval Shipyard, where *Swordfish* was built. Undoubtedly, as Barrows came to the yard for work each day, he would be reminded of its role in *Swordfish's* history and his own trials aboard the boat. Even today, the launch areas stand as sentinels recalling the yard's past glory. On a personal note, Barrows had married Margaret Claxton in 1937, and in 1947 she gave birth to a son, Frank L. Barrows Jr. In summation, Frank Barrows' loyalty to the Navy and to his country were consistent and evident.[116]

However, for the crew of *Swordfish*, the ninth patrol left a deep and lasting impression. They remembered vividly the trials of the patrol. Although they had sympathy for the luckless Barrows, morale had sunk to a low point.[117] Submarine crews took a certain pride when a boat was successful in inflicting damage on the enemy, and *Swordfish* had the reputation for being very successful. Pride in the boat also contained an ingredient of competition with the other members of the submarine fleet. In boat after boat, there were photographs of crews surrounding a battle flag full of Japanese symbols for ships sunk—the more the better.

Barrows and his superior, Joseph Connolly, were concerned about transfers of experienced men from the boat. In his patrol log, Barrows called the condition of personnel only "fair." He asserted that there were many new and inexperienced crewmen aboard *Swordfish* and that routine transfers should not be mandatory. He recommended setting aside the general practice in the Submarine Service for a portion of experienced crew members to be rotated to other assignments, where they could "show the ropes" to newcomers. Barrows wrote, "It is recommended that after such a short patrol the normal personnel transfers should not be required as there has not been sufficient time to qualify new people."[118] Connolly agreed. He would not require the usual transfers of personnel. In his recommendation to Admirals Nimitz and Lockwood, he requested that the only required transfers from *Swordfish* should be key personnel for rest purposes. He added, "Key men transferred to Relief Crew at end of previous patrol would be returned to their ship in exchange for equivalent ratings among key men who are due for a rest."[119]

In addition to finding a new skipper and maintaining a sufficiently experienced crew, there was yet another factor impeding a quick return of *Swordfish* to sea. The numerous material defects on *Swordfish* could not be ignored. Sensitive to the problems that had ruined his patrol, Frank Barrows pointed to what he perceived to be a fundamental flaw in *Swordfish*. Barrows wrote, "It is believed that there is some structural defect in the after part of the vessel."[120] The dejected commander cited the three major patrol stoppers which were the basis for his notion of a flaw. Propeller shaft noises had developed since leaving the Navy Yard in June 1943, the rudder started binding about the same time, and lastly, during the patrol the stern planes had jammed.[121] Barrows cited additional problems. There was an excessively noisy trim pump, a malfunctioning bathythermograph, and numerous leaks in the steering system. He also mentioned the burned-out armature in the main hydraulic pump motor and the breakdown of the ventilation supply blower impeller.[122]

Rejecting Barrows' theory of a fundamental defect in the aft part of *Swordfish*, Joseph A. Connolly termed the jammed stern planes, the chattering rudder, and the noisy propellers a "coincidence." Nevertheless, he recognized that a realignment of the hull attachments aft might be in order and, as he put it, "all efforts will again be made to eliminate the possibility of faulty operation of internal machinery."[123] Connolly also made it clear that he wanted to avoid the kind of extended repair period that preceded the ninth patrol: "It is anticipated that normal refit period will be required to complete all repairs."[124]

Even the gods seemed to be turning their backs on *Swordfish*. During the refit at Midway, severe weather caused external damage to her hull. Donald Gaither described the scene: "The boat was beaten against the dock quite fiercely, causing the sides of the fuel tanks and ballast tanks to be pushed in slightly between the frames with the superstructure of the boat being battered up against the dock."[125]

Swordfish had reached a pivotal point in her career. She was wearing down, her discouraged crew needed experienced men, and once again her command position was vacant. The cohesive combination of an effective commander, an experienced and enthusiastic crew, and a well-functioning boat, formerly associated with Chester Smith, was fading away. The next commander of *Swordfish* would have to contend not only with the stark challenge of war, but also with conditions detrimental to the well-coordinated parts, human and mechanical, that defined an effective submarine. He would be sailing against a very strong current.

5

Hensel's Finest Hour

Riding the wave of momentum provided by the victories at Midway and Guadalcanal, in 1943 the U.S. Navy in the Pacific pursued offensive operations primarily based upon the aggressive use of aircraft carriers and submarines. In a vigorous island-hopping campaign, U.S. naval forces pierced the outer perimeter of Japan's island empire in the Solomons and in the Central Pacific. Allied forces also advanced against the Japanese in New Guinea. Meanwhile, American submarines throughout the Pacific pursued Japanese merchant ships in a relentless quest to choke off logistical support for the far-flung empire. By the end of 1943, U.S. submarines had sunk 308 Japanese merchant ships totaling over 1,366,962 gross tons capacity, a loss that an island empire could ill-afford. In fact, Japan was losing more tonnage than it could replace.[1]

On the other side of the globe in the Battle of the Atlantic, 1943 was also a pivotal year. American shipyards were producing Liberty ships at a greater rate than German U-boats could sink them. Moreover, as American Merchant Marine convoys received better escort protection, successful Atlantic crossings increased. In particular, fast, mobile "jeep" aircraft carriers with submarine-spotting aircraft hunted down the U-boats, which marked a decline in the threat to the American Merchant Marine. The American buildup of supplies in Britain in preparation for the Allied liberation of Europe was proceeding. Nevertheless, in both the Atlantic and Pacific theaters of operations, U.S. naval leaders had no illusions about achieving a quick victory. The progress of the war up to that point indicated that there would be a long, hard struggle ahead.[2]

Impeding the advance of the U.S. Navy in the Pacific was the Japanese stronghold of Truk in the Caroline Islands group. Known as the "Gibraltar of the Pacific," Truk was a major anchorage for the Japanese Combined Fleet and was situated in a key forward position. However, located 1,800 miles south of Tokyo, Truk depended upon a long, tenuous supply line. Starting in 1942, American submarine patrols attacked Japanese ships all along the route to the sprawling naval base, and in December 1943, it was *Swordfish's* turn to raise havoc in the Tokyo-Truk sea lanes.[3]

During *Swordfish's* refit period, workmen addressed the major defects in the

5. Hensel's Finest Hour

Bow view of USS *Swordfish*, trials in San Francisco Bay, 13 June 1943. *National Archives, San Bruno.*

steering system, the stern planes, the hydraulic system, and noise coming from the propellers and rudder. One bright spot was the installation of a new model SJ-A radar transmitter. With this model specifically designed for sweeping the surface for targets, Navy technicians expected the new radar would improve hunting.[4] It remained to be seen how skillful the new commander would be in utilizing this new system at his disposal.

Foul weather had delayed the refitting of *Swordfish*, and in December, Captain Karl G. Hensel came aboard as an interim commander. He presented a marked difference from all the previous commanders. Prior to coming to the Pacific, Hensel was an instructor at the Submarine School in New London, Connecticut. At New London and later as a submarine division commander, Hensel had a reputation for expertise in submarine tactics. He also was known for his unforgiving sternness, blunt language, and demand for high standards of performance. In addition, he was something of a martinet when it came to protocol. He was aware of the rigorous duty that awaited the newcomers to the Submarine Service. Born on 4 November 1901, the nephew of an Annapolis graduate, he graduated from the U.S. Naval Academy and was commissioned an ensign in 1923. Most of his career prior to coming aboard the *Swordfish* alternated between serving in peacetime on submarines or performing the role of Navy instructor, both at his *alma mater* and at the submarine school in New London. His submarine duty had been on the pre-war S class boats, which were considerably more cramped in space than the fleet submarines, such as *Swordfish*.[5]

However, gnawing at Hensel was the fact that he had not participated in a war patrol, yet he was qualifying others for service in the boats and sending them

Members of the 4th Command Class at the U.S. Naval Submarine Base, February 1942. Bottom row, left to right: Mannert L. Abele, Thomas B. Klakring, Karl G. Hensel (Officer in Charge), George W. Patterson, Jr., Jesse L. Hull. Top row, left to right: Howard W. Gilmore, Philip H. Ross, Arthur H. Taylor, Albert C. Burrows, Leonard S. Mewhinney. *National Archives, College Park.*

into combat. Hensel described his motivation for going on patrol: "I had been telling students for so long how it should be done that for my own self I wanted at least one chance to see if I could deliver a creditable patrol." With persistence, he requested the chance to command a submarine on a war patrol, and assignment to *Swordfish* was the result. Hensel had hoped for a newer boat, rather than the aging *Swordfish*, which, in his usual blunt language, he characterized as an "older crate."[6] Nevertheless, Hensel was determined to go on patrol, and he assumed command of the boat on 19 December 1943.

Initially, Karl Hensel did not inspire the crew's confidence, because he came aboard without war patrol experience. Making matters worse, at first Hensel applied his usual sternness to operations while preparing *Swordfish* for the war patrol. Hensel's gruff command style stood in strong contrast to the amiable demeanor of Frank Parker or the quiet personality of his unlucky successor, F. L. Barrows, and it did not sit well with the crew.

Added to his command style were his personal features which, according to those who served with him, were a bit scary. Crewmember William P. O'Briant recalled that Hensel possessed a particularly intimidating stare, which would look right through you. He seemed able to read a subordinate's mind. If Hensel was convinced that he was being told the truth, all was well, but if not, there was hell to pay. Although calm most of the time, when he was excited, his right eye would twitch in a most agitated manner. Leymon Dennis, who sailed with Hensel as Quartermaster, still remembered his stern appearance, with its fierce gaze.[7]

The crew had already had a taste of Hensel's rigid command style while he was their training officer prior to Barrows' patrol, and when the crew learned that Hensel was to be their commander on the next patrol, a minor revolt occurred. As many as 30 experienced crewmembers threatened to transfer off *Swordfish*. It was unusual to have an officer with the rank of Captain as commander of a submarine. As Hensel stated, "they [the crew] knew damn well 4 stripes were too many." Some of the crew believed that Hensel had been sent to, as he put it, "straighten things out."[8] Other crewmen suspected that Hensel was merely attempting to use the patrol to enhance his reputation and, due to his lack of combat experience, perhaps it would be at their peril. In fact, John Hess, *Swordfish*'s executive officer, was very concerned that Hensel would be reckless in his mission to prove his worth as a submarine commander.[9]

Acutely perceptive, Hensel realized he had to modify his obdurate command style. The stiffness of his methods at New London simply would not do aboard the informal environment of the boats. Thus far, the trial period had demonstrated that he had a certain number of seasoned submariners aboard, crewmen who were capable and who still took pride in serving aboard the famous *Swordfish*, even though the ninth patrol had dampened their morale.

During the preparation period, Hensel continued to work on *Swordfish* and on modifying his command style. Taking into greater account the sensitivity of the crew and also their evident ability, Hensel became more considerate and began a process that he continued throughout the patrol. Without diluting the sense of command which he exuded or reducing his high standards of operation, from time to time Hensel openly requested the opinion of the crew and displayed a humility that was most engaging. He asked the crew to postpone transfer requests and to give him a chance to prove his worth as a leader during the remainder of the boat's trial period. He did not want to lose them, and his adroitness in asking the crew to give him a chance had a mollifying effect. Although still skeptical, the crew responded to Hensel's change in behavior and his request for them to stay aboard. He was able to get underway with the major portion of the crew intact. Between the time Hensel assumed command on 19 December and the date of putting to sea, 29 December, out of a crew of 76, only 11 men transferred off *Swordfish*.[10]

An unforeseen gift helped to soften Hensel's image. The famed football player and Harvard football coach, Dick Harlow, gave Hensel a Harvard baseball cap as a good luck piece during the patrol. Hensel proudly wore the cap, which had a large "H" emblazoned on the front. The crew was amused by Hensel's headgear. They thought the "H" stood for Harlow and Hensel. Dick Harlow was on Midway at the time, planning athletic recreational facilities for the men, and he was very popular. Hensel's wearing of the cap reduced the stiffness of his demeanor.[11]

Leaving Midway on 29 December 1943, *Swordfish* embarked on its tenth war patrol. Enroute to the patrol zone, the boat's engines pounded away, and Hensel put the heavily loaded boat through a daily series of dives, drills, and the firing of all guns. Two days into the voyage, the first of a series of malfunctions occurred. The fathometer required repairs, which took three days. Making matters worse, intermittently during the patrol, *Swordfish* encountered foul weather, including December's heavy gales, head seas, rain, hail, and snow. At times, footing could not be maintained on the bridge, and use of the periscope was not always certain.[12] Four months after completion of this patrol, Ensign Floyd M. Cooper, who had served as an enlisted man on five patrols in *Swordfish*, vividly recalled the rough seas as he stated, "This time we had a lot of trouble with water coming entirely over the bridge and down the conning tower hatch. Several times we have had two or three inches of water on the control room deck, sloshing around over the deck, drowning out equipment—grounding various pieces of equipment."[13] Also, the currents in these waters were uncertain and, at times, treacherous. Nevertheless, Hensel was undismayed by such challenges. In fact, he viewed the stormy weather as an opportunity to reawaken in the crew their former confidence by battling and overcoming the elements.[14]

With the analytical skill and zeal of a seasoned professor, Karl Hensel pored over the reports of previous commanders who had patrolled the zone of assignment, the sea-lanes out of Tokyo Bay. Then he plotted on a chart the points of contact with the enemy which the previous commanders had made, as well as the areas where mine fields were observed. Hensel noted which routes were heaviest for merchant vessels and which ones warships used. He focused on the cluster of islands just south of Tokyo Bay, which would constitute his hunting ground: Sagami Nada, Iro Sahi, Owai Saki, Izu Shoto, Mizako, and Koshima. Hensel also surmised that any of these islands could be bases for unfriendly aircraft patrols and patrol boats, making daytime surface action hazardous.

Hensel drew up a course of action. He would concentrate on two Tokyo-to-Truk routes with occasional forays along less important routes. His reasoning was that he'd intercept more enemy ships headed to or from the Truk stronghold. He planned to shift patrol stations daily at night in order to maintain freedom of operation and minimize detection. In particular, he decided to refrain from using radar for spotting aircraft at night, because it would nullify operations by giving away the position of *Swordfish*. Aircraft could trace the radar beam back to *Swordfish*.[15]

After giving these matters much thought and taking evasive action to avoid patrol boats, *Swordfish* entered the patrol zone approximately 200 miles south of Tokyo Bay on 10 January. The submarine dove at daylight for a patrol east of Miyake Shima, across the Truk-Tokyo shipping lanes, intent upon catching a victim.

However, heavy seas and stiff currents impeded progress and made observations via periscope almost impossible. Three patrol boats in the area added to Hensel's concerns. At one point, they had hemmed *Swordfish* in against the shoreline, but Hensel was able to extricate the submarine and shake off the patrol craft. Hensel pushed on, criss-crossing the Tokyo-Truk sea-lanes, fighting the foul weather, and avoiding detection. At one point, the winter seas were so turbulent that *Swordfish* broached, accidentally coming to the surface from a depth of 70 feet. Hensel kept his course.[16]

Yamakumi Maru

Finally, on 13 January at 2223, 15 days into the patrol, *Swordfish* came upon a convoy near Ko Shima, consisting of several ships. Hensel decided to try his luck and started closing at full speed. Due to a bright moon, which threatened to reveal the whereabouts of *Swordfish*, and because some of the targets were barely visible, Hensel started tracking the vessels at 16,000 yards, but found the radar bearings poor. Initially, Hensel thought the convoy was headed for Tokyo, but he later concluded that it had stopped. He began his attack on the surface using radar tracking at extreme range. At 9,800 yards, Hensel had taken the boat to a radar depth of 40 feet to avoid detection, and at 6,500 yards he dove deeper and proceeded by periscope alone. He also ordered the crew to prepare to fire torpedoes via the Torpedo Data Computer. Ten minutes prior to firing, *Swordfish* was slowed to silent speed, and Hensel noted the choice of targets. There was one large well-deck freighter, another merchant ship with a low stern, and one or two freighters farther away. The convoy was protected by one destroyer and two smaller escorts that were circling at slow speed. Judging by the telltale observation of heavy smoke, one of the smaller escorts was burning coal.[17]

Hensel's aggressive instincts surfaced. Initially, Hensel chose to attack the destroyer, which he termed "troublesome." He wanted to close to 1,500 yards and send two torpedoes at it, as well as two at the well-deck freighter, and then use the stern tubes for a "long shot" at one of the more distant merchant ships. The bow tubes were set to send the torpedoes off at a five-foot depth setting. Suddenly the two smaller patrol craft headed toward *Swordfish*, and the destroyer veered to a new course, taking it out of contention as a target. With lightning speed, Hensel shifted his attention to the nearest merchant ship. The submarine skipper concluded, "Although range was about 3,000 yards it was now or never."[18] Hensel made his move. In a hurried attack, at 0037 on 14 January, *Swordfish* sent off a spread of four torpedoes intended to achieve at least two hits. All torpedoes ran well.[19]

The two smaller escorts had detected the American submarine by echo ranging at 2,000 yards and were moving in for their counter-attack. In spite of a faulty flooding mechanism, *Swordfish* went deeper and awaited results. Two minutes later, everyone aboard *Swordfish* learned the outcome of their efforts. The crew heard two timed explosions of high impact. Both sound operators picked up the telltale sounds of their target breaking up until 0054, when the sea silently claimed the stricken merchantman. Because the moon was down, Hensel could not conclusively identify his target; light was poor through the periscope. But he made out some of the lines of the merchant ship, which had a raked bow and a composite structure amidships.[20]

Hensel's first kill was the armed passenger-cargo ship, *Yamakumi Maru*, of 6,921 tons, which had been taken into naval service. In retrospect, Hensel surmised that the sunken freighter was part of a convoy that was forming up to go south and that the ship was fully loaded. In fact, it was part of Japanese convoy number 4102.

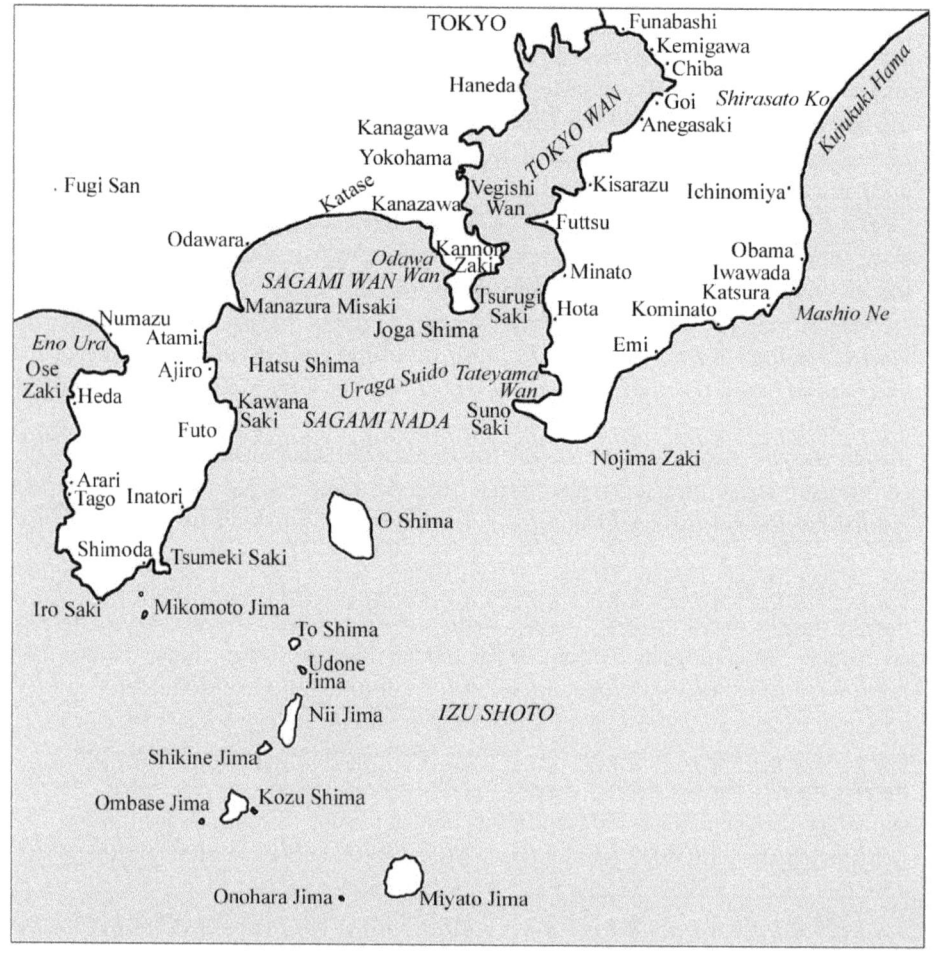

Approach to Tokyo Bay. *Map by Eliz Alahverdian.*

The merchantman was towing the forward half of *Yamabiko Maru*, which the USS *Steelhead* had torpedoed on 10 January and which now also went to the bottom. The sinking of *Yamakumi Maru* resulted in the loss of 18 Japanese seafarers.[21]

The Japanese would be busy with losses on 14 January. The same day as Hensel's first sinking, U.S. submarines made other attacks. *Scamp*, *Albacore*, *Guardfish*, and *Seawolf* sank Japanese ships in other convoys. Scattered far and wide, the attacks revealed the precarious nature of the Japanese sea-lanes to their island empire, as well as the growing effectiveness of the American commerce war on Japanese shipping.[22]

Japanese escorts lost little time in attacking *Swordfish*. At 0045 and 0054, the Japanese let loose with two depth charges, which Hensel described in vivid language: "These two depth charges were lollapaloozas and fairly knocked our teeth loose along with throwing tools, paint and cork all over."[23] Hensel sought the cover of a thermocline layer below 320 feet, thus foiling Japanese sound devices. It was known that variations in sea temperature layers could distort sound, and Hensel took full advantage of this phenomenon. By 0344, the last of 24 depth charges had been endured, the results of which included a foot of water and damaged items in the conning tower, as well as other damage that did not reveal itself until later that night. In bright moonlight, at 0415 *Swordfish* surfaced and started to clear the area at full speed on two engines. A minute later, one of the convoy escorts, approximately 5,000 yards astern of the submarine, challenged *Swordfish* with a yellow blinker light. Hensel quickly cleared the area, which was dotted with nearby Japanese bases. He headed east with the current and recharged the battery.[24]

A Memorable Dive

With his appetite whetted by his initial success, Hensel prepared his boat for another foray, which very nearly caused the end of *Swordfish*. The forward torpedo tubes were reloaded in preparation for further action. However, at 0530 *Swordfish* contacted by radar a small Japanese boat at 3,600 yards, pursuing *Swordfish* at eight knots. To shake off the as yet unsighted vessel, Hensel opened *Swordfish* up to full power, creating a gap of 6,500 yards, and then dove at 0548.

Fate knocked on Hensel's door, as he described: "A memorable dive. It was the biggest angle downward and biggest up I ever hope to see. Everything went wrong—on the diving signal we lost all power and had fires in pump room and in the maneuvering room. Caused by depth charge damage which caused short circuits of main power."[25] Among the problems created by the prolonged depth charge attack was an emergency power cable that had jarred loose in the pump room. During the dive, the loose cable slid up against other equipment, causing a disabling electrical ground. Ensign Floyd Cooper described the disastrous state of affairs: "In the confusion of having all the lights out, the fire in the pump room and the fire in the maneuvering space and, at the same time, of course, the hydraulic plant went out, and the escort only 14,000 yards away and closing in on us. We took an exceedingly large down angle which Captain Hensel described as a 'kalolapaloozer,' the biggest down angle he had ever seen in all his years of submarine experience, and at the same time, the bow planes and stern planes stuck."[26] The fire in the pump room raged from 0555 to 0610.[27] Although Cooper's recollection of the distance of the pursing Japanese escort differed from what Hensel reported above, the danger, in either case, was clearly evident to everyone aboard the helpless *Swordfish*. Most likely, the differing estimates of the distance resulted from calculations made at different points in the chase.

The crew took desperate measures to prevent a sinking. In order to get the boat back to the surface, they closed all vents and blew in air for the bow buoyancy tank and numbers one and two main ballast tanks. As Cooper related, "we surfaced with a much larger up angle than the angle we had when we went down."[28] By the time the submarine bobbed up to the surface, all power was gone, and the boat was dead in the water. The disabled submarine wallowed in the sea 12 to 15 miles from nearby Japanese islands. Making matters critical, day was breaking and with it easier visibility for the pursuing enemy patrol boat, which was now zigging around in the vicinity, first at 10,000 yards, then 8,000 yards astern of the powerless *Swordfish*.[29]

Hensel had three choices of action. He could order the manning of the deck guns and try to fight the enemy on the surface. Such action, however, was very risky. Without maneuverability, *Swordfish* could not train its torpedoes on the enemy, and she was an easy target for attacking ships and aircraft from the nearby islands, as well as the patrol boat already closing in on the submarine. In general, devoid of armor plate or heavy weaponry, submarines on the surface were easy prey for warships and aircraft, as the German submarine force learned in the Battle of the Atlantic. Admiral Karl Doenitz, supreme commander of the German submarine force, encouraged U-boat officers to fight it out with aircraft while on the surface, with disastrous results. On the other hand, profiting from the German debacle, Vice Admiral Charles Lockwood, commanding the U.S. Pacific Fleet submarine force, discouraged American submariners from taking such action.[30]

Another course of action, which Hensel considered, was to attempt to achieve a balance (neutral buoyancy) 200 feet below the surface, without power. Although flooding the tanks would allow *Swordfish* to submerge, remaining in a stable position was questionable. Unknown currents might carry the boat in an undesirable direction or disturb her trim. Essentially, the boat would be adrift at 200 feet down, not the most desirable of conditions. Add to this situation the possibility of buffeting and bouncing from a depth charge attack, and *Swordfish's* powerless state presented to the skipper and crew a very desperate scene.[31]

Only feverish repair work and a large parcel of luck offered the third possibility, restoring propulsion. Remaining calm, Hensel strode aft to inform the electricians working on motor repairs that they had approximately ten minutes before the pursuing enemy patrol boat would be upon them. He then made an almost casual remark to the repairmen, stating, "I can get down on one propeller."[32] Turning around, Hensel marched toward the control room, knowing that the crew would work hard to solve the problem. And work they did! The men seized upon Hensel's remark and focused on getting one propeller in operation. Just as the Japanese patrol vessel was close astern at approximately 6,000 yards, the crew found a way to restore power to the starboard propeller shaft. As Hensel returned to the control room, the propeller began churning up the sea and drove *Swordfish* into the depths, out of sight.[33] The chief of the boat on this patrol, Paul Marvin, gave his reaction to the turn of events in an interview later that year: "Boy, I thought my time was up right then and there! But somehow or other the Japanese didn't see us or were afraid to come in, and we finally got the boat under the water, diving it by hand."[34] Like disappointed fishermen, all the pursuing Japanese could do was peer out at the swirling foam where *Swordfish* had been moments earlier and bemoan the loss of the great American "fish" that had gotten away. The entire episode lasted approximately 20 minutes, but Hensel experienced a different time frame. "It was quite a period of years," he reported.[35] Observing Hensel's actions, one of the crewmen, Arthur Myers, noted, "Hensel might've been scared, but he certainly didn't show any agitation. He was cool-headed."[36]

All day *Swordfish* ran deep on one propeller and followed evasive courses to elude two patrol boats. Once down to 200 feet, to revive his men, Hensel broke out a supply of whisky and distributed two ounces to each man aboard. Meanwhile, Hensel and his crew sought a tranquil spot in the eastern portion of their patrol area. Here, they hoped to pause and repair the damages of the depth charge attacks, and especially to "chase" the electrical grounds that had threatened propulsion. That evening, before moonrise, *Swordfish* surfaced and lay-to, while the crew tested the electrical equipment. After the crew finished putting the port shaft and number four engine back into commission and making other repairs, as Hensel expressed, with "baling wire and glue," *Swordfish* returned with a vengeance to the center of the assigned patrol zone.[37]

Fourth of July Fireworks

On 15 January, *Swordfish* took up patrolling the warship lanes between Tokyo and Truk, approximately 12 miles east of Mikura Shima and 25 miles from the previous day's attack on the convoy. Again, lady luck came forward. By afternoon, the seas had moderated, allowing for continuous periscope observations in place of intervals of every 15 minutes. At 2216, the crew picked up echo sounds to the north in the direction of Tokyo, and a minute later radar contact was made at 14,000 yards. Manning the tracking stations, the crew held the target to 12,000 yards because *Swordfish* was silhouetted against the moon, which was three-quarters full. The submarine ran at full power on three engines.[38]

Hensel began to maneuver into position for a shot. At 2247, in order to avoid an escort vessel that was detected by radar at 8,850 yards, he decided to cross ahead of his intended victim, to its starboard side. The escort boat was on the port side of the target, and the moon was still a beacon to detection. There was too much light for a surface attack, especially because now two escort vessels were recognized, one on each beam of the sought-after prey. Hensel had gained position ahead of his target, and at 2350 he ordered battle stations. *Swordfish* headed toward the Japanese ship, which it sighted at 9,500 yards, with an angle on the bow of five degrees to port. Three minutes into 16 January, the submarine dived to radar depth and utilized radar ranges and periscope bearings until it closed to 6,200 yards, when it reached a periscope depth of 64 feet.[39]

At this point, Hensel realized he was in a classic position of advantage, as well as danger. He had eased *Swordfish* inside the port screen, precisely between the Japanese escorts and the merchant ship they were trying to protect. Hensel was about to turn *Swordfish* away from the intended prey and order stern shots when the target changed course, opening the chance for a frontal shot. One of the Japanese escorts crossed *Swordfish's* bow, and the other her stern. Seizing the opportunity, Hensel commenced the second attack of the patrol at 0020. *Swordfish* fired from the bow three torpedoes on a 70-degree track for a run of 1,500 yards, with a 300-foot spread and a depth of five feet. The plan was to achieve three hits, "if reasonably lucky," as Hensel put it. The crew had watched the course and speed very carefully. Evidence of success was clear-cut. The first of the three hits was seen and heard. Fifteen seconds after the torpedoes ripped open the ship, it was obscured in smoke rising 200 feet. Secure in a hit, Hensel took *Swordfish* deep. Beset with the boat's noisy trim pump, Hensel took *Swordfish* to 340 feet in search of a protective gradient to foil enemy detection gear. Finding none, he returned to 330 feet and prepared for the expected Japanese counter-attack with depth charges.[40]

The next few moments were a mixed blessing. The depth charge attack did, indeed, begin at 23 minutes after midnight, but two minutes after that, the stricken Japanese merchant ship, in Hensel's words, "blew all to hell." He characterized the many explosions that were heard through the submarine's hull as a "Fourth of July celebration."[41] Explosions from within the sinking vessel resounded for 15 minutes, and Hensel speculated that the ship was laden with ammunition. The emotional impact on the crew of *Swordfish* was astonishing. The commander noted that the successful attack had given the crew a great "lift," after the previous "working over" during the depth charge attack two days before.[42] Hensel believed *Swordfish* had attacked a *Chile Maru*-class merchantman and that it sank 40 minutes past midnight.

However, *Swordfish* had actually sunk a 2,205-ton Japanese Q-ship, *Delhi Maru*. Originally a conventional merchant ship, *Delhi Maru* now had concealed guns, depth charge launchers, water tight compartments, and a specially trained navy crew. Coming out of Nagaura, Japan, on her maiden voyage, *Delhi Maru* sailed with the mission of killing submarines. Posing as a vulnerable merchant ship, the Japanese hoped to entice submarines to come close to her, which the Q-ship then would attack. Hensel obliged, but the outcome was not what the Japanese expected. Hensel had not received any messages warning him of the Q-ship, but he guessed that from the wild explosions that he might have hit a type of gunboat. A torpedo had hit the portside of the Q-ship, snapping it in two. The forward section sank immediately, and the aft section later. A total of 161 Japanese personnel perished.[43]

By coincidence, Karl Hensel was not the only *Swordfish* skipper to sink an enemy ship on 16 January. On the same day, Acey Burrows, commander of the unsuccessful fifth patrol of *Swordfish* and now in command of *Whale*, succeeded in sinking the Japanese cargo ship, *Denmark Maru*. In addition, *Whale* sank *Tarushima Maru*, a transport that was previously damaged by the submarine *Seawolf*. Admiral Lockwood's faith in Burrows' ability and the admiral's assessment of the fifth patrol of *Swordfish*, as a result of inexperience, was bearing out. Several other U.S. submarines were successful on 16 January, and the only mishap was the grounding of the submarine *Flier*, while it attempted to transit the channel at Midway Island.[44]

Delhi Maru had been accompanied by two patrol boats, the escorts that Hensel had side-stepped on the way to his target. Desperately attempting to destroy the spoiler of the Q-ship scheme, the irate Japanese pursuers began depth-charging *Swordfish*. Hensel realized that drastic action would be needed to escape from the patrol craft, which were proving hard to shake off. The location of the attack and the direction of the current made it obvious where *Swordfish* would eventually have to surface, and one of the pursuing patrol craft moved slowly along with the

Karl Hensel aboard *Swordfish* on the tenth patrol. By permission of Katherine Wikstrom & David Fields.

submarine, poised for an attack. From time to time, *Swordfish* had to circle in order to keep the enemy boat astern. The submarine commander knew that it was important to surface before daylight and escape to the east before additional enemy vessels arrived on the scene to keep *Swordfish* submerged. While under the surface, *Swordfish* gradually increased speed to 100 revolutions per minute to widen the gap with the patrol boat.[45]

Making a break, *Swordfish* surfaced at 0315, and four minutes later the Japanese patrol craft was spotted four miles astern. Hensel believed that it was probably a Chidori class of armed patrol vessel. *Swordfish* continued to increase to full speed on battery drive, and when the range was six miles, he brought the "smoky" Winton diesel engines into operation. Clearing the area at high speed, *Swordfish* widened the gap with the pursuit craft to 35 miles and then dived to the anonymity of the ocean depths, out of harm's way. The episode concluded with Hensel's remark, "Ran deep all day, to south, and all hands got a needed rest."[46]

As *Swordfish* proceeded, the crew would have time to reflect upon the recent experiences with their commander. In the early days of the patrol, Hensel had displayed an uncanny sense of where to find the enemy ships, which he expeditiously ferreted out. When he located a convoy, his aggressive tactics were evident. During the recent brush with destruction, when the boat had lost power, he displayed a remarkable steadiness under pressure.[47] Together, these experiences revealed to the crew a deep-seated characteristic of Karl Hensel, his iron-bound determination. Everyone aboard *Swordfish* could take pride in what they had accomplished, and their confidence in the ability of their skipper grew. Memories of the dismal ninth patrol were fading before the vividness of the present one. By the same token, Karl Hensel could acknowledge the unmistakable spirit inherent in the crew of *Swordfish*. The boost in morale of the two successful attacks was clearly evident.[48] Also, the crew had responded to his orders without any serious missteps, and he could be confident in their actions. Two sunken Japanese ships were the result of their efficient teamwork. They understood their mission—sink enemy ships—and under Hensel, they were confident in achieving it. Altogether, the commander, the crew, and the boat had welded into a very lethal fighting machine.

After the crew reloaded the torpedo tubes and performed repairs on the number three main engine, *Swordfish* resumed the hunt. However, Hensel discovered yet another problem. As a result of the recent depth charge attacks after sinking *Delhi Maru*, three of four underwater sound heads, used for hearing enemy ships, were out of commission and would be for the rest of the patrol.

A Fine Chance

One of the best-kept secrets of the war was the U.S. Navy's coded message system known as Ultra (short for Ultra Secret). As intelligence information on Japanese ship movements and activities was gathered, it was relayed to affected personnel, especially submarine commanders, who would use the information to locate targets. Elaborate precautions were taken to keep both the code and the system secret. The Navy required personnel involved (including submarine skippers) to sign an oath declaring they would never reveal the details of Ultra in their lifetimes. On patrol, when a submarine received an Ultra communiqué, only the commanding officer decoded the message, and the cipher strips were destroyed.

It was such an Ultra message which spurred *Swordfish* into her next foray against the enemy. On 17 January, Hensel received an Ultra transmission informing him that a *Shokaku*-class aircraft carrier and four destroyers were headed for his patrol area. Pushing on west of Hachijo Shima Island, Hensel heard a series of 63 distant, random depth charges in the direction of Tokyo. He reasoned that this was in preparation for the expected task force movement through the area. The Japanese were "plastering" the entire Isu Shoto island chain.[49] By the time *Swordfish* surfaced at 1756 beneath a heavy overcast and dark sky, Hensel concluded that whatever had been en route had passed from the scene and that all was clear. However, a radar contact at 15,000 yards quickly changed his thinking. He ordered battle stations. Although the radar was not working well and had limited range, Hensel could determine that his prey was making 18.5 knots at an angle of ten degrees starboard, with four to five ships present, one 4,000 yards closer than the largest ship. The submarine commander surmised that this was the task force of the aircraft carrier and escorts that he had been expecting, especially in view of its high speed and the previous random dropping of depth charges that afternoon. Tensions mounted.

Working in a pitch-black night with no horizon visible and heavy clouds overhead, Hensel groped forward. Peering through his binoculars, at 1845 he saw a blurred hull approaching at a range of 10,800 yards. At 1845, *Swordfish* dove to 38 feet. Achieving a radar fix at 10,300 yards while diving, Hensel knew the target was on bow five-to-ten degrees starboard. He decided to proceed on the present course to permit six tubes to be fired in quick succession. Hoping for good tracks and short runs, by 1849 the crew had all tubes readied. However, three minutes later, an inconvenient interruption in the form of a Japanese destroyer dead ahead at 1,200 yards spoiled his timing. In order to allow the destroyer to sail by without spotting the periscope shears of *Swordfish*, Hensel ordered the submarine to dip quickly to 60 feet. A minute and 30 seconds later, in his eagerness to resume his pursuit, Hensel brought the boat back to 38 feet, as he put it, "a hair too soon." His executive officer, John Hess, muttered under his breath, "Oh God."[50] The destroyer "whizzed" by close to the submarine's port side, indeed, a little too close for comfort.

Hensel looked for the original target. Although the dip to 60 feet lasted barely a minute and a half, Hensel found that the intended target had changed bearing and had zigged to starboard. Hensel decided to, as he put it, "shoot the works."[51] However, the sound of screws close aboard to port and on the starboard bow had obliterated any opportunity to follow a target by sound. Making matters worse, with so many targets at close range, the radar was practically blanked out, and the Plan Position Indicator, used in fixing locations on the radar screen, was, in Hensel's words, "a ball of fire."[52] To his dismay, Hensel also discovered that the darkness of the evening prevented his spotting a target by periscope. Sensing that a task force of ships was all around *Swordfish*, Hensel desperately sought out a clear-cut target. At 1859, a large "pip" (image) appeared on the Plan Position Indicator at 2,400 yards, and a smaller one at 3,500 yards astern. Quickly checking for setup and verifying his bearings a couple of times, Hensel fired a spread of torpedoes from the four stern tubes. Alas, no hits. The crew rigged for depth charges. Hard on the heels of the attack, the Japanese counter-attacked with four blockbuster depth charges that were not very close, and a destroyer gave *Swordfish* more "attention," as Hensel put it. Reaching a protective thermocline layer of ocean at 340 feet, *Swordfish* eluded her pursuers.[53]

Mulling over his unsuccessful attack on the Japanese task force, Hensel characterized the situation as follows: "This was a tough setup. We were extremely fortunate to be in such an ideal position. We had a good organization. A very slender string separated us from success." Hensel had planned on being able to see the darkened mass of the main target through the periscope when the range was 1,500 yards or even 1,200 yards. The commander believed that these circumstances alone would have been sufficient, as he expressed it, "to hit, and to hit plenty."[54]

As was characteristic of him, Hensel speculated about why the attack had failed. He believed it was quite possible that he had fired at the wrong target. That is, he had fired the torpedoes at the largest intelligible "pip" (image) on the radar screen, which was further out in range, while, in fact, the largest ship in the task force had possibly passed by the submarine much closer at a range of 500 yards. If this was the case, the torpedoes most likely missed ahead of the larger, closer ship, and they were set too deep to hit an escorting destroyer further out (the larger image on the radar). On the other hand, mused Hensel, perhaps *Swordfish* had fired at the correct target, the largest ship, but had simply missed. Possibly, the intended target made a wide zig and increased speed after its radar made contact with the submarine. If that was the situation, the alerted escorting destroyers alone had converged on *Swordfish*.[55]

Hensel concluded that for continuity of information, it would have been better if he had kept the radar fixed on the target throughout the approach, rather than using it only intermittently. He acknowledged that his reluctance to keep the radar trained on the target, in order to avoid enemy detection, probably played into the hands of misfortune. There was no definite indication that the enemy ship had discovered the submarine before firing the "fish." In conclusion, he wrote, "If the destroyers had been equipped with radar they would certainly have tried to ram us so it appears they, at least, did not have radar." Hensel expressed the prevalent emotions: "We felt pretty low about this attack."[56] No matter how much Karl G. Hensel speculated on what action he might have taken that murky night, everyone aboard *Swordfish* realized that a golden opportunity had been lost. Later, a decoded communication from Commander Submarines Pacific confirmed that the most desirable of targets, an aircraft carrier, was probably part of the missed task force. Another American submarine, *Tautog*, alerted the Command headquarters that it had come across a carrier and four escorts, and the position given indicated to Hensel that it was the same group that he encountered.[57] The one consolation was that *Swordfish* was still intact and could fight again another day. Surfacing, *Swordfish* cleared the area.

Karl Hensel had, indeed, come against the 30,000-ton Japanese aircraft carrier, *Shokaku*, a veteran of the Pearl Harbor attack. *Tautog* had fired three torpedoes at the ship, but also missed. For several more months, *Shokaku* led a charmed life, until 19 June 1944, when the American submarine, *Cavalla*, caught up with her during the Battle of the Philippine Sea. *Cavalla* slammed three torpedoes into her hull, and the flattop sank in a matter of minutes. Its crew numbered 1,660.[58]

After surviving the Japanese convoy, Hensel pressed on with his patrol of the Tokyo-Truk sea-lanes, circling the adjacent islands. Determined more than ever to achieve another strike, he stationed four lookouts and two officers on the bridge, and he noted that the lookouts and sound operators were, as he stated, "doing a fine job."[59] As a quartermaster aboard *Swordfish*, Leymon Dennis had frequent contact with Captain Hensel, and the quartermaster related the extraordinary lengths that Hensel went to, in order to bag a prey. Dennis reported to the author that often Hensel would have him set up a makeshift bunk in the conning tower near the plotting desk in order to be near the center of action, an arrangement similar to that of Jack Lewis. Rather than sleep in the commander's quarters, Hensel would half-doze and half-listen to conversations and reports of the sailors on watch, telling them not to be bothered by his presence. "Drinking it all in," so to speak, Hensel was constantly absorbing data and, as was his nature, continually assessing the situation, as well as achieving a closer bond with his crew.[60]

For several days, only patrol craft were discovered. Hensel elected to catch, if possible, a larger target. He was still looking for an aircraft carrier. At times, very heavy seas and faulty radar apparatus prevented closing in on what appeared to be decent targets.[61]

Boredom

While hunting for prey, the crew of *Swordfish* had to contend with another enemy—boredom. Although a continuous plague of defects and malfunctions, such as leaking pipes and stuck valves, was a challenge to those members of the crew involved in maintenance, others aboard the boat, such as the watchstanders, had to contend with the tedium of daily routines that were their lot when not summoned to battle stations. Day after day, they carried out their humdrum duties. Not content to put up with any crew member that he considered inexperienced, Hensel saw to it that the crewmen's "down time" was utilized. Ever the educator, Hensel embarked on a program to qualify as many of the crew as he could, requiring the sailors to have a basic knowledge of all shipboard operations. The tenth patrol began with 38 unqualified men, and before the end of the patrol, 22 had achieved official qualifications as submariners.[62]

The variety of food served aboard *Swordfish* offered a diversion to routines. Submarine food was generally considered superior on the boats, and Hensel termed the food on his patrol as "excellent." He was especially enamored with frozen vegetables and fruit. He also noted that baking was done daily and was of high quality.[63] Earlier a cook for Frank Parker's eighth patrol, Robert L. Harrington, described the variety of food on hand. He remembered cooking steaks, pork chops, ham, chicken, and meatloaf, along with soup and eggs. Harrington especially enjoyed baking pies, although he jokingly referred to times when he burned the food. Nevertheless, Harrington advanced from Cook 3rd class to Cook 2nd class.[64] On the other hand, a long-time member of the crew, Lloyd Henry Faye, offered a dissenting vote. He did not like the food aboard *Swordfish*, but he enjoyed the comradeship of the crew.[65]

In addition to a variety of food, a submarine at the outset of a patrol usually presented a full warehouse of edibles. At the beginning of the tenth patrol, personnel had to crawl over the tops of full potato crates to pass through the passageways. Karl Hensel described to his son his joy during the third week of the patrol, when the potatoes had been eaten and the passageways were free of the crates. Perishable food was consumed first, then the frozen, canned, and finally powdered food, such as powdered eggs and milk.[66] Toward the end of a patrol, stores became scarce, and the reader may recall Acey Burrows' predicament when he wanted to extend his patrol on *Swordfish*, but each day resulted in a growing shortage of food.

Another momentary diversion occurred one afternoon when *Swordfish* came within viewing distance of snow-capped Mount Fujiyama. Hensel remarked at seeing the mountain, "I got a thrill." The commander allowed time for all hands to take a look at the landmark through the periscope.[67]

Another Target—Another Chance

Finally, on the dark and rainy evening of 27 January, Hensel had an opportunity to make up for the missed chance of ten days before. At 2153, *Swordfish* heard echo ranging and later made radar contact with a ship traveling southward near Inamba Shima. The submarine began tracking the potential target, which was sailing at between five and eight knots. Turning a semi-circle around the Japanese ship, *Swordfish* closed to 4,500 yards. Radar showed just one ship, and Hensel concluded it was an old destroyer or smaller Chidori patrol vessel. The submarine commander elected not to act but to see what else might come his way.[68]

Hensel's hunch paid off. Approximately one hour after contact with the advance vessel, contact was made with another ship, at 14,000 yards, which seemed to be a more desirable target. An elated Hensel wrote, "This is it."[69] But the intended victim was not cooperative. The wary Japanese skipper proceeded on an evasive tack, zigzagging between 120 and 180 degrees on the compass at a speed of 12 knots. Running southward with the enemy ship, Hensel twice commenced an attack, only to be thwarted by the target zigging away. At 8,000 yards, the executive officer of *Swordfish*, John Hess, reported that the target as it appeared on the radar screen did not seem very large, and he advised setting the torpedoes at a depth of seven feet, which was done.

Matters worsened when *Swordfish*'s radar picked up contact with the earlier patrol vessel, five to six miles ahead of the intended target and being overtaken by it. A few minutes later, the radar revealed a second patrol boat 2,000 yards on the target's starboard side or, perhaps, astern of it.[70] Unfazed by the presence of the escorts, Hensel pressed on with a night surface attack. The commander made out the dim image of his target through his binoculars 4,500 yards in the distance. Crewman Paul Marvin described the scene, "On our tenth patrol we got in a Japanese convoy on the surface one night and we had the convoy so fouled up that they didn't know whether we were a part of their convoy or not and they were signaling us with lights and running so close that we almost collided with one."[71] Slowing to 13 knots, Hensel opened the muzzle doors forward and let loose four torpedoes from the bow.

Unfortunately, just as the torpedoes were launched, the enemy ship swung toward *Swordfish* and, upon seeing the submarine, tried to evade with a zig. The torpedoes missed ahead of the ship as a result of the ship's evasive action. In frustration, Hensel explained, "I botched this first salvo badly due mostly to communication difficulties."[72] The bridge loudspeaker was not in commission, and use of a pair of headphones was not satisfactory. The possibility of losing another target surely pumped up Hensel's adrenaline. Remaining on the bridge and knowing the bow tubes were empty, Hensel quickly positioned the submarine for a stern shot. Calling for "emergency ahead," he opened the outer doors of the stern tubes and ordered right full rudder to pass across the enemy ship track for a port shot. While swinging the boat around, Hensel entered into the Torpedo Data Computer calculations of two eye-estimated bearings and angles on the bow. After three or four more checks of bearings from the bridge, with last-minute calculations, he barked out orders to quickly fire four torpedoes from the stern tubes. He counted on a 1,000-yard run to the target. Hensel described the results: "First of three hits heard. The first hit was seen right in her middle and a few seconds later all hell broke loose. A big sheet of flame went up from the hits and a very heavy explosion came simultaneously which shook us badly."[73]

The aroused but badly confused Japanese retaliated with vehemence. The rear escort started closing on *Swordfish*'s port beam at 3,200 yards and attacked with a deck gun. On the submarine, the battle lookouts scrambled below, while Hensel on the bridge asked for whatever additional speed that could be mustered.[74] Chief Paul Marvin captured the tenseness of events: "When the lookouts came off the bridge after the attack, after we had gotten away, the lookouts were so scared that they couldn't even talk, and that's no lie, they came off the bridge and their eyes were popping out and they couldn't say a word for about two or three minutes."[75]

However, instead of diving, Hensel decided to remain on the surface. Depth charges started to go off, and one minute after the torpedo explosions, another huge explosion went off, quickly followed by a third, 30 seconds later. Hensel related the impact: "They really shook the *Swordfish* and for a moment I thought they were firing depth charges at us with a big bertha."[76] Hoping to destroy the American submarine, either submerged or on the surface, the Japanese continued a stream of depth charges and gun flashes. Hensel wrote, "The Japs again exhibited a tendency to throw depth charges at random following a surface attack. This was odd in view of the fact that the near escort was repeatedly firing in our direction and should have sighted us, unless the charges were to counter-mine our torpedoes, discourage us, or save face."[77] Hensel watched the pyrotechnics and called them "thrilling" and "worth seeing,"[78] Undoubtedly, they were.

The Japanese attackers had followed designated procedures for protecting a damaged ship. Orders were to throw out the depth charges as quickly as circumstances permitted. When the depth of the submarine was unknown, procedures called for vigorous retaliation with the firing of depth charges at staggered depths, usually in a salvo of five or six charges. A Japanese anti-submarine manual urged the following: "In any situation attacks must be pressed continuously with maximum accuracy and in order to strike terror into the hearts of the enemy."[79] Unfortunately for the Japanese, they were dealing with a submarine commander who was unfazed by the "terror" of a counterattack.

However, there was no time for celebrations. The two escort vessels were closing in on *Swordfish*. The near escort was on the port beam at 3,000 yards, and the other was 6,000 yards on the starboard side of the submarine. Still on the surface, the submarine changed course 080 degrees. Hensel called for flank speed, and the crew brought all four main engines up to top speed. The submarine held the closer

5. Hensel's Finest Hour   131

of the two pursuers at 2,800 yards. After following *Swordfish* for some time, the Japanese ships began to fall behind. Within 16 minutes after the successful attack, both pursuers had lost either heart or the location of *Swordfish*.[80]

At last, Hensel and his crew could savor their latest success. At a radar range of 4,000 yards, the target had disappeared from the screen, and Hensel recorded the demise of the 3,140-ton *Kasagi Maru*, at 2354. Confirming the sinking were the commander, the executive officer, the radar officer, and a technician, who witnessed the "blip" disappear from sight. The *Kasagi Maru* had left Yokosuka, Japan, on 26 January and was bound for Marcus Island with 474 military personnel aboard. The sinking cost the lives of six Japanese crewmen and 468 troops aboard.

Hensel indicated the effect of the sinking on *Swordfish's* crew: "At about this time the morale was terrific. As others have remarked, a night surface attack is like a tonic, especially when the depth charging can be watched from the surface."[81] Hensel's daring in this attack and the crew's superb execution of orders were a perfect combination. In addition, the skillful use of radar for the night surface attack had a marked effect. The end result was yet another victory in the relentless commerce war against Japan.

With only one torpedo left, Karl Hensel decided to depart the patrol area. According to one crewmember, as was his custom, the commander wanted to know the sentiments of the crew. In a poll, the crew had agreed that it was time to return to home port.[82] Leaving the Tokyo-Truk sea-lanes, *Swordfish* headed for home on 28 January 1944. On the way to Pearl Harbor, Hensel and his crew could look upon their patrol with great satisfaction.[83] *Swordfish* had sunk three enemy ships for a total of 12,270 tons, and they did so in close proximity to the Japanese mainland. Moreover, much of the tonnage they had sent to the bottom was most likely headed for the naval base at Truk. *Swordfish* arrived at Pearl Harbor on the morning of 7 February 1944.[84]

Ten days later, the Japanese on Truk faced a time of reckoning as aircraft from a carrier task force of Admiral Raymond A. Spruance's Fifth Fleet, with ships led by Spruance himself, descended upon the island bastion. Admiral Nimitz had hoped to draw out the Japanese Combined Fleet berthed at Truk for a decisive battle, but during the previous week, Admiral Mineichi Koga, commander of the Combined Fleet, had ordered his ships to leave the port. Nevertheless, American surprise attacks, on 17 and 18 February 1944, destroyed 190,000 tons of Japanese naval and merchant shipping, 250 to 275 aircraft, numerous island installations and, with the destruction, Truk's fabled impregnability.[85] Participating in the operation were U.S. submarines, *Skate, Sunfish, Tang, Aspro, Burrfish, Permit, Dace, Darter Gato, Searaven*, and *Seal*. Confirming the value of submarine involvement in the strike, *Tang* succeeded in attacking an escaping convoy 130 miles from Truk and sank *Gyoten Maru*, an army cargo ship, and the merchant tanker, *Kuniei Maru*. *Searaven* performed essential lifesaving duties by rescuing three American naval aviators from the clutches of the sea. In general, the attack on Truk was so devastating that the island ceased to be part of strategic planning, and invasion was deemed unnecessary. Truk would be bypassed in the advance toward Japan.

For Hensel's crew, the success of the tenth patrol had a special meaning. Hot on the heels of the dismal ninth patrol, the crew now returned to base with their heads held high. They had met the enemy and had defeated him. The crew's self-confidence, their self-worth as submariners, and their pride in serving on the famous *Swordfish* were restored.[86] They had not let the old boat down. The commander and crew had added a new chapter to the legend of *Swordfish*.

By this point in the war, Admiral Lockwood had put into place a special routine for greeting submarines returning from a war patrol. Waiting on the dock, Admiral Lockwood or one of his assistants would be present to welcome the seafarers. A band would play rousing patriotic music, and the crew would receive a warm welcome. Ready for distribution to the men were crates of fresh fruit and containers of ice cream. However, the most important items were the waiting sacks of mail. After mail call, the sailors would often go to some quiet corner to read letters from loved ones and family. Later, they would break off into small groups and go into town for liberty.[87]

Admiral Lockwood's interest in the bands went beyond the receiving ceremonies for returning submarines. He recognized the power of music as a morale booster, and he arranged with Commander Eddie Peabody, a well-known musician and Navy morale officer, to have bands play for resting submariners at the Royal Hawaiian Hotel in Honolulu. Lockwood also had a hand in sending bands to far-flung submarine bases in the Pacific, to raise morale in those remote areas.[88]

The Navy provided exclusive accommodations for members of the Submarine Service in the Royal Hawaiian Hotel, a landmark of luxury on Oahu's beachfront. The hotel offered good food, excellent recreational facilities, and very comfortable quarters. Painted bright white and ornate as a castle, this "grand dame" of architectural design was a welcome oasis for the patrol-weary submariners. They could escape, at least temporarily, from the close quarters of their boat and memories of the tense moments while on patrol. Nearby bars and social night spots offered additional pleasures of port. On their arrival, *Swordfish's* crew received a rousing welcome and a much-deserved rest.[89]

The success of *Swordfish* was all the more remarkable when Hensel listed the problems encountered. In the summary to his war patrol report, Hensel described the numerous malfunctions which had challenged the ingenuity of the crew, including the drastic loss of main and auxiliary power while crash diving on 14 January. In addition to this "close call," Hensel noted persistent problems with the steering system that compromised his ability to achieve a stealthy attack and silent escape afterward. Despite attempts to repair the system prior to the patrol, it still sucked in air, which caused a rumbling noise and which jammed the rudder. Also, there was still a chattering noise when submerged and while moving the rudder. Even the most fundamental problem of keeping out the sea was a challenge.

Karl Hensel with the officers and crew aboard *Swordfish* after the tenth war patrol, 1944. *Courtesy of the Submarine Force Library, Groton Connecticut.*

During a storm, approximately 25 gallons of sea water had entered the control room and accumulated so much on a roll as to damage equipment. A defective hatch was the culprit. In all, Hensel pointed out over 20 instances of damage or malfunctions, many lasting a good part of the voyage.[90]

Hensel believed that some of the equipment malfunctions could have been avoided. He noted that at least two of them were caused by carelessness during the previous refit work at Pearl Harbor. For instance, while *Swordfish* made a fast speed run after the successful attack of 27 January, a jammed injector control prevented the number two main engine from achieving full speed for the escape from the scene. A stray nut had blocked the travel of fuel to the engine, and Hensel concluded, "This is probably a souvenir of the last refit crew work."[91] Similarly, while on patrol, the number four engine lost lubrication because of an errant rag probably left by the refit crew. The engine was out of service for two days.

C. B. "Swede" Momsen, Commander of Submarine Squadron Four, praised Hensel for the thoroughness of his report. Momsen called the war patrol report a model for all submariners, and he wrote, "The Commanding Officer has included every essential observation and given a concise statement of his reasoning on important decisions."[92] As the mastermind of the undersea rescue in 1939 of crewmen from the USS *Squalus*, a sister ship to *Swordfish*, Momsen was familiar with the capabilities and limitations of the boat. Momsen was also inventor of the "Momsen Lung," a significant piece of rescue apparatus. He was keenly aware of what might have developed from the various problems with equipment that challenged the ingenuity of Hensel and his crew aboard *Swordfish*. Momsen also knew that the sea did not willingly release hapless mariners in its grip. In the concise language of a submariner, Monsen termed the patrol "well executed,"[93] and he complimented the officers and crew.

Recognition for Hensel continued with the award of a Navy Cross for his extraordinary heroism. The citation accompanying the award duly noted the rigors of the patrol: "In spite of adverse weather conditions, material failures, and being forced to dive his ship to evade ... depth charging, outstanding ship-control and the performance of a well-trained crew enabled his ship to escape and return safely to port."[94] The Navy also recognized Hensel's inspiring leadership and decorated several other officers and crewmen, including Paul Marvin.[95]

The highest compliment was issued by the most demanding of taskmasters, the Commander Submarine Force, Pacific Fleet, Admiral Charles A. Lockwood. Known for expecting aggressive action on the part of his submarine commanders, Lockwood bestowed upon the tenth patrol a coveted distinction. Lockwood declared, "This patrol is designated as successful for combat Insignia Award."[96] The results-minded Lockwood was especially pleased with the way Hensel and his crew persisted in their attack on the night of 27 January, when the first salvo of torpedoes from the bow tubes missed the target, but by quick maneuvering *Swordfish* was able to sink the Japanese ship with stern shots.[97] Clearly, Lockwood wanted his submariners to draw blood.

As in Ernest Hemingway's novel, *The Old Man and the Sea*, where an aged fisherman demonstrated tremendous willpower in catching a big fish, so too the 42-year-old Hensel, old by submarine command standards, displayed his strength of will and showed that he was up to the task of commanding a submarine on a war patrol. In fact, the tenth patrol resulted in Hensel becoming the oldest submarine commander to go into combat in World War II. However, while the hapless fisherman in Hemingway's novel returned home with a mere fish skeleton, eaten away by sharks, Hensel's quest had a better outcome. He, too, had caught fish, in the form of Japanese merchant ships, but he was quite content to leave his "catch" at the bottom of the sea, certain that they would never reach their destinations. No doubt, both he and Lockwood derived much satisfaction from that knowledge.[98]

As meaningful as the recognition was for Hensel, the success of the patrol had deep personal benefits. The war patrol earned him credibility, and it erased his concern about not seeing action. Returning to his regular duties as commander of a submarine division, Karl Hensel now had first-hand knowledge of the dangers he would ask young commanders to face while on patrol. Undoubtedly, the informality of crew relations, the quick-changing circumstances while tracking a target, the challenge of hostile weather, the task of addressing frequent mechanical failures, and the "hair raising" episodes before, during and after attacks provided Hensel with real insight into the conditions of a war patrol. His subordinates thereafter knew he was issuing orders based upon his own journey into harm's way. He understood. He was leading by example. Inspired by his training and leadership, the submarine commanders in his division went on 43 war patrols, in which they sank 68 enemy ships and damaged 40 to 50 more. Their success was part of the legacy of Hensel's own war patrol.[99]

Another dividend of the patrol was a lasting friendship with veterans of *Swordfish*. At the time of the patrol, Hensel gave his assessment of his crew: "Our personnel throughout, officers and men, showed themselves to be what we have always known them to be—the world's finest."[100] The crew returned the compliment many-fold with their steadfast admiration and friendship. Whenever he attended annual gatherings of the U.S. Submarine Veterans of World War II, Hensel proudly sat at the table reserved for *Swordfish* crew. In his subsequent naval career and retirement years, Karl Hensel had a loyal band of submariners who had shared in the rigors and success of the tenth patrol. Leymon L. Dennis, the Quartermaster of *Swordfish*, summed up the crew's sentiments when he wrote, "Capt. Hensel became one of the 'best liked' CO's of *Swordfish*, and remained a friend of every man who made the 10th patrol."[101] In later years, Hensel hosted dinners for his fellow *Swordfish* crew members in his home.[102] One of the veterans of *Swordfish* supplied the author with a photograph of Karl Hensel in advanced age, wearing his admiral's uniform. Although his visage showed the toll of time, even then the fierce eyes of the old sea warrior gaze out at the observer, still giving evidence of the steely inner determination that shaped the outcome of the tenth patrol.[103]

In his postwar naval career, Hensel pursued posts of leadership that required either strong administrative ability or a marked interest in education, or both. He held several posts connected with the Office of the Commander of Submarine Forces, Pacific Fleet, and in June 1945 he was placed in charge of the Submarine Desk in the Office of the Chief of Naval Operations. However, his interest in education was resurrected again, in August 1946, when he reported to the National War College in Washington, D.C., as a student in the first class, and he remained as a member of the faculty until July 1948. After filling several administrative positions, including in the Office of Naval Operations, on 1 July 1953, Hensel retired with the rank of Rear Admiral, in recognition of his combat experience. Nevertheless, the Navy would not let him go entirely, and he was kept on active duty until 1 February 1958, as Special Assistant to the Chief of Naval Research.[104]

Finally retiring in earnest, Admiral Hensel settled in Florida, where he kept in touch with fellow World War II submariners of all ranks. In 1989, he corresponded with Joe Parks, former torpedoman from *Swordfish*, and described his close association: "I try to go to every bi-monthly meeting of our local chapter—the SW Florida Chapter of Subvets of WWII. I think they are as fine a group of men, and their wives (the Dinky Di's), and as patriotic, as I ever knew. And they have been so thoughtful and have given me such a warm welcome."[105]

Hensel could look back upon his 35 years of Navy service with a high degree

Oil painting on cover of *POLARIS* magazine entitled "Swordfish (SS-193) Sinks Delhi Maru, 16 January 1944," by C. Mike Carmody. *Courtesy of the artist, a submarine veteran.*

of satisfaction. He had helped win the war in the Pacific, and in the postwar era, he helped the Navy prepare for the challenges of the Cold War. His numerous meritorious duties had earned him much recognition. However, the veterans of the tenth patrol had no doubts as to when Karl Hensel was at his best. For them, his brilliant command of *Swordfish* was Hensel's finest hour.[106]

6

New Commander—Old Submarine

By 1944, over 100 American submarines were on patrol on various assignments, such as reconnaissance and lifeguard duty, rescuing downed American airmen from the sea. But the central mission of the boats was to continue the destruction of Japanese merchant shipping, and Karl Hensel's replacement would have to scour his patrol area to locate viable targets.

The submarine command tapped Lieutenant Commander Keats Edmund Montross to be the next skipper. Born in 1912 to a long-established Michigan family, Montross graduated from Annapolis in 1935. Known as "Monty" by family and friends, Keats Montross had many interests, especially music. He played the piano, but since he could not bring such a bulky instrument aboard a boat, he settled for playing the concertina while at sea. Montross was short in stature, and at the Naval Academy students labeled him a "sandblower," which is a midshipman's slang for someone so short that sand must be blown out of the way for him or her to breathe. Later on, aboard the confined spaces in submarines, Montross' short stature would be an asset. Unlike Frank Parker, who made up for his lack of height by his loquaciousness, Keats Montross was spare with words. However, his most striking feature was his youthful (boyish) appearance. Without uniform insignia, he could be easily mistaken for a freshly "minted" ensign, which militated against a commanding appearance.

After serving aboard the USS *Nevada* and later as a communications watch officer on the staff of the Commander, Battleships, he found his real interest in the submarine service. He graduated from submarine school in December 1938, and his first submarine assignment was the USS *S-41*. The boat was part of America's naval presence in China, and Montross observed conditions in Asian waters.[1] He subsequently gave his evaluation of the Japanese Navy: "I have a high regard and high opinion of the Japanese Navy. This was first formed on my tour of duty in China. I was very impressed by their enlisted personnel—they seemed alert, smart, and well disciplined." He added that before the war, many people thought the Japanese would be, as he put it, "a cinch to knock off," but his tour of duty in the Far East and his observations of Japanese Navy personnel and their warships convinced him that they would be both intelligent and aggressive.[2]

After qualifying to command a submarine, Montross transferred to the USS *O-4*, where he eventually took command. The Submarine School in New London scheduled the sailings of *O-4* while Montross was in command. The boat sailed daily with instruction for two to three officers and ten to 15 enlisted personnel. Normally, there were four separate dives in the morning and four in the afternoon. While in command of *O-4*, Montross gained valuable knowledge which equipped him to handle inexperienced newcomers who would come aboard *Swordfish*. The 'O" class submarines were an older class that had been recommissioned in 1941 to train World War II submariners. Montross' *O-4* had been launched in December 1916 and recommissioned in February 1941. Later, the Navy assigned him to a war patrol aboard USS *Muskellunge* for training as a prospective commanding officer. His first test as commander would come with his next assignment as skipper of *Swordfish*. All his previous training and experience would be measured by the outcome of the war patrol aboard this boat.[3]

To veterans of *Swordfish*, Montross appeared calm, level-headed, and knowledgeable. He did not possess as forceful a personality as Karl Hensel, but the youthful-looking Montross was assertive enough in his own quiet, unassuming way to achieve respect and exercise command. Quartermaster Leymon Dennis called him a Glenn Ford type.[4] One of the crew, Quartermaster Arthur C. Myers, played poker with both Karl Hensel and Keats Montross, and he recollected their differences in temperament. Both Hensel and Montross required discipline of their crews, but while at sea, Hensel took suggestions from the men and asked their opinions. He wanted feedback. On the other hand, Montross was not so willing to ask the opinion of the crew about operations while on patrol. Nevertheless, Montross was likeable and, as Meyers stated, "a good submarine sailor."[5]

Montross relieved Karl Hensel the day after *Swordfish's* return on 7 February 1944. Many of the crew would have preferred Hensel to continue as commander and, following Hensel's very successful patrol, there was an added emphasis on Montross doing well.[6] Montross presided over the refit of the submarine, which included installation of new range radar. However, in addition to a new commander, *Swordfish* would have a large number of inexperienced crewmen for its 11th patrol. Montross observed that during the last two refits, 32 men had transferred, and 16 of these men had six war patrols or more. There were 33 replacements, but of that number, 29 men had no war patrols at all. Montross added, "Altho [sic] every effort has been made to train men for key positions, it is impossible to substitute training alone for experience; and the loss this time of 15 to 18 experienced men for inexperienced men will leave the ship below a minimum of trained and experienced submariners."[7] There were only eight days of instruction for the new commander and crew, as well as two days of convoy exercises.[8]

With a crew populated with newcomers, Keats Montross took *Swordfish* to sea for her 11th patrol on 13 March 1944. After topping off with fuel and water at Johnston Island, *Swordfish* headed for the assigned patrol area west of the Mar-

6. New Commander—Old Submarine

Vice Admiral Charles A. Lockwood, Jr., awarding Silver Star to Keats Edmund Montross. *National Archives, College Park.*

ianas, which was reached 13 days later. Montross inspired his lookouts to search for sightings by promising cash prizes based on a point system. Points would be awarded for ships and aircraft spotted, as well as objects in the water.[9]

Contact with the enemy was made on the morning of 4 April, while the submarine was patrolling on the surface. A lookout spied what appeared to be a small ship at 10,000 yards, emerging from a rain squall. The submarine's radar picked up the same ship simultaneously. When range was closed to 5,600 yards, it was realized that the "small ship" was a destroyer. Five minutes after the first sighting, radar picked up three additional "pips" at a range of 18,000 to 15,000 yards. *Swordfish* began the tedious task of tracking a small convoy, but at dawn the convoy veered away from *Swordfish* and slipped out of range of an attack. With his appetite whetted, the commander looked for other quarry.

Montross did not have to wait long. At 1227 on the same day as the first sighting, smoke from another convoy was spotted, and a 24-hour sea chase began. Montross proceeded with an end run around the convoy. The presence of patrolling aircraft and abrupt zigzagging by the convoy prevented a daylight attack. He planned a night surface radar-directed attack once the moon had set. Undeterred by three escorts on the dark side of the convoy, at 0439 on 5 April, Montross reported, "Started in for attack."[10] Thirty-four minutes later, *Swordfish* fired four torpedoes at one of five merchant ships. The attacked ship was low in the water with a flush deck, single mast, and high funnel. Its weight was estimated to be

5,000 tons. In quick succession, Montross ordered the firing of four "fish" from the stern tubes at yet another freighter, larger than the first and estimated to be 5,000 to 5,500 tons. He saw his torpedoes hit both targets in timed detonations. The two targets were seen burning, but they were not sinking.[11]

When the convoy escorts started dropping depth charges, *Swordfish* retired from the scene. At a range of 5,000 yards, fires were still seen, but the fiercest fire ceased four minutes after launching the torpedoes. Montross wanted to attack again but was deterred when, during the reload of "fish," crewmen discovered that the outer door to torpedo tube number seven would not close. It was a perilous situation, if the torpedo was jammed in the tube. Fortunately, none was present, but by the time the torpedomen had investigated the damage and closed the outer door, the convoy was out of sight.

But Keats Montross would not quit. With depth charges sounding in the distance, he risked an end run on the surface in search of the convoy in hazy daylight. However, fate intervened in the form of a Japanese warship. Appearing out of the haze, it headed straight for *Swordfish,* and Montross barked orders for a crash dive and battle stations. He tried to maneuver for a stern shot at what was identified as a *Mutsuki* class destroyer. The destroyer passed out of decent range, approximately 4,000 yards astern of *Swordfish,* and dropped six depth charges where the Japanese suspected the submarine was located, but was not.[12]

Montross pressed on with his search for the convoy, which he came to realize was composed of five merchantmen, two destroyers, and two small escorts. At mid-afternoon, Montross again sighted it. When a small escort headed toward the submarine, *Swordfish* avoided detection by going deep. Montross reported, "Could not see if any ships were missing from last night's attack."[13] Later in the afternoon, *Swordfish* came closer to the surface and searched for the enemy by periscope. In the haze, initially all appeared clear, when suddenly the same destroyer appeared. Montross

Portrait of Keats Montross with medal. *National Archives, College Park.*

wrote, "Didn't know we had been sighted but on leveling off at periscope depth saw destroyer coming in fast."[14] *Swordfish* dove for the second time, but the chagrined Montross was bent on retaliation. He ordered the boat to periscope depth and the crew to battle stations. Fifteen minutes later, *Swordfish* fired three torpedoes in haste. All missed. Going deep, the crew rigged for depth charges. Eight rained down in the Japanese counter-attack, but none were close to the submarine. Again *Swordfish* eluded its pursuer, but not without a price. The depth-charging had damaged a switch for the SJ radar, which Montross used for surface searches and in particular for night surface attacks. However, the skipper also realized that as the enemy proceeded to install radar on their navy ships, it would be difficult to mount a night surface attack via a radar approach without being detected. From Montross's viewpoint, submariners would have to return more and more to a submerged approach with the periscope.[15]

The Sea Chase

The commander and crew of *Swordfish* had little time for rest. On the next day, 6 April, Montross was offered another chance at success. At 1959, radar revealed another convoy, or perhaps another image of the first convoy. Looking out from the bridge of the submarine into a night brightly lit by a full moon, Montross discerned two destroyers underway, with a convoy trailing 6,000 to 8,000 yards behind them. Hoping to ward off a submarine attack, the ships were swinging back and forth in a zigzag pattern between 180 and 120 degrees, every 20 to 30 minutes. *Swordfish* began what turned out to be a pursuit lasting two days. By morning of the following day, *Swordfish* was racing to gain a favorable position for an attack ahead of the convoy.[16]

However, a clear-cut approach to the convoy was spoiled by the sighting of an airplane headed for the submarine. Seeking to nullify the threat that American submarines posed to their convoys, the Japanese were busy writing formal instructions for aerial anti-submarine tactics against American submarines. Specific flight patterns for search-and-destroy missions were mapped out in manuals, along with descriptions of how aircraft could distinguish between periscope wakes and ocean whitecaps. The flier was urged to look for a triangular formation where, typically, the periscope wake joined the whitecaps.[17]

Because of the hostile aircraft, any aspirations Montross had for either a surface or submerged attack had to be abandoned temporarily. As the boat dove to 175 feet, the crew discovered yet another equipment casualty. A blow regulator valve for a main ballast tank began to leak badly, making it very inadvisable to go deep. Nevertheless, the crew made temporary repairs and *Swordfish* resumed the pursuit.[18] Committed to getting at the convoy, at 2230 Montross had *Swordfish* perform an audacious maneuver. Montross reported, "Passed right between the two leading destroyers. Could see one to port and one to starboard."[19] The submarine commander believed he had positioned his boat 6,000 yards ahead of the convoy in preparation for an attack. However, again the convoy eluded him, as it passed by too far away, probably by zigging.[20]

Not willing to let go, Montross continued the sea chase into the next day, but circumstances began to turn against *Swordfish*. In the morning, an enemy aircraft approached, and *Swordfish* was forced down again as the crew rigged for the enemy attack. The Japanese plane dropped a bomb which knocked out apparatus for operating the stern planes, and a second bomb exploded further away. After *Swordfish* returned to the surface later that afternoon, either the same airplane or another aircraft again attacked the boat, which hastily dove into the depths. A bomb exploded, as Montross reported, "fairly close," damaging three torpedo spindles as the impact jarred the "fish" in their tubes. Making matters worse, the previously damaged main ballast tank blow regulator valve still leaked. Plagued with mounting equipment problems, at 1930 on 8 April, Montross reluctantly broke off the pursuit in order to make repairs. The 48-hour chase was over.[21]

From here on, the patrol deteriorated as patrolling Japanese aircraft again drove *Swordfish* from the surface on 14 and 16 April. The submarine command ordered *Swordfish* to end the patrol after four more days of fruitless searching. While en route to the port of Majuro, the submarine encountered two more aircraft, but without incident. Finally, on 29 April, *Swordfish* entered Majuro. The 11th patrol had ended in disappointment, but *Swordfish* had survived and would renew her sea hunt another day.[22]

The members of the submarine command were well-satisfied with Keats Montross. The "rookie" commander had tracked targets with patience and tenacity. He had shown great promise. Even Karl Hensel, that hard task-master, congratulated Montross and his crew for damaging two enemy vessels. No doubt, Montross's passage between two Japanese destroyers while tracking a convoy reminded Hensel of his own weave between two enemy patrol boats while in command on the tenth patrol. Montross had been aggressive while also maintaining a cool disposition, two desirable characteristics for a successful submarine commander.[23]

At Majuro, *Swordfish* refitted while tied up next to the tender, *Sperry*, and the crew went to a rest camp to unwind. The camp at Majuro was surprisingly commodious and well-organized. There was ample time for loafing around in the sun and for swimming. The food was good, and there was plenty of beer. Movies nightly in an open-air theater brought an end to each day of leisure. Although the camp was not removed from naval activities, it did provide a chance to recover from a wearisome patrol.[24]

Michael Billy Meets the Grand Dame

The condition of *Swordfish* was another matter. When Motor Machinist Mate Michael Billy stepped aboard *Swordfish* in May 1944, he was setting foot

6. New Commander—Old Submarine

on a legendary submarine, but she was past her prime. In the space of five years, old SS-193 had endured the ravages of 11 war patrols, traveled thousands of miles, and had numerous encounters with enemy depth charges and bombs. *Swordfish* was older than *Gunnel*, *Barb*, *Blackfish*, or *Drum*, boats to which Billy had been assigned in various capacities prior to transferring to *Swordfish* on 13 May 1944.[25] Initially as a Fireman and now as a Motor Machinist's Mate, Michael Billy had had two years' experience in the Submarine Service, and while on duty aboard *Blackfish*, he was authorized to wear the Submarine Combat Insignia with a star.[26]

On board *Swordfish*, Keats Montross listed the numerous problems that plagued *Swordfish* during the 11th patrol, and Billy and his new shipmates grappled with the equipment casualties. There was damage that could be repaired temporarily while on patrol, such as a broken head bolt for number four main engine and a cracked liner related to the number two engine. High voltage and weakened insulation caused a short-circuiting of the armature for the number two after-battery. Also, the auxiliary engine outboard exhaust valve had stiffened during operations, requiring heavy lubrication. Operations were also hampered when a section of the main motor cooling water line was damaged, resulting in flooding of the pump motor. The cause was a line strained at the time of installation. The crew fashioned a makeshift patch. Montross complained about yet another installation defect, caused while the submarine was previously refitted by the crew of the submarine tender USS *Holland*. A newly-installed, solenoid-operated clutch in the stern plane line shafting gave "trouble" when two bearings seized. The shaft floated axially an excessive amount and various components were out of alignment. Montross wrote, "Cause: Careless installation."[27]

Other installation defects included numerous electrical grounds that occurred in the Mark 18 torpedo-charging panels. Montross suggested better insulation of the tie bolts, and additional torpedo issues had arisen while on patrol. As noted earlier, an aerial bombing had jarred three torpedoes in their tubes, bending three gyro-setting spindles. Also, when the outer door to torpedo tube number seven failed to close following an attack, there was, as Montross expressed it, "some anxiety" as to the possibility of there being a "fish" jammed in the tube. The cause was a jammed lever; fortunately, there was no stuck torpedo.[28]

Wearing-out components on the aging *Swordfish* were noted. The commander pointed out that the blow regulator valve for one of the main ballast tanks had sheared two deteriorated brass studs, which held it to the pressure hull. While they were submerged, the crew put in place a metal plate to shore up the valve, and later, when surfaced, they put in place two studs. In addition, Montross observed that, as he stated, "antique insulation" had caused the steering motor brake wires to short-circuit. Montross also complained that the steering motor was out of alignment with the steering pump, causing three coupling failures during the 11th patrol. A relief crew from the USS *Sperry* commenced repairs. Meanwhile, the regular crew of *Swordfish* engaged in rest and recuperation.[29]

One fundamentally sound feature of *Swordfish* was the General Motors Winton engines. When Michael Billy went to sea on his war patrol aboard the USS *Gunnel* with its commander, Lieutenant Commander John S. McCain, Jr., Billy witnessed breakdowns of the poorly-designed H.O.R. diesel engines, while *Gunnel* was serving as a beacon ship for the North Africa landings in 1942. The submarine had to limp back to home port in Scotland on power from her auxiliary engine. As someone who was charged to help maintain the engines on *Swordfish*, Mike Billy knew the Wintons were far more reliable.[30] They were masterpieces of engineering. When properly tuned and maintained, the 16 cylinders in each engine would purr rather than clatter. They were a pure manifestation of power.[31]

In addition to a new submarine commander, Michael Billy would meet new officers and crewmen, and the process of fitting into a new group would start with the first day aboard the boat. However, Billy was not alone in the acclimation process. As previously mentioned, Keats Montross had noticed the substantial loss of 32 personnel prior to the 11th patrol. Now, on the eve of the 12th patrol, there was further attrition of men familiar with the peculiar characteristics of *Swordfish*. In particular, Montross bemoaned the departure of Lieutenant W. N. Brown and Ensign J. J. Lorenz, regarded by the commander, in his words, as "key officers." Montross added sarcastically, "For replacements I got two ensigns, Ensign Nixon

Some of the crew of *Swordfish* around the deck gun, 1944. *Courtesy Janice Langley.*

6. New Commander—Old Submarine

and Ensign Janes." No doubt the newcomers would do their best, but their experienced predecessors were missed.[32]

Admiral Lockwood noticed a decrease of experienced officers throughout the Submarine Service. An exasperated Lockwood wrote to Commander R. H. Rice, his Submarine Detail Officer, "As you know from looking at our rosters of submarines, the percentage of Naval Academy officers is dropping very low and the captain of the ship is in most cases the only man who can claim to have reached years of discretion, while the rest are practically children."[33] Lockwood envisioned a further drop in experienced skippers as they rotated to new ship construction, and he saw the portents of, in his words, "operational and battle losses."[34]

Along with new officers, new crewmen had come aboard *Swordfish*. In addition to the arrival of Michael Billy, ten other replacements joined the crew for the 12th patrol. As a routine procedure, the Navy rotated submariners. Mixing new crewmen with veterans on the boats allowed the newcomers to work side-by-side with experienced hands and to learn submarine operations quickly. However, the extra challenge of going out on patrol with a substantial number of new hands, relatively unfamiliar with *Swordfish*, could be daunting for a new commander. The number of veteran crewmen who could "show the ropes" had dropped.[35]

Montross Finds a Destroyer

Nevertheless, Keats Montross was determined to resolve the unfinished business from the 11th patrol—sinking enemy ships. After a short period of three days' training from 16 to 18 May 1944, and a final loading of provisions on 19 and 20 May, *Swordfish* was ready to go. Departing Majuro on 22 May, with the submarine USS *Grouper* and the USS *Weaver*, a destroyer, as escort, *Swordfish* embarked on her 12th war patrol. A day later, the *Swordfish* parted company with her companions and proceeded independently toward her assigned patrol area near the Bonin Islands. A main objective was to interdict traffic along the Tokyo-Chichi Shima route, as part of the overall objective of securing the Bonins.[36]

Montross was to take part in a new operations plan known as "Dunker's Derby." Encouraged by Admiral Lockwood and Captain Richard G. Voge, Dunker's Derby was one of several operations designed to equalize attack opportunities and divide up the burdens of patrol within a general area. The end goal was to step up attrition of Japanese merchant shipping by concentrating more submarines in an area, somewhat similar to the wolf packs that German U-boats used in the Battle of the Atlantic. A major difference was that Lockwood did not bring as many submarines into any one area.[37] Code names for other concentrated patrol areas included "Hit Parade," "Speedway," and "Maru Morgue." By 30 May, *Swordfish* had reached its designated patrol area and was ready to participate in Dunker's Derby. The submarine was replacing *Skate*. Other boats at work in the area were *Plaice*,

Gar, *Kingfish*, and *Archerfish*. Once in the patrol area, *Swordfish* sighted enemy sea and air patrols, and building on the experience of the previous patrol, Montross was careful to avoid detection.[38]

Finally, in the afternoon of 8 June, Montross had the chance to make up for the fruitless pursuits of the previous patrol. *Swordfish* sighted a destroyer. Hoping that the destroyer was escorting a convoy, Montross looked in vain for other ships, but nothing appeared. Still, through the periscope he kept his eyes peeled on the destroyer. At 2323, initial radar contact was made with two ships at 16,000 yards distant. In the bright moonlight of the evening, six vessels came into view: three freighters, the destroyer, and two other escorts.[39]

Swordfish raced to get ahead of the convoy, and at 0315 on 9 June, the crew went to battle stations near Chichi Shima. Intent upon attacking a freighter, Montross selected his target. Bathed in the light of a full moon, the merchant ship was clearly visible. Montross started his final approach at periscope depth, but the escorting Japanese destroyer must have spotted the submarine. It headed for *Swordfish* while taking the precaution of zigzagging. Not to be disappointed, rather than dive, Montross quickly shifted the torpedo set-up for a direct shot at the destroyer. When the fast-approaching destroyer closed to 1,200 yards at an angle on the bow of just ten degrees port (almost head on), *Swordfish* fired four Mark 18 electric torpedoes. The torpedoes were calculated to run the short distance of 920 yards. Because they were electric torpedoes, they left no telltale wake, and the men on the bridge of the destroyer had no time to alter course. Within a minute of going deep, the submarine crew heard two timed torpedo explosions. Another explosion appeared to be a depth charge that probably was jolted off the destroyer when the torpedoes hit. A few minutes later, listening gear aboard the submarine picked up the sounds of the destroyer breaking up, and her screws and echo ranging had ceased.[40] *Swordfish* had sunk the Japanese destroyer *Matsukaze*, a 1,270-ton ship of the *Kamikaze* (Divine Wind) class. It had a normal complement of 148 men, but the actual number lost is unknown. Previously in October 1943, during the Solomons campaign, the *Matsukaze* participated in the evacuation of Japanese troops from Vella Lavella.[41]

Montross' use of the Mark 18 electric-propelled torpedo was part of a growing trend in their application. After the Navy "debugged" initial defects in the Mark 18s, they gradually caught on as the torpedo of choice. Their advantage in leaving no wake, which could be traced back to the firing submarine, was especially advantageous. By the end of December 1944, American submarines had fired 1,487 Mark 18 torpedoes for 448 hits, with a success rate of a little over 30 percent. The hits sank 183 ships and damaged 72 more vessels. In terms of tonnage, the Mark 18s sank 1,076,000 tons of enemy shipping and damaged another 523,700 tons. The increased favor attached to the Mark 18 torpedo was revealed in loading figures. In April 1944, submarines took on board 132 Mark 18s, whereas in October 1944 submarines loaded on 640 Mark 18 torpedoes. By January 1945, the Mark 18s constituted 75 percent of the "fish" on American boats.[42]

6. New Commander—Old Submarine

For the immediate time being aboard *Swordfish*, use of the Mark 18s for another attack fell behind the higher priority of evading a Japanese counter-attack. Hearing distant depth charges, presumably from one of the other escorts, and sighting an aircraft five miles distant, Montross kept *Swordfish* under the surface. Still intent on attacking one of the freighters in the convoy, Montross finally ordered "surface" at 0735 and renewed the chase. It was too late. The convoy was near port at Chichi Shima, and another patrolling aircraft finalized matters by making it prudent for *Swordfish* to dive once more. Montross would have to be satisfied with sinking a destroyer—his first "kill."[43]

For several days, *Swordfish* was plagued with the sightings of five more aircraft contacts, but persistence in the search of enemy ships paid off. In the afternoon of 14 June, the submarine sighted smoke, and a convoy came into view. It consisted of four ships and five escorts. Montross decided to trail the ships and make a night surface attack. The escorts formed a protective perimeter around the convoy. Two lead escorts were a substantial distance ahead of the convoy, and an additional pair of escorts was farther back on each side, with a smaller escort astern. For a brief period, *Swordfish* lost sight of the convoy, but Montross doggedly held course, surfaced, and caught up with the convoy in the evening. He approached for an attack.[44]

When it appeared that the submarine would traverse too close to the bow of the second escort on the port side of the convoy, Montross changed direction. He pointed *Swordfish* toward the lead escort on the starboard side, and the submarine stealthily wove its way 1,200 yards astern of the escort. The submarine commander had planned to attack the leading freighter, but sailing on a phosphorous-laden sea, *Swordfish* left a visible wake. Montross believed that the second escort on the starboard side of the convoy detected the intruder, either by sight or by sound gear, and two of the escorts turned on red lights. Then the first escort on the starboard side fired a white rocket. Montross recorded his reaction: "We knew we had been sighted, but decided to continue in."[45]

The first merchant ship failed to take evasive action by zigzagging, and Montross seized the opportunity at 2256 to fire four torpedoes quickly from tubes one through four. The sound gear picked up the explosion of one of the "fish," but no hits. Two minutes later, an escort suddenly closed to within 200 yards of the submarine. Montross described the close encounter, "We picked him up at about 500 yards and he closed to 200 yards and there were a few frightful moments there whether we were going to ram him, or he ram us."[46] *Swordfish's* radar had missed picking up the small ship earlier, probably the rear escort. Montross was able to avoid a collision and described the tense outcome: "Fortunately we were able to turn out of the way and make good our escape."[47] The escorts did not retaliate with depth charges.

Instead, the starboard escort was sending up white warning flares and the convoy was dispersing. Montross singled out a merchantman that seemed to be separated from the rest. She was protected by one escort ahead and a smaller one aft. Unfazed by the now-alerted escorts, Montross ordered four torpedoes fired from the bow tubes for a 1,500-yard run. Again, all missed. Two torpedo explosions were heard, and the trailing escort fell behind to investigate, but again, no depth charges were heard. Montross took this as a signal to mount another attack. Early the next morning, the fleeing ship came into range, and once again *Swordfish* dispatched four "fish" from the bow tubes, this time for a run of 1,000 yards. Success at last! Within a minute after firing, Montross saw and heard three torpedoes slam into the merchant ship, while a fourth torpedo sped ahead of the target. Montross described the final minutes of the Japanese ship:

> Bow quickly settled in water. Escort now turned back. Target last seen with only stern out of water. Radar kept contact with target with pip getting smaller and smaller until at 0118 radar pip on target disappeared at range of 4,500 yards.[48]

An escort dropped a few depth charges and then circled the target to pick up survivors. The crew of *Swordfish* had sent to the bottom *Kanseishi Maru*, a merchant ship of 4,804 tons of the *Buzyon* class. Two torpedoes found their target on the maru's port side, killing two of the crew. Unrealized at the time, a dividend came out of the attack. *Swordfish's* attack raised havoc in the convoy, and apparently one of the ships, *Toyokawa Maru*, was damaged when it collided with another Japanese ship that was trying to avoid the torpedoes.[49] At 0154, Montross elected to cease pursuit of the convoy because its course was uncertain. The grim work of sinking enemy ships was finished for the day.

If Keats Montross had ordered his crew to head for home port that day, his war patrol would have been judged successful by his superior officers. *Swordfish* had sunk a Japanese naval ship and a merchantman. Montross did not have to go further. However, the exigencies of war and his evident sense of duty did not allow for a respite. His mandate was to seek targets, and he did so with vigor.

For six days, the tedium of searching for prey and evading hostile aircraft was *Swordfish's* lot, but the seventh day ushered in previously spurned targets. Finding large enemy ships had been difficult, and smaller vessels were considered. *Swordfish* surfaced and came across two trawlers, each estimated at 475 tons. Using night radar, tracking commenced. By 2225, the submarine had come ahead of the trawlers and, as Montross reported, "With stern pointed at target, and on targets track, let target come up astern gradually working off track and keeping stern to target until at 2310 fired tubes 7 and 8."[50] The torpedoes were set to run 1,800 yards in a divergent spread in the hopes of "catching" a target. Even though the TDC setup was well worked out, the torpedoes detonated but had missed their target. The "rookie" commander realized his error. He wrote in the patrol log, "After firing 2 torpedoes with what appeared to be a perfect set-up on the TDC and missing, it was not considered advisable to fire more torpedoes at such a small target."[51] Montross had wasted two torpedoes, but had learned a lesson: save them for bigger game.

6. New Commander—Old Submarine 149

Four days later on 26 June, Montross applied what he had learned. Sighting six enemy trawlers strung out in a column, Montross declared, "Decided to attack by gunfire."[52] In a night surface attack, at a range of 1,000 yards, *Swordfish* fired all guns at the last trawler. Montross had in mind coming up astern and on the port quarter of the column and firing at each vessel as the submarine passed by.[53] Two minutes into the engagement, Montross reported, "Ceased firing—pulled away to clear jam on 3"/50 cal. gun. The 20mm fire was very effective. Saw a small fire start on ship fired on. He stopped and dropped from column. Now planned to try and cripple another and then finish both of them off."[54] As the flaming trawler projected an eerie reflection upon the shimmering water in this ink-black night, the crew worked vigorously to clear the jammed 3"/50.[55]

Resuming the attack at ten minutes after midnight, *Swordfish* fired all guns at a range of 900 yards. Montross described this second attack: "From now until 0120 made runs on target at ranges of 1,000 yards to 500 yards and finally stopping 300 yards from target and blasting away. First hit made with 3" at 0022."[56] Turning his attention to the other trawlers, the submarine commander realized that the four unscathed trawlers had increased speed, and they would escape to Chichi Shima before they could be intercepted. The second trawler fired upon was

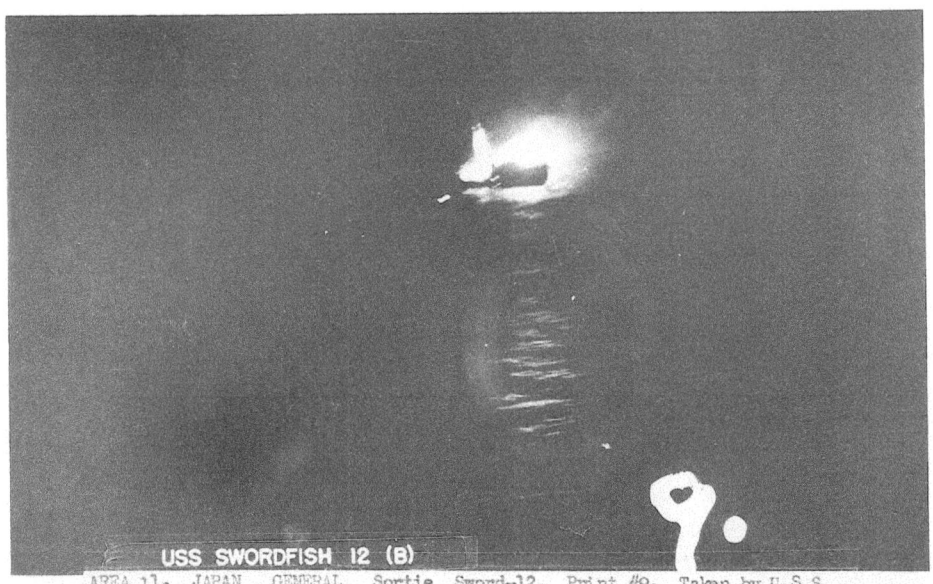

Photograph of unidentified burning Japanese trawler after *Swordfish*'s night surface sortie of 26 June 1944. *Courtesy of Submarine Force Library, Groton, Connecticut.*

Large portion of crew of *Swordfish*, 1944. *Courtesy Janice Langley.*

the 148-ton *Hokuryu Maru* #10, employed as a cargo vessel. Montross reported the boat as "afire from stem to stern and the main deck was awash." Three Japanese seamen perished in the conflagration.[57] *Swordfish* left the burning hulk and searched for the first damaged target, but it had slipped into the night, and a 55 minute search proved fruitless. The engagement was a great success in terms of morale. After the Japanese ship was set afire, members of the *Swordfish* crew were able to come topside to see the results of their efforts, an opportunity which usually did not occur in submarine attacks.[58] Toward daylight, *Swordfish* dove into the anonymity of the depths. Later that morning, three planes were spotted through the periscope, and in the afternoon, a patrol boat was seen. For the time being, the ordeal of combat was over.

The next day, more enemy planes were noted, and that evening the course was set for Midway. The patrol was finally nearing its end. Crewmen could think of home port and shore leave. However, when the masts of three small trawlers came into view on June 30, any thoughts the crew had of home were quickly dispelled by their zealous commander's order, "battle stations." The deck crew scrambled topside to man the surface weapons. *Swordfish's* guns trained on the rear trawler, *Chiyoda Maru* #8, and at 2027, firing commenced. Montross provided a picture of the fierce fire fight:

6. New Commander—Old Submarine   151

Enemy promptly returned fire with small caliber machine guns. 20mm. soon silenced his fire. From now until 2145 made runs on target at ranges of 1000 yards to 500 yards. Target's speed about 10 knots. Each time we would come in, target would give us a 180 degree angle on the bow. Once he attempted to ram.[59]

Montross added that fire from the 3"/50 caliber gun was "wild," with about ten hits on the target.[60] By 2150, it was all over. The crew secured from battle stations. The enemy ship was down by the stern, and sea water had risen up to claim the deckhouse amidships. The trawler was listing at 20 degrees and was still burning, with a loss of 24 seamen. The other two trawlers had fled the scene at the beginning of the attack. Noting the low supply of ammunition on hand, Montross elected not to pursue the enemy and headed for home port.[61]

Swordfish, with her battle-weary crew, slipped into her berth at Midway on 5 July, thus concluding her 12th war patrol. Staying at Midway for less than a day, the submarine sailed on to Pearl Harbor and arrived there just past noon on 9 July. The officers and crew finally received their respite from the danger and stress of going on patrol.[62]

Worn and battle-scarred, the aged *Swordfish* went into the shipyard at Pearl for a major overhaul. Montross described damage that had occurred while on patrol. On number four main engine, a piston, liner, and head had cracked when a piece of liner had lodged on top of the piston, cracking the cylinder head before the engine could be stopped. Also, on engine number four, dirt in the fuel had caused the injector plunger to seize. Excessive pressure caused a roller bearing to jam and damage other components.[63] Additional breakdowns of equipment occurred during the four-day trip from Midway to Pearl Harbor. Bilge water had flooded the auxiliary generator and caused it to completely ground out. Montross complained that personnel had not kept the bilges free of water and had not wired closed a drain valve. A second problem was a cracked cylinder head on number two main engine. The skipper attributed this casualty to both engine fatigue and unequal stresses on bolts that held down the cylinder head. Another mechanical problem involved a burned-out connecting-rod bearing and badly scored crankshaft journal, with no forewarning of the damage. Montross noted that there was evidence of a restricted flow of lube oil and that the oil had been in the engine for 997 hours. Clearly, the mainstays of propulsion, the *Swordfish*'s diesel engines, along with other components, would need a close inspection during the planned overhaul.[64] Apparatus for firing torpedoes was also a matter of concern. While on patrol, during several approaches to targets, the gyro-setting indicator regulator did not work properly, and firing on two occasions had to be done by local control. Montross recommended the replacement of the regulator.[65]

In contrast to the regrettable failure of equipment, the performances of Keats E. Montross and his crew were lauded by their superior officers. The 12th war patrol was hailed as successful, and the patrol endorsements recounted *Swordfish*'s sinking of the enemy's destroyer, merchant ship, and trawlers. Montross and his officers and crew were praised for their aggressive war patrol. For Montross, a final stamp of approval came in the form of a medal. On 9 October 1944, he was awarded the Navy's Silver Star. The citation read in part, "For gallantry and intrepidity in action in the performance of his duties as Commanding Officer of the USS *Swordfish* during vessel's Twelfth War Patrol from 30 May 1944 to 28 June 1944."[66] The citation described the successful sinkings and added, "By skillful evasive tactics he was able to successfully evade severe enemy countermeasures and avoid damage to his ship."[67] Admiral Charles Lockwood pinned the medal onto the uniform of Montross. Similarly, Michael Billy and his shipmates were included in the recognition for the successful patrol. For their service in the Bonin Islands campaign, the sailors were authorized to wear combat engagement stars on their Asiatic-Pacific Area campaign ribbons.

After commanding two war patrols against the enemy, Keats Montross also had some words to say. In assessing the submariner's main target, the Japanese merchant marine, Montross gave his evaluation. He termed the Japanese merchant marine as excellent, and he called attention to the Japanese as a seafaring people and their expertise at navigation. Then, on a more personal level, he reflected, "Their conduct under attack—I often times believe that they are just as scared as we are, when we go in to make an attack."[68] Regardless of his inner feelings when going into harm's way, Keats Montross had done it right. He had taken the aging *Swordfish* to sea with a relatively new crew, and he had closed with and destroyed the enemy. In so doing, he had contributed to the success of Dunker's Derby, which had severed Japanese shipping routes to the Bonin Islands.[69] Montross had significantly enhanced his career, and he had added one more set of accolades to the illustrious image of the legendary *Swordfish*. For Keats Montross, the future looked bright.

Dorothy Heath Clary. *Courtesy John Clary and Cynthia E. Clary.*

7

The Thirteenth Patrol

In summer 1944, the crew of *Swordfish* returned from their war patrol, and the discipline, tedium, and alternate terror of combat were supplanted with merriment. As sailors have done throughout the ages, these young men on leave enjoyed the pleasures of port. But another element crept into their behavior—whimsy. Eleven members of *Swordfish* from Texas were eager for news from their home state and, commenting that Texas had beautiful women, in an open letter to the *Dallas Morning News*, the Texans pleaded for pretty girls back home to send letters and photographs, which would be delivered to the single men in the crew.[1]

Illustrating the concerns of many individuals on the home front, Dorothy Heath responded to the sailors' request. As a 17-year-old freshman at Southern Methodist University, she wrote to the crewmen. Her motivation was typical of many of the folks back home. She viewed her correspondence as a way of doing her part to boost morale and help the war effort. She believed she was being patriotic.[2] One Texan in the crew, Fred M. Cauley, Jr., began to write to Heath regularly as a kind of "pen pal," and she, in turn, sent him cookies and photographs of herself.[3] Apparently Cauley shared Dorothy Heath's photos (and cookies) with his shipmates, because in December 1944 the crew sent another letter to the *Dallas Morning News*. The letter requested that Ms. Heath become their pin-up girl because she reminded them of the "girl next door."[4]

Heath recalled her positive reaction to the letter, as the sailors preferred her for their pin-up girl because she reminded them of the reasons for which they were fighting: home, family, and the future of America.[5] Knowing that it was customary for servicemen to have pin-ups in World War II, Dorothy Heath complied with this innocent, morale-building gesture. She posed modestly in her swimsuit photo session in freezing December weather.[6] On the following day, her swimsuit photograph appeared in the *Dallas Morning News*, along with an insert of the *Swordfish* battle flag. The accompanying article was entitled, "Sub Crew Chooses Dallas Girl As Favorite for Pin-Up Photo."[7] Later, a tabloid newspaper distributed Heath's photograph to Texas servicemen throughout the world. For a while, Dorothy Heath was a kind of international celebrity and a heroine to Texas servicemen.[8]

The Ravages of Time and War

On the other hand, another celebrity, the venerable USS *Swordfish*, was contending with the ravages of time and 12 war patrols. Navy officials recognized that the old *Swordfish* needed an extensive overhaul. From 11 July to 6 October 1944, the boat was in the Pearl Harbor Navy Yard, undergoing what amounted to a complete "makeover." At least 79 parts of the submarine were either modernized, replaced, repaired, or serviced. Among the items affected were the valves, vents, gauges, pumps, piping, and cables throughout the boat. The overhaul crew worked on the numerous tanks for air, water, and fuel, as well as the conning tower, antennas, periscope, propulsion machinery, torpedo loading hatches, SJ radar, batteries, auxiliary plane angle indicators, propeller shafts, announcing system, JP sonar equipment, radio equipment, new air conditioning units (in the conning tower), and a long list of other components. A unique piece of new equipment was the installation of an Identification, Friend, or Foe Mark III radar system. The IFF electronic system was designed to determine the friend-or-foe status of a radar target, especially aircraft.[9] One of the "casualties" was particularly noticeable. In July 1944, Keats Montross reported that during the overhaul of number three main engine, the crew discovered seven cracked cylinder heads. Montross stated that prior to the overhaul, the engine had been flooded, resulting in the cracks. Charles Lockwood duly noted the report.[10]

Apparently there was the expectation of possible surface action on the next patrol, because plans also called for the fabrication of compartments for ammunition storage for 20 mm guns and 4"/50 caliber ammunition on the port side below the platform deck. Indeed, navy personnel quickly made use of the new ammunition storage compartments. They took on board, from the Naval Ammunition Depot in Oahu, 90 rounds of various types of 4"/50 ammunition, 30 boxes of 20 mm ammunition, eight boxes of .30 caliber ammunition, and ten boxes of .50 caliber cartridges, including tracer and armor-piercing types. The boat also took on Mark 18 torpedoes. Lastly, they loaded on two boxes of .45 caliber cartridges. *Swordfish* may have been worn down, but it was not slated for decommissioning.[11]

Coming out of overhaul, *Swordfish* was now put to the test in a variety of courses and speeds. The boat also performed diving procedures, including a slow, stationary dive. The crew fired practice torpedoes from tubes one, two three, and four. In addition, the submarine was monitored while operating under both battery and main engine propulsion. The course of action had been routine, except on 9 October when *Swordfish* scraped against the starboard propeller of the USS *Kingfish* (SS-234), while approaching a berth at the Pearl Harbor Submarine Base.[12] There was no appreciable damage.

A more puzzling discovery after the overhaul at Pearl Harbor necessitated additional work. In a memorandum to the Chief of the Bureau of Ships dated

7. The Thirteenth Patrol

3 January 1945, E. R. Swinburne, Commanding Officer of the Naval Submarine Base, reported: "Subsequent to overhaul by the Navy Yard, Pearl Harbor, the starboard reduction gear on the USS *Swordfish*, (SS193), was damaged by miscellaneous foreign matter passing through the gears."[13] The boat's reduction gears were an integral part of the power train between the boat's engines and her propellers. The foreign matter in the starboard gear consisted mainly of metal, such as a steel lock washer and metal chips. The materials found in the gear casing and had caused the gear to be noisy, an unforgivable condition for a submarine. Swinburne could not account for the damage, but described the repair of the reduction gear, which was performed in mid–December at a shop in Pearl Harbor. Workmen cut one-and-a-half inches out of part of the gear and smoothed out adjacent areas to quell the noise. The gear was then re-installed aboard the boat.[14]

During a follow-up dock trial run, the gear made two distinct knocks per revolution, and the noise level was deemed still too high. Further work was performed. The gear underwent lapping (smoothing), filing, and grinding. The reduction gear was re-installed again. Tooth contact was good, but an underway test on 15 December revealed, as reported, "comparatively high sound level at creeping speeds."[15] The submarine was worked on for another two days, and a sound test was performed on 18 December. Operating sounds from the gear had dropped by an average of two decibels, with a reading of 82 decibels at 50 revolutions per minute. Swinburne concluded, "It was believed no further improvement in the sound level was feasible by work on the starboard reduction gear. The submarine departed for patrol."[16]

From 18 to 31 January 1945, Swinburne's report of the reduction gear incident passed through the hands of several Bureau of Ships officials. The officials offered written comments on a routing slip that accompanied Swinburne's report. One official believed the damage was not accidental, and another called for an investigation. However, no firm recommendations for action were cited, because there was a question as to whether or not the Commander of Submarines Pacific, Admiral Lockwood's office, was aware of the incident and was already looking into the matter. In searching the historical records, the author has found no additional references to the reduction gear incident. This lack of any further documentation suggests that the matter may have been set aside and ultimately dropped, especially since the boat's officers and crew were no longer available to give testimony after *Swordfish* went to sea.[17]

However, district intelligence reports covering the Pearl Harbor Navy Shipyard cited shipyard incidents similar to that of *Swordfish*. In the report of 30 September 1944, there were 41 reported cases of shipboard mechanical damage since December 1941. In 12 cases, foreign matter was introduced by carelessness, and in only three instances was there a determination of sabotage. In one of the three sabotage cases, a blocked fuel line on the USS *Pensacola* was linked to the negligence of a disgruntled worker. In another situation, two employees damaged a fire main on the USS *Saratoga*, in the hopes of discrediting their supervisor. In yet another case, two enlisted men caused a collision and damage by locking a rudder post on an LST, in the hope of obtaining extra liberty during the repair period.[18] In a similar intelligence report of 26 January 1945, Captain Peyton Harrison, District Intelligence Officer, stated that during 1944, the Intelligence Office had investigated 41 incidents classified as "sabotage" and nine as "espionage." In reviewing the data, Harrison stated, "No evidence of enemy-inspired sabotage or espionage was found in these."[19] The details of the intelligence reports suggest a large variety of causes of shipyard damage, including material failure and factory defects, as well as carelessness and deliberate sabotage, as noted concerning *Pensacola* and *Saratoga*. The shipyard was doing its job of returning ships to sea, but there were problems of quality control.

The problems at the Navy Yard at Pearl Harbor were not unique. At Mare Island, California, there were problems too. Leo L. Pace, a Navy officer, gave his evaluation of difficulties at that facility. Pace reported to Lockwood: "Navy Yard overhauls continue to have their troubles. The worst offence is having Navy Yard work going on right up to the moment of departure."[20] Quality control problems were further compounded by the normal expansion of overhaul facilities during the course of the war. A large number of inexperienced personnel were brought into the yards, and the need to work fatiguing overtime shifts inevitably led to errors in workmanship.[21]

The reader might well ask, why would Charles Lockwood order to sea older submarines of the fleet, including *Swordfish*? Clearly *Swordfish* was past prime condition, even with the extensive makeover. Numerous other boats, such as the "S" class boats, were even older. In a letter to Captain Joseph A. Fowler at the Office of the Assistant Industrial Manager, dated 9 January 1945, Lockwood provided insight into his sense of urgency. He railed against delays of submarines coming out of the Bethlehem Shipyard in San Francisco. Referring to the liberation of Luzon in the Philippines and to subsequent submarine operations, an exasperated Admiral Lockwood wrote:

> We have needed all possible boats so badly at times and no doubt we have seemed over impatient. Our problem has been to knock off all possible transports and supplies before our troops went into the Luzon end of things.... After Luzon there will be other places which we must isolate, places that American boys in landing craft must take. How many of them are killed and wounded in so doing is almost a direct function of how many of their [Japanese] reinforcements and supplies our submarines can prevent reaching these outlying places—or in fact the Japanese homeland.... This is a bit long winded, Joe, but if all repair yards, building yards, torpedo factories, etc., could fully realize these facts, maybe there would be more earnest effort and less looking out for No. 1 all around.

Lockwood concluded: "On the whole, your gang and all the gangs around the Bay have done a fine job—as have our lads here [Pearl Harbor] and in advanced bases. I realize the difficulties you encountered along the lines of inexperienced workmen, incompetence, political complications, etc., and I know that you will deal with them as though the lives of your own kith and kin depended on your success—as indeed they do."[22] For Charles Lockwood, the submarine patrols were a matter of saving lives as much as defeating the enemy. Indeed, in Lockwood's way of thinking, there was a direct link between the two objectives.

No Substitute for Experience

In addition to the reduction gear issue, the lack of experienced crewmen aboard *Swordfish* became acute. As noted earlier, when Montross embarked on the 11th war patrol, he bemoaned the fact that during the last two refit periods, a total of 32 members of the crew had transferred off the boat. Of that number, 16 men had experienced six patrols or more.[23] The exodus continued. Between patrols 11 and 12, another ten experienced crew members bid farewell to *Swordfish*.[24]

The muster rolls of the crew for *Swordfish* reveal the outcome of the exodus from the submarine. Of the 77 regular crewmen who set sail in December on the 13th patrol, 51 (66 percent of the crew) came aboard in 1944 as newcomers. The degree of inexperience among the 51 sailors is magnified further when counting the men of that group who arrived after the 12th patrol. Between 5 July and 22 December 1944, 24 replacements (31 percent of the crew) came aboard for the first time. That is, after 5 July, a staggering 26 crew members transferred, never to return to the boat. In addition, two Navy photographers on special mission reported for duty in December 1944, raising to 26 the total of new arrivals since the 12th patrol, but not adding to the hands available to operate the boat. To be sure, many of the newcomers had war patrol experience on other submarines, but they had to learn the peculiar characteristics of old *Swordfish*. The officers and the more experienced crew members who remained would be busy instructing the newcomers while on the 13th war patrol. Given the addition in 1944 of so many newcomers, the prospects for smooth ship operations were reduced.[25]

No doubt, reasons for the transfers varied. The Submarine Service had routinely transferred a select number of experienced crewmen in order to "pepper" the crews of new boats under construction with "old hands," who could show newcomers the best methods and procedures. Many of these men had gone on numerous patrols and were due for a change of duty. Also, sailors are traditionally a superstitious lot, and the number "13" is often considered unlucky. The prospect of going into harm's way on the 13th patrol surely influenced some of the men to transfer off *Swordfish*.[26]

Swordfish was a prized boat with a famed past. Nevertheless, it was evident that basic machinery on the boat, such as the main engines, was wearing out. The extensive rehabilitation was somewhat reassuring, but how well newly-installed components would "mesh" with older parts was uncertain. The boat was seaworthy, but was it battle worthy? As new crewmen came on board after each patrol, experienced crew members could not know for certain how the new crew members would handle emergency situations in a boat where breakdowns were a real possibility.[27]

Attitudes toward the skipper, Keats Montross, may have come into play. It was evident that Montross was willing to close with and destroy the enemy. His daring exploits on the 12th patrol had won him the coveted Silver Star medal, and he was making his mark. Yet he was still a relatively new commander, and how he would fare in all manner of emergencies with an inexperienced crew was an open question. Perhaps some of the crew did not want to remain on board to find out the answer.

While their boat was being overhauled, the crewmen of *Swordfish* went on leave. Michael Billy had an opportunity to see his sisters and brothers in New Jersey. Typical of members of the Silent Service, Mike did not discuss his Navy assignments, but before taking leave of his siblings, he expressed his doubts about returning home safely from the pending war patrol. Billy's sentiments were similar to those expressed by numerous other submariners who were about to go out on patrol. They were keenly aware of the perils that could befall them. In 1944, Donald Gaither described the prevalent mood prior to departure: "I have asked fellows on the *Swordfish* and other boats and they all seem to have that same feeling, that when we went out we never expected to come back."[28] As a veteran of 12 war patrols aboard *Swordfish*, Gaither could back his words with experience.

A Challenging Assignment

When Keats Montross took *Swordfish* to sea on 22 December 1944, for her 13th patrol, he had an assignment fraught with risks. He was ordered to patrol the waters in the area of the Nansei Shoto, alternately known as the Ryuku Islands, an island chain extending south from Japan in an arc of a circle toward the Philippine Sea. In addition, Montross had a second special assignment. *Swordfish* was to conduct photo reconnaissance off the shores of Okinawa Jima, the largest island in the group. The photography was in preparation for the amphibious strike known as Operation ICEBERG.

Even without the presence of hostile forces, Okinawa's natural characteristics are a problem for approach by sea. Extending 70 miles in length and seven miles in width, the island possesses a heavily indented coastline fringed by reefs which constrict access to harbors. Shoals are present, and tidal currents vary in direction and strength. Adding to the chance for a mishap, depths of the water near the coastline are not consistent. In confined areas, coastal depths can range from less than 30 feet (five fathoms) to more than 240 feet (40 fathoms). Modern Sailing Directions give this warning: "Caution should be exercised when approaching Okinawa Jima. A landfall should not be attempted during the hours of darkness or poor visibility."[29] To get into a close-up position for a day of photographs, *Swordfish* would have to take risks.

There was yet another peril. Added to the extremes in depths off the Okinawan coast is a nearby geologic gash in the seabed known as the Ryuku Trench. Within 35 miles east of Okinawa, the depth reaches 6,000 feet (1,000 fathoms). As part of the earth's tectonic plate system, the crevices in the Trench descend even deeper further east, reaching down in numerous places to more than 18,000 feet (3,000 fathoms). The hull of a disabled submarine sinking into the trench area would succumb to the crushing sea pressure long before hitting bottom, and no submarine commander would want to test these depths.[30]

Initially, Navy planners in the Fifth Amphibious Force had asked that *Swordfish* disembark a landing party, which would reconnoiter the lengthy offshore reefs and beaches of Okinawa. However, Admiral Raymond A. Spruance, the task force commander, vetoed the idea. Although Spruance was cognizant of the value of on-site exploration, he believed the danger of compromising the location of the planned landings, via loss of the scout party or the submarine, outweighed the possible information gathered. Instead, Spruance ordered *Swordfish* to proceed only with visual reconnaissance and photographs. Prior to the recent invasion of Iwo Jima, the *Spearfish* had moved close in and had provided valuable photographs of Mount Suribachi which helped guide the Marines ashore. Spruance wanted *Swordfish* to perform a similar mission.[31]

Approaching a hostile island in shallow waters, *Swordfish* would have to expose its periscope for periods of time sufficient to allow photographers to take photographs of shore installations. The possibility of detection from land-based observers augmented the Japanese aircraft and coast patrols that scrutinized the approaches to the shoreline, especially by harbor facilities. Stealth, the strongest aspect of submarine operations, would be deliberately compromised in order to allow the two Navy photographers to capture on film those details not available from air photographs.

Even patrolling in the general vicinity of Nansei Shoto was dangerous. Japanese land-based aircraft were looking for the slender hulls of American submarines, and the Japanese determination to stave off invasion of the home islands stiffened as American forces came ever closer. The dual missions of the patrol, seeking targets along the Nansei Shoto chain and photographing Okinawa, would pose a challenge to Keats Montross, his crew, and the old *Swordfish*. Nevertheless, Montross had already demonstrated a willingness to take risks during his previous two war patrols, and he had been successful.

Departing Pearl Harbor, *Swordfish* proceeded to Midway Island, where she topped off her fuel tanks on 26 December. She left the same day for her patrol area. But there was a change in plans. On 2 January 1945, Montross received orders to stay clear of Nansei Shoto until a carrier-based air strike had ended. Instead, the submarine was directed to patrol in the general vicinity of latitude 30 degrees-00' North, longitude 132 degrees-00' East until she received new orders. *Swordfish* acknowledged the switch in orders on 3 January. This acknowledgment was the final message received directly from *Swordfish*.

The main purpose of the war patrol was to commence on 9 January, with the orders for *Swordfish* to carry out her special mission: photo reconnaissance of the Okinawa installations. Although there was no set time limit for performing this task, the estimated time for completion was seven days after arriving off Okinawa. The general timetable was for the boat to reach her assigned station on 11 January. After completing approximately seven days of reconnaissance, she was to proceed to the American-held island of Saipan. There was an alternative. If for some reason *Swordfish* was unable to transmit messages, she was directed to proceed to Midway after completion of her mission. At normal cruising speeds, *Swordfish* should have reached Midway on or about 29 January. There were several failed attempts to reach *Swordfish* by radio. When the boat became overdue at Midway, the ominous suspicion was that she was lost in enemy-controlled waters.[32]

The exact circumstances of the loss of *Swordfish* remain a mystery. However,

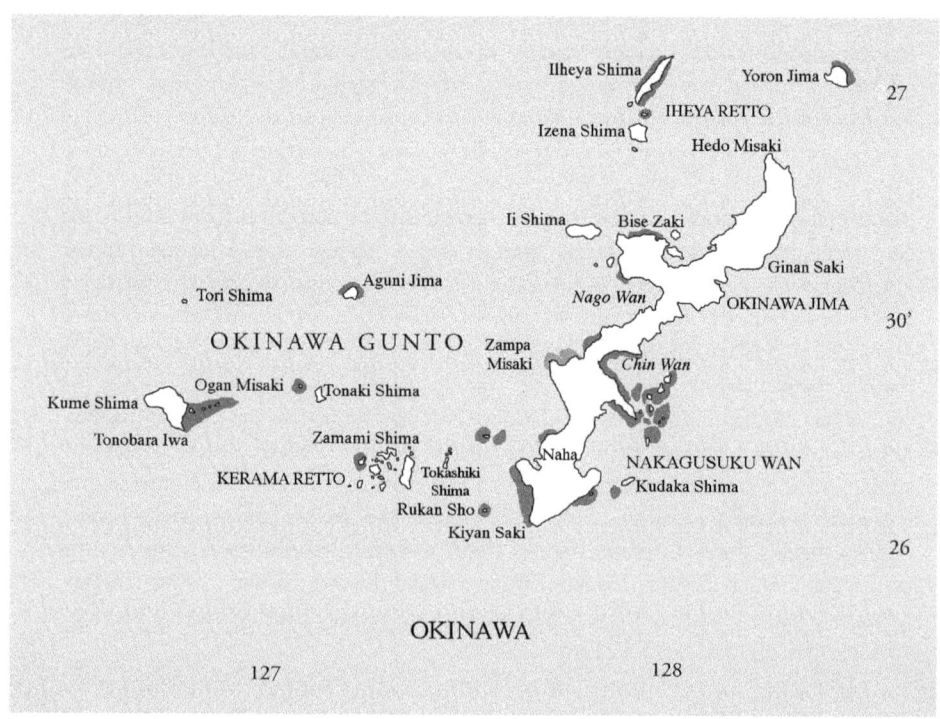

Okinawa. *Map by Eliz Alahverdian.*

7. The Thirteenth Patrol

"USS Swordfish SS-193," pen & ink and acrylic painting by Thomas Denton. *Courtesy of the artist, a submarine veteran.*

the log of the American submarine, USS *Kete*, provides additional facts that may be relevant. *Kete* was patrolling in the vicinity of Okinawa under the command of Commander Royal L. Rutter. He reported in his war patrol log, at 0508 on 12 January, that friendly radar interference had been picked up. He believed *Kete's* radar had contacted *Swordfish* in the area of Latitude 27–10' North, Longitude 128–40' East. Then, at 0949 Rutter wrote in his log, "Heard about 15 distant depth charges—Patrol craft were still around."[33] Lockwood recorded in his personal diary similar information, including the fact that the radar contact was probably *Swordfish* heading westward and that the depth charges were possibly in the vicinity of Latitude 27–20,' North, Longitude 128–20' East. He also noted that the Japanese were now setting their depth charges for 350 feet.[34] Whether or not the distant explosions were related to *Swordfish* is uncertain.

At this point, the historical evidence is supplanted by conjecture as to what caused the demise of *Swordfish*. A number of outcomes are plausible. It is possible that the explosions heard aboard *Kete* on 12 January were the result of a depth charge attack on *Swordfish*. The submarine was in the vicinity, and Japanese patrol craft and airplanes were looking for American ships. Previously, on 5 January, while serving as a convoy escort, Japanese coast defense ship number four (*Kaibokan 4*) commenced anti-submarine tactics. At 1705, a torpedo had slammed into the bow of *Shoto Maru* at Latitude 29–35' North, Longitude 141–07' East, while in a convoy out of Chichi-Jima, killing six crew members. By 1906, the ship had sunk. Meanwhile, the escort vessel counter-attacked. The Japanese warship dropped depth charges and claimed to have sunk *Swordfish*. However, if *Kete* had, indeed, picked up "friendly" radar interference from *Swordfish* on 12 January, as Rutter had suspected, then *Swordfish* was still operating subsequent to the attack of the convoy escort. Summoning the facts as they are presently known, there is no definite evidence that an actual attack on *Swordfish* had occurred either on 5 January or 12 January or that *Swordfish* had attacked *Shoto Maru*.[35]

An alternative possibility is that *Swordfish* hit a sea mine. As the war progressed and their fleet was destroyed, the Japanese employed sea mines with greater frequency to defend harbors and probable landing sites.[36] The Japanese had dispersed many mines off Okinawa, and *Swordfish* did not have mine-detection equipment aboard. *Kete* sighted an old Japanese MK6-type mine on 19 January. The crew expended 600 rounds from a 20 millimeter gun in order to pierce and sink it.[37] *Kete*, herself, was lost sometime after 20 March 1945.[38] Later in the war, submarines, such as USS *Spadefish* and USS *Tunny*, were equipped with detectors in the form of FM sonar. Whenever a mine came within proximity, a loud alarm bell would sound. The mine detectors were popularly known as "hell's bells."[39] As with *Kete*, *Swordfish* had entered mined waters without "hell's bells." Traveling submerged near mines would be a very chancy endeavor. *Swordfish* veteran Leymon Dennis believes that the boat probably struck a mine. He reasons that if a Japanese ship had successfully depth-charged the submarine, the Japanese would have gloated over the fact, such as via an announcement by Tokyo Rose. The lack of any announcement or definitive entry in Japanese records leads him to conclude that the culprit was a mine.[40] An alternative explanation for the boat's loss is put forward by another *Swordfish* veteran, Robert E. Dyer. Although he has no evidence, Dyer theorizes that a kamikaze aircraft may have swooped down low and, before the submarine's crew could react, the plane may have crashed into the boat.[41] It is more likely that the Japanese would have sent an aircraft to attack *Swordfish* with bombs and depth charges.

Contributing factors for *Swordfish*'s loss may have resided within the submarine. As *Swordfish* veteran Lloyd Henry Faye points out, the crew was full of newcomers who would not be familiar with the peculiarities of the grand old boat. It took time to sense when operations were not running normal, and in emergency situations, familiarity with the boat was vital. Keats Montross, relatively new to *Swordfish* himself, may not have succeeded with his usual daring, especially while dependent upon a crew populated with so many newcomers. Faye believes the crew's inexperience was a fundamental factor in the boat's demise.[42]

Faye, a motor machinist's mate, also asserts that the condition of *Swordfish* must be considered. He believes the boat was worn out.[43] True, it had been extensively overhauled with over 79 repairs. However, as with any mechanical work, there lurked the possibility that all was not done correctly, no matter how thorough the quality control. It should be recalled that Karl Hensel discovered careless workmanship from the previous rehabilitation during the tenth patrol. The discovery of unaccounted-for damage to the reduction gear was an added factor. The reduction gear problem was addressed before departure, but was there any assurance that its noise level would not rise during operations? One or more of these factors may have contributed trouble during the patrol.

With the passage of time, *Swordfish's* silence raised anxiety. On 24 January 1945, Admiral Lockwood wrote, "I am worried about *Swordfish*." The admiral also commented that USS *Tunny* had FM sonar, capable of detecting small objects, such as mines, in proximity to the submarine. He added, "She is our best bet to take over *Swordfish* job."[44] Two days later, Lockwood expressed his concerns in a letter to Captain Frank C. Watkins in the Office of the Chief of Naval Operations. Lockwood noted that while performing photo reconnaissance at Okinawa, *Swordfish* had not answered any calls. He added that the submarine *Tinosa* had gone into Okinawan waters to survey for mines using FM sonar, and she detected a string of them southwest of Okinawa, but reported the rest of the coast clear. Lockwood observed, "Whether a mine got *Swordfish* or not of course we don't know … such is possibly the case. However, other forms of A/S [anti-submarine warfare] are also active there, especially radar planes." In the same letter to Watkins, Charles Lockwood vented his frustrations. He wrote: "Can we get someone to get the lead out of their pants and really work on some project which will give us a mine detector? …We are losing too many ships to view calmly the lack of these defensive gadgets which we have tried so long to obtain." Lockwood concluded with an expression of his inner feelings: "Sorry my last two letters have been sobs, but sometimes I get a bit discouraged."[45]

In March, *Tunny* provided additional evidence of the prevalence of mines in the waters off Okinawa, while carrying out the mission of the photo reconnaissance originally assigned to *Swordfish*. On 14 March, *Tunny's* FM sonar detected 230 mines while patrolling at a depth of 150 feet.[46] Without the benefit of FM sonar, *Swordfish* would not have been so fortunate.

Whatever the reasons for *Swordfish's* demise, on 15 February 1945, Admiral Lockwood reluctantly designated her as lost. *Swordfish* had left an impressive record of accomplishment. At the time, Admiral Lockwood gave *Swordfish* credit for sinking 115,580 tons of Japanese shipping and damaging 47,706 additional tons of enemy shipping.[47] The JANAC board subsequently reduced the total tonnage sunk by *Swordfish* to 47,928 tons, and JANAC allowed no credit for damaged tonnage.[48] Admiral Chester W. Nimitz, Commander in Chief of the United States Pacific Fleet, summed up the record of the submarine in his endorsement to Admiral Lockwood's action report: "Forwarded, with profound regret. Starting with the first days of the war *Swordfish* has turned in a splendid record. The Pacific Fleet has lost a potent fighting ship."[49]

The Telegram

Between 1 and 5 March, the Navy Department sent to the next of kin the telegram most dreaded by a submariner's family, stating that their loved one was overdue in returning from sea, and the presumption was that he was lost. Because the actual date of the loss was unknown, for administrative purposes the Navy set the date of 29 January 1945. Notices went out literally across the nation. They were sent to families in 33 states and the District of Columbia. A more formal letter was sent to the families in May 1945. The Navy had a special department dedicated to the sad task of notifying the next of kin concerning the loss of a relative. Indeed, before *Swordfish* embarked on the 13th patrol, on 22 December 1944, the Navy had on hand a listing of everyone who sailed and the names and addresses of their next of kin.[50]

Relatives and friends of the missing officers and crew gradually came to the reluctant realization that their servicemen were truly not coming back to port. Some family members held out hope for an eventual return. Dorothy Montross, wife of the skipper, applied to the Navy for the names of the relatives of the missing officers and crew. At first, the Navy was reluctant to divulge private information but promised to supply the list at a later time, which it did.[51] Undaunted by the months of no news, in June 1945, Mrs. Montross corresponded with the next of kin of her husband's crew. She expressed her sympathy for their common sorrow and uncertainty. She then wrote that she could not give up hope for their return. Mrs. Montross noted that some submariners had become prisoners of the Japanese, and reports appeared many months after they were missing. She noted that there had been extraordinary escapes from damaged submarines. Alluding to the coming end of the war in the Pacific, she expressed her hope that good news might come. She added that the Navy Department would not provide any details, but if she received more details, she would write again.[52]

Unfortunately, with the passage of time even the remote possibility of a return of the crew of *Swordfish* diminished. On 17 January 1946, the Navy drew up a more definitive statement regarding the deaths of the crewmen, which was the basis for subsequent letters to the relatives.[53] No longer bound by the concern for secrecy due to the war's end, on 31 January 1946, a Navy Department letter was sent to the next of kin, such as Michael Billy's sister. The letter cited the meager facts known about the loss of *Swordfish*. Then the letter stated:

> In view of the length of time that has now elapsed since your brother was reported to be missing and because there have been no official nor unconfirmed reports that any of the personnel of the vessel survived or were taken prisoner of war, I am reluctantly forced to the conclusion that your brother is deceased.[54]

The letter closed with condolences. Subsequently, the Navy notified the families that each crew member was awarded the Purple Heart posthumously.[55] Families were left with memories and photographs to fill the void.[56] In the case of Keats Montross, he left behind his wife, Dorothy MacMurray Montross, and a baby daughter, Ridgley R. Montross, who had been born in 1943. Subsequently, Dorothy Montross married another Navy officer, Captain Eugene C. Rider, who helped raise young Ridgley.[57]

For some of the individuals concerned, there was no letter of notification. Because Dorothy Heath was not a family member, her realization of *Swordfish's* loss was delayed. Shortly after New Year's 1945, one of her letters to her friend aboard *Swordfish*, Fred Cauley, was returned. Knowing that the conditions of war often interrupted communication with the war fronts, she continued to write with the expectation that eventually he would reply. Later, a mail handler in Hawaii came across her pin-up photos and advised her that *Swordfish* was "overdue." The crew never received Heath's pin-up shots, and Dorothy Heath never had the pleasure of meeting Fred Cauley or his shipmates. Heath described her initial reaction to the crew's loss as one of disbelief at such a tragedy, then deep sorrow.[58] As the weeks passed, a flood of new letters began to arrive from family members of the missing crew, including the mother of Fred Cauley. Dorothy Heath wrote to the various family members, and later in 1945 she visited Fred Cauley's mom. By then, the Navy had changed the official status of *Swordfish* to "presumed lost." As time passed, the correspondence with family members diminished. Heath gradually stepped out of the spotlight, resuming her role of private citizen and marrying a Navy serviceman. Public memory of Dorothy Heath had faded along with that of *Swordfish*.[59]

Circumstances were particularly difficult for *Swordfish* crewmen who had rotated off before the final patrol. Although they could find relief in the knowledge that they had stepped out of harm's way, many of them had close friends aboard the boat. In one instance, the toss of a coin determined who would remain on *Swordfish*. After the tenth patrol, Quartermaster 1st Class Leymon Dennis and Quartermaster 1st Class William Russell were both eligible to become chief of the boat, but only one quartermaster could remain. Dennis lost the toss of the coin and moved on to new construction. Russell stayed on *Swordfish* for patrols 11, 12 and 13.[60]

One *Swordfish* veteran, Arthur Myers, expressed his grief in December 1949 by composing a poem in memory of his lost shipmates. The poem is entitled "I'll Never Forget," and the last two stanzas of the poem are as follows:

> Some were noisy, some were quiet
> Some were loud and course and rough
> Some just needed a dare to try it
> They never learned the word "enough"
>
> There are *many* of my shipmates
> Who I'll never see again
> But to God I'm giving thanks
> For having known those glorious men.

Myers was aboard *Swordfish* for the ninth and tenth patrols.[61]

It was not unusual for a submarine crewman to feel remorse that he had survived while other members of the crew had perished. Some submarine veterans from World War II requested a U.S. Navy burial at sea so they can rejoin their lost comrades. An example of such sentiments was expressed by a former crew member of *Swordfish*, Seaman Robert Frank Harris, who voiced to the author his intention to join his lost shipmates by arranging, after his death and cremation, for the scattering of his ashes at sea.[62] In addition, at meetings of the Submarine Veterans of World War II, there is a ceremonial tolling of the bells in which the names of the 52 lost submarines, including *Swordfish*, are read aloud with solemnity.

In a rather unique manner, William Warren called notice to the loss of *Swordfish*. Warren's father, William Rufus Warren, related to his son his experiences aboard *Swordfish*. The elder William was not assigned to *Swordfish* for her 13th patrol, but he remembered with deep regret his fellow shipmates who never returned. He kindled in his son a desire to remember the lost crewmen. William Warren, the son, asked himself, "How about commemorating those young guys on the *Swordfish* who never got a chance to live the life that they were fighting for?"[63]

USS *Swordfish* Memorial, St. Paul, Minnesota. *U.S. Naval History & Heritage Command.*

7. The Thirteenth Patrol

A scholarship honoring the lost crewmen of *Swordfish* germinated as the answer to this question. William Warren, Jr., funded the scholarship at his *alma mater*, the University of Mississippi. The *Swordfish* memorial scholarship was awarded to a student in 2006.

Commemorating the loss of *Swordfish* and her crew after the war became the special mission of the Viking Squadron (chapter) of the Submarine Veterans of World War II in Minnesota. On Sunday, 13 June 1965, the Viking Squadron, along with other veterans groups, as well as Navy units and family members connected to the lost men of the boat, participated in dedicating a memorial to the USS *Swordfish*. The memorial consisted of a World War II torpedo and memorial plaques that are currently on display in Como Park in St. Paul, Minnesota. The plaques provide a brief history of *Swordfish*, a list of the names of her lost officers and crew, and a listing of the other 51 U.S. submarines lost during the war.[64] The submarine veterans are determined to keep alive the memory of their lost shipmates and boats.

Following an honorable tradition of christening new ships with the names of predecessors, the U.S. Navy forged a link with the past by naming a new

USS *Swordfish*, stern view, trials in San Francisco Bay, 13 June 1943. *National Archives, College Park.*

nuclear-powered submarine, *Swordfish* (SSN-579). Adding to the link with the past, Keats Montross's widow, Dorothy Montross, now Mrs. Eugene C. Rider, christened the new *Swordfish* on 27 August 1957. Ridgely R. Montross, the daughter of Keats and Dorothy Montross, also attended the ceremony. Following her commissioning in 1958, *Swordfish* went to the Pacific, and in January 1960 she patrolled the western Pacific. She became the first American nuclear submarine to enter those waters. During her tours of duty in the Pacific, the nuclear *Swordfish* was involved in Cold War espionage activities, such as tracking the movements of Soviet submarines and listening to Russian military communications. In recognition of her service, the Navy awarded the nuclear *Swordfish* several Navy Unit Commendations. Finally, on 2 June 1989, *Swordfish* was decommissioned, ending the Navy's use of "*Swordfish*" as the name for a submarine.[65]

Today, the fate of the World War II submarine, *Swordfish* (SS-193), remains a mystery. No one can say for sure how the submarine met her end. It is not known whether she sank in combat with an enemy warship, because of a brush with a sea mine, or as victim of some other disaster. Her whereabouts is uncertain, but advances in undersea exploration and technology may one day unlock the riddle of *Swordfish*. Since 2007, six lost World War II submarines have been found. They are USS *Flier*, USS *Grunion*, USS *Logarto*, USS *Perch*, USS *Wahoo* and USS *S-28*.[66] Perhaps one day the location of *Swordfish* will be discovered. When she is found, clues as to why she sank may come to light. In the meantime, the sea holds onto *Swordfish*, and the 89 men aboard must continue their Eternal Patrol.

Appendix A: USS *Swordfish*

Hull SS-193 (initially designated S-12)
Built at: Mare Island Naval Shipyard
Hull laid: 27 October 1937
Launched: 1 April 1939
Delivered: 22 July 1939
1st Commanding Officer: Lt. Chester Carl Smith
Sponsor: Miss Louise Shaw Hepburn
Sargo Class Fleet Submarine
Length: 310 feet, 1 inch
Beam: 26 feet, 10 inches
Displacement: Standard: 1450 tons
              Submerged: 2350 tons
Design Speed: Surface: 20 knots
              Submerged: 8.75 knots
Complement: 5 officers, 50 men
Armament: One three-inch/50 caliber deck gun
        Two .50 caliber machine guns (replaced with two 20mm machine guns prior to 12th patrol)
        Two .30 caliber machine guns
        Eight 21-inch Triple torpedo tubes
Propulsion: Diesel Electric Drive
        Four diesel engines: General Motors (Winton) Model 16–248 diesel engines 16 cylinders—"V" type, 8½" diameter, 10½" stroke, 2 cycles\1,535 B.H.P. at 750 r.p.m.
    (NOTE: B.H.P = Brake Horse Power)
        Two auxiliary General Motors 4 cycle engines, model 241
        Two main General Electric generators
        Two auxiliary generators, 258 KW
    Four main General Electric motors, 685 HP
Surface cruising range: 11,000 miles

Commanders

    Lt. Chester Carl Smith
    LCDR Albert Collins Burrows

LCDR Jack Hayden Lewis
LCDR Frank Mahlon Parker
LCDR Frank Lloyd Barrows
CAPT Karl Goldsmith Hensel
LCDR Keats Edmund Montross

Note: The Navy promoted Chester C. Smith to LCDR while he was commanding the *Swordfish*. Similarly, the Navy promoted Keats Montross to CDR while he commanded the submarine.

Swordfish Decorations

1 star, PHILIPPINE ISLAND OPERATION: 8–27 Dec 1941; 16 Jan—9 Mar 1942
1 star, GUADALCANAL (THIRD SAVO): 5 Nov—12 Nov 1942
1 star, CAPTURE AND DEFENSE OF GUADALCANAL: 9 Jan—8 Feb 1943
1 star, MARIANAS OPERATIONS
    2nd Bonins Raid: 24 June 1944
SUBMARINE WAR PATROLS, PACIFIC:
1 star, 15 May—4 Jul 1942
1 star, 29 Jul—20 Sep 1943
1 star, 9 Dec 1943–7 Feb 1944
1 star, 13 Mar—29 Apr 1944
American Defense Service Medal with Fleet Clasp: 8 Sep 1939–7 Dec 1941
Philippine Defense Ribbon—8–27 Dec 1941; 16 Jan—9 Mar 1942
Philippine Republic Presidential Unit Citation Badge: 8–27 Dec 1941; 16 Jan–9 Mar 1942

Data Sources

Alden, *The Fleet Submarine in the U.S. Navy: a Design and Construction History*.
Friedman, *U.S. Submarines Through 1945: an Illustrated Design History*.
Jane's Fighting Ships, 1941.
USS *Swordfish*. War Patrol Reports 1–12. Naval Historical Center.
Winton-Diesel Engine Model 16-248: Instructions for the Care and Operation of the Engine.

Appendix B: USS *Swordfish* (SS-193) Crew List of the Thirteenth Patrol

Abrahamson, Arthur—CCS
Arold, Roy G.—MoMM2
Baeckler, Donald—PhoM3
Baker, Gilbert S.—MoMM1
Basta, Joseph J.—RM1
Bates, Mack—F1
Baughman, Daniel S., Jr.LCDR
Benbennick, Claude J.—S1
Billy, Michael—MoMM2
Blanchard, Joseph R.L.—RM3
Bleasdell, Le Roy J.—MoMM2
Bogdan, Wesley C.—MoMM2
Braley, Andrew E.—MoMM3
Brown, Robert J.—SC1
Cauley, Fred M., Jr.—CRT
Clark, Allen D.—EM2
Connors, Timothy J.—TM3
Cox, Marshall E., Jr.—RM3
Daly, Robert F.—LT
Davis, Herman W.—EM2
Delladonna, J.V.—LT
Dillon, William—TM2
Draga, Gordon K.—S1
Duncan, Loris H.—EM2
Dunton, Emory W., Sr.—MoMM1
Echols, Leonard O.—Bkr3
Edwards, George V.—TM2
Emmingham, Robert L.—EM3
Fausset, Eugene R.—GM3
Feiss, Kenneth F.—S1
Forsythe, Eugene J.—TM1
Fowler, John G.—S1
Funk, Nick—EM1

Galley, Emery A., Jr.—SM2
Gambrell, Dee E., Jr.—QM2
Garza, Eleazar—MoMM3
Geraghty, Bernard J., Jr.—S1
Gilfillan, Howard M.—MoMM2
Graf, John V.—MoMM1
Graham, George P.—RM3
Grandy, William P.—StM1
Hafter, Ralph L.—EM1
Hall, Charles E.—CEM
Haserodt, Ralph W.—MoMM1
Haskins, Winslow C.—EM3
Haynes, Jack E.—TM3
Holland, Ray—MoMM2
Hoopes, R.D., Jr.—LT
Hrynko, Fred A.—MoMM3
Janes, Robert L.—LTJG
Johnson, Robert E.—MoMM3
Johnson, Stephen J.—PhoM3
Kelly, John R.—F1
Kirk, Vernon—St3
Kohler, William E.—MoMM3
Kremer, Richard B.—MM2
Kroll, Roy E.—TM3
Lauderdale, Hollie O.—F1
Lindsay, Douglas C.—MoMM3
Looney, Gerald A.—CY
Lo Presti, Russell—S1
Madden, John J., Jr.—TM3
McCaffrey, Morriss F.—RT3
Mayfield, James M.—EM2
Marvin, Paul—ENS
Meacham, William T., Jr.—FC2

Appendix B: USS *Swordfish* (SS-193) Crew List

Montross, Keats E.—CDR-CO
Pence, Kenneth E.—GM2
Petty, Fremont—BM2
Plourd, Gordon R.—PhM1
Pollard, Claude L.—ENS
Preston, Earl W., Jr.—S1
Pye, John B.—LCDR-XO
Robinson, Harry N., Jr.—MoMM3
Russell, William E.—CQM
Schwendener, K.D.—LT
Siskaninetz, William—Cox
Skeldon, James A.—QM3
Slater, Clifford F.—CMoMM
Soffes, Mike—MoMM2
Spencer, Frank H., Jr.—EM3
Statton, Wally G.—MoMM1
Stone, Harold A.—TM2
Tarbox, Fred A.—EM3
Taylor, James F.—S1
Van Horn, Elwood K.—TM3
Wagner, Arnold J.—TM2
William, Thurman A.—TM1
Wren, Joseph E.—EM3

Source: U.S. Naval History Division, *United States Submarine Losses: World War II* (Washington, D.C.: U.S. Naval History Division, 1963), 134.

Appendix C: USS *Swordfish*— Ships Sunk or Damaged

Sources of Data:
Alden, John D. and Craig R. McDonald, *United States and Allied Submarine Successes in the Pacific and Far East During World War II,* 4th edition, 2009.
Joint Army-Navy Assessment Committee, *Japanese Naval and Merchant Shipping Losses During World War II by All Causes,* 1947.
USS *Swordfish,* War Patrol Reports Nos. 1 to 12, 1941–1944.

Appendix C: USS *Swordfish*—Ships Sunk or Damaged

War Patrol No. 1

Date	Name	Vessel Type	Tonnage	Location	WPR Claim	Janac Assessment	Alden Assessment
9-Dec-41	unidentified	cargo	est. 3900	14-30N, 119-00E	sunk	0	probably no hit/no damage
14-Dec-41	unidentified	cargo	est. 9200	18-05N, 109-18E	sunk	0	probably no hit/no damage
14-Dec-41	KASHI MARU	cargo	8407	18-08N, 109-22E	sunk	0	confirmed damaged
16-Dec-41	ATSUTASAN MARU	cargo	8662	18-06N, 109-44E	sunk	sunk	confirmed sunk

War Patrol No. 2

Date	Name	Vessel Type	Tonnage	Location	WPR Claim	Janac Assessment	Alden Assessment
24-Jan-42	MYOKEN MARU	gunboat	4124	01-25N, 126-10E	sunk	sunk	confirmed sunk
24-Jan-42	KATSURAGI MARU (was in Ambon force 30 Jan., STURGEON sank it Oct. 42)	converted cargo	8033	01-25N, 126-10E	sunk	0	probably no hit/no damage
14-Feb-42	AMAGISAN MARU (sunk at Truk)	cargo	7620	06-45N, 126-54E	sunk	0	damaged
19-Feb-42	unidentified	tanker	est. 3100	14-32N, 12-08E	sunk	0	probably no hit/no damage

War Patrol No. 3

—no damage—

War Patrol No. 4

Date	Name	Vessel Type	Tonnage	Location	WPR Claim	Janac Assessment	Alden Assessment
23-May-42	unidentified	cargo	est. 6500	09-21S, 118-34E	damaged	0	possible light damage

Appendix C: USS Swordfish—Ships Sunk or Damaged

Date	Name	Vessel Type	Tonnage	Location	WPR Claim	Janac Assessment	Alden Assessment
29-May-42	TATSUFUKU MARU	cargo	1946	07-33N, 116-18E	sunk	sunk	sunk, joint credit
NOTE: JANAC gave full credit for sinking an unknown maru, 29 May, est. 1900 tons. Alden gave joint credit with SEAL for sinking TATSUFUKU MARU, 29 May.							
6-Jun-42	unidentified	cargo	est. 6500	05-00N, 104-00E	damaged	0	probably no hit/no damage
12-Jun-42	BURMA MARU	cargo	4582	10-08N, 102-34E	sunk	sunk	Sunk

War Patrol No. 5
—no damage—

War Patrol No. 6

Date	Name	Vessel Type	Tonnage	Location	WPR Claim	Janac Assessment	Alden Assessment
13-Nov-42	unidentified	cargo	est. 6300	05-27S, 152-29E	damaged	0	probably no hit/no damage
17-Nov-42	unidentified	tanker	est. 4400	05-00S, 152-21E	sunk	0	probably no hit/no damage

War Patrol No. 7

Date	Name	Vessel Type	Tonnage	Location	WPR Claim	Janac Assessment	Alden Assessment
19-Jan-43	MYOHO MARU	cargo	4122	05-25S, 156-00E	sunk	sunk	Sunk

War Patrol No. 8

Date	Name	Vessel Type	Tonnage	Location	WPR Claim	Janac Assessment	Alden Assessment
22-Aug-43	NISHIYAMA MARU	transport	3016	02-40N, 137-10E	damaged	sunk	sunk
22-Aug-43	unidentified	transport	est. 8500	02-40N, 137-10E	damaged	0	probably no hit/no damage
5-Sep-43	TENKAI MARU	passenger cargo	3203	01-10N, 142-01E	sunk	sunk	Sunk

Appendix C: USS *Swordfish*—Ships Sunk or Damaged

War Patrol No. 9
—no damage—

War Patrol No. 10

Date	Name	Vessel Type	Tonnage	Location	WPR Claim	Janac Assessment	Alden Assessment
14-Jan-44	YAMAKUNI MARU	cargo	6921	33-16N, 139-30E	damaged	sunk	sunk
14-Jan-44	YAMABIKO MARU	repair ship	6799	33-17N, 139-40E	0	0	sunk, joint credit

NOTE: the YAMAKUNI MARU was towing the bow half of the YAMABIKO MARU, previously hit by the USS STEELHEAD, 10 Jan 44

| 16-Jan-44 | DELHI MARU | Q-ship | 2182 | 34-04N, 139-56E | sunk | sunk | sunk |
| 27-Jan-44 | KASAGI MARU | gunboat | 3140 | 33-31N, 139-36E | sunk | sunk | Sunk |

War Patrol No. 11

Date	Name	Vessel Type	Tonnage	Location	WPR Claim	Janac Assessment	Alden Assessment
5-Apr-44	unidentified	cargo	est. 5000	20-23N, 141-22E	damaged	0	probably no hit/no damage
5-Apr-44	unidentified (2nd ship)	cargo	est. 5000	20-23N, 141-22E	damaged	0	probably no hit/no damage

War Patrol No. 12

Date	Name	Vessel Type	Tonnage	Location	WPR Claim	Janac Assessment	Alden Assessment
9-Jun-44	MATSUKAZE	destroyer	1270	26-59N, 143-13E	sunk	sunk	sunk
15-Jun-44	KANSEISHI MARU	cargo	4804	29-30N, 141-11E	sunk	sunk	sunk

Appendix C: USS Swordfish—Ships Sunk or Damaged

Date	Name	Vessel Type	Tonnage	Location	WPR Claim	Janac Assessment	Alden Assessment
15-Jun-44	TOYOKAWA MARU	cargo	5123	29-30N, 141-11E	0	0	damaged
	NOTE: possible collision with another ship in convoy while evading torpedo.						
26-Jun-44	unidentified	trawler	est. 400	27-25N, 141-55E	damaged	0	repeated attack on 27 Jun 44
27-Jun-44	HOKURYU MARU #10	trawler	148	27-10N, 141-57E	sunk	0	sunk
30-Jun-44	CHIYODA MARU #8	trawler	127	28-20N, 153-24E	sunk	0	Sunk

War Patrol No. 13

Date	Name	Vessel Type	Tonnage	Location	WPR Claim	Janac Assessment	Alden Assessment
5-Jan-45	SHOTO MARU	cargo	572	29-35N, 141-07E			sunk

NOTE: at about 1705 on 5 Jan, the SHOTO MARU was hit in bow by a torpedo, and it sank by 1906. Six were killed. Coastal Defense Ship No. 4 claimed sinking a submarine in a counterattack. SWORDFISH ordered to Okinawa on 9 January and USS KETE received possible radar contact presumably with the SWORDFISH on 12 January.

TOTAL SHIPS SUNK OR DAMAGED: 29 | 12 | 18 + 2 joint credit

Appendix D: U.S. Submarines SS 188–193—Compartments and Tanks

U.S. Submarines SS 188–193, Compartments and Tanks (National Archives)

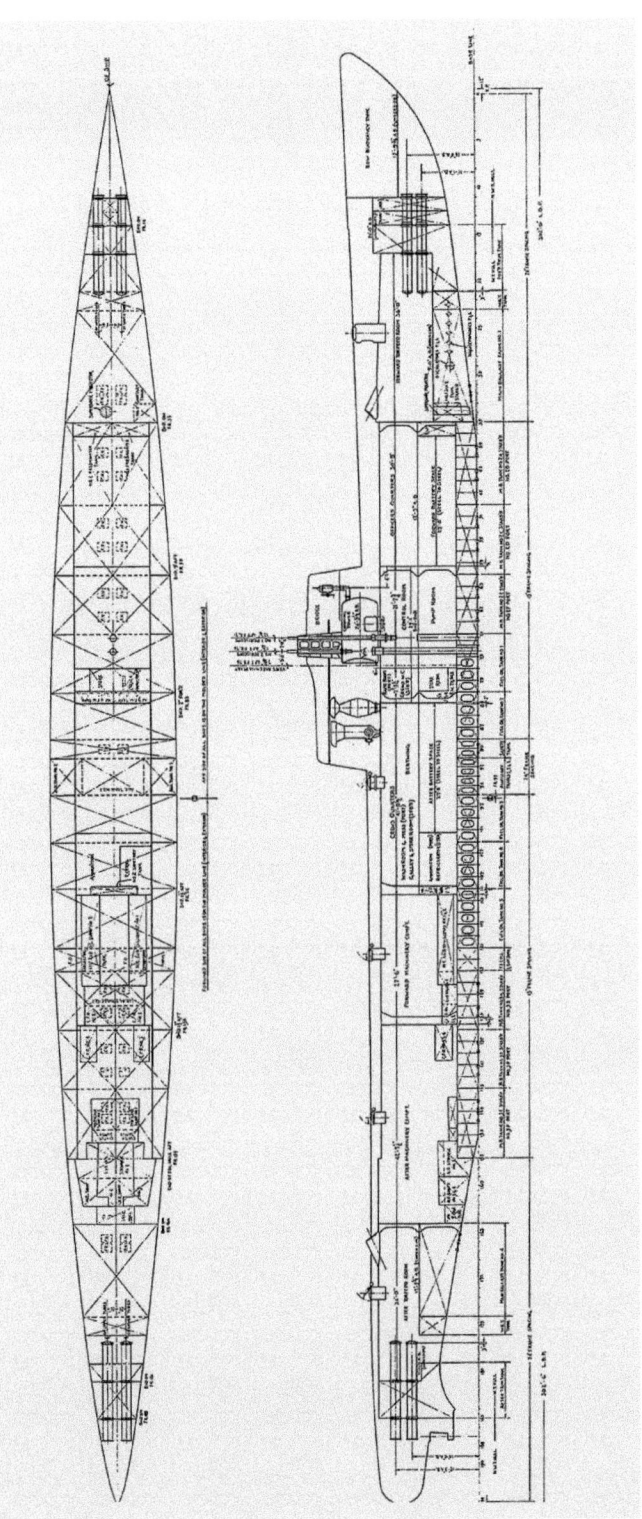

Glossary

Abaft—a term always used relative to another part of the ship and which indicates the direction toward the stern, e.g., "abaft the wheel house" designates a position between the wheel house and the stern.

Abaft the Beam—Behind a horizontal line drawn through the middle of a ship at right angles to the keel.

AK—cargo vessel.

Amidships—the middle part of a vessel, as measured between stem and stern in the fore and aft direction or on the centerline of a vessel in the athwartships direction. Same as midships.

Angle on the Bow—the angle formed by a target ship's direction of travel and the line of sight of that ship from a viewing vessel.

Arm—to make a weapon ready to fire or explode.

Ashcan—depth charge.

Bathythermograph—an instrument which records sea temperature at a submarine's depth. A bathythermograph can indicate changes in gradient capable of distorting or reflecting echo ranging.

Beam—width of a vessel.

Bearing—direction in which an object lies from an observer.

Big Bertha—a heavy artillery piece or a general reference to any heavy explosive ordnance. The term originally referred to an extra-heavy German howitzer in World War I.

Blow—emptying a tank by forcing air into it and, thereby, forcing water out.

Broach—an involuntary or unexpected rise to the surface.

Chidori—a class of Japanese vessels employed in anti-submarine warfare and frequently employed for convoy protection.

CO—Commanding Officer.

Composite Structure—a vessel in which the upper or freeboard deck is covered from stem to stern by a continuous superstructure deck.

COMSUBLANT—Commander Submarine Force, U.S. Atlantic Fleet.

Glossary

COMSUBPAC—Commander, Submarine Force, U.S. Pacific Fleet.

Conning Tower—a submerged control station in a submarine, which in World War II enabled higher extension of the periscope.

Crash Dive—an emergency or quickly executed dive.

DD—Navy designation for a destroyer.

Density Layer—a layer of seawater characterized by a thick density and useful in thwarting enemy anti-submarine detection devices.

Fairwater—(1) a conical cap covering the after side of the hole of a propeller which takes the end of the tail shaft; (2) any casting or plate fastened to a ship's hull designed to maintain a smooth, streamlined flow of water.

Fathom—a measure of length equal to six feet and used in gauging the depth of water by soundings.

"Fish"—torpedo.

Flank Speed—highest possible speed.

Forecastle—a short superstructure located over the bow. In merchant ships, the foremast cabin was used as crew accommodations.

Goal Post—a type of mast and cargo-handling apparatus whose main components consist of two vertical steel posts and a transverse girder which connects the upper ends of the two posts. A topmast is often placed amidships on the transverse girder.

Gyro—any rapid spinning device sufficient to establish stability of motion.

Gyro Angle—the angle set into each torpedo's gyro by the TDC so its steering mechanism will keep the torpedo on course to hit the point of aim, the target.

Hatch Skirt—the side plate of a ship hatch.

Head Sea—a sea in which the waves run counter to a ship's direction or course.

Hot Bunk—AKA Hot Rack—a scheduled rotation of bunk use by two or more crew members.

In Ballast—a ship carrying extra ballast in the form of rocks or water in special tanks and designed to prevent the ship from floating too high in the water, usually because it is empty of cargo.

JANAC—Joint Army-Navy Assessment Committee.

Jury Rig—a makeshift or temporary arrangement of rigging of equipment usually associated with expedient measures in time of emergency or disabled equipment.

Kaibokan—coast defense ship (Japanese term).

Keel—the backbone of a vessel, consisting of the main center-line structural member which runs fore and aft the bottom of a ship.

King Post—a short, heavy mast which supports a boom.

Lay To—stop the motion of a vessel and cause her to become stationary.

Glossary

List—the leaning or inclination of a vessel, which is contrary to being upright.

Maru—a Japanese merchant ship (Japanese term). Originally the word was derived from a Chinese character meaning circle or circular in shape. The term usually appears as a suffix to the proper name of a Japanese ship.

Midships—the middle, same as amidships.

Momsen Lung—an underwater breathing device employed by submariners as emergency escape gear.

Periscope Depth—the depth under the surface that a submarine maintains while maximizing the use of a periscope, but still remaining concealed.

Periscope Shears—the supporting structure for the periscope which projects from the top of the conning tower.

Ping—the sending (transmission) of an electronic pulse signal of an echo-ranging indicator (associated with sonar).

Pip (Blip)—a dot or some other indication on a radar screen representing a target, via a radar return (echo) from the target.

Plan Position Indicator (PPI)—a radar screen that displayed a map-like image, with the center of the screen indicating the position of the ship (boat) and any targets represented by a small dot known as a "pip."

Plank Owner—a member of the crew at the time of the ship's commissioning.

Poop Deck—a short, raised deck located in the stern of a ship.

"Pull the Plug"—an expression indicating the act of diving.

Rack—bunk.

Rake—the overhang of a vessel forward or aft.

Reduction Gear—special gears which transferred the power of the high-speed motors to the propeller shaft.

Relative Bearing—a direction in relation to the fore-and-aft line of a vessel.

S—Designates the first class of submarines with a significant number built to U.S. Navy designs.

SD Radar—radar designed for air searching (aircraft detection).

SJ Radar—radar especially designed for surface searches.

Soundhead—a container for a transmitting device and listening hydrophones.

Spread—a multiple salvo of torpedoes calculated to diverge in tracks in order to ensure a hit.

SS—Submarine—U.S. Navy symbol.

SSN—Submarine, Nuclear Powered—U.S. Navy symbol.

Glossary

Stick (of Bombs)—a quick succession of bombs released at pre-determined intervals from an aircraft.

Strike—remove torpedoes from storage.

TDC—Torpedo Data Computer—an early shipboard computer that sets the track that a torpedo must follow in order to hit a moving target. The TDC can program the torpedo to alter directions after leaving the submarine while heading for the target.

Thermocline—an ocean layer of quickly changing temperature while at a small change in depth. Submariners depended upon thermocline variations to fend off detection.

Tin Can—destroyer (Navy ship).

Tin Fish—torpedo.

Trim—the condition of a ship regarding her longitudinal position in the water, that is, the difference between the draft forward and aft.

Track—the path or course a target is expected to follow, as determined by the sequential changes in the target's position.

Ultra—short for Ultra Secret, a covert U.S. communications system based upon decoded enemy messages.

Well Deck—the open deck (main deck) running between the forecastle and the bridge-house.

Yaw—inability to hold a steady course, usually because of wind or sea conditions.

Zig-Zag—the calculated changing of a ship's course by short turns in alternate directions as an effort to prevent an enemy vessel from determining the ship's bearings in preparation for an attack. An evasive maneuver.

Note Abbreviations

AHC—American Heritage Center

JANAC—Joint Army-Navy Assessment Committee

LC—Library of Congress

MD—Manuscript Division

NARA—National Archives and Records Administration, College Park

NARA San Bruno—National Archives and Records Administration, Pacific Region, San Bruno

NHHC—Naval History and Heritage Command

NPRC—National Personnel Records Center

RG—Record Group

WPR—War Patrol Report

Chapter Notes

Preface

1. Randy Papadopoulos, "Between Fleet Scouts & Commerce Raiders: Submarine Warfare Theories and Doctrines in the German and U.S. Navies, 1935–1945," *Undersea Warfare* 7, no. 4 (Summer 2005): 28–33; Clark G. Reynolds, *Command of the Sea: The History and Strategy of Maritime Empires* (New York: Morrow, 1974), 521, 525, 542. For a discussion of the history of the strategy of the *guerre de course*, see Theodore Ropp, "Continental Doctrines of Sea Power," *Makers of Modern Strategy: Military Thought from Machiavelli to Hitler*, edited by Edward Mead Earle. (Princeton, NJ: Princeton University Press, 1953, 1971), 446–456. For a comprehensive study of the U.S. Navy's Pacific war plans prior to World War II, see Edward S. Miller, *War Plan Orange: The U.S. Strategy to Defeat Japan, 1897–1945* (Annapolis, MD: Naval Institute Press, 1991).

2. Mark P. Parillo, *The Japanese Merchant Marine in World War II* (Annapolis, MD: Naval Institute Press, 1993), 207, 224; Clay Blair, Jr., *Silent Victory: The U.S. Submarine War Against Japan* (Philadelphia: Lippincott, 1975), 17, 879. See also *Triumph in the Pacific: The Navy's Struggle Against Japan*, edited by E. B. Potter and Chester W. Nimitz (Englewood Cliffs, NJ: Prentice-Hall, 1963), 133, 153.

3. Three comprehensive works that describe episodes in the history of *Swordfish* in World War II are: Clay Blair, Jr., *Silent Victory: The U.S. Submarine War Against Japan* (Philadelphia: Lippincott, 1975); W. J. Holmes, *Undersea Victory: The Influence of Submarine Operations on the War in the Pacific* (Garden City, NY: Doubleday, 1966); and Theodore Roscoe, *United States Submarine Operations in World War II* (Annapolis, MD: United States Naval Institute, 1949). Concise details of *Swordfish*'s attack were covered in John D. Alden and Craig McDonald, *United States and Allied Submarine Successes in the Pacific and Far East During World War II*, 4th ed. (Jefferson, NC: McFarland, 2009). For additional brief accounts of *Swordfish*, see *United States Submarine Losses: World War II* (Washington, D.C.: U.S. Navy History Division, 1963). See also Harry Holmes, *The Last Patrol* (London: Airlife, 1994, 1997 reprint), and U.S. Naval History Division, *Dictionary of American Naval Fighting Ships* (Washington, D.C.: Government Printing Office, 1976), Vol. VI, 703. For the reference to the USS *Swordfish* (SS-193) in the online edition of the *Dictionary of American Naval Fighting Ships*, see http://www.history.navy.mil.danfs/s21/sword_fish-i.htm. Accessed 9 September 2014.

Chapter 1

1. George V. Brown, "The Launching of the *Swordfish*," *Our Navy* (Mid-May 1939), 64.

2. Ibid.

3. See *On Eternal Patrol: The Lost Boats of Mare Island* (Mare Island, CA: Mare Island Historic Park Museum), 40; Joyce Giles, Director, Mare Island Historic Park Museum, interview by author, Mare Island, 25 October 2008. Research Trip: Mare Island Naval Shipyard, 25 October 2008. The navy designated *Swordfish* with hull number SS-193.

4. John D. Alden, *The Fleet Submarine in the U.S. Navy: A Design and Construction History* (Annapolis, MD: Naval Institute Press, 1979), 68, 210–211; Erminio Bagnasco, *Submarines of World War Two* (Annapolis, MD: Naval Institute Press, 1977), 223; Norman Friedman, *U.S. Submarines Through 1945: An Illustrated History* (Annapolis, MD: Naval Institute Press, 1995), 204, 293; *Jane's Fighting Ships, 1941*, edited by Francis E. McMurtrie (New York: Macmillan, 1942), 481; U.S. Naval His-

tory Division, *Dictionary of American Naval Fighting Ships* (Washington, D.C., 1969), Vol. VI, 703; *On Eternal Patrol*, 40; Gary E. Weir, "Silent Defense: 1900–1940," *Undersea Warfare* 1, no. 4 (Summer 1999): 15. See also Gary E. Weir, *Building American Submarines, 1914–1940* (Washington, D.C.: Naval Historical Center, 1991), 115–116. See also ship engineering drawings: U.S. Submarines SS 188–193, Inboard Profile and Plans, Contract Plan No. 4: Navy Department, Bureau of Construction and Repair, Washington, D.C., June 22, 196, C&R No. 244420; U.S. Submarines SS 188–193, Outboard Profile and Plans, Contract Plan No. 3: Navy Department Bureau of Construction and Repair, Washington, D.C., June 22, 1936, C&R No. 244419. U.S. Submarines SS 188–193, Compartments and Tanks Type Plan: Navy Department, Bureau of Construction and Repair, Washington, D.C., June 22, 196, C&R No. 244427. RG19, Bureau of Ships, Portfolio SS-193, ALPHA *Swordfish* SS-193, NARA.

5. George Valentine Brown, "Through Hell and High Water: Memories of a Wartime Sub Skipper," *Shipmate* 47, no. 5 (July–August 1984): 23–24.

6. Robert E. Dyer, telephone interview by author, 25 January 2001.

7. *Ibid.*

8. Robert E. Dyer to author, correspondence, 24 August 2000.

9. *Ibid.*

10. Donald Baxter Smith (son of Chester C. Smith), telephone interview by author, 17 February 2010. Chester C. Smith Biography File, Naval History and Heritage Command. References to the Naval History and Heritage Command hereafter NHHC.

11. Harley F. Cope, *Serpent of the Seas: The Submarine* (New York: Funk & Wagnalls, 1942) 201.

12. Donald Baxter Smith, interview, 17 February 2010.

13. Chester C. Smith, Biography File, NHHC; Cope, 90

14. U.S. Naval History Division, *Dictionary*, Vol. VI, 703.

15. Chester C. Smith, USS *Swordfish*, Priority Message, 21 August 1941, U.S. Navy, Bureau of Ships, General Correspondence, 1940–1945, RG 19, Entry 1266, Box 1915, File CSS-193, National Archives and Records Administration, hereafter NARA and refers to College Park, MD, branch unless noted otherwise.

16. USS *Swordfish*, Chester C. Smith to Chief of Naval Operations, Post Repair Trial-Additional Report, Serial 041, 25 August 1941, U.S. Navy, Bureau of Ships, General Correspondence, 1940–1945, RG 19, Entry 1266, Box 1915, File CSS-193/S8, NARA; USS *Swordfish*, Route Slip and Brief, 2 September 1941, U.S. Navy Bureau of Ships, Route Slip and Brief, RG 19, Entry 1266, Box 1915, File CSS-193/S8, NARA; Gerold Frank and James D. Horan, with J. M. Eckberg, *U.S.S. Seawolf: Submarine Raider of the Pacific* (New York: G. P. Putnam's Sons, 1945), 54.

17. Dyer to author, 24 August 2000; Cope, 200.

18. Carl L. Carmer, *The Jesse James of the Java Sea* (New York: Farrar & Rinehart, 1945), 3. Smith's associates' formal names: Dudley Walker ("Mush") Morton; Morton Claire Mumma, Jr.; Richard George Voge; Frederick Burdette Warder; William Leslie ("Bull") Wright. Donald Baxter Smith interview, 17 February 2010; Donald Baxter Smith to Tom Bolan, correspondence, 24 January 1996; George V. Brown, "*Swordfish* Scored History's First Ship Sinking by a U.S. Submarine," *San Diego Union*, 4 December 1977, C0–4; Clair Blair, *Silent Victory*, 131, 135.

19. James Fife reminiscences, 1962, 211, Oral History Collection, Columbia University; Joel Holwitt, "Unrestricted Submarine Victory: The U.S. Submarine Campaign Against Japan," in *Commerce Raiding: Historical Studies, 1755–2009*, Naval War College Papers No. 40, edited by Bruce A. Elleman and S. C. M. Paine (Washington, D.C.: U.S. Government Printing Office), 226–230; Joel Ira Holwitt, *"Execute Against Japan," The U.S. Decision to Conduct Unrestricted Submarine Warfare* (College Station: Texas A&M University Press, 2009), 148. Holwitt offers a very detailed analysis of the evolution of American naval strategy and the decision to engage in unrestricted submarine warfare.

20. Holwitt, "Unrestricted Submarine Victory," 230. See also Theodore Ropp, "Continental Doctrines of Sea Power," *Makers of Modern Strategy*, edited by Edward Meade Earle (Princeton: Princeton University Press, 1971), 446–456.

21. Lloyd Henry Faye, telephone interview by author, 28 February 2003.

22. Dyer, interview, 25 January 2001.

23. Vernon Fields, USS *Swordfish*—Submarine Activities Southwest Pacific, Narrative, Recorded 4 June 1943, Film No. 81, 1, NHHC.

24. Chester C. Smith, interview by Clay Blair, Jr., Audiotape Number Two, Clay Blair

Notes—Chapter 1

Collection, Accession 8295, American Heritage Center. References to the American Heritage Center, hereafter AHC.

25. Lloyd Faye, interview, 28 February 2003.

26. Robert Hargis, *U.S. Submarine Crewman, 1941–45* (Botley, England: Osprey, 2003), 2–26; *Swordfish*, Preliminary War Patrol Report 1, 1, NHHC. References to War Patrol Reports, hereafter WPR. The Navy had promoted Smith to the rank of Lieutenant Commander.

27. Michael Billy, Military Personnel Records, National Personnel Records Center. References to the National Personnel Records Center, hereafter NPRC. Marie Billy (Michael Billy's sister-in-law), interview by author, Rahway, New Jersey, 3 July 1984; Peter Zeleznik (Michael Billy's brother-in-law), interview by author, Rahway, New Jersey, 12 March 2001; Ann Kirkman (sister-in-law of Michael Billy), interview by author, East Brunswick, New Jersey, 30 July 2000.

28. Michael Billy, Military Personnel Records, NPRC; Marie Billy (Michael Billy's sister-in-law), interview by author, Rahway, New Jersey, 3 July 1984; Peter Zeleznik (Michael Billy's brother-in-law), interview by author, Rahway, New Jersey, 12 March 2001; Ann Kirkman (sister-in-law of Michael Billy), interview by author, East Brunswick, New Jersey, 30 July 2000.

29. Michael Billy, Military Personnel Records, NPRC. USS *Gunnel* (SS-253) Muster Rolls, 30 September 1942 to 15 January 1943, Microfilm Reel number 1806, RG24, NARA; John McCain, *Faith of Our Fathers*, with Mark Salter (New York: Random House, 1999), 79–82. See also Biography of Rear Admiral Karl G. Hensel, Clay Blair Collection, Accession Number 8295, Box 79, File Folder 28, Folder Title: "Research Files—U.S. Pacific Ocean Submarine Fleet." *Swordfish*, 1957, 1972, AHC. See also Blair, *Silent Victory*, 264–266. Note: LCDR John S. McCain, Jr., was the father of John S. McCain III, U.S. Senator from Arizona.

30. Leyman Dennis, telephone interview by author, 17 January 2001. Dennis was a Quartermaster on *Swordfish*. Dyer, interview, 25 January 2001; Lloyd H. Faye to author, correspondence, 12 March 2003; Fred Kramer, telephone interview by author, 18 January 2001. Kramer served aboard *Swordfish* from 28 June 1941 to 23 December 1943 as an Electricians Mate; Robert MacDonald (USS *Gunnel* veteran), telephone interview, 19 July 2001.

31. Ronald H. Spector, *At War at Sea: Sailors and Naval Combat in the Twentieth Century* (New York: Viking, 2001), 288; Dyer, interview, 25 January 2001; Dennis, interview, 17 January 2001.

32. William Shakespeare, "Julius Caesar," Act 3, Scene 1, line 273, in *The Complete Works of William Shakespeare* (London: Oxford University Press, 1955), 833.

33. *Swordfish*, WPR NO. 1, p. 3, NHHC. See also *Swordfish*, Preliminary WPR No. 1, p. 1, NHHC.

34. *Ibid.*

35. Faye, interview, 28 February 2003.

36. Floyd M. Cooper and Donald Gaither, "War Patrols of USS *Swordfish* and USS *Sargo*," Narrative, Recorded 23 June 1944, Transcribed at Pearl Harbor, Film No. S-77, NHHC.

37. Fields, narrative, 1.

38. Fred Kramer, telephone interview by author, 25 January 2003; Fields, 1.

39. *Swordfish*, WPR No. 1, Details of Attacks Made, 3, NHHC. For Smith's additional comments on this first encounter, see Chester C. Smith, "USS *Swordfish*, Early War Patrols," Narrative, Recorded 19–20 November 1943, transcribed at Pearl Harbor, Film No. S-18, 2, NHHC.

40. Donald Baxter Smith, interview, 17 February 2010.

41. *Swordfish*, Preliminary WPR No. 1, 2, NHHC.

42. *Ibid.*

43. Charles Lockwood, *Down to the Sea in Subs* (New York: Norton, 1967), 200–201); Blair, *Silent Victory*, 65.

44. *Swordfish*, Preliminary WPR No. 1, 3, NHHC.

45. *Swordfish*, WPR No. 1, Details of Attacks Made, 4, NHHC. See also *Swordfish*, Deck Log, 14 December 1941, 729, RG 24, NARA.

46. *Swordfish*, Preliminary WPR, No. 1, 4, NHHC; Cooper and Gaither, 4.

47. *Swordfish*, WPR No. 1, Details of Attacks Made, 5, NHHC.

48. *Swordfish*, Preliminary WPR No. 1, 5, NHHC.

49. *Ibid.*

50. *Swordfish*, WPR No. 1, Details of Attacks Made, 5, NHHC.

51. *Swordfish*, Preliminary WPR No. 1, 6, NHHC; *Swordfish*, Deck Log, 16 December 1941, 733, RG 24, NARA.

52. *Swordfish*, Preliminary WPR No. 1, 6, NHHC.

53. Dyer, interview, 25 January 2001; Dennis, interview, 17 January 2001.

Notes—Chapter 1

54. *Swordfish*, Preliminary WPR No. 1, 6–7, NHHC.
55. *Ibid.*, 7.
56. *Ibid.*
57. *Ibid.*
58. Alden and McDonald, *United States Submarine*, p. 28. *Japanese Merchant Ships: ONI-J (revised)* (Washington, D.C.: United States, Office of the Chief of Naval Operations, 1942), 86; Joint Army-Navy Assessment Committee, *Japanese Naval and Merchant Shipping Losses: During World War II by All Causes* (Washington, D.C.: Government Printing Office, February 1947), 29, 47, hereafter referred to as JANAC; Roger W. Jordan, *The World's Merchant Fleet: 1937, the Particulars and Wartime Fates of 6,000 Ships* (Annapolis, MD: Naval Institute Press, 1999), 256, 540; *Lloyd's Register of Shipping, 1940–41* (London: Lloyd's Register of Shipping, 1940).
59. *Swordfish*, Preliminary WPR No. 1, 7, NHHC.
60. Fields, 1, NHHC.
61. *Swordfish*, Preliminary WPR No. 1, 7, NHHC; *Swordfish* Deck Log, 19 December 1941, 739, RG 24, NARA.
62. Cooper and Gaither, 2, NHHC.
63. *Ibid.*
64. *Ibid.*
65. Milton Seltzer (veteran of the USS *Steelhead*), interview by author, 3 June 2002, Garden City, NY; Joseph Librizzi (veteran of the USS *Balao*), interview by author, Garden City, NY, 22 May 2007.
66. Faye, interview, 28 February 2003.
67. Fred Kramer, interview, 25 January 2003; Seltzer, interview, June 3, 2002.
68. *Swordfish*, Preliminary WPR No. 1, 7, NHHC.
69. Chester C. Smith, "USS *Swordfish*, Early War Patrols," 7, NHHC.
70. *Swordfish*, Preliminary WPR No. 1, 7–8, NHHC.
71. Fred Kramer, interview, 25 January 2003.
72. Chester C. Smith, "USS *Swordfish*, Early War Patrols," 8, NHHC.
73. David E. Cohen, "The Mk-XIV Torpedo: Lesson for Today," *Naval History* 6, no. 4 (Winter 1992): 34–36; Larry Kimmett and Margaret Regis, *U.S. Submarines in World War II: An Illustrated History* (Seattle: Navigator Publishing, 1996), 30–31.
74. *Swordfish*, Preliminary WPR No. 1, 8, NHHC.
75. Cohen, 34–36.
76. *Ibid.;* Blair, *Silent Victory*, 435–439.
77. Charles A. Lockwood, *Sink 'Em All: Submarine Warfare in the Pacific* (New York: E. Dutton, 1951), 85, 111–114. See also Lockwood, *Down to the Sea*, Chapter 22; Blair, *Silent Victory*, 435–439.
78. Lockwood, *Down to the Sea*, 289–295; Kimmett and Regis, 30–31; Anthony Newpower, *Iron Men and Tin Fish: The Race to Build a Better Torpedo During World War II* (Westport, CT: Praeger Security International, 2006), 29, 156–161, 173–174, 182–183, 190.
79. *Swordfish*, Patrol Report No. 1, "Major Defects and Casualties, Mark VI Exploders," 8, NHHC.
80. *Swordfish*, Preliminary WPR No. 1, 9, NHHC.
81. *Ibid.*
82. *Ibid.*
83. *Ibid.* See also, *Swordfish*, Deck Log, 22 December 1941, 745, RG 24, NARA.
84. *Swordfish*, Preliminary WPR No. 1, 9, NHHC. See also USS *Swordfish*, Deck Log, 22 December 1941, 745, RG 24, NARA.
85. *Swordfish*, Preliminary WPR No. 1, 9, NHHC. See also USS *Swordfish*, Deck Log, 22 December 1941, RG 24, NARA.
86. Chester C. Smith, "USS *Swordfish*, Early War Patrols," 11, NHHC.
87. *Swordfish*, Preliminary WPR No. 1, 9–10, NHHC.
88. Fields, 2, NHHC.
89. Cooper and Gaither, 1, NHHC; Donald Gaither served on *Swordfish* for 11 war patrols.
90. *Swordfish*, Preliminary WPR No. 1, 10, NHHC; Chester C. Smith, "USS *Swordfish*, Early War Patrols," 20, NHHC.
91. Chester C. Smith to Arthur L. Smith, correspondence, 25 December 1941 (provided by Donald Baxter Smith, son of Chester Smith).
92. Frank and Horan, with J. M. Eckberg, ix, 55. The authors quote Bull Kiser, but the muster roll of the *Swordfish* lists the radioman as Kenneth J. Keyser. USS *Swordfish*: Muster Roll, 31 December 1941, 2, Microfilm Reel No. 7434, NARA.
93. JANAC, 1, Appendix, 47; Alden and McDonald, *United States*, 6, 28.
94. *Swordfish*, Preliminary WPR No. 1, 10, NHHC. See also *Swordfish*, Deck Log, 28 December 1941, 757, RG 24, NARA.
95. Cooper and Gaither, 5, NHHC.
96. Blair, *Silent Victory*, 135; Potter and Nimitz, *Triumph*, 5–10.
97. Blair, *Silent Victory*, 132–134; Richard Connaughton, *MacArthur and Defeat in the*

Philippines (Woodstock, NY: Overlook Press, 2001), 162–178; W. G. Winslow, *The Fleet the Gods Forgot* (Annapolis, MD: Naval Institute Press, 1982), 7–10.
 98. Blair, *Silent Victory*, 135.
 99. Frank and Horan, with Eckberg, *Seawolf*, 56. See also Blair, *Silent Victory*, 135–152.
 100. U.S. Defense Mapping Agency Hydrographic/Topographic Center, *Sailing Directions (Enroute) for the Philippines*, Publication 162 (Washington, D.C.: U.S. Defense Mapping Agency Hydrographic/Topographic Center, 1979), 41–42. Also, author's on-site research at Manila Bay, 20–27 March 1999.
 101. Blair, *Silent Victory*, 153–154, 160.
 102. Blair, *Silent Victory*, 153–155.
 103. Wilkes took with him on board *Swordfish* the following: W. M. Percifield, S. S. Murray, W. T. Jones, S. B. Wright, C. S. Osborne, A. Enrico, E. Lancaster, J. S. Patrick, and J. W. Stier. See *Swordfish* Deck Log, 31 December 1941, 763, RG24, NARA; Blair, *Silent Victory*, 154–155, 160.
 104. *Swordfish*, Deck Log, 6–8 January 1942, 13–15, RG 24, NARA.
 105. Cooper and Gaither, 6, NHHC.

Chapter 2

1. Valentine Brown, "Through Hell," 24.
2. *Ibid.*
3. *Swordfish*, WPR No. 2, 2, and Major Defects and Casualties, 1, NHHC.
4. Celebes Island, currently known as Sulawesi, and Lembeh Strait, currently known as Selat Lembeh. U.S. Defense Mapping Agency, *Sailing Directions (Enroute) for Borneo, Jawa, Sulawesi and Nusa Tenggara*, Pub. 163 (Washington, D.C.: U.S. Defense Mapping Agency, 1979), 276–277; U.S. National Imagery and Mapping Agency, Teluk Tomini and North Coast to Sulawesi, Nautical Chart No. 73012 (Washington, D.C.: U.S. National Imagery and Mapping Agency, 2003).
5. Chester C. Smith, "USS *Swordfish*, Early War Patrols," 15; *Swordfish*, WPR No. 2, 3, NHHC.
6. *Swordfish*, WPR No. 2, 3, NHHC.
7. Alden and McDonald, *United States Submarine*, 71; John Cressman, *The Official Chronology of the U.S. Navy in World War II* (Annapolis, MD: Naval Institute Press, 2000, 71.
8. *Swordfish*, WPR No. 2, Details of Attacks Made, 1, NHHC; Chester C. Smith, "USS *Swordfish*, Early War Patrols," 16, NHHC. See also Thomas M. Dykers and Chester C. Smith, "The Swordfish Story," Videorecording, DVD (Annapolis, MD: United States Naval Academy, Multimedia Support Center, 1958, 2003).
 9. *Swordfish*, WPR No. 2, 3, NHHC. See also Alden and McDonald, *United States*, 30.
 10. *Swordfish*, WPR No. 2, 4, NHHC. See also *Swordfish*, WPR 24 January 1942, 49, RG 24, NARA.
 11. Chester C. Smith, "USS *Swordfish*, Early War Patrols," 17, NHHC.
 12. *Ibid.*
 13. Cressman, 71.
 14. *Swordfish*, WPR No. 2, 5, NHHC.
 15. *Ibid.*
 16. *Ibid.*, Weather, n.p.
 17. *Ibid.*, 6
 18. *Ibid.*
 19. *Ibid.*, 9
 20. *Ibid.*
 21. *Ibid.*
 22. *Ibid.*
 23. *Ibid.*
 24. *Ibid.*
 25. *Ibid.*, 11.
 26. *Ibid.*, 12.
 27. *Ibid.*, 13; Details of Attacks, 2.
 28. Alden and McDonald, *United States Submarine*, 31.
 29. *Swordfish*, WPR No. 2, 13, NHHC.
 30. *Ibid.*, 15.
 31. *Ibid.*; Details of Attacks Made, 3.
 32. *Ibid.*, 16, NHHC; Edward C. Whitman, "Submarines to Corregidor," *Undersea Warfare* 4, no. 3 (Summer 2002): 28–31; U.S. Defense Mapping Agency Hydrographic/Topographic Center, *Sailing Directions (Enroute) for the Philippines*, Publication 162 (Washington, D.C.: U.S. Defense Mapping Agency Hydrographic/Topographic Center, 1979), 42.
 33. Carlos Romulo, *I Saw the Fall of the Philippines* (Garden City, NY: Doubleday, 1946), 182.
 34. The Quezon group included Vice President Sergio Osmena, Chief Justice Santos, General Basilio J. Valdes, Colonel Nieto, and Captain Ortiz, a chaplain. *Swordfish*, WPR No. 2, 16, NHHC. See also *Swordfish*, Deck Log, 20 February 1942, 105-a, NARA, RG 24; Carlos Romulo, 186–187; Gerald Astor, *Crisis in the Pacific* (New York: Dell, 1996), 178; Robert L. Underbrink, *Destination Corregidor* (Annapolis, MD: United States Naval Institute, 1971), 159; Connaughton, 266; Dyer, interview, 25 January 2001.

35. George Valentine Brown, "Traveling Down Memory Lane with Val Brown, Ye Olde and Ancient Mariner," *Klaxon* (February 1978). The author thanks the St. Marys Submarine Museum staff for sending this article and other information from their USS *Swordfish* Information File.

36. *Swordfish*, WPR No. 2, Major Defects and Casualties, 1, NHHC. Faye, interview, 28 February 2003.

37. Blair, *Silent Victory*, 174; Underbrink, 159.

38. *Swordfish*, WPR No. 2, 16, NHHC; *Swordfish*, Deck Log, 22 February 1942, 109, RG 24, NARA. Romulo, 186–187.

39. Romulo, 188.

40. In adult life, William Graves was editor of the *National Geographic* magazine. Other members of the Sayre party included Woodbury and Amea Willoughby, Evett D. Hester, Cabot Coville, James J. Saxon, Janet White, and Anna Bell Newcombe. *Swordfish*, WPR No. 2, 17, NHHC; *Swordfish*, Deck Log, 24 February 1942, 112, RG 24, NARA. See also Underbrink, 159–160.

41. Blair, *Silent Victory*, 174–175; William Graves, "Corregidor Revisited: 43 Years after the Siege" *National Geographic* 170, no. 2 (July 1986): 118; Chester C. Smith, interview by Clay Blair, Jr., Audiotape Number Three, Clay Blair Collection, Accession 8295, AHC.

42. Elizabeth E. Sayre, "Submarine from Corregidor: Manila Goes Under," *The Atlantic* 170, no. 2 (August, 1942): 25–28.

43. Elizabeth E. Sayre, "Submarine from Corregidor: The Escape," *The Atlantic* 170, No. 3 (September 1942): 40.

44. Amea Willoughby, "Undersea Escape from Corregidor," *The Best 100 True Stories of World War II* (New York: Wise, 1945), 58.

45. *Ibid*.

46. Sayre, "Submarine...The Escape," 43; William Graves, Diary, 10, Submarine Force Library, USS *Swordfish* reference binder; William Graves, "Corregidor Revisited: 43 Years After the Siege," *National Geographic* 170, no. 2 (July 1986): 130; Joe Parks to author, correspondence, 21 June 2001.

47. Sayre, "Submarine...The Escape," 41–42; Willoughby, "Undersea Escape," 59.

48. Sayre, "Submarine...The Escape," 42.

49. Willoughby, 62.

50. Sayre, "Submarine...The Escape," 42.

51. Willoughby, 60.

52. *Ibid*., 59–60.

53. Sayre, "Submarine...The Escape," 43.

54. Graves, "Corregidor Revisited," 130.

55. Sayre, "Submarine...The Escape," 43.

56. Kramer, interview, 8 February 2001.

57. Faye, interview, 28 February 2003.

58. Kramer, interview, 8 February 2001.

59. *Ibid*.

60. Faye, interview, 28 February 2003.

61. *Swordfish*, WPR No. 2, Major Defects and Casualties, 1. The "guests" obtained some relief toward the end of the trip when they were permitted to come to the bridge in a brief but welcome pattern of rotation. [Sayre, "Submarine...The Escape," 45.]

62. *Ibid*., 43–44.

63. Willoughby, 60.

64. *Ibid*., 62.

65. *Ibid*., 62–62.

66. Sayre, "Submarine...The Escape," 45.

67. *Swordfish*, WPR No. 2, 19, NHHC.

68. Sayre, "Submarine...The Escape," 45.

69. *Ibid*., 46.

70. Willoughby, 67.

71. *Swordfish*, WPR No. 2, 20. For additional details concerning the special missions of U.S. Navy submarines in Philippine waters early in World War II, see Charles Dana Gibson and E. Kay Gibson, *Over Seas: U.S. Army Maritime Operations 1898 Through the Fall of the Philippines* (Camden, ME: Ensign Press, 2002), Chapter 16.

72. Chester C. Smith to Mary Baxter Smith, telegram, 17 March 1941.

73. Cooper and Gaither, "War Patrols of USS *Swordfish*," 7, NHHC.

74. Dyer, interview, 14 November 2001.

75. Kramer, interview, 24 September 2001; Dennis, interview, 7 September 2003.

76. *Swordfish*, WPR No. 2, Major Defects and Casualties, 1, NHHC.

77. *Ibid*., 1–2.

78. *Ibid*., 2.

79. *Ibid*., 1.

80. *Ibid*., 1–3.

81. Chester C. Smith, interview by Clay Blair, Jr., Audiotape Number Two, Clay Blair Collection, Accession 8295, AHC.

82. Louis Morton, *The Fall of the Philippines*, Series: U.S. Dept. of the Army, Office of Military History, United States Army in World War II (Washington, D.C.: Office of the Chief of Military History, Dept. of the Army, 1953), 399; Kramer, interview, 25 January 2003.

83. Chester C. Smith, interview by Clay Blair, Jr. Audiotape Number Three, Clay Blair Collection, Accession 8295, AHC.

84. Fife, reminiscences, 1962, 267–268,

Oral History Collection of Columbia University. Fife served as John Wilkes' chief of staff and subsequently was commander of the submarine base at Brisbane, Australia. Blair, *Silent Victory*, 131, 348, 371–372.
    85. Faye, interview, 28 February 2003.
    86. *Swordfish*, WPR No. 3, 3, NHHC.
    87. Edward C. Whitman, "Submarines to Corregidor," *Undersea Warfare* 4, no. 3 (Summer 2002): 31. See also Edward C. Whitman, "Suicide Run: MacArthur's Guerrilla Submarines," *Sea Classics* 39, no. 2 (February 2006), 34–41; Kramer, interview, 25 January 2003.
    88. *Swordfish*, WPR No. 3, 1, 4–7, NHHC.
    89. *Swordfish*, WPR No. 3, 9; Major Defects Experienced, 2, NHHC.
    90. *Ibid.*, 10. See also Cooper and Gaither, 7–8, NHHC; Chester C. Smith, interview by Clay Blair, Jr., Audiotape Number 2, Clay Blair Collection, National Heritage Center, Accession 8295, AHC.

Chapter 3

    1. *Triumph in the Pacific*, 7–15.
    2. William P. O'Briant, telephone interview by author, 21 December 2000. Submariners possess special traits which author and submarine veteran Captain Edward L. Beach describes as "the sense of loyalty to his ship and an indefinable oneness with, and deep understanding of the sea." The submariner appreciates the complexity of the sea and its chimerical nature. This recognition of a sea that is ever changing reinforces his sense of duty and loyalty to his shipmates. As Beach writes, "The submariner is always aware that an error during underwater operations jeopardizes everyone's life." Nevertheless, the sea can also be the submariner's protector. As Beach also writes, "The depths of the ocean are always inviting to a submariner. It is only the surface of the sea that is sometimes harsh." Whether on the surface or submerged, the deep bond among the crewmen is unmistakable. See Edward L. Beach, *Submarine!* (New York Pocket Star Books, 2004), 2. See also Edward L. Beach, *Dust on the Sea* (New York: Zebra Books, 1989), 282.
    3. Kramer, interview, 18 January 2001; Dyer, interview, 25 January 2001. See also Robert J. Casey, *Battle Below: The War of the Submarines* (Indianapolis: Bobbs-Merrill, 1945), 15–17.
    4. Blair, *Silent Victory*, 877. See also Williamson Murray and Allan R. Millett, *A War to Be Won: Fighting the Second World War* (Cambridge, MA: Belknap Press/Harvard University Press, 2000), 224; Robert MacDonald (*Gunnel* veteran), telephone interview by author, 19 July 2001; Parks to author, correspondence, 21 June 2001.
    5. Kramer, interview, 18 January 2001.
    6. O'Briant, interview, 21 December 2000; Casey, 15.
    7. Emil Schoonjans, telephone interview by author, 2 November 2009. Torpedoman 3rd Class Schoonjans served on the USS *Burrfish*. See also Willoughby, 67; Casey, 15–16.
    8. Brown, "Through Hell," 23–23; Dennis, interview, 17 January 2001; Kramer, interview, 25 January 2003; O'Briant, interview, 5 June 2000; Parks to author, 21 June 2001.
    9. Kramer, interview, 18 January 2001; Charles A. Lockwood, Jr., *History of Submarine Operations in World War II* (1946), Vol. I, 168–201 (original pagination), Ben Bastura Collection, St. Mary's Submarine Museum, Chapter E, 10.
    10. *Swordfish*, WPR No. 4, Enclosure A, 1, NHHC.
    11. *Swordfish*, WPR No. 4, Enclosure A, 2, and Enclosure G, 1, NHHC. There was the possibility that one torpedo hit toward the bow to cause slight damage. Alden and McDonald, *United States*, 38.
    12. *Swordfish*, WPR No. 4, Enclosure A, 4, NHHC.
    13. *Seal*, WPR No. 3, 9, 20, Submarine Force Library.
    14. *Ibid.*, 9–10.
    15. *Swordfish*, WPR No. 4, Enclosure A, 4–5; Enclosure E, 1; and Enclosure G, 1, NHHC.
    16. *Seal*, WPR No. 3, 10, Submarine Force Library.
    17. *Swordfish*, WPR No. 4, Enclosure A, 5; Enclosure E, 1, NHHC.
    18. *Ibid.*, Enclosure E,1; Enclosure G, 1.
    19. *Ibid.*, Enclosure A, 5.
    20. *Seal*, WPR No. 3, 10, Submarine Force Library.
    21. *Ibid.*
    22. Charles A Lockwood, Endorsement to USS *Seal*, WPR No. 3, FF6-4/A16-3, Serial S-0019, 27 July 1942, Submarine Force Library.
    23. Charles A. Lockwood, Endorsement to USS *Swordfish*, WPR No. 4, FF-4/A16-3, Serial S-C016, 25 July 1942, NHHC.
    24. JANAC, 32; Appendix 40, 47.
    25. *Swordfish*, WPR No. 4, 5, NHHC. Chester C. Smith to Clay Blair, Jr., Correspon-

Notes—Chapter 3

dence, 25 March 1972, Clay Blair Collection, Accession Number 8295, Box 70, Folder Number 3, Folder Name: Research File, *Silent Victory*, Skippers of the U.S., World War II, Pacific Ocean, Submarine Patrols 1941–1943, Si-Sto, AHC.

26. *Seal*, WPR No. 3, 8–10, 20, Submarine Force Library; *Swordfish*, WPR No. 4, Enclosure A, 4–5; Enclosure E, 1, NHHC.

27. See Alden and McDonald, *United States*, 4th ed., 38–39. Alden and McDonald support the idea that *Seal* and *Swordfish* were jointly responsible for the sinking of *Tatsufuku Maru*.

28. *Ibid*.

29. *Swordfish*, WPR No. 4, Enclosure A, 7, and Enclosure G, 2, NHHC.

30. *Swordfish*, Action Report, 4 June 1942, RG 38, Box 1460, NARA.

31. *Swordfish*, WPR No. 4, Enclosure I, 3–4, NHHC.

32. *Ibid.*, Enclosure A, 7.

33. *Ibid.*, Enclosure G, 2.

34. *Ibid.*, Enclosure H, 1.

35. *Ibid.*, Enclosure I, 1.

36. *Ibid.*, Enclosure A, 8, and Enclosure E, 2.

37. *Ibid.*, Enclosure A, 8, and Enclosure G, 2. See also, *Swordfish*, Action Report, 6 June 1942, RG 38, Box 1460, NARA.

38. *Swordfish*, WPR No. 4; Enclosure G, 3.

39. *Ibid.*, Enclosure A, 9.

40. *Ibid.*

41. *Ibid.*

42. *Ibid.*, Enclosure A, 9, and Enclosure J, 1–2.

43. *Ibid.*, Enclosure A, 10.

44. *Ibid.*, Enclosure J, 1–2.

45. *Ibid.*, Enclosure A, 10–11; Enclosure G, 3; Alden and McDonald, *United States*, 39.

46. *Swordfish*, WPR No. 4; Enclosure A, 11; Enclosure G, 3, NHHC.

47. *Ibid.*, Enclosure G, 3. See also *Swordfish*, Action Report, 12 June 1942, RG 38, Box 1460, NARA; JANAC, Appendix, 47; Alden and McDonald, *United States*, 39.

48. *Swordfish*, WPR No. 4; Enclosure A, 11; NHHC.

49. *Ibid.*, Enclosure J, 2.

50. *Ibid.*, Enclosure A, 12.

51. *Ibid.*, Enclosure J, 2.

52. *Ibid.*, Enclosure A, 15.

53. *Ibid.*, Enclosure A, 16.

54. *Ibid.*

55. Charles A. Lockwood, First Endorsement, 25 July 1942, FF6-4/A16-3, Serial S-0016 in *Swordfish*, WPR No. 4, NHHC.

56. Blair, *Silent Victory*, 818.

57. Charles A. Lockwood to C. W. Styer, 24 May 1942, Box 12, Charles A. Lockwood Papers, Official Correspondence, Naval Historical Foundation Collection, Manuscript Division, Library of Congress, Washington, D.C. Reference to the Manuscript Division, Library of Congress, hereafter MD, LC.

58. *Swordfish*, WPR No. 4, Enclosure J, 1, NHHC; Alden and MacDonald, *United States*, 38, 39.

59. *Swordfish*, WPR No. 4, Enclosure J, 2, NHHC.

60. *Ibid.*

61. Lockwood to Styer, May 24, 1942, Box 12, Charles A. Lockwood Papers, Official Correspondence, Naval Historical Foundation Collection, MD, LC.

62. Charles A. Lockwood to W. J. Suits, 14 November 1942, Box 12, Official Correspondence, Charles A. Lockwood Papers, Naval Historical Center Foundation Collection, MD; LC. Charles A. Lockwood, Jr., *History of Submarine Operations in World War II*, Vol. I, 168–201 (original pagination, Naval Historical Foundation Collection), Ben Bastura Collection, St. Mary's Submarine Museum, Chapter E, 9. See also Samuel Eliot Morrison, *History of United States Naval Operations in World War II: Coral Sea, Midway, and Submarine Actions, May 1942-August 1942*. (Edison, NJ: Castle Books, 1949), Vol. IV, 222–223.

63. *Ibid.*

64. Cooper and Gaither, 8, NHHC.

65. *Ibid.*

66. *Swordfish*, WPR No. 4, Enclosure I, 1–3, NHHC.

67. Donald Baxter Smith, telephone interview by author, February 17, 2010; Chester C. Smith to Clay Blair, Jr. Correspondence, 25 March 1972, Clay Blair Papers, Accession Number 8275, Box Number 70, Folder Number 3, Folder Title: "Research File, *Silent Victory*, Skippers of the U.S., World War II, Pacific Ocean Submarine Patrols, 1941–1973," Si-Sto; Chester C. Smith, interview by Clay Blair, Jr., audiotape, Clay Blair Collection, Accession 8295, NHHC.

68. Valentine Brown, "Through Hell," 24; Clay Blair, Jr., *Silent Victory*, 288.

69. Albert Collins Burrows Biography File, NHHC; *The Lucky Bag 1928* (Annapolis, MD: First Class, U.S. Naval Academy, 1928), 124.

70. Cooper and Gaither, 10; *Swordfish*, WPR No. 5, 1, NHHC.

71. *Ibid.*

72. Dyer to author, 24 August 2000, and

Notes—Chapter 3

interview, 25 January 2001; Dennis, interview, 17 January 2001; Faye, interview, 28 February 2003.
73. *Swordfish*, WPR No. 5, 3–4, NHHC.
74. *Ibid.*, 4.
75. *Ibid.*
76. *Ibid.*, 6.
77. *Ibid.*
78. *Ibid.*, 7. 21.
79. *Ibid.*, 7.
80. *Ibid.*, 8.
81. *Ibid.*
82. *Ibid.*
83. *Ibid.*
84. *Ibid.*, 8–10.
85. *Ibid.*, 12.
86. *Ibid.*, 13.
87. *Ibid.*, 14–15.
88. *Ibid.*, 15.
89. *Ibid.*
90. *Ibid.*
91. *Ibid.*, 22.
92. *Ibid.*
93. *Ibid.*, 16.
94. Paul Marvin, "War Patrols of the USS *Swordfish*," narrative, Pearl Harbor, Film No. S-93, Recorded 20 October 1944, 17, NHHC.
95. Kramer, interview, 25 January 2003.
96. Faye, interview, 28 February 2003.
97. *Swordfish*, WPR No. 5, 22, NHHC.
98. *Ibid.*, 18, 22, 27, and First Endorsement, 2; Kramer, interviews, 18 January 2001 and 25 January 2003; Dennis, interview, 17 January 2001.
99. *Swordfish*, WPR No. 5, First Endorsement, 1, NHHC.
100. *Ibid.*
101. *Ibid.*
102. *Ibid.*; First Endorsement, 2.
103. *Ibid.*; Second Endorsement, 1.
104. *Ibid.*
105. *Ibid.*; Second Endorsement, 2.
106. Charles A. Lockwood to James Fife, 8 March 1943, Box 14, Charles A. Lockwood Papers, Naval Historical Foundation Collection, MD, LC.
107. Clay Blair, Jr., *Silent Victory*, 410.
108. James Fife to Charles A. Lockwood, 12 May 1943, Official Correspondence, Box 13, Charles A. Lockwood Papers, Naval Historical Foundation Collection, MD, LC.
109. Burrows Biography File, NHHC; Albert C. Burrows Citation, Navy Cross Citation, CinC Pac Serial 36, NHHC.
110. Albert C. Burrows, USS *Whale*, Citation for Gold Star in lieu of 2nd Silver Star Medal by Cinpac, ltr Pac-052-jls P15/BA-Serial 0185—dated 14 Jan. 1944 (Cinpac Serial 45), Burrows Biography File, NHHC.
111. Edward L. Beach, *Submarine!* (New York: Pocket Star Books, 1980), 99.
112. Burrows Biography File, NHHC; Dyer, interview, 25 January 2001; *Lucky Bag*, p. 124.
113. *Swordfish*, WPR No. 6, 1, NHHC.
114. *Ibid.*; Enclosure I, Food, Habitability, and Health, 1.
115. *Ibid.*; Enclosure I, Food, Habitability, and Health, 1–2.
116. *Ibid.*; Enclosure I, Food, Habitability and Health, 1.
117. *Ibid.*; Enclosure H, Major Defects and Casualties, 1.
118. Parillo, 92–93; *Swordfish*, WPR No. 6, Enclosure A, 5–6, and Enclosure F, Details of Action, 1–2, NHHC. See also *Swordfish*, Action Report, 13 November 1942, RG 38, Box 1460, NARA.
119. *Swordfish*, WPR No. 6; Enclosure A, 6; Enclosure G, Enemy Anti-submarine Measures, 1, NHHC.
120. *Ibid.*; Enclosure G, Enemy Anti-submarine Measures, 1.
121. *Ibid.*; Enclosure A, 6.
122. *Ibid.*
123. *Ibid.*; Enclosure A, 7.
124. *Ibid.*
125. *Ibid.*; Enclosure F, Details of Action, 2.
126. *Ibid.*
127. *Ibid.*; Enclosure G, Enemy Anti-submarine Measures, 2.
128. *Ibid.*; Enclosure F, Details of Action, 2.
129. *Ibid.*
130. *Ibid.*; Enclosure F, 3.
131. *Ibid.*; Enclosure G, 2. See also *Swordfish*, Action Report, 17 November 1942, RG 38, Box 1460, NARA.
132. *Swordfish*, WPR No. 6, Enclosure G, 2, NHHC. Admiral Christie noted that "Smithy," as Christie called him, had been patrolling the area; Ralph Christie to Charles Lockwood, 23 November 1942, Box 12, Official Correspondence, Charles A. Lockwood Papers, Naval Historical Foundation Collection, MD, LC.
133. *Swordfish*, WPR No. 6, Enclosure A, 13, NHHC.
134. *Ibid.*; Enclosure A, 16.
135. *Ibid.*; Enclosure A, 13–20.
136. *Ibid.*; Ralph Waldo Christie, Comments, Serial 00141, 21 December 1942.
137. *Ibid.*; William Frederick Halsey, First

Endorsement, A16-3/(11), Serial 0036, 8 January 1943.
138. Chester C. Smith, Biography File, NHHC.
139. Charles A. Lockwood to W. J. Suits, 14 November 1942, Box 12, Official Correspondence, Charles A. Lockwood Papers, Naval Historical Foundation Collection, MD, LC.
140. Chester C. Smith, Biography File, NHHC; Chester C. Smith, interview by Clay Blair, Jr. Audiotape Number Three, Clay Blair Papers, Accession 8295, AHC.
141. *Ibid.*
142. Chester C. Smith, Biography File, NHHC.
143. Chester C. Smith, "Silver Star Medal," Press Release, 4 February 1946, Smith Biography File, NHHC.
144. Cope was Smith's commanding officer when Smith was second officer on the old S-40 in the Far East; Cope, 200, 203.
145. Clay Blair, Jr., *Silent Victory*, 343, 877–879, 903, 910, 920; JANAC, ii, Appendix 47.
146. See Casey, 227. See also Corwin Mendenhall, *Submarine Diary* (Annapolis, MD: Naval Institute Press, 1991), 47.
147. Blair, *Silent Victory*, 143, 353, 407–408, 510–511, 911. See also Carl LaVo, "Commanding Officer Breaking Down," *Naval History* 6, no. 3 (Fall 1962): 29–34.
148. Valentine Brown, "Through Hell," 24.
149. *Ibid.*
150. *Swordfish*, WPR No. 6; Enclosure H, 2, NHHC.
151. *Ibid.*, Enclosure H, 3.
152. *Ibid.;* Enclosure A, 1; Enclosure H, 1.
153. Cooper and Gaither, 9, NHHC.
154. Charles A. Lockwood to M. Collins, 23 December 1942, Official Correspondence, Box 12, Charles A. Lockwood Papers, Naval Historical Foundation Collection, MD, LC.
155. *Ibid.*

Chapter 4

1. The figures refer to all vessels sunk, military and merchant. See Charles A. Lockwood, Commander, Submarine Force, Pacific Fleet to Submarine Force, Pacific Fleet, 26 February 1943, World War II Command File, Tactical Information Bulletin No. 2, Box 358, NHHC.
2. See Parillo, 204.
3. *Swordfish*, WPR No. 7, 1, NHHC; Clair Blair, Jr., *Silent Victory*, 247–248; Beach, *Submarine!*, 6; Beach, *Salt and Steel: Reflections of a Submariner* (Annapolis, MD: Naval Institute Press, 1999), 92–96; Blair, *Silent Victory*, 247–248; Edward L. Beach, *Salt and Steel: Reflections of a Submariner*, Annapolis, MD: Naval Institute Press, 1999), 131.
4. Beach, *Salt and Steel*, 130–131; Edward L. Beach, interview by the author, Naval Submarine League Annual Conference, Alexandria, Virginia, 13 June 2001; *The Lucky Bag 1927*, 392.
5. Blair, *Silent Victory*, 380; *The Lucky Bag 1927*, 392; Jack Hayden Lewis Biography File, NHHC.
6. Lewis, Jack H. Lt JG, USN Between Wars 1931 to 1941, SECNAV Letter of Commendation, Jack H. Lewis Biography file, NHHC.
7. *Swordfish*, WPR No. 7, 1–3, NHHC.
8. *Ibid.*, 27
9. *Ibid.*, 30.
10. Richard B. Frank, *Guadalcanal: The Definitive Account of the Landmark Battle* (New York: Penguin Books, 1990, 1992 reprint), 545.
11. *Ibid.*, 4.
12. *Ibid.*, 5.
13. *Ibid.*, 26.
14. *Ibid.*, 6, 24. See also Commander Submarine Force, Pacific Fleet, Action Report, Serial 0401, 24 March 1943, USS *Swordfish*, RG 38, Box 742, NARA.
15. *Swordfish*, WPR No. 7, 6–7, NHHC. See also Commander Submarine Force, Pacific Fleet, Action Report, Serial 0401, 24 March 1943, USS *Swordfish*, RG 38, Box 742, NARA.
16. *Swordfish*, WPR No. 7, NHHC.
17. Alden and McDonald, *United States,* 62. See also JANAC Appendix, 47; Frank, *Guadalcanal,* 545.
18. *Swordfish*, WPR No. 7, 12, NHHC.
19. *Ibid.*, 22.
20. Fields, 4, NHHC.
21. *Swordfish*, WPR No. 7, 13, 22, NHHC.
22. *Ibid.*, 14; Kramer, interview, 18 January 2001.
23. Commander Submarine Force, Pacific Fleet, Serial 0276, 1 March 1943, "Strafing of USS *Swordfish* by USAAF Plane," Action Report, RG 38, Box 742, NARA.
24. *Swordfish*, WPR No. 7, 14–15, NHHC.
25. *Ibid.*, 14, 26. See also Fields, 5, NHHC.
26. *Swordfish*, WPR No. 7, 15, NHHC.
27. *Swordfish*, WPR No. 5; Charles A. Lockwood, Second Endorsement, 5 October 1942, 1, NHHC.
28. *Swordfish*, WPR No. 7, 16, NHHC. See also Commander Submarine Force, Pacific Fleet, Serial 0276, 1 March 1943, "Strafing of USS *Swordfish* by USAAF Plane," Action Report, RG 38, Box 742, NARA.

Notes—Chapter 4

29. *Swordfish*, WPR No. 7, 18, NHHC.
30. *Ibid.* 19. The track chart for the seventh war patrol indicates the area that *Swordfish* had patrolled, ranging from north of the Ninigo Island Group to the area west of Bougainville. See U.S.S. *Swordfish*, Seventh War Patrol Track Chart, January 16–February 7, 1943, RG313, NARA.
31. *Swordfish*, WPR No. 7, 26–28, NHHC; *Ibid.*, 26–28. See also *Swordfish*, WPR No. 6, Enclosure H, 1–3, NHHC.
32. *Swordfish*, WPR No. 7, 27–29, NHHC.
33. *Ibid.*, 33.
34. Charles A. Lockwood, Endorsement, Serial Number 273, 1 March 1943 in *Swordfish*, WPR No. 7, NHHC.
35. Jack H. Lewis, U.S. Navy Board of Decorations & Medals, Letter of Commendation (Ribbon) by CINPAC, D4TH End File, p151/83 conf., Serial 01914, 5 March 1945, Rec'd Board of Decorations & Medals, 16 March 1945, Lewis Biography File, NHHC; Kramer, interview, 18 January 2001.
36. Commander Submarine Force, United States Pacific Fleet, Administration, "Patrol Incidents, Dragonet First," Box 18, Charles A. Lockwood Papers, Naval Historical Foundation Collection, MD, LC; Clay Blair, *Silent Victory*, 806. See also Roscoe, 428–429.
37. U.S. Navy Board of Decoration & Medals, Jack H. Lewis, bronze Star Medal by Cin Pac, 4th End File, P15/SS Conf. Serial 01847, 3 March 1945. Rec'd Bd. D&M 14 March 1945, Jack H. Lewis Biography File, NHHC.
38. VADM Charles A. Lockwood, letter dated 15 June 1955; Jack H. Lewis, Ser. 434 of 27 June 1955, Approved by SECNAV on 28 July 1956, in Lewis Biography File, NHHC; J. Reilly Lewis (son of Jack Hayden Lewis), telephone interview by author, 6 February 2013; Jack Hayden Lewis Biography File, Letter of Commendation, 23 August 1945, NHHC; *Ibid.* J. Reilly Lewis (son of Jack Hayden Lewis), telephone interview by author, 6 February 2013.
39. *Swordfish*, WPR No. 7, Commander, Submarine Division 42, Endorsement, Serial No. 04, 25 February 1943, NHHC.
40. Cooper and Gaither, 10–11, NHHC.
41. *Ibid.*, 11.
42. *Ibid.*, 10.
43. *Ibid.*, 15; *Swordfish*, WPR No. 8, 1, NHHC; Friedman, 235–236.
44. *Swordfish*, WPR No. 6, Enclosure H, 2, NHHC.
45. *Swordfish*, Patrol Report No. 7, 33, NHHC.
46. Holmes, *Undersea Victory*, 164–166.
47. Frank M. Parker, USS *Argonaut*, Letter of Commendation, Cinpac File P15 (2) / (05) Serial 02733, 15 September 1942, Parker Biography File, NHHC.
48. Walter Karig, "The Makin Island Raid," *United States Naval Institute Proceedings* 72. no. 10 (October 1946): 1282.
49. *The Lucky Bag*, 1932, 76; Frank Mahlon Parker, biography File, NHHC.
50. *Swordfish*, WPR No. 8, 1, NHHC.
51. *Ibid.*, 1–2.
52. *Ibid.*, 2–4.
53. *Ibid.*, 4, 23.
54. *Ibid.*, 4–5.
55. *Ibid.*, 5, 12–13.
56. *Ibid.*, 12, 21.
57. Alden and McDonald, *United States*, 94. See also JANAC, Appendix, 47.
58. *Swordfish*, WPR No. 8, 21–24, NHHC.
59. Faye believed *Swordfish* was wearing out. Faye, interview, 28 February 2003.
60. *Swordfish*, WPR No. 8, 5, 21, NHHC.
61. *Ibid.*, 5.
62. *Ibid.*
63. Dennis, interview, 17 January 2001.
64. *Swordfish*, WPR No. 8, 5, NHHC.
65. Leymon Dennis, Audio tape recording, 5 September 2000; Dennis, telephone interview by author, 17 January 2001.
66. *Swordfish*, WPR No. 8, 7, NHHC.
67. *Ibid.*, 21.
68. *Ibid.*, 8.
69. *Ibid.*, 21.
70. *Ibid.*
71. *Ibid.*, 8, 21.
72. *Ibid.*, 21.
73. *Ibid.*, 9, 21.
74. Alden and McDonald, *United States*, 97. See also JANAC, Appendix, 47.
75. *Swordfish*, WPR No. 8, 9–10, NHHC.
76. *Swordfish*, WPR No. 8, 10, 18–19, NHHC.
77. *Ibid.*, 10, 22.
78. Kramer, interview, 18 January 2001; O'Brient, interview, 21 December 2000.
79. Kramer, interview, 18 January 2001; Dennis, interview, 17 January 2000.
80. Kramer, interview, 18 January 2001.
81. Kramer, interview, 18 January 2001; O'Brient, interview, 21 December 2000; Dennis, interview, 17 January 2001.
82. J. A. Connolly, Commander Submarine Division Twenty-two, 23 September 1943, Endorsement, FB5–22/A16–3(Serial 045b) in *Swordfish*, WPR No. 8, NHHC.
83. Robert Lee Harrington, telephone interview by author, 22 November 2000.

84. *Swordfish*, WPR No. 8, 10, 20, 22, NHHC.

85. J. B. Griggs, Acting Commander Submarine Force, Pacific Fleet, Third Endorsement, 3 October 1943 Serial 01387 in *Swordfish*, WPR No. 8, NHHC. See also C. W. Styer, Commander Submarine Force, Pacific Fleet, Subordinate Command No. 1504, Second Endorsement Letter, 20 September 1943, SS 193/A9/A16–3 serial in *Swordfish*, WPR No. 8, NHHC. The track chart for Parker's patrol illustrates his steadfast pursuit of targets. Also, there's an inset map for the region around Manokwarei. See U.S.S. *Swordfish*, Track Chart, Eighth War Patrol, 9/30/43, Area Ten Able. RG313, NARA.

86. J. A. Connolly, Commander Submarine Division Twenty-two, Endorsement, 23 September 1943, FB5–22/A16–3 Serial (045B) in *Swordfish*, WPR No. 8, NHHC. See also Parker, Biographical File, NHHC.

87. O'Briant, interview, 21 December 2000; Leymon Dennis, interview by author at U.S. Submarine Veterans of World War II Annual Meeting, St. Louis, Missouri, 24 August 2001.

88. J. A. Connolly, Commander Submarine Division Twenty-two, Endorsement, 23 September 1943, FB5–22/A16–3 Serial (045B), in *Swordfish*, WPR No. 8, NHHC.

89. *Ibid.*

90. Cooper and Gaither, "War Patrols of USS *Swordfish* and USS *Sargo*," 11, NHHC.

91. *Swordfish*, WPR No. 9, 1, NHHC.

92. *Ibid.*, 1–2.

93. *Ibid.*; Kramer, interview, 18 January 2001; O'Briant, interview, 21 December 2000.

94. Parker, Biographical File, NHHC.

95. O'Briant, interview, 21 December 2000; Kramer, interview, 18 January 2001.

96. *Swordfish*, WPR No. 9, 2, NHHC.

97. Frank Lloyd Barrows, USS *Gudgeon*, Silver Star Medal—by CINPAC Serial 39. Cinpac letter dated 17 August 1943, File Pac-08-rel P15/B4 Ser. 2590, in Frank M. Barrows, Biography File, NHHC.

98. Frank L. Barrows, USS *Gar*, "Awarded Gold Star in Lieu of Second Silver Star Medal." ComSubForPaFile FF12–10/P15 Serial 2118 Dtd 6 October 1947 Recd Bd D&M 2 c 1947, in Barrows Biography File, NHHC. See also, Frank Lloyd Barrows, Officer Biography Sheet, NAVPERS 9.9 (Rev. 5–53), in Barrows Biography File, NHHC; *The Lucky Bag 1935*, 288.

99. O'Briant, interview, 21 December 2000; Dennis, interview, 17 January 2001.

100. *Swordfish*, Patrol Report No. 9, 2–3, NHHC.

101. *Ibid.*, 12.

102. *Ibid.*

103. O'Briant, interview, 21 December 2000; Dennis, interview, 17 January 2001.

104. Kramer, interview, 25 January 2003.

105. *Swordfish*, WPR No. 9, 3–5, NHHC.

106. *Ibid.*, 5.

107. *Ibid.*

108. *Ibid.*

109. *Ibid.*, 6, 11.

110. *Ibid.*, 6, 9.

111. *Ibid.*, 6.

112. *Ibid.*, 7.

113. *Ibid.* Barrows patrolled the region between Moroto Zaki and Ichie Saki. See USS *Swordfish*, Ninth War Patrol Track Chart, November 1943, Area Six, RG313, NARA.

114. Leymon Dennis to author, correspondence, 9 August 2000; Dennis, tape recording, 5 September 2000; Dennis, interview, 24 August 2001. See also Michael Sturma, *The USS Flier: Death and Survival on a World War II Submarine* (Lexington, KY: 2008), 21.

115. Frank Lloyd Barrows, Officer Biography Sheet, NAVPERS 9.9 (Rev. 5–53), 15 October 1953, Barrows Biography File, NHHC. Blair, *Silent Victory,* 533; U.S. Naval History Division, *Dictionary of...*, Volume IV, 435; O'Briant, interview, 21 December 2000.

116. *Lucky Bag 1935*, 288; Frank Lloyd Barrows Biography File, NHHC.

117. O'Briant, interview, 21 December 2000; Dennis to author, 9 August 2000 and interview, 17 January 2001; Kramer, interview, 25 January 2003; Faye, interview, 28 February 2003; *The Lucky Bag 1935*, 288; Frank Lloyd Barrows Biography File, NHHC.

118. *Swordfish*, WPR No. 9, 13, NHHC.

119. Joseph A. Connolly, First Endorsement, 6 December 1943, FB5–45/A16–3, Serial 092(B) in *Swordfish*, WPR No. 9, NHHC.

120. *Swordfish*, WPR No. 9, 13, NHHC.

121. *Ibid.*

122. *Ibid.*, 11–12.

123. Joseph A. Connolly, First Endorsement, 6 December 1943, FB5–45/A16–3, Serial 092(B) in *Swordfish*, WPR No. 9, NHHC.

124. *Ibid.*

125. Cooper and Gaither, 13, NHHC.

Chapter 5

1. *The Great Sea War: The Story of Naval Action in World War II*, edited by E. B. Potter and Chester W. Nimitz (Englewood Cliffs,

NJ: Prentice-Hall, 1960), 284–309, Chapter 11; Nimitz and Potter, *Triumph in the Pacific*, 72; Clark G. Reynolds, *The Fast Carriers: the Forging of an Air Navy* (Annapolis, MD: Naval Institute Press, 1968), Chapters 3 and 4; Lockwood, *Sink 'Em All*, p. 155. Bernard Ireland, *Jane's Naval History of World War II* (New York: Harper Collins, 1998), 110.

2. John Bunker, *Heroes in Dungarees: The Story of the American Merchant Marine in World War II* (Annapolis, MD: Naval Institute Press, 1995), Chapters 5 and 9. See also R. A. Bowling, "Mahan's Principles and the Battle of the Atlantic," in *To Die Gallantly: The Battle of the Atlantic*, eds. Timothy Runyan and Jan M. Copes (Boulder, CO: Westview Press, 1994), 249; George J. Billy and Christine M. Billy, *Merchant Mariners at War: An Oral History of World War II* (Gainesville: University of Florida Press, 2008), Chapters 3, 4, and 5. For detailed accounts of U-boat operations and conditions aboard the German boats, see Clay Blair, Jr., *Hitler's U-boat War: The Hunters, 1939–1942*, Volume 1 (New York: Random House, 1996); and Clay Blair, Jr., *Hitler's U-boat War: The Hunted, 1942–1945*, Volume 2 (New York: Random House, 1998). See also Timothy Mulligan, *Neither Sharks Nor Wolves: The Men of Nazi Germany's U-boat Arm, 1939–1945* (Annapolis, MD: Naval Institute Press, 1999). For the story of Allied deciphering of the German Navy's secret codes, see David Kahn, *Seizing the Enigma: The Race to Break the German U-boat Codes, 1939–1943* (New York: Barnes and Noble, 1991, 1998).

3. Potter and Nimitz, *Triumph in the Pacific*, 72–73. See also Clay Blair, Jr. *Silent Victory*, 308–309; *Swordfish*, WPR No. 10, 3, NHHC.

4. J. A. Connolly, First Endorsement, A16-3 Conf Letr. of 5 December 1943, in *Swordfish* WPR No. 9, NHHC. *Swordfish*, WPR No. 10, 2.

5. *Swordfish*, WPR No. 10, 2, NHHC; Karl G. Hensel to Clay Blair, Jr. Correspondence, 15 May 1972, Clay Blair Papers, Accession Number 8295, Box 79, Folder 68, Folder Title: "Research File, *Silent Victory*, Skippers of U.S. World War II, 1944–1967, 1971–1972, Pacific Ocean Submarine Patrols, He-Hol," AHC. See also U.S. Navy, "Rear Admiral Karl G. Hensel Retired," Hensel Biography File, August 31, 1974, 1, NHHC; Blair, *Silent Victory*, 533; Lockwood, *Sink 'Em All*, 93–94; W. J. Holmes, *Undersea Victory*, 287.

6. Karl G. Hensel to Clay Blair, Jr., Correspondence, 15 May 1972, Clay Blair Papers, Accession Number 8295, Box 68, Folder Number 2, Folder Title, "Research File, *Silent Victory*, Skippers of U.S. World War II, 1944–1967, 1971–1972, Pacific Ocean Submarine Patrols, He-Hol," AHC.

7. Two crewmen of *Swordfish* who became quite familiar with Captain Hensel on the tenth patrol were William P. O'Briant, Yeoman First Class (called "OB" by fellow crewmen), and Leymon L. Dennis, Quartermaster First Class (called "Denny" by fellow crewmen). O'Briant, interview, 21 December 2000; Dennis to author, 9 August 2000; Dennis, Audiotape, 5 September 2000. Although Lockwood did not name Hensel, Lockwood described Hensel's request to go on a war patrol in his autobiographical account of his war experiences and bemoaned the fact that he was not able to go on patrol himself. See Lockwood, *Sink 'Em All*, 83. See also Blair, *Silent Victory*, 463; W. J. Holmes, *Silent Victory*, 287.

8. Karl G. Hensel to Clay Blair, Jr., Correspondence, 15 May 1972, Clay Blair Papers, Accession Number 8295, Box Number 68, Folder Number 2, Folder Title: "Research Files, *Silent Victory*, Skippers of U.S. World War II, 1944–1967, 1971–1972, Pacific Ocean Submarine Patrols, He-Hol," AHC.

9. Blair, *Silent Victory*, 533.

10. *Swordfish*, Muster Roll of the Crew, Report of Changes, 29 December 1943 and 31 December 1943, Reel No. 7434, RG24, NARA; Dennis, interview, January 17, 2001; O'Briant, interview, 5 June 2000; Karl G. Hensel to Clay Blair, Jr., Correspondence, 15 May 1972, Clay Blair Papers, Accession Number 8295, Box Number 68, Folder Title: "Research File, *Silent Victory*, Skippers of U.S. World War II, 1944–1961, 1971–1972, Pacific Ocean Submarine Patrols, He-Hol," AHC. See also W. J. Holmes, *Undersea Victory*, 287. U.S. Navy.

11. Karl Hensel, video interview by Katherine Wikstrom, granddaughter of Karl Hensel, 7 September 1991, McLean, Virginia, DVD.

12. *Swordfish*, WPR No. 10, 2–3, NHHC.

13. Cooper and Gaither, 17, NHHC.

14. Karl G. Hensel to Clay Blair, Jr., Correspondence, 15 May 1972, Clay Blair Papers, Accession Number 8295, Box Number 68, folder Number 2, Folder Title: "Research File, *Silent Victory*, skippers of U.S. World War II, 1944–1967, 1971–1972, Pacific Ocean Submarine Patrols, He-Hol," AHC.

15. Karl Hensel, video interview by Katherine Wikstrom, 7 September 1991; *Swordfish*, WPR No. 10, 3–4, NHHC.

16. *Swordfish*, WPR No. 10, 5–6, NHHC.
17. *Ibid.*, 6–7.
18. *Ibid.*, 7, 26.
19. *Ibid.*
20. *Ibid.*, 7–8, 26.
21. *Ibid.*, 8. See also JANAC, Appendix, 48; Alden and McDonald, *United States*, 125.
22. Cressman, 205.
23. *Swordfish*, WPR No. 10, 8, NHHC.
24. *Ibid.*; See also Cooper and Gaither, 17.
25. *Swordfish*, WPR No. 10, 8, NHHC.
26. Cooper and Gaither, 18.
27. *Swordfish*, Deck Log Operational Remarks (War Diary), 14 January 1944, 14, RG24, NARA.
28. Cooper and Gaither, 18.
29. *Ibid. Swordfish*, WPR No. 10, 8, NHHC; Paul Marvin, Narrative, "War Patrols of USS *Swordfish*," Recorded 20 October 1944, Transcribed at Pearl Harbor, Film No. S-93, p. 20, NHHC.
30. Lockwood, *Sink 'Em All*, 123.
31. *Swordfish*, WPR No. 10, 8, NHHC.
32. Karl Hensel, video interview by Katherine Wikstrom, 7 September 1991; O'Briant interviews, 21 December 2000 and 14 January 2002; *Swordfish*, WPR No. 10, 8, NHHC.
33. *Swordfish*, WPR No. 10, 8, 37, NHHC; Marvin, 20.
34. Marvin, 20.
35. *Swordfish*, WPR No. 10, 8, NHHC.
36. Arthur Myers, telephone interview by author, 27 July 2001.
37. Blair, *Silent Victory*, 534; *Swordfish*, WPR No. 10, 9, NHHC; Karl Hensel, interview by Katherine Wikstrom, 7 September 1991.
38. *Swordfish*, WPR No. 10, 9, NHHC.
39. *Ibid.*, 9, 26.
40. *Ibid.*, 9, 27.
41. *Ibid.*, 9, 28.
42. *Ibid.*, 9–10, 28–29.
43. JANAC, Appendix, 48; Alden and McDonald, *United States*, 126; *Swordfish*, WPR No. 10, 10, NHHC; Karl G. Hensel to Clay Blair, Jr. Correspondence, May 15, 1972, Clay Blair Papers, Accession Number 8295, Box 68, Folder 2, Folder Title: "Research Files, *Silent Victory*, Skippers of U.S. World War II, 1944–1967, 1971–1972, Pacific Ocean Submarine Patrols, He-Hol," AHC. See also Blair, *Silent Victory*, 534; W. J. Holmes, *Silent Victory*, 288–289. Submarine veteran C. Mike Carmody (USS *Pampanito*) commemorated *Swordfish's* success by painting "*Swordfish* (SS193) Sinks Delhi Maru, 16 January 1944." The oil painting appeared as the cover illustration of *Polaris* magazine. See *Polaris* 52, no. 4 (October 2007): cover.
44. Charles Lockwood, Second Endorsement, SSWP/A16-3, Serial S-0063, 5 October 1952, in *Swordfish*, WPR No. 5, NHHC. See also Cressman, 205.
45. *Swordfish*, WPR No. 10, 10, NHHC; *Swordfish*, Deck Log Operational Remarks (War Diary), 16 January 1944, 16, RG 24, NARA.
46. *Swordfish*, WPR No. 10, 10, NHHC. For information on the Chidori Class patrol vessels, See *Conway's All the World's Fighting Ships, 1922–1946*, eds. Robert Gardiner and Roger Chesneau (New York: Mayflower Books, 1980), 197.
47. O'Briant, interview, 21 December 2000.
48. *Swordfish*, WPR No. 10, 10, NHHC.
49. *Ibid.*, 10–11; Karl G. Hensel to Clay Blair, Jr., Correspondence, May 20, 1972, Clay Blair Papers, Accession Number 8295, Box 68, Folder Number 2, Folder Title: "Research Files, *Silent Victory*, Skippers of U.S. World War II, 1944–1967, 1971–1972, Pacific Ocean submarine Patrols, He-Hol," AHC; Blair, *Silent Victory*, 87, 259.
50. Karl Hensel, video interview by Katherine Wikstrom, 7 September 1991, McLean, Virginia, DVD; *Swordfish*, WPR No. 10, 11, HHC.
51. *Ibid.*
52. *Ibid.*, 12.
53. *Ibid.*; See also *Swordfish*, Deck Log Operational Remarks (War Diary), 17 January 1944, 17, RG24, NARA.
54. *Swordfish*, WPR No. 10, 12, 30, NHHC.
55. *Ibid.*, 12, 30–31.
56. *Ibid.*, 12.
57. *Ibid.* See also Blair, *Silent Victory*, 535.
58. Blair, *Silent Victory*, 535; Prados, John, *Combined Fleet Decoded: The Secret History of American Intelligence and the Japanese Navy in World War II* (Annapolis, MD: Naval Institute Press, 1995), 533; William T. Y'Blood, *Red Sun Setting: The Battle of the Philippine Sea* (Annapolis, MD: Naval Institute Press, 1981), 128; Cressman, 237. See also *Conway's All the World's...*, 181.
59. *Swordfish*, WPR No. 10, 14, NHHC.
60. Dennis, interview, 24 August 2001. Karl Hensel was not the only skipper who set up a bunk in a conning tower. David Welchel, commander of the USS *Steelhead*, maintained a bunk in the conning tower. Milton Seltzer, *Steelhead* veteran, interview by author, 6

Notes—Chapter 5

December 2004, Garden City, NY. Marvin G. Kennedy, early skipper of the *Wahoo*, also had a bunk in the conning tower. See George Grider, *War Fish* (Boston: Little, Brown, 1958), 72; Blair, *Silent Victory*, 333. As previously noted, Jack Lewis also utilized a bunk in the conning tower while aboard *Trigger*.

61. *Swordfish*, WPR No. 10, 15–18, NHHC.
62. Ibid., 43.
63. Ibid.
64. Robert L. Harrington, telephone interview by author, 22 November 2000.
65. Faye, interview, February 28, 2003. For a detailed discussion of the food and cooking aboard submarines, see Phillip T. Rutherford, "Pig Boats, Fleet Boats, and Mystery Meat: U.S. Submarine Food, 1941–1945," *Undersea Warfare* (Fall 2011): 22–27.
66. David Hensel (son of Karl Hensel) to author, email, 19 June 2008.
67. Karl G. Hensel, interview by Katherine Wikstrom (granddaughter of Karl Hensel), 7 September 1991, McLean, VA, DVD.
68. Ibid., 18.
69. Ibid.
70. Ibid., 19.
71. Marvin, 21.
72. *Swordfish*, WPR No. 10, 19, NHHC.
73. Ibid.
74. Ibid.
75. Marvin, 21.
76. *Swordfish*, WPR No. 10, 19, NHHC.
77. Ibid., 36.
78. Ibid., 19.
79. Training Reference Materials #5, Reference Materials on Anti-submarine Warfare, CINPAC-CINPOA #B-16493, 23 April 1944, Records of Naval Operating Forces Command Submarine Force, Pacific Fleet, Confidential General Administrative Files, Flag Files (Blue 440), 1942–1945, RG 313, File A8(2), Box 14, DC 313-A1(223) 6, NARA.
80. *Swordfish*, WPR No. 10, 19–20, NHHC; *Swordfish*, Deck Log Operational Remarks (War Diary), 27 January 1944, RG 24, NARA.
81. *Swordfish*, WPR No. 10, 20, NHHC; JANAC, Appendix, 48; Alden and McDonald, *United States*, 4th ed., 130.
82. Dennis to author, correspondence, 3 July 2000. Also successful that day, the USS *Thresher* "bagged" two enemy ships southwest of Formosa. See Cressman, 208.
83. Dennis, Audio tape to author, 5 September 2000.
84. *Swordfish*, WPR No. 10, 20, NHHC; JANAC, Appendix, 48. For the location of Hensel's attacks, see USS *Swordfish*, Tenth War Patrol Track Chart, January 1944, Area Four. RG313, NARA. The chart shows where the *Swordfish* patrolled on the surface and where submerged.
85. Dan van der Vat, *The Pacific Campaign: World War II, The U.S.-Japanese Naval War, 1941–1945* (New York: Simon & Schuster, 1991, 1992), 306–307; H. P. Wilmott, *The Second World War in the East* (London: Cassell, 1999), 127, 215; Reynolds, *The Fast Carriers*, 136–141.
86. Without exception, all the *Swordfish* veterans interviewed by the author displayed an intense pride in their boat and her record of service.
87. Seltzer, interview, 6 December 2004; Eddie Peabody to Charles A. Lockwood, 20 May 1944, Official Correspondence, Box 14, Charles A. Lockwood Papers, Naval Historical Foundation Collection, MD, LC.
88. Peabody to Lockwood, 20 May 1944, Box 14, Charles A. Lockwood Papers, Naval Historical Foundation, MD, LC.
89. Ensign Floyd M. Cooper remembered the enjoyable stint of relaxation. Cooper and Gaither, 13, NHHC. In July 1944, Lockwood expected the Royal Hawaiian Hotel to accommodate a peak load of relaxing personnel that would include 135 officers and 1125 enlisted men. With some alterations, the hotel could accommodate even more personnel. Commander Submarine Force, Pacific Fleet to Vice Admiral J.H. Towers, 18 July 1944, Official Correspondence, Box 14, Charles A. Lockwood Papers, Naval Historical Foundation Collection, MD, LC.
90. *Swordfish*, WPR No. 10, 37–38, NHHC.
91. Ibid., 38.
92. Charles R. Momsen, Second Endorsement to *Swordfish* Conference Letter, SS193/A9/A16-3, Ser. 1 dated 7 February 1944 in *Swordfish*, WPR No. 10, NHHC. For accounts of Momsen's rescue of crewmen of *Squalus*, a sister ship of *Swordfish*, see Peter Maas, *The Terrible Hours: The Man Behind the Greatest Submarine Rescue in History* (New York: HarperCollins, 1999); and Nathaniel A. Barrows, *Blow All Ballast! The Story of the Squalus* (New York: Dodd, Mead, 1940).
93. Momsen, Second Endorsement in *Swordfish*, WPR No. 10, NHHC. In addition, Admiral Christie asked Admiral Lockwood to tell Hensel how very pleased the submarine personnel were with the success of Hensel's patrol. Charles A. Lockwood to Captain J. B.

Longstaff, Commander Submarine Squadron Fourteen, 12 July 1944, Box 14, Charles A. Lockwood Papers, Naval Historical Foundation Collection, MD, LC.
  94. U.S. Navy, Cinc Pac, "Hensel, Karl G, Capt. USN, SWORDFISH," Awarded: Navy Cross by Cinc Pac ltr., 18 April 1944, File Pac-052-rel P15/BA Serial 01489, Confidential (Cinc Pac Serial 56) Rec'd Bd D&M 4–29–44, Hensel Biography File, NHHC.
  95. Marvin, 20.
  96. Charles A. Lockwood, Jr. COMSUBSP.C., Endorsement to Patrol Report No. 363, USS *Swordfish*-Tenth War Patrol, 7 February 1944 in *Swordfish*, WPR No. 10, NHHC.
  97. Ibid.
  98. Ernest Hemingway, *The Old Man and the Sea* (New York: Scribner's, 1952, 1980), 122.
  99. U.S. Navy, "Rear Admiral Karl G. Hensel," 3, Hensel Biography File, NHHC.
  100. *Swordfish*, WPR No. 10, 43, NHHC.
  101. Dennis to author, Correspondence, 9 August 2000.
  102. *Ibid.* Fred Kramer was an Electrician's Mate First Class; Kramer, interview, 18 January 2001; Fred Kramer, USS *Swordfish* Memorabilia Book, unpublished; O'Briant, interview, 21 December 2000.
  103. Photograph of Rear Admiral Karl G. Hensel, Fort Myers, Florida, in Kramer, Memorabilia Book.
  104. U.S. Navy, "Rear Admiral Karl G. Hensel," 2–3, Hensel Biography File, NHHC.
  105. *Ibid.*; Karl G. Hensel to Joe Parks, Correspondence, 3 July 1989 (provided by Joe Parks).
  106. Dennis to author, 9 August 2000; Kramer, interview, 18 January 2001.

Chapter 6

  1. Lockwood, *Sink 'Em All,* 155; Ruth Smith (sister-in-law of Keats Montross), telephone interview, 24 September 2009; *The Lucky Bag*, 1935, 281.
  2. Keats E. Montross, "War Patrols of the USS *Swordfish*," Narrative, Recorded 22 September 1944, Transcribed at Pearl Harbor, Film No. S-87, 19, NHHC.
  3. *Ibid.,* 19–20; Keats Edmund Montross Biography File, Pers-5323a-rra 75109, NHHC. See also John Wilson Taylor and Eva Mills (Lee), *Montross: A Family History: Pierre Montross and His Descendants, a Record of 300 Years of the Montras-Montross-Montrose-Montress Family in the United States and Canada* (Staunton, VA: McClure Printing, 1958), 143, 236, 592–593; Friedman, 97, 288.
  4. O'Briant, interview, 21 December 2000; Dennis, interview, 17 January 2001.
  5. Arthur C. Myers, telephone interview with author, 27 July 2001.
  6. Dennis, interview, 24 August 2001.
  7. *Swordfish*, WPR No. 11, 18, NHHC.
  8. *Ibid.*
  9. Montross, "War Patrols of USS *Swordfish*," 3, NHHC.
  10. *Swordfish*, WPR No. 11, 3, NHHC.
  11. Ibid., 11. USS *Swordfish*, Administrative Remarks, 5 April 1944, 5, RG 24, NARA.
  12. *Swordfish*, WPR No. 11, 4, NHHC.
  13. *Ibid.*
  14. *Ibid.*, 5.
  15. Keats E. Montross, "War Patrols of USS *Swordfish*," 3, NHHC.
  16. *Swordfish*, WPR No. 11, 5, NHHC.
  17. "Japanese Aerial Anti-submarine Tactics," United States Pacific Fleet and Pacific Ocean Areas, CINCPAC-CINCPOA Special Translation, 23 December 1944, No. 18, p. 27. Records of the Japanese Navy and Related Documents, 1940–1960, Vol. 4, File Item 18, NHHC. See also "Protection of Convoys from Submarines," Allied Translator and Interpreter Section, Current Translations, 16 July 1944, 32–33, Records of the Japanese Navy and Related Documents, 1940–1960, Box 59, File ATIS IX-129, No. 1386, NHHC.
  18. *Swordfish*, WPR No. 11, 5–6, NHHC.
  19. *Ibid.*, 6.
  20. *Ibid.*
  21. *Ibid.*, 6–7.
  22. *Ibid.*, 7–8. The track chart for the 11th war patrol indicates 15 encounters with aircraft. See USS *Swordfish*, Eleventh War Patrol Track Chart, RG313, NARA.
  23. Karl G. Hensel, Submarine Division 101, First Endorsement, FB-101/A16–3, Series 023, 29 April 1944, in *Swordfish*, WPR No. 11, NHHC. See also C. F. Erck, second Endorsement, FC5–10/A16–3(5), Serial 090, 29 April 1944 in *Swordfish*, WPR No. 11, NHHC.
  24. Cooper and Gaither, "War Patrols of USS *Swordfish* and USS *Sargo*," 13, NHHC.
  25. Michael Billy, Personnel File, NPRC.
  26. Commander Submarine Squadron Fifty (J. D. Watson for H. C. Tucker) to F/c Michael Billy, FC5–50/15, 2 August 1943, Michael Billy, Personnel File, National Service Records Center, St. Louis, Missouri; Michael Billy Personnel File, "Transfer to USS *Swordfish* for

Duty," 13 May 1944, National Service Records Center, St. Louis, MO. National Personnel Records Center, hereafter cited as NPRC.

27. *Swordfish*, WPR No. 11, 15, NHHC.

28. *Ibid.*, 14–15.

29. *Ibid.*, 8, 14–15. See also *Swordfish*, WPR No. 12, 1, NHHC.

30. John M. McCain and Mark Salter, *Faith of My Fathers* (New York: Random House, 1999), 79–82; Blair, *Silent Victory*, 264–266.

31. On 22 October 2010, fireboat personnel from New York Fire Department Marine Company Number 9, Staten Island, New York, operated one of two GM Winton engines aboard the fireboat, *Firefighter*, identical to the engines on *Swordfish*. The author thanks Firemen Martin Gray and Ray Geara for interviews and for permitting the author to see and hear the Wintons in operation. For information on *Firefighter*, see Norman J. Brower, *The International Register of Historic Ships*, 3d ed. (Peekskill, NY: Sea History Press, 1999), 291.

32. Montross, "War Patrols of the USS *Swordfish*," 12, NHHC.

33. Charles A. Lockwood to R. H. Rice, Submarine Detail Officer, 19 October 1944, Box 14, Charles A. Lockwood Papers, Naval Historical Foundation Collection, MD, LC.

34. *Ibid.*

35. *Swordfish*, Muster Roll of the Crew, Report of Changes, 22 May 1944, Reel No. 7434, RG24, NARA; Hargis, 19; Dennis to author, correspondence, September 9, 2000.

36. *Swordfish*, WPR No. 12, 1–2, NHHC.

37. Lockwood, *Sink 'Em All*, 23.

38. Montross, "War Patrols of USS *Swordfish*," 13, NHHC; Roscoe, 324, 388, 449. A broad history of U.S. submarine wolf packs is provided in Steven Trent Smith, *Wolfpack: The American Submarine Strategy that Helped Defeat Japan* (New York: Wiley, 2003).

39. *Swordfish*, WPR No. 12, 3, NHHC.

40. *Ibid.*, 3–4, 16.

41. JANAC, Appendix, 48. *Japanese Naval Vessels at the End of War*, Compiler: Shizuo Fukui, Administrative Division, Second Demobilization Bureau, 25 April 1947, 32, Records of the Japanese Navy and Related Documents, 1940–1960, Vol. 4, NHHC; Alden and McDonald, *United States*, 165; Paul S. Dull, *The Battle History of the Imperial Japanese Navy (1941–1945)*(Annapolis, MD: Naval Institute Press, 1978), 296. See also Anthony J. Watts, *Japanese Warships of World War II* (Garden City, NY: Doubleday, 1966, 1967), 122; Freeman Westel, "Japan's Deadly WWII Destroyer Fleet," *Sea Classics* 43, no. 5 (May 2010): 20–25; Tameichi Hara, Fred Saito, and Roger Pineau, *Japanese Destroyer Captain* (New York: Ballantine Books, 1961, 1965), 214–225.

42. Lt. F. W. Allcorn to VADM C. A. Lockwood, Jr., Memorandum, 11 January 1945, Clay Blair Papers, Accession Number 8295, Box 57, Folder 4, Folder title: "*Silent Victory—Administration of U.S. Pacific Fleet—Jan.-Feb. 1945*," AHC. See also Clay Blair, Jr., *Silent Victory*, 508, 511 and 818.

43. *Swordfish*, WPR No. 12, 3–4, 16, NHHC.

44. *Ibid.*, 5–6.

45. Montross, "War Patrols of USS *Swordfish*," 14, NHHC. See also *Swordfish*, WPR No. 12, 5–6, NHHC.

46. Montross, "War Patrols of the USS *Swordfish*," 14, NHHC.

47. *Swordfish*, WPR No.12, 6, 17, NHHC.

48. *Ibid.*, 6.

49. JANAC, Appendix, 48; Alden and McDonald, *United States*, 166.

50. *Swordfish*, WPR No. 12, 8, NHHC.

51. *Ibid.*

52. *Ibid.*, 10.

53. *Ibid.*, 21.

54. *Ibid.*, 10.

55. Photograph, USS *Swordfish* 12(B), Area 11. Japan-General. Sortie Sword-12. Print #9. Caption: "Taken by USS *Swordfish* on the 12TH War Patrol. Taken 26 June 1944. Shows unidentified trawler burning. For data sheet covering this print, see ONI #338654. ONI (P-5) #338–666." USS *Swordfish* Reference File, Submarine Force Library Archives, Groton, CT. See also Alden and McDonald, *United States*, 169.

56. *Swordfish*, WPR No. 12, 10, 22, NHHC.

57. *Ibid.*, 10; Alden and McDonald, *United States*, 170.

58. Montross, "War Patrols of USS *Swordfish*," 6, NHHC. See also *Swordfish*, WPR No. 12, 10, NHHC.

59. Swordfish, WPR No. 12, 11, NHHC.

60. *Ibid.* 23.

61. *Ibid.*, 11, 23; Alden and McDonald, *United States*, 172. For a detailed discussion of surface attacks which other submarines conducted in World War II, see Michael Sturma, *Surface and Destroy: The Submarine Gun War in the Pacific* (Lexington: University of Kentucky Press, 2011). During the 12th patrol, Montross crisscrossed a well-defined area, for the most part between Latitude 30 degrees and 25 degrees North and between Longitude 140

degrees and 144 degrees East. See Twelfth War Patrol Track Chart, RG313, NARA.
62. *Swordfish*, WPR No. 12, 11–12, NHHC.
63. *Ibid.*, 4. See also USS *Swordfish*, Log, July 10, 1944, RG 24, NARA. The log entry reads, "Undergoing Navy Yard Overhaul."
64. *Swordfish*, WPR No. 12, 24–25, NHHC.
65. *Ibid.*, 25.
66. Keats Montross, Silver Star Citation, Cincpac ltr. P15/BA Serial 05480, 9 October 1944, conf. rec'd bd. Dtm 10–24–44 (Cincpac Serial 76), Montross Biography File, NHHC.
67. *Ibid.*
68. Montross, "War Patrols of USS *Swordfish*," 19, NHHC.
69. Roscoe, 324, 388 and 449.

Chapter 7

1. "From Sailing Texans," *Dallas Morning News*, 16 April 1944, Section 2, 8; Elizabeth Hudson, "Dallas Woman Remembers *Swordfish* Fondly," *Navy Times*, 2 February 1987, 42.
2. Hudson, "Dallas Woman...," 42.
3. Dorothy Heath Clary, telephone interview by author, 17 November 2000. See also Dorothy H. Clary Memoirs, WWII, Mss 202c, Series 2, Folder 2, Texas Woman's University, Woman's Collection and University Archives.
4. Hudson, "Dallas Woman...," 42–43.
5. Dorothy H. Clary Memoirs, WWII, Mss 202c, Series 2, Folder 2, 6, Texas Woman's University, Woman's Collection and University Archives.
6. Hudson, "Dallas Woman...," 43; Clary, interview, 17 November 2000.
7. "Sub Crew Chooses Dallas Girl as Favorite for Pin-Up Photo," *Dallas Morning News*, 8 December 1944, Section 2, 1.
8. Clary, interview, November 17, 2000. See also Clary Memoirs, Texas Woman's University.
9. J. R. Moore to Commandant, Navy Yard, Mare Island, California, Subject: USS *Swordfish*-Alterations Authorized, SS-193/L9 (815), 9 June 1944, U.S. Navy Bureau of Ships, General Correspondence, 1940–1945, Vol. 4, RG 19, Entry 1266, Box 1914, NARA; USS *Swordfish*, SS-193, Report of Work Released, 22 March 1945, U.S. Navy, Bureau of Ships Correspondence, 1940–1945, Vol. 4, RG 19, Entry 1266, Box 1914, NARA.
10. Keats E. Montross to Chief of the Bureau of Ships, USS *Swordfish*, SS193/S41, 17 August 1944, U.S. Bureau of Ships, General Correspondence, 1940–1945, Vol. 4, RG 19, Entry 1266, Box 1914, NARA; Charles A. Lockwood, Jr., to Chief of the Bureau of Ships, Subject: Defective Cylinder Heads-G.M. Engine Model 16–284, FF12–10/S41/(C70), Serial 1789, 24 August 1944, U.S. Navy, Bureau of Ships, General Correspondence, 1940–1945, Volume 4, USS *Swordfish* (SS-193), RG19, Entry 1266, Box 1914, NARA.
11. USS *Swordfish*, Deck Log-Remarks Sheet, 8 October 1944, 8, RG 24, NARA.
12. USS *Swordfish*, Deck Log-Remarks Sheet, 9 October 1944, 9, RG 24, NARA; USS *Swordfish*, Deck Log-Remarks Sheet, 12 October 1944, 12, RG 24, NARA.
13. E. R. Swinburne to Chief of the Bureau of Ships, 3 January 1945, NB14/S42 (55-jn), U.S. Navy, Bureau of Ships, General Correspondence, 1940–1945, Volume 4, USS *Swordfish* (SS-193), RG19, Entry 1266, Box 1914, NARA.
14. *Ibid.* As a part of the gear train, reduction gears were used to lower the speed of power emanating from the main propulsion motors and before going to the boat's propeller shafts. In general, reduction gears were characteristically noisy. Kenneth Jacobs (USS *Queenfish* veteran), interview by author, Garden City, NY, 3 December 2007; Albert LaRocca (USS *Spadefish* veteran), interview by author, Garden City, NY, 3 December 2007; Joseph Librizzi (USS *Balao* veteran), interview by author, Garden City, NY, 3 December 2007.
15. E. R. Swinburne to Chief of the Bureau of Ships, 3 January 1945, NB14/S42 (55-jn), U.S. Navy, Bureau of Ships, General Correspondence, 1940–1945, Volume 4, USS *Swordfish* (SS0–193), RG19, Entry 1266, Box 1914, NARA.
16. *Ibid.*
17. *Ibid.* In connection with the damaged reduction gear incident, the author has searched the records of the National Archives and Records Administration in College Park, MD, and the National Archives and Records Administration branch at San Bruno, CA, which holds documents related to operations at the Pearl Harbor Naval Shipyard. In addition, the author has examined the Charles A. Lockwood Papers, MD, LC. Note: the National Archives and Records Administration branch at San Bruno, California, hereafter cited as NARA San Bruno.
18. Pearl Harbor Naval Shipyard, General Correspondence, 1941–1945,10, 181–58–3404, Box 9305/V9375A, Counter Intelligence

Summary for the Month Ending 30 September 1944, File No. A8-5/LL, RG181, NARA San Bruno.

19. Pearl Harbor Naval Shipyard Correspondence, 1941-1945, 181-58-3404, Box 9305/V9375A, Counter Intelligence Summary for the Month Ending 30 December 1944, p. 8, 181-58A, Box 9305/V9375A, File No. A8-5/LL, RG181, NARA San Bruno.

20. Leo L. Pace to Charles A. Lockwood, 8 November 1944, Official Correspondence, Box 14, Charles A. Lockwood Papers, Naval Historical Foundation Collection, MD, LC.

21. Lockwood, "History of Submarine Operations in World War II" (unpublished, 1946), Vol. II, 489-504 (original pagination), Ben Bastura Collection, St. Mary's Submarine Museum, Chapter O, 4.

22. Lockwood to J. W. Fowler, 9 January 1945, Official Correspondence, Box 14, Charles A. Lockwood Papers, Naval Historical Foundation Collection, MD, LC.

23. *Swordfish*, WPR No. 11, 18, NHHC.

24. U.S. Navy, Bureau of Personnel, "Muster Roll of the Crew of the *U.S.S. Swordfish* (SS 193)," 30 June 1944, 30 September 1944 and 31 December 1944, Reel No. 7434, RG24, NARA; Dennis, interview, 17 January 2001.

25. U.S. Navy, Bureau of Personnel, "Muster Roll of the Crew of the *U.S.S.* Swordfish (SS 193)," quarterly rolls for 30 June 1943, 30 September 1943, 31 December 1943, 31 March 1944, 30 June 1944, 30 September 1944; "Report of Changes of *U.S.S. Swordfish* (SS 193)" for 31 October 1944, 30 November 1944, 22 December 1944 and "Report of Changes (SS 193)" with notes: "This report shows final disposition of entire crew, ship was lost on thirteenth patrol," and "missing in action, 1-29-45; changed to presumed dead, 1-30-46," Reel No. 7434, RG24, NARA. For an online listing of the crew with capsule biographies and photographs, see the following website: Charles R. Hinman, "USS *Swordfish* (SS-193)," On Eternal Patrol: http://www.oneternalpatrol.com/uss-swordfish-193.htm, USS *Bowfin* Submarine Museum and Park, Honolulu, Hawaii.

26. The superstition of a crew leery of sailing on a boat's 13th patrol is described by Edward L. Beach in his book, *Salt and Steel*, 155.

27. Dennis, interview, 17 January 2001; Faye, interview, 28 February 2003.

28. Cooper and Gaither, "War Patrols of USS *Swordfish* and USS *Sargo*," 3, NHHC; Margaret Cudwadie (sister of Michael Billy),

interview by author, 31 October 2004, Hazelton, PA.

29. U.S. Defense Mapping Agency Hydrographic/Topographic Center, *Sailing Directions (Enroute) for Japan Volume I: East Coasts of Hokkaido, Honshu, and Kyushu Including Nanpo Shoto and Ryuku Islands*, Publication 158 (Washington, D.C.: U.S. Defense Mapping Agency Hydrographic/Topographic Center, 1980), 160; U.S. Defense Mapping Agency Hydrographic/Topographic Center, *Asia-East Coast of China, Shenquan Gang to Sanmen Wan Including Taiwan to Okinawa Jima, Loran C*, Nautical Chart No. 94002 (Washington, D.C.: U.S. Defense Mapping Agency Hydrographic/Topographic Center, February 1967).

30. U.S. Defense Mapping Agency Hydrographic/ Topographic Center, *Asia-East Coast of China...* Nautical Chart No. 94002.

31. W. J. Holmes, *Undersea Victory*, 436-437.

32. Charles A. Lockwood, Jr. Commander Submarine Force, Pacific Fleet, "Loss of USS *Swordfish*, 12 January 1945," USS *Swordfish*, Action Report, Serial 0008, 15 February 1945, RG 38, Box 744, NARA.

33. *Kete*, WPR No. 1, 6, NHHC. See also Lockwood, "Loss of USS *Swordfish* (SS 193)," Charles A. Lockwood to Commander-in-Chief, U.S. Pacific Fleet, FF12-10/A4-1, 15 February 1945, 2, RG 38, Box 744, NARA.

34. Charles A. Lockwood, "Notes for Guam," Diary, April 1944 to February 1945, Entry numbers 24 and 29, Box 1, Charles A. Lockwood Papers, Naval Historical Foundation collection, MD, LC.

35. John D. Alden, *United States*, 253; Jurgen Rohwer, *Chronology of the War at Sea, 1939-1945: The Naval History of World War Two*, Third Edition (Annapolis, MD: Naval Institute Press, 2005), 382.

36. *Japanese Sea Mines*, "Know Your Enemy!" CinPac-CinCPOA Bulletin 49-45, 19 February 1945, 1, Records of the Japanese Navy and Related Documents, 1940-1960, Box 128, No. 8, NHHC.

37. *Kete*, WPR No. 1, 7, 15, NHHC.

38. See Harry Holmes, *The Last Patrol*, 163-164.

39. Stephen L. Moore, *SPADEFISH: On Patrol with a Top-Scoring World War II Submarine* (Dallas: Atriad Press, 2006), Chapter 18.

40. Dennis, interview, 17 January 2001.

41. Dyer, interview, 25 January 2001.

42. Faye, interview, 28 February 2003.

43. *Ibid.*

44. Charles A. Lockwood, Jr., to Rear Admiral Brown, Commander Comstock, Captain Voge, and Captain Yeomans, "Unfinished Business as of 24 January 1945," Secret, Box 14, Official Correspondence, Charles A. Lockwood Papers, Naval Historical Foundation Collection, MD, LC.

45. Lockwood to Captain Frank C. Watkins, Secret, 26 January 1945, Box 14, Charles A. Lockwood Papers, Naval Historical Foundation Collection, MD, LC.

46. U.S. Department of the Navy, Naval Historical Center, *Dictionary of ...,* 342.

47. Commander Submarine Force, Pacific to Commander-in-Chief, United States Fleet and Commander-in-Chief, U.S. Pacific Fleet, Ltr. FF12–10/A4, Serial 0008, USS *Swordfish*—loss of, 15 February 1945, in USS *Swordfish* (SS-193) WWII Patrol File, NHHC.

48. JANAC, Appendix, 47–48.

49. Commander in Chief, U.S. Pacific Fleet to Commander in Chief, United States Fleet), First Endorsement, 23 February 1945, Serial Number 0005537, in *USS Swordfish* (SS-193) WWII Patrol File, NHHC.

50. Lt. Lee B. Cottrell, Pers-5321-Mrb, 5 March 1945, Records of the Bureau of Naval Personnel, Casualty Assistance Branch, Ships, Stations, Units, and Incidents Casualty Information, Records, 1941–45, RG 24, Box 89, NARA; Cdr. Vernon Long Lowrence, Commander, Submarine Division Forty Five to Veronica Puletier (Michael Billy's sister), Ltr., 6 May 1945, Service Personnel File for Michael Billy, NPRC.

51. Cdr. H. B. Atkinson to Mrs. Keats Edmund Montross, correspondence, March 30, 1945, 5109, Pers-5320-aeb, U.S. Navy, Records of the Bureau of Navy Personnel, Casualty Assistance branch, Ships, Stations, Units and Incidents Casualty Information Records, 1941–1945, RG 24, Box 89, NARA.

52. Dorothy Montross to Mary Sturtz (Michael Billy's sister), Correspondence, 12 May 1945. Provided by Michael Sturtz.

53. Statement Concerning Finding of Death, Pers-5326-cmt, 17 January 1946, Records of the Bureau of Personnel, Casualty Assistance Branch, Ships, Stations, Units, and Incidents Casualty Information, Records 1941–45, 1950–60, RG 24, Box 89, NARA.

54. Navy Department, to Veronica Puletier, correspondence, Number 223 78 68, 31 January 1946. Records file of Michael Billy, NPRC.

55. Lt. Cdr. Joe H. Floyd to Veronica Puletier, Pers-102H-PHR, MM/223 78 68, 16 August 1948, Navy Department Bureau of Personnel, Records File of Michael Billy, NPRC. Billy, Michael MoMM2c, Died: Missing—29 Jan. 1945; Presumptive—30 Jan. 1946; USS *Swordfish*, to next of kin: Veronica Puletier (sister), Purple Heart medal and certificate. Fwd: 16 August 1946, Michael Billy Biography File, NHHC.

56. Mary Gladding (niece of James Mayfield, EM2 of *Swordfish*), telephone interview by author, 25 October 2000.

57. Keeley, interview, 24 March 2010; Nocera, interview, 16 September 2009; Ruth Smith, interview, 24 September 2009.

58. Hudson, "Dallas Woman...," 43; Clary, interview, 17 November 2000.

59. Clary, interview, 17 November 2000.

60. Dennis, interview, 17 January 2001.

61. Arthur C. Myers, "I'll Never Forget," *Memories from World War II*, unpublished, 1949. Printed with permission of Arthur C. Myers.

62. Robert Frank Harris, telephone interview by author, 9 November 2000. Harris was a Seaman 1st Class aboard *Swordfish*.

63. Chris Schultz, "Alum Seeds Scholarship Commemorating Lost WWII Submarine USS *Swordfish*," http://www.umf.olemiss.edu/home/print.php?id=172, retrieved 17 November 2011 (Oxford: University of Mississippi Foundation, 2006); William Warren, telephone interview by author, 22 November 2011.

64. George R. Pokorny, U.S. Submarine Veterans of World War II, Minnesota Viking Squadron to Bureau of Naval Personnel, Correspondence, "Information on locating next of kin of the crew of the *U.S.S. Swordfish*," Records of the Bureau of Naval Personnel Casualty Assistance Branch; Ships, Stations, Units, and Incidents Casualty Information Records, 1941–45, 1950–60, RG24, Box 89, NARA. See also Ernie Carley, "*Swordfish* (SS 193) Memorial Dedicated," *Polaris* (July 1965), 19–20. The author thanks the St. Mary's Submarine Museum for sending information concerning the *Swordfish* memorial. The author also thanks Susie L. Hoeller for sending information and photographs of the memorial. Many towns had their own ways of remembering the individual servicemen who did not return. Some cities erected monuments with lists of the war dead. In addition to setting up a marker, in November 1997, Michael Billy's native city, Rahway, New Jersey, dedicated a newly created street, Billy Court, in memory of their native son. Members of Michael Billy's family and various veterans groups attended; Liane Ingalls, "City Dedicates

Street to a WWII Submariner," *Rahway Progress,* 20 November 1997, 2.

65. U.S. Naval History Division, *Dictionary of...*, Vol. VI, 703–704. Naval Sea Systems Command, Shipbuilding Support Office, "*Swordfish* (SSN 579): Submarine (Nuclear-powered)," *Naval Vessel Register*, http://www.nvr.navy.mil/nvrships/details/SSN579.htm, 21 November 2011; Taylor and Mills, 593; *Jane's Fighting Ships, 1963–1964* (Great Missenden, England: Jane's Fighting Ships Publishing, 1964), 367. For references to the new *Swordfish's* clandestine activities, see Sherry Sontag and Christopher Drew, with Annette Lawrence Drew, *Blind Man's Bluff: The Untold Story of American Submarine Espionage* (New York: Public Affairs, 1998), 79–80n, 172–173, 279.

66. Matt Grills, "On Eternal Patrol," *Legion* 168, no. 4 (April 2010): 22–32; Walter Lee, "A Matter of Faith: 65-year Search for the Lost Submarine *Grunion*," *Sea Classics* 41, no. 2 (February 2008): 22–25; "A Warrior's Final Resting Place Is Located," *The Klaxon* (March 2008), 1, 4; "*Logarto* Wreck Discovered," *Naval History* 19, no. 5 (October 2005): 10–11.

Bibliography

Archival Materials

Columbia University Libraries, Columbia Center for Oral History, New York: Oral History Collection: The Reminiscences of James Fife, 1962. Transcript.

Library of Congress Manuscript Division: Naval Historical Center Foundation Collection, Charles A. Lockwood Papers:
  Box 1—Diaries
  Box 12, 13, 14—General Correspondence
  Box 18—Subject Files

National Archives and Records Administration, College Park, Maryland
  Record Group 19: Bureau of Ships:
    General Correspondence, 1940-1945. USS *Swordfish* (SS-193), Entry 1266, Box 1915.
    LCM SS-193 Photographic Prints.
    Portfolio, SS-193, ALPHA *Swordfish* SS-193 (Ship Engineering Drawings).
  Record Group 24: Records of the Bureau of Naval Personnel:
    Casualty Assistance Branch, Ships, Stations, Units and Incidents Casualty Information Records, 1941-1945, 1950-1960, USS *Swordfish* (SS-193), Box 89.
    USS *Gunnel* (SS-253), Muster Rolls, 30 September 1942 to 15 January 1943, Microfilm Reel Number 1806.
    USS *Swordfish* (SS-193), Deck Log.
    USS *Swordfish* (SS-193), Muster Rolls, 22 July 1939 to 1 January 1945, Microfilm Reel Number 7434.
  Record Group 38: Records of the Office of Naval Operations:
    USS *Swordfish* (SS-193), Action Reports, Boxes 742, 744 and 1460.
  Record Group 80G, GX: Navy Ships and Personnel—Still Pictures.
  Record Group 313: Records of Naval Operating Forces:
    Command Submarine Force, Pacific Fleet, Confidential General Administrative Files, Flag Files (Blue 440), 1942-1945.
    Training Reference Materials Number 5, Reference Materials on Anti-Submarine Warfare, CINCPAC-CINPOA #B-16493, 23 April 1944, File A8 (2), Box 14, DC 313-A1 (223).
    USS *Swordfish* SS-193 War Patrol Track Charts—CINPAC.

National Archives and Records Administration, Pacific Region, San Bruno, California
  Record Group 181: Pearl Harbor Naval Shipyard, General Correspondence, 1941-1945, Box 9305/V9375A:
    Counter Intelligence Summary for the Month Ending 30 September 1944, 181-58-3404, File Number A8-5/LL.
    Counter Intelligence Summary for the Month Ending 30 December 1944, 181-58A, File Number A8-5/LL.

National Personnel Records Center, St. Louis, Missouri
  Billy, Michael. Military Personnel Records.

Naval History and Heritage Command, formerly Naval Historical Center, Washington, D.C.
  Biography Files:
    Barrows, Frank Lloyd
    Billy, Michael
    Burroughs, Albert Collins
    Hensel, Karl Goldsmith
    Lewis, Jack Hayden
    Montross, Keats Edmund

Parker, Frank Mahlon, including photograph
Smith, Chester Carl
Narratives:
Cooper, Floyd M., and Gaither, Donald. "War Patrols of USS *Swordfish* and USS *Sargo*," Narrative, recorded 3 June 1944. Transcribed at Pearl Harbor, Film No. S-77.
Fields, Vernon. "USS *Swordfish*—Submarine Activities Southwest Pacific." Narrative, recorded 4 June 1943, Film No. 81.
Marvin, Paul. "War Patrols of the USS *Swordfish*." Narrative, recorded 20 October 1944, Pearl Harbor, Film No. S-93.
Montross, Keats E. "War Patrols of the USS *Swordfish*." Narrative, recorded 22 September 1944. Transcribed at Pearl Harbor, Film No. S-87.
Smith, Chester C. "USS *Swordfish*, Early War Patrols." Narrative, recorded 19-20 November 1943. Transcribed at Pearl Harbor, Film No. S-18.
Records of the Japanese Navy and Related Documents, 1940–1960.
World War II Command File:
Charles A. Lockwood, Commander, Submarine Force, Pacific Fleet to Submarine Force, Pacific Fleet, 26 February 1943. World War II Command File, Tactical Information Bulletin No. 2, Box 358.
World War II Patrol File:
USS *Kete* (SS-369) War Patrol Report No. 1 (NRS 108).
USS *Swordfish* (SS-193). Loss of, Correspondence (NRS 1979-10).
USS *Swordfish* (SS-193). War Patrol Reports Numbers 1 to 12 (NRS 1979-10).

Nimitz Library, U.S. Naval Academy
Dykers, Thomas M., and Chester C. Smith. "The *Swordfish* Story," DVD. Annapolis, Maryland, United States Naval Academy, Multimedia Support Center, 1958, 2003.

St. Marys Submarine Museum, Ben Bastura Collection, St. Marys, Georgia
Lockwood, Charles A. "History of Submarine Operations in World War II," unpublished, 1946.

Submarine Force Library Archives, Groton, Connecticut
USS *Seal* War Patrol Report No. 3
USS *Swordfish* Reference File:
Graves, William, Diary
Photograph: Burning Trawler, Sortie 12, Print #9, 6 June 1944.

Texas Woman's University, Denton, Texas
Woman's Collection and University Archives Digital Collection
Dorothy H(eath) Clary. Memoirs World War II, Mss. 202c, Series 2, Folder 2.

University of Wyoming. American Heritage Center. Laramie, Wyoming
Clay Blair Collection, Accession 8295:
Karl G. Hensel, correspondence
Chester C. Smith, correspondence and audiotaped interviews.

Swordfish Crewmen: Interviews by Author, Correspondence, Audiotapes

Dennis, Leymon:
Audiotape sent to author, 5 September 2000.
Correspondence, 13 July 2000; 8 August 2000.
Interview at U.S. Submarine Veterans of World War II Annual Meeting, St. Louis, Missouri, 24 August 2001.
Telephone interviews, 17 January 2001; 8 August 2001; 7 September 2003
Dyer, Robert E.:
Correspondence, 24 August 2000.
Telephone interviews, 25 January 2001, 14 November 2001.
Faye, Lloyd Henry:
Correspondence, 12 March 2003.
Telephone interview, 28 February 2003.
Harrington, Robert L., Telephone interview, 22 November 2000.
Harris, Robert F., Telephone interviews, 1 November 2000, 9 November 2000.
Kramer, Fred:
Telephone interviews, 18 January 2001, 8 February 2001, 24 September 2001, 25 January 2003.
USS *Swordfish* Memorabilia Book, n.p., n.d.
Myers, Arthur C., Telephone interviews, 27 July 2001, 30 September 2004.
O'Briant, William P., Telephone interviews, 5 June 2000, 21 December 2000, 14 January 2002.

Parks, Joe, Correspondence, 12 June 2001; 21 June 2001.

Additional Interviews by Author and Correspondence

Beach, Edward L., Interview, Naval Submarine League Annual Conference, Alexandria, Virginia, 13 June 2001.
Billy, Marie (sister-in-law of Michael Billy), Interview, Rahway, New Jersey, 3 July 1984.
Clary, Dorothy Heath, Telephone interview, 17 November 2000.
Cudwadie, Margaret (sister of Michael Billy), Interview, Hazelton, Pennsylvania, 31 October 2004.
Gierer, Ray (Fire Department of New York Marine Company Number 9, Staten Island, New York) Interview, 22 October 2010.
Giles, Joyce (Director, Mare Island Historic Park Museum), Interview, Mare Island, California, 25 October 2008.
Gladding, Mary (niece of James Mayfield, EM2 of USS *Swordfish*), Telephone interview, 25 October 2000.
Gray, Martin (Fire Department of New York Marine Company Number 9, Staten Island, New York), Interview, 22 October 2010.
Hensel, David (son of Karl Hensel), Correspondence, 19 June 2008.
Jacobs, Kenneth (USS *Queenfish* veteran), Interview, Garden City, New York, 3 December 2007.
Keeley, Thomas (son-in-law of Keats Montross), Telephone interview, 24 March 2010.
Kirkman, Ann (sister-in-law of Michael Billy), Interview, East Brunswick, New Jersey, 30 July 2000.
LaRocca, Albert (USS *Spadefish* veteran), Interview, Garden City, New York, 3 December 2007.
Lewis, J. Reilly (son of Jack Hayden Lewis), Telephone interview by author, 6 February 2013.
Librizzi, Joseph (USS *Balao* veteran), Interviews, Garden City, New York 22 May 2007; 3 December 2007.
Nocera, Wyatt R. (family relation of Keats Montross), Telephone interview, 16 September 2009.
MacDonald, Robert (USS *Gunnel* veteran), Telephone interview, 19 July 2001.
Schoonjans, Emil (USS *Burrfish* veteran), Telephone interview, 2 November 2009.
Seltzer, Milton (USS *Steelhead* veteran), Interview, Garden City, New York, 3 June 2002.
Smith, Donald Baxter (son of Chester C. Smith), Telephone interview, 17 February 2010.
Smith, Ruth (sister-in-law of Keats Montross), Telephone interview, 24 September 2009.
Warren, William, Telephone interview, 22 November 2011.
Zeleznik, Peter (U.S. Navy, brother-in-law of Michael Billy), Interview, Rahway, New Jersey, 12 March 2001.

Miscellaneous Sources

Carmody, C. Mike (USS *Pampanito* veteran). "*Swordfish* (SS-193) sinks *Delhi Maru*, 16 January 1944." Oil Painting. POLARIS (October 2007), Volume 52, Number 4, cover.
Denton, Thomas (USS *Francis Scott Key* veteran). "USS Swordfish (SS-193)." Acrylic Painting.
Hensel, Karl G., Interview by Katherine Wikstrom (granddaughter of Karl Hensel), McLean, Virginia, 7 September 1991, DVD. Provided by Katherine Wikstrom.
_____, Photograph, Fort Myers, Florida. Provided by Fred Kramer, Kramer Memorabilia Book.
_____ to Joe Parks, correspondence, 3 July 1989. Provided by Joe Parks.
Hoeller, Susie L. Photographs of *Swordfish* Memorial, Como Park, St. Paul, Minnesota.
Montross, Dorothy (wife of Keats Montross), to Mary Sturtz (sister of Michael Billy), correspondence, 12 May 1945. Provided by Michael Sturtz.
Research Trip: *Firefighter* (Fire Boat): witnessed operations of GM Winton diesel engine. Fire Department of New York Marine Company Number 9, Staten Island, New York, 22 October 2010.
Research Trip: Manila Bay, Philippines, author's on-site visit, 20–27 March 1999.
Research Trip: Mare Island Naval Shipyard, California, author's on-site visit, 25 October 2008.
Research Trip: Pearl Harbor, Hawaii, author's on-site visit, 28 October 2008.
Research Trip: Sydney Harbor, Australia, author's on-site visit, 31 October 2008.
Scull, Walter (USS *Aulick* veteran) to Marie Billy (sister-in-law of Michael Billy), Correspondence, 10 July 1996. Provided by Marie Billy.
Smith, Chester C. to Arthur L. Smith, Correspondence, 25 December 1945. Provided by Donald Baxter Smith.

_____ to Mary Baxter Smith, Telegram, 17 March 1942. Provided by Donald Baxter Smith.
Smith, Donald Baxter to Tom Bolan, correspondence, 24 January 1996.

Books, Articles, DVDs and Published Documents

Alden, John D. *The Fleet Submarine in the U.S. Navy: A Design and Construction History*. Annapolis, MD: Naval Institute Press, 1979.
_____, and Craig R. McDonald. *United States and Allied Submarine Successes in the Pacific and Far East during World War II*. 4th edition. Jefferson, NC: McFarland, 2009.
Astor, Gerald. *Crisis in the Pacific*. Garden City, NY: Dell, 1996.
Bagnassso, Erminio. *Submarines of World War Two*. Annapolis, MD: Naval Institute Press, 1977.
Barrows, Nathaniel A. *Blow All Ballast! The Story of the Squalus*. New York: Dodd, Mead, 1940.
Beach, Edward L. *Dust on the Sea*. New York: Zebra Books, 1989.
_____. *Salt and Steel: Reflections of a Submariner*. Annapolis, MD: Naval Institute Press, 1999.
_____. *Submarine!* New York: Pocket Star Books, 1980.
Billy, George J., and Christine M. Billy. *Merchant Mariners at War: An Oral History of World War II*. Gainesville: University of Florida Press, 2008.
Blair, Clay, Jr. *Hitler's U-boat War: he Hunters, 1939–1942*, Volume 1. New York: Random House, 1996.
_____. *Hitler's U-boat War: The Hunted, 1942–1945*, Volume 2. New York: Random House, 1998.
_____. *Silent Victory: The U.S. Submarine War against Japan*. Philadelphia: Lippincott, 1975.
Bowling, R. A. "Mahan's Principles and the Battle of the Atlantic," In *To Die Gallantly: The Battle of the Atlantic*, edited by Timothy Runyan and Jan M. Copes. Boulder, CO: Westview Press, 1994.
Brower, Norman J. *The International Register of Historic Ships*. 3rd edition. Peekskill, NY: Sea History Press, 1999.
Brown, George V. "The Launching of the Swordfish," *Our Navy* (mid–May 1939), 64.
_____. "*Swordfish* Scored History's First Ship Sinking by a U.S. Submarine," *San Diego Union*, December 4, 1977, C-4.
_____. "Through Hell and High Water: Memories of a Wartime Sub Skipper," *Shipmate* 47, no. 5 (July–August 1984): 23–24.
_____. "Traveling Down Memory Lane with Val Brown, Ye Ole and Ancient Mariner," *Klaxon* (February 1978).
Bunker, John. *Heroes in Dungarees: The Story of the American Merchant Marine in World War II*. Annapolis, MD: Naval Institute Press, 1995.
Carley, Ernie. "*Swordfish* (SS193) Memorial Dedicated," *Polaris* (July 1965): 19–20.
Carmer, Carl L. *The Jesse James of the Java Sea*. New York: Farrar & Rinehart, 1945.
Casey, Robert J. *Battle Below: The War of the Submarines*. Indianapolis: Bobbs-Merrill, 1945.
Cohen, David E. "The MK-XIV Torpedo: Lessons for Today," *Naval History* 6, no. 4 (Winter 1992): 34–36.
Connaughton, Richard. *MacArthur and Defeat in the Philippines*. Woodstock, NY: Overlook Press, 2001.
Conway's All the World's Fighting Ships, 1922–1946, edited by Robert Gardiner and Roger Chesneau. NY: Mayflower Books, 1980.
Cope, Harley F. *Serpent of the Seas: The Submarine*. New York: Funk & Wagnalls, 1942.
Cressman, Robert J. *The Official Chronology of the U.S. Navy in World War II*. Annapolis, MD: Naval Institute Press, 2000.
Dull, Paul S. *The Battle History of the Imperial Japanese Navy (1941–1945)*. Annapolis, MD: Naval Institute Press, 1978.
Frank, Gerold, and James D. Horan, with J. M. Eckberg. *U.S.S. Seawolf: Submarine Raider of the Pacific*. New York: G. P. Putnam's Sons, 1945.
Frank, Richard B. *Guadalcanal: The Definitive Account of the Landmark Battle*. New York: Penguin Books, 1990.
Friedman, Norman. *U.S. Submarines Through 1945: An Illustrated Design History*. Annapolis, MD: Naval Institute Press, 1995.
"From Sailing Texans," *Dallas Morning News*, 16 April 1944, Section 2, 8.
Gibson, Charles Dana, and E. Kay Gibson. *Over Seas: U.S. Army Maritime Operations 1898 Through the Fall of the Philippines*. Camden, ME: Ensign Press, 2002.
Graves, William. "Corregidor Revisited: 43 Years after the Siege," *National Geographic* 170, no. 2 (July 1985): 118.
The Great Sea War: The Story of Naval Action in World War II, edited by E. B. Potter and

Chester W. Nimitz. Englewood Cliffs, NJ: Prentice-Hall, 1960.

Grider, George. *War Fish*. Boston: Little, Brown, 1958.

Grills, Matt. "On Eternal Patrol," *Legion* 168, no. 4 (April 2010): 22–32.

Hara, Tameichi, Fred Saito, and Roger Pineau. *Japanese Destroyer Captain*. New York: Ballantine Books, 1961, 1965.

Hargis, Robert. *U.S. Submarine Crewman, 1941–45*. Botley, England: Osprey, 2003.

Hemingway, Ernest. *The Old Man and the Sea*. New York: Scribner's, 1952, 1980.

Holmes, Harry. *The Last Patrol*. London: Airlife, 1994, 1997.

Holmes, W. J. *Undersea Victory: The Influence of Submarine Operations on the War in the Pacific*. Garden City, NY: Doubleday, 1966.

Holwitt, Joel Ira. *"Execute Against Japan": The U.S. Decision to Conduct Unrestricted Submarine Warfare*. College Station: Texas A & M University Press, 2009.

———. "Unrestricted Submarine Victory: The U.S. Submarine Campaign against Japan." *Commerce Raiding: Historical Case Studies, 1755–2009*. Naval War College Newport Papers No. 40, edited by Bruce A. Ellerman and S. C. M. Paine. Washington, D.C.: U.S. Government Printing Office, 235–238.

Hudson, Elizabeth. "Dallas Woman Remembers Swordfish Fondly," *Navy Times*, 2 February 1987, 42.

Ingalls, Liane. "City Dedicates Street to a World War II Submariner," *Rahway Progress*, 20 November 1997, 2.

Ireland, Bernard. *Jane's Naval History of World War II*. New York; HarperCollins, 1998.

Jane's Fighting Ships, 1941, edited by Francis E. McMurtrie. New York: Macmillan, 1942.

Jane's Fighting Ships, 1963–64. Great Missenden, England: Jane's Fighting Ships Publishing, 1964.

Japanese Merchant Ships: Recognition Manual, ONI 208-J (revised) United States. Washington, D.C.: Navy Department, Office of the Chief of Naval Operations, 1942 revised edition.

Joint Army-Navy Assessment Committee. *Japanese Naval and Merchant Shipping Losses During World War II by All Sources*. Washington, D.C.: U.S. Government Printing Office, February 1947.

Jordan, Roger W. *The World's Merchant Fleet: 1937, the Particulars and Wartime Fates of 6,000 Ships*. Annapolis, MD: Naval Institute Press, 1999.

Kahn, David. *Seizing the Enigma: The Race to Break the German U-boat Codes, 1939–1943*. New York: Barnes and Noble, 1991, 1998.

Karig, Walter. "The Makin Island Raid," *United States Naval Institute Proceedings* 72, no. 190 (October 1946): 1277–1284.

Kimmett, Larry, and Margaret Regis. *U.S. Submarines of World War II: An Illustrated History*. Seattle: Navigator Publishing, 1996.

La Vo. "Commanding Officer Breaking Down," *Naval History* 6, no. 3 (Fall 1962): 29–34.

Lee, Walter. "A Matter of Faith: 65 Year Search for the Lost Submarine *Grunion*," *Sea Classics* 41, no. 2 (February 2008): 22–25.

Lloyd's Register of Shipping, 1940–41. London: Lloyd's Register of Shipping, 1940.

Lockwood, Charles A. *Down to the Sea in Subs*. New York: Norton, 1967.

———. *Sink 'Em All: Submarine Warfare in the Pacific*. New York: Dutton, 1951.

"*Logarto* Wreck Discovered," *Naval History* 19, no. 5 (October 2005): 10–11.

The Lucky Bag 1927, 1928, 1932, 1935. Annapolis, MD: First Class, United States Naval Academy, 1927, 1928, 1932, 1935.

Maas, Peter. *The Terrible Hours: The Man Behind the Greatest Submarine Rescue in History*. New York: HarperCollins, 1999.

McCain, John M., and Mark Salter. *Faith of My Fathers*. New York: Random House, 1999.

Mendenhall, Corwin. *Submarine Diary*. Annapolis, MD: Naval Institute Press, 1991.

Miller, Edward S. *War Plan Orange: The U.S. Strategy to Defeat Japan, 1896–1945*. Annapolis, MD: Naval Institute Press, 1991.

Moore, Stephen L. *Spadefish: On Patrol with a Top-Scoring World War II Submarine*. Dallas: Atriad Press, 2006.

Morrison, Samuel Eliot. *History of United States Naval Operations in World War II: Coral Sea, Midway, and Submarine Actions, May 1942–August 1942*, Volume IV. Edison, NJ: Castle Books, 1949.

Morton, Louis. *The Fall of the Philippines*: U.S. Department of the Army, Office of Military History, United States Army in World War II. Washington, D.C.: Office of the Chief of Military History, Department of the Army, 1953.

Mulligan, Timothy. *Neither Sharks nor Wolves: The Men of Nazi Germany's U-boat Arm, 1939–1945*. Annapolis, MD: Naval Institute Press, 1999.

Murray, Williamson, and Allan R. Millett. *A War to Be Won: Fighting the Second World War, 1937–1945*. Cambridge, MA: Belknap Press/Harvard University Press, 2000.

Myers, Arthur C. "I'll Never Forget," *Memo-*

ries from World War II, unpublished, 1949. Printed with permission of Arthur C. Myers.

Newpower, Anthony. *Iron Men and Tin Fish: The Race to Build a Better Torpedo During World War II*. Newport, CT: Praeger Security International, 2006.

On Eternal Patrol: the Lost Boats of Mare Island. Mare Island, CA: Mare Island Historic Park Museum, undated.

Papadoulos, Randy. "Between Fleet Scouts and Commerce Raiders: Submarine Warfare Theories and Doctrines in the German and U.S. Navies, 1935–1945." *Undersea Warfare* 6, no. 4 (Summer 2005): 28–33.

Parillo, Mark P. *The Japanese Merchant Marine in World War II*. Annapolis, MD: Naval Institute Press, 1993.

Prados, John. *Combined Fleet Decoded: The Secret History of American Intelligence and the Japanese Navy in World War II*. Annapolis, MD: Naval Institute Press, 1995.

Reynolds, Clark G. *Command of the Sea: The History and Strategy of Maritime Empires*. New York: Morrow, 1974.

_____. *The Fast Carriers: The Forging of an Air Navy*. Annapolis, MD: Naval Institute Press, 1968.

Rohwer, Jurgen. *Chronology of the War at Sea, 1939–1945: The Naval History of World War Two*. 3d ed. Annapolis, MD: Naval Institute Press, 2005.

Romulo, Carlos. *I Saw the Fall of the Philippines*. Garden City, NY: Doubleday, 1946.

Ropp, Theodore. "Continental Doctrines of Sea Power." In *Makers of Modern Strategy: Military Thought from Machiavelli to Hitler*, edited by Edward Mead Earle. Princeton, NJ: Princeton University Press, 1943, 1971, 446–456.

Roscoe, Theodore. *United States Submarine Operations in World War II*. Annapolis, MD: Naval Institute Press, 1949.

Rutherford, Phillip T. "Pig Boats, Fleet Boats, and Mystery Meat; U.S. Submarine Food, 1941–1945," *Undersea Warfare* (Fall 2011): 22–27.

Sayre, Elizabeth E. "Submarine from Corregidor: Manila Goes Under," *The Atlantic* 170, no. 2 (August 1942): 22–28.

_____. "Submarine from Corregidor: The Escape," *The Atlantic* 170, no. 3 (September 1942): 40–46.

Shakespeare, William. "Julius Caesar." In *The Complete Works of William Shakespeare*. London: Oxford University Press, 1955.

Smith, Steven Trent. *Wolfpack: The American Submarine Strategy That Helped Defeat Japan*. New York: Wiley, 2003.

Sontag, Sherry, and Christopher Drew, with Annette Laurence Drew. *Blind Man's Bluff: The Untold Story of American Submarine Espionage*. New York: Public Affairs, 1998.

Spector, Ronald H. *At War at Sea: Sailors and Naval Combat in the Twentieth Century*. New York: Viking, 2001.

Sturma, Michael. *Surface and Destroy: The Submarine Gun War in the Pacific*. Lexington: University of Kentucky Press, 2011.

_____. *The USS Flier: Death and Survival on a World War II Submarine*. Lexington: University of Kentucky Press, 2008.

"Sub Crew Chooses Dallas Girl as Favorite for Pin-Up Photo," *Dallas Morning News*, 8 December 1944, Section 2, 1.

Taylor, John Wilson, and Eva Mills (Lee). *Montross: A Family History: Pierre Montross and His Descendants, Record of 300 Years of the Montras-Montross-Montrose-Montress Family in the United States and Canada*. Staunton, VA; McClure Printing, 1958.

Triumph in the Pacific: The Navy's Struggle Against Japan, edited by E. B. Potter and Chester W. Nimitz. Englewood, NJ: Prentice-Hall, 1963.

Underbrink, Robert L. *Destination Corregidor*. Annapolis, MD: United States Naval Institute, 1971.

U.S. Defense Mapping Topographic Agency. *Asia-East Coast of Chian, Shenquan Gang to Saumen Wan Including Taiwan to Okinawa Jima, Loran C*. Nautical Chart No. 94002. Washington, D.C.: U.S. Defense Mapping Agency Hydrographic/ Topographic Center, February 1967.

_____. *Sailing Directions (Enroute) for Borneo, Jawa, Sulawesi and Nusa Tenggara*. Publication 163. Washington, D.C.: U.S. Defense Mapping Agency, 1979.

_____. *Sailing Directions (Enroute) for Japan, Volume 1: East Coasts of Hokkaido, Honshu, and Kyushi Including Nanpo Shoto and Ryuku Islands*. Publication 158. Washington, D.C.: U.S. Defense Mapping Agency Hydrographic/Topographic Center, 1980, 160.

_____. *Sailing Directions (Enroute) for the Philippines*. Publication 162. Washington, D.C.: U.S. Defense Mapping Agency Hydrographic/Topographic Center, 1979.

U.S. National Imagery and Mapping Agency. *Teluk Tomini and North Coast to Sulawesi*. Nautical Chart No. 73012. Washington, D.C.: U.S. National Imagery and Mapping Agency, 2003.

U.S. Naval History Division. *Dictionary of American Naval Fighting Ships*, 9 volumes.

Washington, D.C.: Government Printing Office, 1969.
———. *United States Submarine Losses: World War II*. Washington, D.C.: U.S. Naval History Division, 1963.
Van der Vat, Dan. *The Pacific Campaign: World War II, the U.S.-Japanese Naval War, 1941–1945*. New York: Simon & Schuster, 1991, 1992.
"A Warrior's Final Resting Place Is Located," *The Klaxon* (March 2008), 1, 4.
Watts, Anthony J. *Japanese Warships of World War II*. Garden City, NY: Doubleday, 1966, 1967.
Weir, Gary E. *Building American Submarines, 1914–1940*. Washington, D.C.: Naval Historical Center, 1991.
———. "Silent Defense: 1900–1940," *Undersea Warfare* 1, no. 4 (Summer 1999): 13–15.
Westel, Freeman. "Japan's Deadly WWII Destroyer Fleet," *Sea Classics* 43, no. 5 (May 2010): 20–25.
Whitman, Edward C. "Submarines to Corregidor," *Undersea Warfare* 4, no. 3 (Summer 2002): 28–31.
———. "Suicide Run: MacArthur's Guerrilla Submarines," *Sea Classics* 39, no. 2 (February 2006): 34–41.
Willoughby, Amea. "Undersea Escape from Corregidor," *The Best 100 True Stories of World War II*. New York: Wise, 1945.
Wilmott, H. P. *The Second World War in the East*. London: Cassell, 1999.
Winslow, W. G. *The Fleet the Gods Forgot*. Annapolis, MD: Naval Institute Press, 1982.

Winton-Diesel Engine Model 1G-248: Instructions for the Care and Operation of the Engine. Washington, D.C.: U.S. Navy, undated.
Y'Blood, William T. *Red Sun Setting: The Battle of the Philippine Sea*. Annapolis, MD: Naval Institute Press, 1981.

Internet Websites

Hinman, Charles R. "USS *Swordfish* (SS-193), On Eternal Patrol, http://www.oneternalpatrol.com/uss-swordfish-193.htm. USS *Bowfin* Submarine Museum and Park, Honolulu, Hawaii. Accessed 8 August 2012.
Naval History and Heritage Command. "USS Swordfish (SS-193) 1939–1945," Dictionary of *American Naval Fighting Ships*. http://www.history.navy.mil/danfs/s21/swordfish-i.htm. Washington Navy Yard. Accessed 8 August 2012.
Naval Sea Systems Command, Shipbuilding Support Office. "*Swordfish* (SSN579): Submarine (Nuclear Powered)." Naval Vessel Register. http://www.nvr.navy.mil/nvrships/details/SSN579.htm. Norfolk Naval Shipyard, Norfolk, Virginia. Accessed 21 November 2011.
Schultz, Charles. "Alum Seeds Scholarship Commemorating Lost WWII Submarine USS *Swordfish*," http://www.umf.olemiss.edu/home/print.php?id=172. Oxford, Mississippi: University of Mississippi Foundation, 2006. Accessed 17 November 2011.

Index

Numbers in **_bold italics_** indicate pages with illustrations

Abele, Mannert L. 114
Abrahamson, Arthur 171
Adams, R.D. 80
Adelaide, Australia 82
Albacore, USS (SS-218) 119
Aleutian Islands 85
Amagiri class 57
Amagisan Maru 37, 174
Ambon 32, 174
Ambulong Island 69
Annapolis 5, 64, 66, 85–86, 95, 113, 137; *see also* United States Naval Academy
Aoga Shima 106
Archerfish, USS (SS-311) 146
Argonaut, USS (SS-166) 94–96, 105, 197
Arold, Roy G. 171
Asiatic Fleet 5, 7, 12, 27, 81
Asiatic-Pacific Area campaign ribbon 152
Asiatic Submarine Force 27
Aspro, USS (SS-309) 131
Atsutasan Maru **_19_**, 20, 26, 81–82, 174

B-17 bomber 91
B-25 bomber 77
Baeckler, Donald 171
Baker, Gilbert S. 171
Balabac 53–54, 60
Barb, USS (SS-220) 14, 143
Barrows, Frank Lloyd ("Butch") 105–108, **_109_**, 170
Basta, Joseph J. 171
Bataan Peninsula 27–28, 38, 49, 51
Bates, Mack 171
Battle of the Atlantic 2, 5, 120, 145
Baughman, Daniel S., Jr. 171
Beach, Edward L. 72, 84–86, 93, 193n2
Benbennick, Claude J. 171
Bethlehem Shipbuilding Company 93
Billy, Michael 2, 12, **_13_**, 14–15, 142–145, 152, 158, 164, 171
"Black Swan" 46
Blackfish, USS (SS-221) 14, 143
Blanchard, Joseph R.L. 171
Blandy, William H.P. 23
Bleasdell, Le Roy J. 171

Boeing B-17 *see* B-17 bomber
Bogdan, Wesley C. 171
Boise, Idaho 26
Bonin Islands 145, 152, 170
Bougainville Island 73, 89, 197
Braley, Andrew E. 171
Brisbane 73, 78, 86, 193
Britain *see* Great Britain
British navy 9
Brown, George Valentine 3–6, 17–18, 30, 40, 46, 63, 81–82
Brown, Robert J. 171
Brown, W.N. 144
Buka Island 88
Buna 77–78
Bureau of Ordnance *see* Ordnance, Bureau of
Bureau of Ships *see* Ships, Bureau of
Burma Maru 59, 81, 175
Burrfish, USS (SS-312) 131, 193, 211
Burrows, Albert Collins ("Acey") 63–64, **_65_**, 66–73, 91, **_114_**, 123, 128, 169
Buzyon class 148

Canal Zone 86
Canopus, USS (AS-9) 28
Cape Hanpan 88
Cape Merah *see* Tanjung Merah
Cape St. George 87
Cape San Agustin 36
Capetown, South Africa 96
Caroline Islands 112
Cauley, Fred M., Jr. 153, 165, 171
Cavalier, USS (APA-37) 105
Cavalla, USS (SS-244) 127
Cavite 27
Cebu 49
Celebes Island 30–31, 60, 191
Celebes Sea 60
ChiChi Shima 145–147, 149
Chidori 124, 129, 181, 200
Chile Maru 122
China Station 5
Chiyoda Maru #8 150, 177
Christie, Ralph W. 71, 78, 195n132
Clark, Allen D. 171

217

Index

Clark, J.S. 77
Clarke, J.E. 44
Clarke, Jim 31
Cold War 10, 136, 168
Collins, M. 82, 196n154
commerce war *see guerre de course*
commissary officer 12
communications officer 12
Como Park 167
Connolly, Joseph A. 104, 110
Connors, Timothy J. 171
Cooper, Floyd 29, 46, 62, 93–94, 116, 119–120
Cope, Harley F. 81
Coral Sea, Battle of 51
Corregidor 26–28, 37–42, 44, 48, 51, 65
Cox, Marshall E., Jr. 171
crew rotations 52
Currie, Dora C. 86

Dace, USS (SS-247) 131
Dallas Morning News 153
Daly, Robert F. 171
Darter, USS (SS-227) 131
Davao 30, 33, 36–37
Davao, Gulf of 36
Davis, Herman W. 171
Delhi Maru 122–124, 136, 176
Delladonna, J.V. 171
Denmark Maru 123
Dennis, Leymon ("Denny") 46, 65–66, 98, 108, 115, 127, 135, 138, 162, 165
depth charge, characteristics 21
Dillon, William 171
Dinky Di's 135
distillery (alcohol) 103, 105–106
diving officer 12
Doenitz, Karl 120
Doolittle, James 51
Draga, Gordon K. 171
Dragonet, USS (SS-293) 92–93
Drum, USS (SS-228) 14, 143
Duncan, Loris H. 171
"Dunker's Derby" 145, 152
Dunton, Emory W., Sr. 171
Dutch navy 28–29
Dyer, Robert E. 4, 10, 66, 162

Echols, Leonard O. 171
Edwards, George V. 171
Emmingham, Robert L. 171
engineering officer 12
Evans, James 62
executive officer 12
Exmouth Gulf 45

Fausset, Eugene R. 171
Faye, Lloyd Henry 10, 15, 21, 44, 70, 98, 128, 162
Feiss, Kenneth F. 171
Fields, Vernon 10, 15, 20, 25, 89
Fife, James 23, 49, 70, 72
Fifth Amphibious Force 159

Flier, USS (SS-250) 108, 123, 168
Flusser, USS (DD-368) 12–13
FM sonar 162–163
food 128
Forsythe, Eugene J. 171
Fowler, John G. 171
Fowler, Joseph A. 156
Fremantle 45, 47, 49–50, 52, 60, 62- 63, 65, 70, 82
"friendly fire" 60
Fujiyama, Mount *see* Mount Fujiyama
Funk, Nick 171

Gaither, Donald 15, 17–18, 20–21, 25, 27, 62, 65, 82, 110, 158
Galley, Emery A., Jr. 171
Gambrell, Dee E., Jr. 171
Gar, USS (SS-206) 106, 146
Garza, Eleazar 171
Gato, USS (SS-212) 87, 89, 131
General Motors Winton *see* Winton engine
Geraghty, Bernard J., Jr. 171
Germany 8
"Gibraltar of the Pacific" 112; *see also* Truk
Gilfillan, Howard M. 171
Gilmore, Howard W. *114*
Glassford, William A. 45
"Gooneyville" 105; *see also* Midway
Graf, John V. 171
Graham, George P. 171
Grandy, William P. 171
Graves, William 41–43
Great Britain 2, 8–9, 75, 112
Griggs, John B. 104
Gross, Roy 72
Grouper, USS (SS-214) 145
Grunion, USS (SS-216) 168
Guadalcanal 76–77, 90, 94, 112, 170
Guardfish, USS (SS-217) 119
Gudgeon, USS (SS-211) 106
guerre de course 1, 9, 187n1
Gulf of Siam 58–59
Gunnel, USS (SS-253) 13–14, 143–144
gunnery officer 30
Gyoten Maru 131

Hachijo Shima 125
Hafter, Ralph L. 171
Hainan Island 10, 17
Hall, Charles E. 171
Halsey, W.F. 78
Hamner, USS (DD-718) 105
Harlow, Dick 115
Harrington, Robert L. 103, 128
Harris, Robert Frank 166
Harrison, Peyton 156
Hart, Thomas C. 7–8, 27–28
Harvard 115
Haserodt, Ralph W. 171
Haskins, Winslow C. 171
Haynes, Jack E. 171

Index

Heath, Dorothy *152*, 153, 165
"hells bells" 162
Hemingway, Ernest: *The Old Man and the Sea* (novel) 134
Hensel, Karl Goldsmith 13, 112–113, *114*, 115–122, *123*, 124–32, *133*, 134–138, 142, 163, 170
Hermit Islands 89
Hess, John 115, 125, 129
Hester, Ed 41
Hirohito 78
"Hit Parade" 145
Hokuryu Maru #10 150, 177
Holland, USS (AS-3) 7, 40, 45, 65, 105, 143
Holland, Ray 171
Holwitt, Joel 8
Hong Kong 27, 67
Honolulu 105, 132
Honshu 106
Hoopes, R.D., Jr. 171
H.O.R. diesel engine 144
hospital ship 89, *90*
hot bunk (hot rack) 42, 182
Hrynko, Fred A. 171
Hull, Jesse L. *114*
Huon Gulf 77
Hurd, Kenneth C. 53–54
Hyde, John 44

Identification, Friend or Foe Mark III radar 154
IFF radar *see* Identification, Friend or Foe Mark III radar
"I'll Never Forget" (poem) 165
Iro Sahi 116
Isu Shoto 125
Iwo Jima 159
Izu Shoto 116

JANAC *see* Joint Army-Navy Assessment Committee
Janes, Robert L. 145, 171
Japanese Combined Fleet 112, 131
Japanese Navy 27, 137
Java 28, 40, 42, 45
Java Sea, Battle of 51
"jeep" aircraft carriers 112
Johnson, Robert E. 171
Johnson, Stephen J. 171
Johnston Island 96, 138
Joint Army-Navy Assessment Committee (JANAC) 10, 55–56, 72, 81, 163, 173–176 182, 185
JP sonar 154
Julius Caesar (play) 15

Kamikaze (Divine Wind) class 146, 162
Kankakee, USS (AO-39) 105
Kanseishi Maru 148, 176
Kasagi Maru 131, 176
Kashii Maru 26
Katsuragi Maru 32, 174
Kavieng, New Ireland 33

Kawanishi 97 aircraft 88
Kelly, John R. 171
Kema 30, 31, 33
Kendari 33
Kete, USS (SS-369) 161–162, 177
Keyser, Kenneth J. 26
Kingfish, USS (SS-234) 109, 146, 154
Kirk, Vernon 171
Klackring, Thomas B. *114*
Ko Shima 117
Koga, Mineichi 131
Kohler, William E. 171
Korean War 79
Koshima 116
Kota Bahru 58
Kramer, Fred 15, 43–44, 102–103, 105, 107
Kremer, Richard B. 171
Kroll, Roy E. 171
Kuniei Maru 131

Lauderdale, Hollie O. 171
Lembeh Strait 31, *32*, 34
Lewis, Jack Hayden 84–85, *86*, 87–94, 127, 170
Liberty ships 112
Lindsay, Douglas C. 171
Lingayen Gulf 27
Lo Presti, Russell 171
Lockwood, Charles A. 23, 55, 61–62, *63*, 64, 68, 70–72, 78, 81–84, 91–92, 110, 120, 123, 132, 134, *139*, 145, 152, 154, 156–157, 161, 163
Logarto, USS (SS-371) 168
Lombak Strait 10
Looney, Gerald A. 171
Lorenz, J.J. 144
LST 156
Lucky Bag 64, 73, 85, 95, 109
Luzon 10, 27, 156

MacArthur, Douglas 27–28, 39–40, 77
Macclesfield Bank 67–68
MacDonald, Robert 14
Madden, John J., Jr. 171
Majuro 142, 145
Makassar Strait 52, 60, 66
Makin Island 94–95
Malay Barrier 27, 49
Malaya 27, 56
Manila 7, 27–28, 30, 39
Manila Bay 12, 26–28, 30, 36, 38, *39*, 41, 79, 82
Manokwari 96
Manokwari Roads 99
Marcus Island 131
Mare Island Naval Shipyard 3–7, 109, 156, 169
Marianas 170
Mariveles 12, 27–28, 38
Mark 6 magnetic exploder 23
Mark 14 torpedo 22–23
Mark 18 torpedo 143, 146–147, 154
"Maru Morgue" 145
Marvin, Paul 70, 121, 129–130, 134, 171
Mary Ann (patrol boat) 41

Index

Maryland, USS (BB-46) 105
Matsukaze, Japanese destroyer 146, 176
Mayfield, James M. 171
McCaffrey, Morriss, F. 171
McCain, John Sidney, Jr. 13, 144, 189n29
McClosky, W.H. 44
Meacham, William T., Jr. 171
Mewhinney, Leonard S. *114*
Midway, Battle of 84–85
Midway Island 85, 87, 92, 101, 104–106, 108, 115–116, 123, 151, 159–160
Mikura Shima 121
Mindanao 30, 36
mines 31, 49, 162–163
Mitsubishi Busan Kaisha, Ltd. 20
Miyake Shima 116
Mizako 116
Moluca Sea 30
Momsen, C.B. "Swede" 134
Momsen Lung 40, 133, 183
Montross, Dorothy MacMurray 164–165, 168
Montross, Keats Edmund "Monty" 137–138, *139*, *140*, 141–52, 154, 157, 159, 162, 165, 168, 170, 172
Montross, Ridgley R. 165
Moray, USS (SS-300) 108–109
Morton, Dudley W. ("Mush") 81
Mount Fujiyama 128
Mount Suribachi 159
Mueller, John C. 41
Mumma, Morton C. 7, 31
Muskellunge, USS (SS-262) 138
Mutsuki class 140
Myers, Arthur 121, 138, 165–166
Myoho Maru 89, 175
Myoken Maru 31, 33, 81, 174

Nansei Shoto 158–160
National War College 135
Nautilus, USS (SS-168) 95
Naval Operations, Chief 8, 73, 135, 163
Neptune 43
Netherlands New Guinea 96
Nevada, USS (BB-36) 137
New Britain Island 74–75
New Guinea 96, 112
New London, Connecticut 5, 13–14, 96, 113, 115, 138
New Mexico, USS (BB-40) 5
Nimitz, Chester W. *109*, 110, 131, 163
Ninigo Islands 89, 197n30
Nishiyama Maru (Seizan Maru) 98, 175
Nixon, Ensign 144
North Africa Campaign 13, 144

O-4, USS (SS-65) 138
Oahu 132, 154
O'Briant, William P. 51, 103–105, 114
Okinawa Jima 158–159, *160*, 161–163, 177
The Old Man and the Sea (novel) *134*
Operation ICEBERG 158

Orange, War Plan 7–8
Ordnance, Bureau of 22–23, 31
Owai Saki 116

Pace, Leo L. 156
Pago Pago 6
Palau 96, 98–99, 101
Panay 40–41
Paracel Islands 67–68
Parker, Cynthia 96
Parker, Frank Mahlon 93–94, *95*, 96–106, 114, 128, 137, 170
Parks, Joe 42, 135
Patterson, George W., Jr. *114*
Peabody, Eddie 132
Pearl Harbor 1, 5–7, 9–10, 12–16, 27, 51, 59, 91, 93, 96, 103–105, 127, 131, 133, 151, 154–156, 159
Pence, Kenneth E. 172
Pensacola, USS (CA-24) 155–156
Perch, USS (SS-176) 168
periscope shears 7, 68, 97, 125, 183
Permit, USS (SS-178) 131
Perth 45–46, 80
Petty, Fremont 172
Philippine Island Operation 46, 170
Philippine Sea 127, 158
Philippines 7, 10, 27–28, 30, 33, 36, *39*, 40–41, 49, 59, 69, 81, 156
Pillsbury, USS (DD-227) 29
"Pink Lady" 103
Piru Bay 30
Plaice, USS (SS-390) 145
Plan D 8
Plan Position Indicator 126, 183
Plourd, Gordon R. 172
Pollard, Claude L. 172
Port Moresby 51
Prattle Island 68–69
Preston, Earl W., Jr. 172
Prince of Wales, HMS (British battleship) 27
Puget Sound 6
Pulo Wai 58–59
Pye, John B. 172

Q-Ship 18, 122–123, 176
Quezon, Dona Aurora 40
Quezon, Manuel, Jr. 40–41
Quezon, Manuel L. 39–41, 48, 191n34
Quezon, Maria 40
Quezon, Zenida 40
Quigley, Francis 86–87
Rabaul 76, 87, 96, 98

Rahway, New Jersey 12
"Rainbow 3" 8
Ranger (tug) 38
reduction gear 155, 157, 163, 183, 204n13, 204n17
relief crews 62
Repulse, HMS (British battlecruiser) 27
Rice, R.H. 145
Rider, Eugene C. 165, 168

Index

Robinson, Harry N., Jr. 172
the "Rock" 39, 41, 49; *see also* Corregidor
Rockwell, Francis W. 41–42
Romulo, Carlos 39
Roosevelt, Franklin D. 8, 41
Ross, Phillip H. *114*
Royal Hawaiian Hotel 132, 201n39
Russell, William E. 165
Rutter, Royal L. 161–162
Ryuku Islands 158–159
Ryuku Trench 159

S class 95, 113
S-14, USS (SS-119) 86
S-15, USS (SS-120) 86
S-21, USS (SS-126) 5
S-23, USS (SS-128) 5
S-28, USS (SS-133) 168
S-30, USS (SS-135) 96
S-31, USS (SS-136) 86
S-40, USS (SS-145) 196n144
S-41, USS (SS-146) 137
Sagami Nada 116
Sailfish, USS (SS-192) 7, 134
St. George's Channel 76
St. Paul, USS (CA-73) 79
St. Paul, Minnesota 166–167
Saipan 160
Salmon, USS (SS-182) 7
Samar 20
Samoan Islands 6
San Diego 7
San Francisco 93, 98–99, 102–103, 113, 156, 167
Sape Strait 45
Saratoga, USS (CV-3) 156
Sargo class 3, 169
Savo Island 76–77, 170
Sayre, Elizabeth E. 41–45, 65
Sayre, Francis B. 41, 45, 79
Scamp, USS (SS-277) 119
Schwendener, K.D. 172
Scotch (beverage) 82–83
SD radar 74, 78, 83, 91, 96, 183
Seadragon, USS (SS-194) 28
Seal, USS (SS-183) 53–56, 64, 72, 175
Sealion, USS (SS-195) 7, 28
Searaven, USS (SS-196) 49, 131
Seawolf, USS (SS-197) 7, 28, 72, 119, 123
Seizan Maru see *Nishiyama Maru*
Sekatung Island 60
Seram Island 30
Shakespeare, William: *Julius Caesar* (play) 15
Shark, USS (SS-174) 28
Shawnee, Oklahoma 64
Shenandoah, USS (AD-26) 73
Ships, Bureau of 7, 23, 154–155
Shokaku (Japanese aircraft carrier) 125, 127
Shoto Maru 162, 177
Sibutu 66
Silversides, USS (SS-236) 87, 89
Singapore 27, 51, 57

Siskaninetz, William 172
SJ radar 94, 97, 99–100, 104, 107, 141, 154, 183
SJ-A radar 113
Skate, USS (SS-305) 131, 145
Skeldon, James A. 172
Skipjack, USS (SS-184) 7
Slater, Clifford F. 172
Sloan, David K., Jr. 44, 59
Smith, Arthur L. 26
Smith, Chester Carl 1, *4*, 5–7, 10, 12, 15–27, 30–42, 44–62, **63**, 64–66, 70, 73–79, **80**, 81–82, 87, 91, 94, 111, 169, 170
Smith, Donald Baxter 5, 7
Smith, Mary Francis Baxter 5, 46
Snapper, USS (SS-185) 34
Soffes, Mike 172
Solomon Islands 73
Solomon Sea 74
South China Sea 52, 60, 68
Southport, Australia 82
Spadefish, USS (SS-411) 162
Spanish American War 7
Spearfish, USS (SS-190) 159
special missions 30, 45–46, 48, 51, 79, 82, 157–158, 160, 192n71
"Speedway" 145
Spencer, Frank H., Jr. 172
Sperry, USS (AS-12) 142–143
Spruance, Raymond A. 131, 159
Squalus, USS (SS-192) 133
Stark, Harold R. 8–9
Statton, Wally G. 172
Steelhead, USS (SS-280) 119, 176
Stingray, USS (SS-186) 45
Stone, Harold A. 172
Strickland, Lyle 44
Sturgeon, USS (SS-187) 7, 32, 174
Subic Bay 33, 38
Submarine Service 1, 5, 7–10, 12–14, 52, 61, 72, 81, 84, 86, 96, 105, 110, 113, 132, 137, 143, 145, 157
Submarine Service School 5, 14, 95, 113, 137–138
Subvets of WWII see US Submarine Veterans of World War II
Suits, W.J. 78
Sulu Sea 66
Sunfish, USS (SS-281) 131
Surabaya, Java 28–30, 42
Suribachi see Mount Suribachi
Sutherland, Richard K. 40
Swan River 46, 61
Swinburne, E.R. 155
Swordfish, USS (SS-193) specifications 3, 169, 178, *179*
Swordfish, USS (SSN-579) 168
Sydney 73

Tang, USS (SS-306) 131
Tanjung Merah 31
Tappahannock, USS (AO-43) 73
Tarbox, Fred A. 172

Index

Tarushima Maru 123
Tassafaronga 77
Tatsufuku Maru 55–56, 81, 174
Tautog, USS (SS-199) 127
Taylor, Arthur H. *114*
Taylor, James F. 172
TDC *see* Torpedo Data Computer
Tenkai Maru 101, 104, 175
Tinosa, USS (SS-283) 163
Tokyo Bay 116, *118*
Tokyo Rose 99, 162
Torpedo Data Computer 16–17, 34, 56, 59, 67, 75, 96, 117, 130, 148, 184
torpedo, defects 22–23
torpedo officer 12
torpedo, transfer 25–26
Toyokawa Maru 148, 177
Trigger, USS (SS-237) 84–87, 92–93, 201n60
Triton, USS (SS-201) 87, 89
Truk 87, 112, 116–117, 121, 127, 131–132, 174
Tunny, USS (SS-282) 162–163
Turner, Richard K. 8

U-boat 2, 112, 120, 145
Ultra (Ultra Secret) 74, 125, 184
United States Naval Academy 106; *see also* Annapolis
University of California–Berkeley 5
University of Mississippi 167
unrestricted submarine warfare 7–9
US Submarine Veterans of World War II (organization) 21, 135, 166, 167

Van Horn, Elwood K. 172
Vella Lavella 146

Viking Squadron (chapter) 167
Voge, Richard G. 7, 81, 145

Wagner, Arnold J. 172
Wahoo, USS (SS-238) 81, 168, 201n60
Wake Island 27
Warder, Frederick B. 7
Warren, William, Jr. 166–167
Warren, William Rufus 166
Washington, D.C. 7, 39, 79, 135
Watkins, Frank C. 163
Weaver, USS (DE-741) 145
Western Electric Corporation 94
Wewak 96, 99, 101
Whale, USS (SS-239) 72–73, 123
Wide Bay 77
Wilkes, John 10, 27–30, 48, 79, 191n103
William, Thurman A. 172
Willoughby, Amea 42–45
Winton Engine 3, 124, 144
World War I 12
Wren, Joseph E. 172
Wright, William L. ("Bull") 7, 81

XO *see* executive officer

Yamabiko Maru 119, 176
Yamakumi Maru 117–118
Yangtze Service Medal 5
Yokosuka 131
Yulinkan 18

Zvanich, Katherine M. 96

www.ingramcontent.com/pod-product-compliance
Ingram Content Group UK Ltd.
Pitfield, Milton Keynes, MK11 3LW, UK
UKHW041949140426
5217IPUK00014B/717